FIGHTING FIREWATE

MW01519925

In *Fighting Firewater Fictions*, Richard W. Thatcher describes and explains the emergence and perpetuation of the 'firewater complex' – the cultural construct of understandings and stereotypes surrounding alcoholism in First Nations reserve communities.

Alcoholism has been considered by many to be an inevitability in the First Nations. Thatcher explores how this attitude has resulted in certain aspects of collective and personal responsibility being neglected in favour of a reliance on therapeutic interventions, often of questionable merit. He argues that this situation has had the effect of relieving government policy makers and reserve leadership from accountability for problematic community development strategies that have long outgrown their usefulness.

Thatcher contends that the conditions that give rise to high alcohol abuse rates in First Nations can be traced to a large extent to feelings of hopelessness associated with multi-generational unemployment. *Fighting Firewater Fictions* calls for community reorganization around a band development policy that looks beyond the reserve, and outlines a strategy that involves a shift from the current emphasis on the treatment of alcoholics towards a more holistic approach, including counselling and non-residential services that address the real needs of potential or actual problem drinkers. This is essential reading for anybody working in, or seeking to understand, aboriginal communities that are experiencing problems with alcoholism.

RICHARD W. THATCHER is the principal consultant and co-owner of Socio-Tech Consulting Services in Craven, Saskatchewan.

Fighting Firewater Fictions

Moving Beyond the Disease Model of Alcoholism in First Nations

Richard W. Thatcher

UNIVERSITY OF TORONTO PRESS
Toronto Buffalo London

© University of Toronto Press Incorporated 2004
Toronto Buffalo London
Printed in Canada

ISBN 0-8020-8985-2 (cloth)
ISBN 0-8020-8647-0 (paper)

Printed on acid-free paper

National Library of Canada Cataloguing in Publication

Thatcher, Richard, 1946–
    Fighting firewater fictions : moving beyond the disease model of
alcoholism in First Nations / Richard Thatcher.

    Includes bibliographical references and index.
    ISBN 0-8020-8985-2 (bound).   ISBN 0-8020-8647-0 (pbk.)

    1. Native peoples – Alcohol use – Canada.   2. Drinking of alcoholic
beverages – Canada.   3. Alcoholism – Canada – Prevention.
4. Alcoholism – Treatment – Canada.   I. Title.

E98.L7T48 2004   362.292' 089' 97071   C2004-902847-2

University of Toronto Press acknowledges the financial assistance to its
publishing program of the Canada Council and the Ontario Arts Council.

University of Toronto Press acknowledges the financial support for its
publishing activities of the Government of Canada through the Book
Publishing Industry Development Program (BPIDP).

Contents

**Part Two: Rebuilding and Renovating Alcohol Prevention Strategies
in First Nations**

FIGHTING FIREWATER FICTIONS

1

Introduction

This book sets out to deconstruct the 'firewater complex,' a cultural construct that embraces the ideological understanding and behavioural dynamics of a drinking style that ravages the reserve communities of First Nations in Canada. It will be argued that this cultural complex, which is a specific set of abiding beliefs and behavioural norms[1] organized around beverage alcohol consumption, is intrinsically integrated into the distinctive political economy of reserve communities. Reinforced by a common stereotype that associates 'Indians' with drunkenness, specific ideas that are implicit in the firewater complex are also integral to the working assumptions of the addictions prevention and intervention workers serving First Nations.

It will be argued that specific, distorted beliefs embraced by the firewater complex have become a central component of the ethnic narrative of First Nations on reserve settlements in Canada. Specific, systemic conditions in the political, economic, and social environment that shape the nature of reserve communities will be described, conditions which combine with a misguided understanding of alcohol problems in First Nations to sustain a specific style of problem drinking. That style severely compromises the health and safety of large numbers of community members and virtually cries out for remediation.

---

1 In this book, 'norm' is used in the sociological sense; it is a standard of behaviour supported widely in society as a whole or within one of its subgroups. In essence, a norm is a behavioural rule defined by the shared expectations of two or more people. That rule or standard can be regarded as deviant and unacceptable by those not sharing the expectation, but it is only a norm if it is a shared understanding of a specific type of conduct, which is also affixed to a commonly understood social context.

The theory, opinion, and evidence presented are not intended solely to stimulate thought and provoke debate; they are presented to encourage fundamental change, both in the realm of ideas and in the adoption of strategies and services. Of itself, critical analysis can be intellectually satisfying, but its value is not truly realized unless it points to plausible alternatives. A revised approach to challenging problem drinking in First Nations is therefore presented in the second part of the book.

The assemblage of fact, theory, and opinion that informs my argument is drawn both from an extensive literature review and from my own applied research background. That background does not include an aboriginal heritage and this fact no doubt sets significant limits on data access and interpretation. However, I have drawn upon almost two decades of work as a social and health policy and program researcher, adviser, and program planner with First Nations. In addition to reading a wealth of written documents, in those years I conversed in local, regional, and national forums with hundreds of elected leaders, administrators, and health and social service workers serving First Nations. I also conducted community health surveys on dozens of reserves in which the information and opinions of reserve residents were polled by local surveyors. It is through the gathering of this latter data that my strongest defence against the 'ignorant outsider' criticism can be mounted. Yet, admittedly, I cannot fully surmount the cultural gap that divides my understanding from the knowledge and sensibilities of First Nations people. I can but apologize in advance for any errors of fact or interpretation in the text that arise from that cultural distance, and invite forgiveness.

The book attempts to sift fact from fiction with respect to the causes of alcohol misuse among the descendants of the first peoples of Canada. It also attempts to explain the genesis of the firewater complex and the social forces that sustain it in public discourse, community organization, development policies, and prevention and intervention messages communicated by paid addictions workers.

Social Problems and Levels of Analysis

While recognizing that there may be critical biological and psychological implications in any alcohol abuse problem, as a clinical sociologist, it was my theoretical preference to analyse destructive drinking patterns in First Nations as a *social problem*. Justification for this approach does not simply follow from personal preference; in this case, it follows from the fact that the subject is one which has an intrinsically sociological nature. The subject is sociological because its central concern is with problem drinking as an ethnic feature rather than an individual problem – a feature that can be altered only through socially organized means. The subject matter is also sociological in that its concern is with the exceptional *rates* of alcohol abuse problems in First Nations and the norms that support and define the meaning of those problems in the collective consciousness of reserve communities.

While there are many operational definitions of a social problem, the simple and straightforward statement offered three decades ago in a popular dictionary of sociology still suffices today. Theodorson and Theodorson define a social problem as 'any undesirable condition or situation that is judged by an influential number of persons within a community to be intolerable and to require group action toward constructive reform' (1969: 392). The authors of that dictionary tell us that standard examples of social problems include crime, ethnic conflict, poverty, prostitution, juvenile delinquency, alcohol and drug abuse, and addiction.

To lend some conceptual order to the task of categorizing the range of potential causes of a social problem, some sociologists and social policy analysts have found it useful to divide the causal spectrum into different analytical levels of analysis. Potential explanatory factors are placed along a continuum stretching from the 'macro- system' through the 'mezzo-' to the 'micro-' level of social systems analysis (see Fischer, 1978: chap. 1; Bruhn and Rebach, 1996: 6–8).

The macro end of the continuum refers to factors and environmental manipulations that have a significant effect on the individual but originate at great physical or organizational distance from him or her. Broad economic patterns and national and regional policies impacting on a particular community of interest are examples of macro-system influences on a social problem. Policy changes are often required to address macro-system problems.

Mezzo-system factors are located in the functioning of community institutions in the immediate environment of those implicated directly in the social problem. Changes in local by-laws or institutional policies, programs, and methodologies are examples of mezzo-level interventions. Mezzo-level issues involve interfaces between social units, such as boundary conflicts between families and institutions, between social classes, and conflicts between units or levels of hierarchies in the organization of businesses or community service organizations. As an example of a mezzo-level social problem, Wolf and Bruhn (1992) documented the relationship between community, family, and individual health, finding that family solidarity and community cohesion tend to be positively associated with indicators of health, while rapid social change and the break-up of family and community solidarity correlate with an increase in illness.

The micro end of the continuum refers to problems residing in and alterable in the individual, such as attitudinal and lifestyle factors that encourage problem drinking. Micro-system factors that encourage health risk behaviours can be altered through direct interventions, such as skill training, counselling, or group therapy.

Obviously, there is significant overlap among all of these systems and, therefore, their boundaries are frequently blurred. More important, in varying degrees, factors in one sphere affect the others. The impact may be almost negligible or it may be so substantial that behaviour in the other spheres is almost wholly explained as a reaction to that influence. A social problem analysis and a strategic problem-solving plan must examine all of these levels of social systems analysis and consider interventions that respond to the actual influence of each sphere.

The description, explanatory and critical analysis, and prevention and intervention strategies presented in this book will climb up and down the causal tiers on this conceptual, analytical hierarchy. However, I will not belabour the process of analysis by repeatedly stopping to identify various explanatory factors or problem-solving strategies as fitting into one of these tiers. It will be left to the reader to recognize that when I am talking about national 'Indian Affairs' policy we are dealing with macro-level analytical factors, and when I am proposing counselling strategies we are dealing with micro-level interventions.

It must also be recognized that social systems are permeable, which is to say that they are 'open systems,' influenced by and, in turn, influencing, factors of a bio-physical and psychological nature. It is part of the challenge of a social problems analysis to incorporate measures of the impacts of non-social factors and, if the evidence warrants, to concede that the social problem under examination is partly or largely an outcome of influences that originate outside of the social sphere.

Macro-System Factors

Macro-system factors examined in this study include traditional cultural influences, the legacy of interactions with non-aboriginal, white settler society, formal 'Indian Affairs' and Health Canada policies, and contemporary social and economic realities. Macro-system factors will also include belief systems that cut across aboriginal cultures and beliefs about alcohol abuse prevention and intervention imported from the occupational culture of North American addictions personnel.

Mezzo-System Factors

Located between the macro and micro level of analysis is the mezzo level of social structure, which includes the immediately visible institutional structures through which routine social intercourse can encourage or discourage problem drinking. Mezzo-level factors include local community organization, social networks of extended family and friends, leadership patterns, social hierarchies, and the dynamics of prevention programs and treatment centres focused on alcohol and drug abuse or directly implicated in it.

Micro-System Factors

At the micro level of the social-analytical continuum are small social units, the smallest of which is the individual, who has or will be socialized into the norms of a particular family, community, and society, as well as the face-to-face, emotionally primary interactions that characterize relationships between lovers, spouses, family members, and friendship networks. Micro-social interventions include counselling, psychotherapy, spiritual healing, assisted learning, skill development and facilitated changes in dysfunctional roles, cognitive styles, social coping skills, and interventions in relationships of abuse and asymmetrical power relationships.

The Need for Fundamental Change at All System Levels

In the analysis presented, essential macro-level problems and changes needed in broad development paradigms targeting on First Nations are examined. It is my firm conviction that, for policy and programming strategies to significantly reduce alcohol-implicated health risks in First Nations, significant structural changes in community life must also occur, as must a sea change in attitudes and received knowledge about alcohol problems and their effective solutions. An attempt is therefore made in the ensuing pages to deconstruct specific features of band organization which function, in systemic terms, to generate and maintain the social conditions that sustain problem drinking patterns.

Key community characteristics are identified that give rise to and sustain destructive drinking comportment. It will be argued that fundamental organizational change is essential. Rather than promoting sober lifestyles, the current structure of resource acquisition and allocation in reserve communities systemically promotes economic dependence; that dependency has created and now perpetuates a bankrupt inventory of adult social roles in reserve communities. Fundamental changes in community organization originate in and demand both macro- *and* mezzo-level changes.

Finally, the book reviews prevention and intervention strategies currently and potentially available to assist individuals and families in maintaining or establishing sober lifestyles. Based on that review, the book advocates the rejection of significant aspects of current prevention and counselling approaches and identifies and recommends the adoption of more empowering and potentially effective alternatives.

An Exclusive Focus on Reserves

Like other Canadians, aboriginal Canadians inhabit a wide range of communities that vary in their size, economic activity, and degree of inclusion in or remoteness from large, urban population centres. The category also includes First Nations people, both on- and off-reserve, Non-Status 'Indians,' French and Scotch Métis, and Inuit peoples. Obviously, an examination of the same problems in all of these communities would be most valuable. However, this analysis is restricted to First Nations people who are either current residents of reserves or who received their primary socialization within the community culture of contemporary reserve life. The necessity of this somewhat limited focus stems from my extensive experience with First Nations and their individual and multi-community shared service programs for alcohol and drug abuse, and from my relative lack of experience with urban Status Indians. It was also encouraged by the comparative abundance of literature on First Nations in a reserve setting and by the relative dearth of relevant information and analytical research literature in the addictions field on other aboriginal groups.

The 'Target' Audience and the 'Anticipated' Readership

Ultimately, the thinking conveyed in this book is directed at those leaders and members of First Nations who are committed to exploring and making changes necessary to improve the health of their people. It is also directed at policy makers in positions that can influence or directly implement change. However, I recognize that the actual readership will be far more limited. This book is decidedly *not* for everybody and is aimed primarily at three groups of readers: (1) academics and policy analysts who influence leadership; (2) students enrolled in university and college courses in aboriginal studies, psychology, sociology, social work, and addiction studies; and (3) professional and paraprofessional counsellors, addictions prevention workers, and other community health and human service personnel serving First Nations directly.

Hopefully, the substance of the book will be diffused to a far wider audience by being passed onto policy makers by policy analysts and, via academics, to students who will become the front-line addictions workers and treatment centre staff, and through them to the wider, grass-roots band membership. The book may also be of interest to those members of the reading public who have an exceptional curiosity about public policy issues in general or the social, cultural, political, and economic interests of contemporary First Nations in particular.

Ruffling Feathers – A *Justified* Mischief

The argument made in this book poses serious challenges for the service delivery system serving First Nations clients throughout Canada – as well as for the clients themselves. And challenged *should* they be! For if there is merit to the case developed in the pages that follow, then until the fictions are set aside and the facts are recognized and incorporated into policies, programs, and core beliefs in the First Nations population, alcohol prevention and intervention strategies will be relatively ineffective.

To be fair, the shift away from the conventional thinking that I have so roundly criticized throughout this book is already beginning to occur. Although at a very slow pace, the changes in theory and practice recommended are already emerging in various First Nations and First Nations programs in many parts of the country. This book is intended to support the efforts of those who are at the forefront of such change.

The perspective presented here does fly in the face of 'conventional wisdom' about aboriginal drinking problems and solutions. Further, the statement of at least some of the problems identified and specific solutions recommended at the level of macro and mezzo systems are likely to evoke an impatient and frustrated reaction from federal government officials who believe that the current entanglement of policy and legal strictures makes fundamental changes in reserve-based band organization a political and legal impossibility. To them I say that, despite the formidable obstacles on the path to change, the alternative of retaining the status quo is not a viable option for the long term. Some of the recommended changes will also offend many community leaders who at least in the short run, the are likely to resist.

The changes in thinking and the therapeutic approaches recommended will probably also be resisted by substance abuse workers, many of whom are firmly, even passionately, committed to a conventional approach to preventing and intervening in alcohol abuse problems. To many, the ideas expressed in this book will be upsetting, but I am convinced that dialogue and debate on these issues is vital to the evolution of services for problem drinkers. I do not enjoy challenging the fundamental beliefs of anyone, especially those who are passionate about their beliefs and habituated to implementing them through their ongoing work. Despite my discomfort, and regardless of the formidable sources of anticipated resistance to much that is presented below, the tragic nature and scope of problem drinking in First Nations surely justifies any such ruffling of feathers.

Fictions of the Firewater Complex to be Challenged

At least ten ideas associated with the firewater complex beg to be challenged by a careful examination of empirical data and to be exposed as fictions or myths rather than facts. As the evidence and arguments in the ensuing text will demonstrate, common views to the contrary, *none* of the following assumptions about alcoholic beverage use by First Nations people living on reserves in Canada are supported by the balance of available evidence:

1 First Nations people have an extraordinary attraction to beverage alcohol, a characteristic that has made them far more likely than other Canadians to be current drinkers.

2 The vast majority of First Nations problem drinkers suffer from the 'disease' of alcoholism. They have a genetic predisposition to alcohol addiction, which is to say they have a special biological predisposition to alcohol dependency which is exhibited through alcohol cravings.

3 If the First Nations attraction to excessive drinking is not explicable in biological terms, it can be attributed to a unique, unwavering, pan-indigenous, sociocultural or psychological predisposition to excessive drinking.

4 First Nations drinkers have a genetic predisposition towards 'out of control,' irresponsible, and often violent behaviour when they are inebriated. Drinking excessive amounts of alcohol and the resulting neurological impairment and lack of inhibition cause much of the brawling that so often that takes place during drinking episodes. It also explains the exceptional rates of spousal battery and various other antisocial, criminal, and negligent behaviours that occur, with such tragic frequency, during or upon the heels of the drinking episodes of First Nations people.

5 The typical, reckless drinking style of First Nations drinkers was, from the outset, fundamentally different from the drinking norms of non-aboriginal, Caucasian Canadians.

6 First Nations problem drinkers in Canada with an addictive pattern of alcohol use will necessarily be permanently afflicted with this problem. They can successfully overcome their abuse pattern only by completely refraining from the recreational use of alcohol. They cannot learn to moderate their use of alcohol.

7 Most problem drinkers from First Nations are best treated by intensive, four- to six-week treatment in in-patient centres intended to promote abstinence.

8 If a problem drinker who has refrained from drinking for an extended period of time has a drinking episode (i.e., 'falls off the wagon'), s/he will begin a relapse which can be effectively addressed only by starting back at the beginning of therapy or at the first step of a twelve-step program.

9 The approach to social problem solving in First Nations intrinsic to the firewater complex is exclusively applied to alcohol abuse.

10 Alcohol abuse in First Nations is purely dysfunctional for all concerned. There are no vested interests in the maintenance of current alcohol abuse patterns in First Nations.

In the pages below, these fictions will be undermined and replaced with facts. The essential elements of a comprehensive strategy will also be presented – a strategy designed to eradicate the abiding problem of binge drinking and injurious drinking behaviour that has long proven so devastating to the people of the First Nations in Canada.

Part One of the book is an exercise in deconstruction. Deconstructive analysis involves a stance of inquiry that is intensely curious and consciously sceptical about prevailing beliefs concerning truth, knowledge, power, the self, and language – beliefs that are often taken for granted as truths, rarely questioned, and which serve as legitimations for various dimensions of social structure and ideology (Foucault, 1975). Deconstruction theory begins with the assumption that human knowledge in its many varieties is a social construction. Formally, the task of social deconstruction originates in the sociology of knowledge[2] and critical social theory,[3] and its most frequent current expression is to be found in 'postmodern' social theory and 'cultural studies.'[4] In accordance with such theory I deconstruct the historical genesis, ideas, and sustaining forces that have defined and maintained the firewater complex among the reserve residents of First Nations in Canada. Part Two then offers a comprehensive set of recommendations for the type of changes which, in my view, are essential to undermine the firewater complex and the physical, social, emotional, psychological, and spiritual destruction that it both activates and rationalizes. These alternative strategies follow from the initial critique.

---

2 The 'sociology of knowledge' is a subdiscipline of sociology concerned with the social underpinnings of human knowledge, especially systems of belief that are routinely taken for granted as truths but which actually function to legitimate the nature of broadly based social arrangements and the groups whose interests they best serve. Interest in the subject was initially aroused by Karl Marx's hypothesis that ruling elites in socially stratified societies developed and coercively promoted idea systems ('ideologies') that served to legitimize existing norms of inequality. The German sociologist Karl Mannheim's collection of essays, *Essays on the Sociology of Knowledge* (1952) is usually considered the seminal work in the subdiscipline.

3 As used in this text, 'critical social theory' refers to any commentary and analysis that calls into question the legitimacy of particular social arrangements or the structure of society as a whole, or that takes issue with the interpretations or explanations of social problems offered by social scientists, prominent or powerful individuals, or corporate or government representatives or which are prevalent as 'taken-for granted truths' in everyday social intercourse. It does not refer to the 'Frankfurt school' or what is sometimes referred to as 'critical theory,' a body of social criticism associated with the German philosophers Theodore Adorno, Herbert Marcuse, and Jürgen Habermas.

4 The term 'cultural studies' is now commonly used to refer to social analyses which consciously (or, in the terminology of its contributors, 'reflexively') attempt to take the biases and social background of the writer/analyst and the subjects of social analyses into account as part of the exploration of a sociocultural phenomenon. A 'deconstructive' analysis is the method employed by those undertaking such an investigation.

Part One

Deconstructing the Firewater Complex

2

'More Dry, More Wet':
Drinking as Pastime and Problem in
First Nations

It is widely believed throughout North America that the members of ethnic groups most commonly known as 'Indians' are frequently afflicted by a pattern of excessive drinking and drunken behaviour. So pervasive is the association in the popular psyche between alcohol abuse and indigenous peoples that, for many, the noun 'Indian' is immediately associated with the adjective *drunken*. In fact, the phrase 'drunken Indian' reflects one of the most common and enduring ethnic stereotypes not only in Canada but in North America as a whole. Whether or not aboriginal North Americans actually have personal problems with drinking, individuals of aboriginal ancestry must constantly reckon with the assumption of others that they have a mysterious and overwhelming inability to manage their use of alcoholic beverages rationally. It has been my experience that, at least in Canada, First Nations people have themselves tended to internalize that same belief.

Origins of the 'Problematic Indian Drinker' View

While some Native North American cultural groups had a tradition of beverage alcohol use prior to their first contact with Europeans, most anthropologists, historians, and First Nations narrators with a specific interest in the subject agree that beverage alcohol was not indigenous to the peoples who resided in what is now Canada. However, it is widely believed that, shortly after contact and the adoption of European wines and spirits, a pattern of excessive drinking and drunken, conflicted, and violent behaviour was established among the indigenous peoples. Reports of problematic drinking patterns among the

First Nations date to the trade in furs between the first Europeans in what is now Canada (Smart and Ogborne, 1986). Such evidence in the historical record is available in documents produced by French explorers and officials, and similar claims were subsequently made by missionaries and, even later, by settlers.

While there is some indication of regional variation in the reception of First Nations people to European alcohol, most evidence suggests that the style of consumption was problematic, primarily for the indigenous hosts themselves. Evidence of an apparent continuity, over time, of troublesome drinking patterns in First Nations is abundant. Consider the following accounts, which take us back over five decades:

- Between 1953 and 1978, accidental deaths in British Columbia were four to five times as common among registered Indians as they were for non-Indians (Hislop et al., 1987). The extent to which alcohol might be implicated in accidental, suicidal, or homicidal deaths was suggested by sociologists Gordon Jarvis and Menno Boldt (1982), whose study of aboriginal suicide indicates that 63 to 100 per cent of Native suicides in British Columbia showed measurable blood alcohol content. The same researchers found key informants reporting drinking as the primary activity immediately preceding death in 80 per cent of a sample of Indians who died at their own hands and 86 per cent who died as a result of homicide (Jarvis and Boldt, 1982).
- A 1971 study in British Columbia showed that the rate of sudden, violent death for aboriginals was four times higher than the figure for non-aboriginals – and approximately 69 per cent of aboriginal deaths were alcohol-related, compared with 26 per cent for non-aboriginals (Cutler and Morrison, 1971).
- A 1977 study by the Saskatchewan Alcoholism Commission of 3,368 people arrested for public drunkenness in Regina found that, despite the fact that in the census aboriginals constituted just 15 per cent of the city's population at the time, of those arrested, 62 per cent were of aboriginal ancestry (Reid, Dewit, and Matonovich, 1980).
- In 1980, a publication funded by the Department of Indian Affairs and Northern Development (DIAND) entitled *Indian Conditions: A Survey* found that alcohol abuse was implicated in between 50 and 60 per cent of all 'Indian' illnesses; it also found that Indians in the twenty-five to fifty-five-year age range were admitted to hospital for alcohol problems at five times the national rate.

This problem has been a North American one. James H. Gray commented acerbically in his social history of beverage alcohol use on the prairies that, as a small army of 'earnest sociologists' discovered during the 1960s, 'there was a pattern to Indian drinking that held consistently from the Gulf Coast to the Arctic' (1982: 127). In a study of drinking patterns and behaviours among selected Indian tribes in the United States, Weisner (1984) noted that 'American Indians' have a higher alcohol consumption rate than all other ethnic groups and subgroups in the country. Another American study suggested that drug and alcohol misuse and abuse may affect 70 per cent of the 'Indian' adolescent population in urban schools and that as many as 86 per cent of suicides among Native Americans involve drugs or alcohol (Schinke et al., 1985). The same study referred to data from a large prison showing that among the 'Indians' convicted of homicide, the homicidal act was almost always alcohol-related, in that perpetrators, victims, or both had ingested excessive amounts of alcohol prior to the act.

Destructive, Alcohol-Related Behaviours Remain a Serious Health Problem in the First Nations Population

Alcohol abuse has long been associated with grave problems for the indigenous peoples in North America, and it continues to be a priority concern of those working to improve the health of the descendants of North America's original denizens. Evidence of the continuance of that problematic drinking pattern is pervasive in impressionistic reports, community studies, and statistical indicators today.

Those descendants of the First Nations who live in what is now Canada continue to perceive alcohol abuse as a primary health problem in their communities and to be directly or indirectly afflicted by severe health, safety, and social problems associated with bouts of alcohol consumption. Let us consider some of the more noteworthy Canadian indicators.

First Nations People in Canada View Alcohol Abuse as One of the Most Significant Health Problems in Their Communities – and the Facts Support Them

A survey of fifty-seven First Nations communities in Manitoba in 1984–5 used a rating scale of 'no problem' and 'major problem' at the extremes of a scale designed to rate the frequency of mental health problems, one of which was alcohol abuse. Fully 86 per cent of the communities rated alcohol abuse as a major or serious mental health problem (Rogers and Abas, 1988).

According to the data retrieved by Statistics Canada in the *1991 Aboriginal Peoples Survey* and published in 1993, First Nations people themselves rank alcohol abuse very high when asked to identify the health problems in their populations and communities. Of those identifying as 'North American Indians' across Canada, 65 per cent reported alcohol abuse as a significant problem for their communities. These data served to confirm the view supported by earlier studies that alcohol abuse was an exceptional and continuing problem among First Nations.

Community health studies and needs assessment studies conducted by the author for First Nations in western Canada support the finding that there is widespread concern about alcohol abuse among Canada's first peoples.[1] In many of these studies, when they are asked to rank health problems, First Nations people living on reserves are most likely to regard alcohol abuse (or alcohol and drug abuse combined) as one of the top three or the 'number one' health problem affecting their people and their communities. Virtually all of the community health workers, police, and human service workers interviewed as key informants in these studies share the view of the ordinary band members surveyed.

A recent national review of an alcohol and drug abuse program funded by Health Canada, the country's national ministry of health, and dedicated to serving First Nations, confirmed the view that First Nations (and Inuit) health workers and addictions prevention workers continue to see alcohol abuse as a leading cause of ill-health in their communities (Jock, 1998).

---

1 I have acted as a consultant or principal investigator for community health studies and evaluations for more than thirty First Nations reserve communities in western Canada. The majority of those studies contain primary data in the form of adult survey information and key informant interview data from health workers. Summaries of this data have consistently indicated that community members and health workers serving First Nation communities continue to regard alcohol consumption and alcohol-related destructive behaviour as either the leading health problem or one of the two or three health problems that warrant concentrated attention by community health service and addictions personnel. Discussion with key informants from across the country and reviews of a variety of regional and national studies confirm that a continuing concern that alcohol abuse is a health problem is the rule in First Nations communities. The problem is typically identified as either the leading health problem or one of the top three health problems.

In the province of Saskatchewan, while approximately 10 per cent of the total population are Status Indians, in 1991/2, 46 per cent of the combined clientele of detoxification services were defined as *aboriginal*, and 67 per cent of that figure were Status Indians (SADAC, 1993). This represents an increase over the equivalent utilization figure tallied in the late 1980s. It should be pointed out that the provincial figures are only part of the picture. The federal government funds a prevention and treatment program network, the National Native Alcohol and Drug Abuse Program (NNADAP), targeting on but not exclusive to First Nations people who reside on reserves.

Death rates from injuries, suicide, and poisonings are especially high in the indigenous population and these high rates are probably at least in part the result of alcohol abuse (Scott, 1997). In testimony submitted to the Royal Commission on Aboriginal People (RCAP), Jacques LeCavalier, executive director of the Canadian Centre on Substance Abuse, reported that one in five admissions to Canadian hospitals for alcohol-related illness is an aboriginal admission, liver disease for aboriginals is three-and-a-half times the national average, and alcohol psychosis occurs among aboriginal people at four times the national average (Royal Commission 1996: 159).

When compared statistically with the Canadian population as a whole, alcohol is disproportionately implicated in family violence and child abuse and neglect and in disproportionately high criminal prosecution and incarceration rates among the aboriginal population.[2] Data gathered as part of the Yukon Alcohol and Drug Abuse Survey (YADS) indicated that indigenous people, especially men, are often heavy and frequent drinkers (Yukon Government, 1991); the incidence of Foetal Alcohol Syndrome (FAS) is also believed to be significantly higher in the indigenous population (Scott, 1997). Nor is the alcohol problem disappearing with the cycle of generational change: aboriginal youth are two to six times as likely to acquire alcohol abuse problems as the youth of non-aboriginals (Scott, 1997).

Problem Drinking versus Alcohol Dependency

A review of community studies available through on-reserve health surveys that I have designed and coordinated indicates that a considerable majority of First Nations drinkers who claim to have problems

---

2 For a review of the studies pointing to these correlations, see Warry (1998: 77–83).

are most accurately viewed as 'problem drinkers,' rather than as alcoholics. While alcoholism itself may be a problem affecting more aboriginal people than non-aboriginal people, in both worlds, alcohol dependency is a minority problem. Most First Nations drinkers exhibiting or admitting to having some problems as a result of drinking are not alcohol dependent.

The fact that most people who admit to having a drinking problem are not alcoholics is consistently reflected in the research literature. For example, Cahalan (1970) found that approximately 15 per cent of men and 4 per cent of women had experienced multiple alcohol problems at some point in their lives; with a more liberal definition, those figures jumped to 43 per cent for men and 21 per cent for women. However, only a small percentage reported experiencing alcohol withdrawal symptoms; in other words, there are a lot of problem drinkers in the general population and the vast majority of them are not alcohol dependent. Hilton (1987 and 1991) found the type of difference, as did Cahalan and Room (1974). A report by the Institute of Medicine to the NIAAA (1990) suggests that the ratio of problem drinkers to those who are seriously dependent is about 4:1.

The High-Risk Drinking Style: An Expected and Tacitly Sanctioned Phenomenon in First Nations

Binge drinking rather than perpetual drunkenness is a central element of the firewater complex. Drinking in 'binges' refers to a drinking style comprising occasional drinking episodes at intervals of varying length, but characterized by consuming alcohol to the point of intoxication and beyond. As one health committee member from the Peepeekisis First Nation in southern Saskatchewan once told me, 'You've got to understand something. When we drink, we drink until we drop!' So compelling is the attraction to the drinking binge that, during times of extreme poverty, such lethal forms of alcohol as vanilla extract, rubbing alcohol, or solvents are often substituted for commercially mixed ethyl alcohol beverages. While resort to beverage alcohol substitutes is now almost exclusively a skid-row behaviour, the emotionally acting out drinking style has long been characteristic of First Nations drinking comportment. As Smart and Ogborne (1986) and Cutler and Storm (1973) have argued, the Canadian First Nations drinking style is similar to the 'skid row' and 'frontier' binge-drinking style.

The 'Indian binge' is social; it is an event announced by the use of the noun 'party' as a verb. To 'go drinking' is to get together with others and 'party.' Participants drink beyond the point of inebriation until all the liquor is gone and there is no cash to replenish the supply. The binge-drinking style characteristically encompasses sex, affection, and extreme sentimentality, insults, anger, and rage. While men are typically the initiator of these binges, women are typically willing participants and they share in the act of excessive drinking. Fighting is expected. As Leo Paul, a former chief of the Onion Lake Reserve on the Alberta/Saskatchewan border north of Lloydminster, once told me, 'Over the years, a lot of bodies have been found in the alley behind those "Indian bars" in the cities.' On reserves there is always the 'party house,' the householder of which is notorious for hosting parties that routinely 'get out of hand' and during which there is 'usually a fight or two,' with at least one person getting well bruised.

Binge drinking has been so much a part of the 'Indian drinking style' for so long that, at least for young adults who have not 'sworn off' drinking altogether, it is virtually expected. Part of that drinking style is the irresponsibility and 'trouble' that follows acts of carelessness that endanger or hurt other people, and violence against persons or property.

Another aspect of the high-risk drinking style at the heart of the firewater complex is the fact that it is tacitly sanctioned. The proof is not to be gained in the telling; one does not hear anybody saying that it is good to get drunk and hurt oneself or someone else. The proof is instead to be found by reading between the lines of discussion after the fact of a brutal assault or even murder. What is frequently observed is a knowing nod and the simple phrase, taken as a complete explanation, 'Yeah, he was drinking.' Drinking becomes the culprit, separated from the person – and personal responsibility – of the individual who committed the crime.

Extended families in reserve communities are very forgiving of their members when it comes to destructive acts committed during a drinking episode. Even the community health system is more than sympathetic. This is best exemplified by the role of the addictions worker, a health service employee, in the court system. Many such workers spend as much as two-thirds of their time going to court on behalf of band members in trouble with the law, automatically trying to 'help' them by convincing the court that alcohol was to blame for the problem. Punishment is therefore not the answer: 'treatment' is required, and the addictions worker will help the 'client' get the treatment he or she needs. The worker and the individual in trouble with the law are as one in their hope that the promise of treatment for alcohol will reduce or eliminate the burden of punishment for the violator.

Comparison of two surveys conducted for regional needs assessment studies in Saskatchewan, one in 1984 (published in 1985) and one in 1993 (published in 1994), indicates that the overall frequency of high-risk drinking patterns appears to have remained relatively unaltered in recent decades.[3] On both surveys, current drinkers were asked how many drinks they normally consumed per session. In both years surveyed, only (approximately) one-quarter of current drinkers reported that an average drinking episode involved the consumption of *fewer* than six drinks. A recently completed needs assessment study of a south Saskatchewan reserve found a similar pattern.[4] These data are supported by survey research from various aboriginal habitation areas in the country. The Northwest Territories Bureau of Statistics Alcohol and Drug Survey (1996) found that 33.3 per cent of aboriginal persons reported drinking heavily as a regular occurrence, compared with 16.7 per cent of non-aboriginals.

Anecdotal data, survey data, and the impressions of key informants gathered by this writer would suggest that heavy drinking and a normative pattern of reckless drinking persist among First Nations drinkers. As various First Nations addictions workers and leaders have indicated to me over the past decade, along with the sniffing of solvents as young teenagers and experimentation with marijuana and hashish, and more recently cocaine and crystalmeth, high-risk drinking and an accompanying antisocial and/or reckless behaviour pattern is a virtual

---

3 The two surveys cited are reported in a study by the Federation of Saskatchewan Indians (FSI) published in 1985 entitled *Alcohol and Drug Abuse among Treaty Indians in Saskatchewan* and prepared for the (then) Federation of Saskatchewan Indians (FSI) Health and Social Development Commission by WMC Research Associates and in a document prepared for the Saskatchewan Regional Advisory Board to NNADAP by Socio-Tech Consulting Services, *Addictions Intervention Needs of First Nations, 1994 and Beyond* (1994).

4 Confidentiality protocol does not allow for the identification of the band or reserve. The survey, conducted as part of a five-year evaluation of the band's self-administered operations under a health services transfer agreement with the federal government, found that 65 per cent of the adults who responded identified as current abstainers. Of those who claimed to be non-abstainers, 87.9 per cent indicated that they drank four or more drinks per setting, with 33.8 per cent indicating that they drank an average of four to six drinks per setting and 54.1 per cent admitting to drinking six or more drinks per setting.

rite of passage into youth subcultures in First Nations communities. The same correspondents suggest that this pattern persists among aboriginal youth whose families have migrated to cities in search of greater educational and employment opportunities.

In short, excessive drinking, by which I refer to drinking to the point of intoxication, and drunken, reckless, and often hostile drinking comportment, continues to be a dominant drinking style among those First Nations people who classify themselves as current drinkers.

First Nations Adults Are Less Likely than Non-Aboriginals to Be Drinkers

Despite the fact that drinking to the point of impairment is widespread among people of the First Nations in Canada, and despite the conventional view that frequent drinking is virtually characteristic of the aboriginal identity, only a tiny minority are daily drinkers. Further, it appears that, compared with the Canadian adult population as a whole, aboriginal Canadian adults are actually less likely to be current drinkers of alcoholic beverages. Survey data from a number of sources indicate that the percentage of regular alcohol consumers in the First Nations population is lower than the percentage distributed among the entire Canadian population. It is true that, in reaction to public stereotyping, first peoples might underreport their drinking because they are defensive when surveyed and less prone than non-aboriginal Canadians to admit to the full force of drinking on their lives. However, several other studies report similar comparisons, all of which suggest that there are relatively more non-drinkers in the aboriginal population than in the non-aboriginal population.

Probably the best primary data of national scope on aboriginal drinking patterns were generated by the 1991 survey conducted as part of the *Aboriginal Peoples Survey* (Statistics Canada, 1993). Profiling self-report data, the APS found that a lower proportion of aboriginal people than Canadians generally drink daily or weekly, and abstinence is almost twice as common among aboriginal people. The finding of the APS that aboriginal Canadians were actually less rather than more likely than the population average to be active drinkers was supported by several community health surveys I conducted. Confirmation of the veracity of these adult survey responses was provided by highly reliable key informants. Similar data were found in the needs assessment study conducted for the Regional (First Nations) Advisory

Board (RAB) to the Saskatchewan Region's National Native Alcohol and Drug Abuse Program (1994).

Evidence of comparatively high First Nations abstinence levels is also found in the *Yukon Alcohol and Drug Abuse Survey* (Yukon Government, 1991) which was based on self-reported answers to survey interviews. The Yukon study found abstinence to be about twice as common among aboriginal people as among other Canadians. The North West Territories Health Promotion Survey cited above provides further evidence of relatively high aboriginal abstinence rates. On that survey, 60.1 per cent of aboriginal adults reported that they had consumed alcoholic beverages in the past year (Northwest Territories Bureau of Statistics, 1996), compared with 85.2 per cent of non-aboriginal adults resident in the territories. Finally, a survey conducted in nine Cree communities in northern Quebec found a similar pattern of greater abstinence among aboriginal drinkers than non-aboriginals (Santé Québec, 1994).

Also contrary to common perceptions, only a small fraction of First Nations drinkers report being 'daily drinkers.' According to the 1991 APS survey, only 1.03 per cent of those respondents identifying as 'North American Indians' indicated that they were daily drinkers (Statistics Canada, 1993).

The available data are consistent: compared with non-aboriginals, First Nations peoples are less likely than the Canadian adult population as a whole to be drinkers. While there is obviously individual, regional and probably cultural variation in this matter, it is also true that those aboriginals both male and female, who do drink tend to engage in a high-risk drinking style.

These facts serve to explode two myths about indigenous North Americans in Canada. Contrary to popular belief:

1 First Nations people are not more likely to be regular drinkers of alcoholic beverages than non-aboriginals; in fact, they are far more likely to be abstainers.
2 First Nations people are not all high-risk drinkers.

However, it remains the case that a high-risk drinking style is much more common in aboriginal communities than in non-aboriginal communities. It appears that drinking to the point of impairment, which can also be referred to as 'high-risk drinking,' is the most common alcohol consumption style among First Nations people who drink alcoholic beverages. This trend of infrequent but excessive intake per drinking episode is also a fact of life in Australia and New Zealand. Referring to the Canadian data in the Aboriginal Peoples Survey, Saggers and Gray note that, 'among those people who do drink, 'heavy drinking is more common than moderate consumption' (1998: 59), as it is among indigenous drinkers in Australia and New Zealand.

We are left with an apparent paradox: First Nations communities are 'drier' than non-aboriginal communities but, in those pockets of the community where drinking does occur, they are 'wetter,' meaning that excessive drinking among First Nation drinkers is far more likely to be the rule rather than the exception. It is my contention that excessive drinking per drinking episode is a longstanding and defining norm of the First Nations drinking culture – and it is a norm that has stubbornly resisted attempts to promote abstinence by addictions workers directly serving the peoples of the First Nation reserve communities. Of those who identify as current drinkers, casual, light drinking of one or two beers or glasses of wine over a lengthy sitting is a style of the very few rather than the many in First Nations. This 'all or nothing' drinking style must be the focus of any analysis of troublesome First Nations alcohol consumption and the target of ideological and behavioural change.

Exceptions to the Rule of High-Risk Drinking

There are many exceptions to the high-risk drinking norm among First Nations. After having worked with First Nations administrators, professionals, and elected leaders for several decades, I have long noted that severe problem-drinking episodes are uncommon within this 'social rung' of First Nations people.

Education and employment appear to be a significant influence on problem drinking in First Nations. Two examples serve to make the point. In 1991/2, prior to the 'health reform' that divided service delivery arrangements in the province of Saskatchewan into health districts which, among other things, maintained their own regional data, Saskatchewan treatment centre data were kept on a provincewide basis. At that time the vast majority of aboriginal clients had failed to complete grade 12 and only 8.6 per cent identified themselves as having full-time employment. A survey I coordinated for the Battlefords Tribal Council Indian Health Services (BTCIHS) that attempted to capture the entire adult population on eight reserves, found that alcohol abuse was apparent from the answers given by 26 per cent of the adults who had a completed Grade 12 who were polled on a survey. In contrast, 36 per cent of those who had not completed high school gave answers that indicated they could be classified as problem drinkers (BTCIHS, 1993).

It is something of an anomaly that aboriginal consumption levels per episode increase statistically with higher levels of education (APS, 1993). However, drunken comportment is extremely rare among employed aboriginal people with completed or partially completed post-secondary education. In my experience some of these well-positioned individuals in First Nations exhibit a behavioural cycle of extremely lengthy abstinence, followed occasionally by a destructive binge that often leads to their fall from grace, in terms of both employment and social prestige. However, this is a rare occurrence: for most members of what might be referred to in sociological terms as a socio-economic status elite, sobriety is the rule, social drinking is an occasional, non-troubling practice, and excessive drinking is either non-occurring or an occasional slip, quickly abandoned for a return to sober living. It is also my observation that substance abuse of any kind is not found among First Nations people who have adopted a 'bicultural' lifestyle, in the sense that they have developed a career and an occupation with which they identify and draw liberally from both modernity and their own First Nation traditions. The acquaintances who can be thus described appear to be comfortable with both selected elements of their aboriginal heritage and many elements of modernity.

A bicultural personal and community stance may actually protect not only aboriginal individuals but also aboriginal communities from a variety of significant social and mental health risks by mediating the potentially disruptive acculturation pressures originating in the surrounding, non-aboriginal society. Evidence at least indirectly in support of this type of interpretation was provided in the work of Levy and Kunitz (1971, 1974) on drinking patterns and homicides in various Southwest, Plains, and Plateau tribes and, more recently, Chandler (2001), who investigated community variation in aboriginal youth suicide rates in British Columbia. Both strands of research are based on community comparisons. Taken together, these studies strongly suggest that continuity with and pride in traditional culture, combined with or protected by socially integrative aspects of contemporary community organization, can reduce risk levels for serious social health problems, including high rates of violent, self-destructive, or antisocial drinking episodes. In the Chandler study, relatively strong self-government organization was associated with low adolescent suicide rates. Contemporary aboriginal self-government includes many characteristics of 'modern' electoral and administrative principles and practices. Local control based on these modernized governance practices can actually reinforce aboriginal social integration. Such governance and administrative technology provides a First Nation or Inuit community with one of several significant means to maintain or reconstruct a positive group identity rooted in traditional indigenous culture while drawing, selectively, upon positive modern and postmodern cultural products and aspects of other traditional non-aboriginal cultures.

3

Alcohol Abuse: A Social Problem Inviting Various Control Strategies

In the services offered to problem drinkers in First Nations, the disease concept of treatment (DCT) of alcoholism prevails – an approach that could more accurately be referred to as the 'bio-spiritual model.' This latter, admittedly more awkward, phrase might be employed because the model itself fuses a genetic explanation with interventions that treat the cause of the problem as a disease and the solution as a medically supported and spiritually motivated pattern of alcohol avoidance. In the DCT, alcohol or, in fact, any other addiction, is viewed as a disease of both the body and the spirit (or soul), with its victims needing a higher power and a this-worldly support group to assist their attempts to cope and avoid the intrusion of an ever-threatening inner craving. In recent decades, the effectiveness and validity of the DCT has been called into question by reputable research and alternative approaches have emerged.

One of the most fundamental distinctions between strategies aimed at addressing problem drinking turns on whether or not the strategy focuses exclusively on the micro-system of individual behaviour, the environment influencing the individual (possibly both the mezzo- and macro-system level), or if it gives equal consideration to the individual (micro-system interventions) and the influencing environment. This chapter will examine the DCT and the disease explanation of alcohol problems and its influence on prevention and remedial services for First Nations people living on reserves. It will also consider the DCT as a public social control perspective and strategy for addressing alcohol abuse as a social problem and other perspectives that reflect fundamentally different core assumptions about how a social problem is appropriately addressed.

The Disease Model: A Basic Synopsis

According to a recent review by Mann and others (2000), the past hundred years have witnessed the formation of the disease concept of alcoholism and, presumably, substantial growth in the knowledge of its causes, course and treatment options. The first half of the twentieth century in Western countries saw attempts to abolish alcoholism through public sanctions. These sanctions included anti-loitering laws, prohibition laws in the United States, and even, in Nazi Germany, proposals for medical procedures to reduce the fertility of alcoholics. As part of this prohibitive approach, Status Indians were not allowed into drinking establishments until the late 1950s because they were perceived to have a distinctive, innate incapacity to handle their liquor. The concept of the 'alcoholic' as a person with a disease with a right to medical treatment and the support of charitably oriented mentors came out of self-organized groups such as Alcoholics Anonymous (AA).

As the Mann et al. review suggests, the current disease concept combines psycho-social and neurobiological causation in its attempt to describe the aetiology of the disease, as well as its predictable consequences. While a detailed description and critical analysis of the disease model will be provided in subsequent chapters, its basic elements need immediate elucidation.

The 'disease of alcoholism' has long been viewed as an addictive-behavioural disease, described by those who advocate its application to problem drinking in the following ways:

- Those who develop the disease of alcoholism are often predisposed to it through a monaminergic dysfunction (i.e., a neurochemical dysfunction). Specific adaptations of the alcoholic's brain chemistry, through extensive alcohol consumption, specifically in the form of depleted dopamine receptors, are thought to play a role in reinforcing the maintenance of the disease.
- Alcoholism is viewed as a disease characterized by a loss of control during an alcohol consumption episode.
- The disease is independent of other problems, whether or not it co-occurs with them. It cannot be traced to childrearing practices or to other factors in the social environment.
- The alcoholic cannot recognize the disease and, in fact, typically denies the problem when confronted with its symptoms. Only with the help of those with a keen understanding of the dynamics of the

disease, including recovered alcoholics, can the individual sufferer come to admit and understand the disease.

- If left to run its course, the disease will progress through a series of predictable changes. While the disease cannot be cured, an alcoholic can recover from its secondary effects and learn to avoid further use. However, the typical cycle of excessive use and destructive physical and psychological outcomes associated with the disease can be interrupted and overcome through concerted treatment by others and significant social support aimed at abstinence – completely eliminating the consumption of beverage alcohol as a behavioural pattern.
- The disease of alcoholism is chronic; it is permanent and sufferers must adapt to its influence and attempt to avoid its manifestations through complete avoidance of alcohol use.
- The disease responds to either or both group treatment provided by those who understand the disease, with AA groups being the most representative of the ideal self-help group, or to an institutionally based, twenty-eight to thirty-five day in-patient treatment program based on the 'Minnesota model' of alcohol treatment, with detoxification arranged prior to treatment and aftercare support provided through a counsellor or self-help group once treatment is completed.
- With specific reference to behaviours associated with their disease, the behaviour of those who suffer from the disease of alcoholism should be exempted from judgment by the ordinary moral standards and codes of expected conduct in the community, and alcoholism should be considered a mitigating factor in the prosecution of criminal offenders who suffer from the disease.[1]

---

1 While summaries of the disease model abound, this listing owes much to the description provided by Stanton Peele (1995: 20–1). Peele makes the point that the original and legitimate use of the term 'disease' is associated with 'first generation' illnesses passed from one to another through microbes. 'Mental illnesses,' the 'second generation' diseases, have some but less scientific warrant. 'Addictions,' which are essentially behaviours resident in numerous environmental causes, are 'third generation' diseases and exist only as metaphor. Peele believes, moreover, that when applied to 'third generation diseases,' the metaphor is, at best, a lengthy stretch from its legitimate meaning. In other writings he argues that the use of the metaphor to describe behavioural problems is a serious error of professional judgment.

The Disease Model and First Nations Alcohol Abuse Services

The disease model continues to dominate much of the thinking and services provided to First Nations people to reduce alcohol abuse rates. This impression was gained from my two decades of professional involvement in the applied study of First Nations addictions issues, and was reinforced by a familiarity with Saskatchewan NNADAP treatment centre programs and a telephone survey conducted in the summer of 2003. The telephone survey, which polled treatment personnel or program managers, was conducted as part of the preparation for this book and provided information of value to consulting assignments I have been involved with on an ongoing basis. The survey indicated that the disease model prevails in all but five of the forty-five adult alcohol and drug abuse treatment programs directly serving First Nations and funded by NNADAP. For example, all but two of the programs either make referrals to AA groups during treatment or as part of termination planning or have AA groups directly incorporated into their program curriculum. It is true that virtually all programs had various cognitive, emotional, skill development, and behavioural goals. However, the polling made it clear that as few as three and possibly five of the forty-five active centres for which Health Canada provided telephone contact numbers regarded abstinence to be the exclusive, primary outcome goal for those elements of treatment focused solely on alcohol use behaviour. Moderate drinking was a clearly defined and encouraged alternative for non alcohol-dependents in only two programs. Spokesperson for three of the five programs offering an alternative to abstinence indicated that, while they did not encourage moderate drinking goals, they were willing to consider them when clients insisted or where circumstances seemed to warrant such a goal.

Assuming that only five of the forty-five NNADAP-funded programs polled provide clients with moderate drinking as an alternative to abstinence, a First Nations client is far more likely to find treatment outcome choices in non-aboriginal centres than in First Nations Centres. The comparison with provincial treatment program providers is quite striking. Health Canada's national province-by-province survey of non-aboriginal Canadian alcohol and drug rehabilitation programs in 1999 found that treatment program providers supported by provincial governments 'increasingly view addiction as a complex bio-psycho-social phenomena, often recognizing a spiritual component' (Health Canada, 1999: 16). The national non-aboriginal program survey also indicated

Figure 3.1 Abstinence-oriented programs: A comparison of First Nations and other Canadian alcohol abuse treatment programs

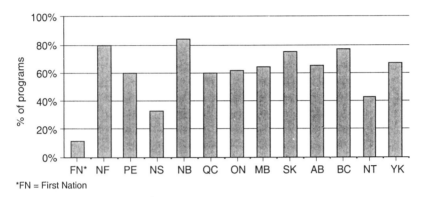

*FN = First Nation

Source: Adapted from Figure 2 of Health Canada's report, *Profile: Treatment and Rehabilitation in Canada*, a 1999 report prepared by Gary Roberts and Alan Ogborne for the Office of Alcohol, Drugs and Dependency Issues in Canada, *Canada's Drug Strategy*, and a 2003 survey of NNADAP treatment centres by the author.

that 51 per cent of all service providers in Canada included primary treatment goals other than abstinence, including moderation management and harm reduction. That included more than 75 per cent of the providers in each of four provinces and territories, and between 60 and 65 per cent of the programs in six other provinces or territories formally offering alternatives to abstinence as primary treatment goals (see figure 3.1).

Background to the Emergence of the DCT in First Nations Services

In the 1960s and early 1970s the established social order was questioned and challenged, with critical sights focused on social inequities and injustices. The organization of protests, demonstrations, and campaigns for change that characterized those years originated with activist students and academics, left-leaning interest group leaders, investigative journalists, and social scientists. In tandem but apart from that pool of activists were advocates speaking for aboriginal peoples throughout Canada, including First Nations. Whiteside's computations show that aboriginal political organizations mushroomed in number in the late 1960s and 1970s (1973: 10). Associations were formed for treaty rights, social issues, and land rights, as well as for developing general administrative policies and 'other general protests.' In the decade and a half running from 1966 to 1980, 'Native Canadian' political associations approximately quadrupled from the number formed in the previous fifteen years, rising from 29 formed between 1940 and 1965 to 120, then dropping again to 28 between 1981 and 1990 (Whiteside, 1973: 10). As a result of the activist ferment of those years, considerable public pressure was applied to government leaders of the day, who were asked to play a far more interventionist role in addressing social problems. The activity associated with the dramatic growth of aboriginal political associations, combined with the sheer numbers of the latter, constituted a significant revival of aboriginal self-confidence and a new and formidable front in aboriginal affairs. Such a presence required government officials to take aboriginal concerns and demands seriously.

Most of the aboriginal organizations were established to give political voice to a desire to overcome disadvantages concentrated so heavily among the country's first denizens (Price, 1978: chaps 17 and 18). In those years, various studies and press reports systematically illuminated the realities of First Nations communities, revealing poor housing conditions, extreme poverty, unemployment, low education levels, substandard health, and strikingly high rates of accidents, injuries, and fatalities.[2] It was hard not to attribute these population health problems to the displacement of traditional lifestyles and economic activity by a combination of Euro-Canadian public policies, social institutions, and predatory capital accumulation that proceeded as if the First Nations and their needs were inconsequential.

As is often the case in culturally undermined, socially dislocated, and economically marginalized communities that are also politically disempowered, alcohol abuse had become widespread. While problem drinking and alcoholism were the most predominant problems, drug abuse and 'inhalant-sniffing' served to increase the suffering of First Nations individuals, families, and communities, ravaging the health, safety, and overall quality of life for the majority of reserve residents.

---

2 Three reports captured many of the basic statistics describing aboriginal health problems that inspired the moral outrage of the time: Hawthorn (1966); Canada (1971); and Adams, Cameron, Hill, and Penz (1970).

Few if any residents were left untouched by problems in which alcohol abuse was implicated.

Revelations in the popular press of the impoverishment, ill-health, and alcohol-related problems of so many indigenous Canadians virtually forced the government to act. After all, in 1964, under the direction of Prime Minister Lester B. Pearson – and heavily influenced by the domestic policies of the democratic administration of Lyndon Johnson in the United States – Canada had declared a 'War on Poverty,' as yet failing to recognize how hard such a war would be to fight in the 'trenches' of social malaise that had become endemic to reserve communities, remote Métis and Inuit communities, and inner-city neighbourhoods. Under the guidance of Pearson's successor, Pierre Elliott Trudeau, the Liberal government declared the goal of building a Just Society. Programs were mounted on many fronts, from economic development and adult education to community infrastructure and housing. Given public sympathy and the relative wealth of government coffers at the time, it was perhaps inevitable that alcohol problems would be given a specific policy and programming focus as well.

NNAP: The First National Alcohol Abuse Program for First Nations

In December 1974, the federal government approved a nationwide pilot project entitled the National Native Alcohol Program (NNAP). The initiative was intended to promote sobriety and prevent alcohol abuse in First Nations reserve communities. Implemented over three years, beginning in fiscal year 1975–6, the pilot program was officially intended to support community-designed and -operated projects in the areas of alcohol abuse prevention, treatment, and rehabilitation.

Run as a joint initiative of the Department of Indian Affairs and Northern Development and the (then) Department of National Health and Welfare, NNAP continued until a proposal for a permanent program operating under Health and Welfare Canada (renamed 'Health Canada' after the department was divided in two) as a stable community service in conjunction with other community health programming was submitted to and met with the approval of the federal Cabinet in 1981–2.

NNADAP and Adjunct Service Development

The National Native Alcohol and Drug Abuse Program, which succeeded NNAP and was expanded to include efforts at preventing drug abuse, has now been in operation for a decade and a half. The fundamental design of NNADAP was anticipated in a Cabinet discussion paper submitted to the Treasury Board in February 1982. The program was appropriately described in a recent federally commissioned review of the program as 'the Federal Government's primary line of attack to combat alcohol and substance abuse in First Nations communities' (Jock, 1998).

NNADAP was designed to provide treatment, prevention, training, and research, with each element being described as part of a comprehensive federal strategy. It was originally proposed, in the founding Treasury Board submission, that the following elements would be included in the program: *non-medical treatment services*, including intensive psychological and therapeutic counselling as well as support oriented towards social and cultural rehabilitation and typically offered in twenty-eight-day cycles; *prevention* activities, including professional and paraprofessional individual and group counselling, community education, self-help groups, and 'complementary' services that would assist individual and group support for families and friends of abusers, Alcoholics Anonymous, and Native cultural and spiritual practices; *support services* that were to include *training* for paraprofessional and professional prevention and treatment workers and program administrators; and *research and development*. It was also intended that *regionally based Indian and Inuit institutions* would be established to provide program support elements. These institutions were to offer local communities and organizations support through technical assistance, training, research, planning, coordination, service evaluation, and funding (Jock, 1998).

Envisioned treatment elements in the original Cabinet document included not only in-patient, residential treatment centres but also half-way houses and community out-patient services. Services of an explicitly 'medical' nature, including detoxification, were expected to be accessed through health services provided through provincial governments under Medicare.

There are now prevention workers, employed by the bands, funded in the primary community reserve settlements of all First Nations and Inuit communities in Canada and over forty treatment programs, almost all of which consist of in-patient programming. Compared with the full continuum of care provided through provincial governments, which includes prevention, brief therapy, detoxification, pre-care, various lengths of in-patient stay, professional out-patient counselling, and aftercare and relapse prevention, most regional NNADAP regions are far less differentiated. In the First Nations system, professional community counselling on an out-patient basis has not been established and in-patient treatment programming is largely restricted to standardized twenty-eight-day to six-week cycles. Prevention workers tend to provide brief counselling and alcohol education workshops and to make referrals and assist clients and the courts in preparing band members experiencing personal crises and conflict with the law for enrolment in an in-patient treatment program.

After 1986, the administration of on-reserve addictions programming began to be transferred from Health Canada administrative offices directly to bands. The program components of NNADAP that are not currently administered under such transfer arrangements are operated by regional coordinating staff, who process funding proposals and coordinate the negotiation of contribution agreements, transfer agreements, provide some educational support and facilitate the distribution of funding – including the funding of most treatment services.

Admittedly, some emphasis in most NNADAP treatment centres and many communities is also now placed on 'cultural' program elements. These latter elements include regular Elder visits and spiritual ceremonies such as sweats, the burning of sweet grass, and pipe ceremonies. These 'traditional' elements, however, are typically minor aspects of the overall therapeutic curriculum in most centres. In one intensive study I conducted, when interviewed, several treatment centre clients complained of the lack of serious cultural programming, with two suggesting that Elders' presentations had little to do with the other aspects of the therapeutic experience. One program participant said that the Elders' input was essentially a mix of spirituality and folk wisdom that was, in both theme and content, completely unconnected to the overall thrust of other aspects of programming.

Individual and group counselling and various other complementary recreational and educational therapy components are also included as part of treatment programming. Nationally, under five hundred bed spaces are allocated annually across the treatment centre network.

In summary, most alcohol abuse programming serving First Nation reserves is essentially a paraprofessional service organized around a standardized, twenty-eight-day to six-week treatment program based on the disease/pathology model of explanation and intervention.

NNADAP treatment centres have done a laudable job in providing temporary respite for alcoholics from circumstances that encourage problem drinking and in successfully assisting thousands of individuals with their efforts to overcome unhealthy drinking practices. Unfortunately, the needs of the non-alcoholic problem drinker have been neglected in the singular emphasis of centres on alcohol dependency and abstinence.

It is also fair to say that the on-reserve NNADAP workers have played a primary, if not exclusive, role in successfully persuading most adults that excessive drinking is destructive and socially unacceptable. However, now that this message has been communicated and is widely accepted in reserve communities, the functions of the prevention workers have not adapted adequately to changing realities. The greatest current need is to challenge problem drinking norms rather than alcoholism, to stem the flow of other illicit, mood-modifying drugs into the reserves, and to focus on other addictive processes, such as gambling. Rather than adequately responding to these needs, however, community prevention workers in First Nations across the country have tended to retain their focus on middle-aged alcohol dependents and on helping young and middle-aged band members with their legal conflicts. Much of the current time budgets of community substance abuse workers now involves providing referrals to treatment centres at the request of the courts and clients and client assistance in accessing residential treatment services.

While sufficiently useful outcome data for NNADAP treatment programming is not yet available to provide a long-term, post-treatment profile of the program, uncontrolled studies suggest that the Minnesota model has been effective with non-aboriginal alcoholics; in other words, its implementation has been associated with reduced drinking and drug abuse and other positive outcomes. Further, one controlled study of the Minnesota model of treatment in Finland showed positive results (Keso and Salaspuro, 1990). However, as Roberts and Ogborne observe in their report for Health Canada on best practices, the key to the success that has been demonstrated for the Minnesota model probably owes more to the fact that it is delivered as part of a full continuum of care, including aftercare and subsequent involvement in a self-help program (Health Canada, 1999c: 17) and that full continuum of care is not available within the First Nations service network.

Additional Support Services

Several problems that came to be understood as being associated with destructive lifestyles in which drinking was implicated were not included in the original Treasury Board submission, and services that were later viewed as being directly implicated causally or as an outcome of alcohol and drug abuse were not directly funded by the program. These included community-based mental health services and services focused on interpersonal abuse, including child emotional abuse and neglect, spousal abuse; sexual abuse; and family violence generally (Whitehead and Hayes, 1998). A relatively substantial 'community-based funding package' providing allocations for these various functions is also now available in most communities.

The problem of community, familial, and individual effects of cultural denigration in residential schools and the effects of physical, emotional, and sexual abuse suffered in the same institutions also went unrecognized. Finally, in 1998 the Aboriginal Healing Foundation was established to address various issues related to the legacy of residential school abuse.

Lack of Research and Development

In practice, research and development in NNADAP never became a systematic effort that enabled ongoing, outcome evaluation (RAB, 2000). Consequently, hard data to demonstrate the effectiveness of the overall program or of specific dimensions of programming has never been available. Ongoing general surveys to identify and observe changes in problem drinking over time have not been employed in a way that would afford a longitudinal estimation of rising or, hopefully, falling, problem drinking rates. Nor has there been any systematic study of treatment outcomes. Instead, research gaps have been partially but unsatisfactorily filled through program evaluations, community surveys associated with the acquisition of local management of community health service delivery.

While its flaws are many, the NNADAP program concept has been and remains a creative and laudable health promotion concept. The program has combined a community-based intervention strategy with a culturally sensitive approach to in-patient (and some out-patient) treatment. The actual delivery of alcohol abuse services is managed by bands, in the case of prevention projects, and/or bands or groups of bands operating as a non-profit corporation to provide treatment services.

How the DCT Was Absorbed into First Nations Country

Owing to the pervasive influence of American publications and professional associations and networks, as well as the enormous influence of

the American-dominated media, Canadian alcohol intervention workers have been overwhelmed by the *alcoholism-as-disease* model that has
dominated in the United States and was championed by private treatment professionals and AA. Being but a small numerical minority
within Canada, First Nations and their service institutions have the
same type of 'elephant and mouse' relationship with Canada, its institutions, and its ideas that Canada as a whole has with the United
States. When the larger neighbour changes its routines, the impact can
be almost suffocating for the smaller one. While cultural sensitivities,
the advice of traditional healers, and ritualistic cleansing ceremonies
traceable to traditional cultures have been reflected in First Nations
alcohol intervention programming in Canada, treatment approaches
have generally borrowed from the mainstream – and that mainstream
has almost wholly adopted the view that alcohol problems reflect an
underlying, primary *disease*.

When NNADAP was established, the Jellinek model of alcohol problems as a singular, progressive disease, coupled with complementary
self-help participation through Alcoholics Anonymous, influenced virtually all alcohol intervention programming in Canada. Consequently,
NNADAP was conceived within that same frame of reference, and the
personnel employed by the program in the communities and the treatment centres became a conduit for the disease model to infiltrate the
collective aboriginal consciousness. As more than one seasoned
NNADAP worker has observed to me, it is not much of an exaggeration to suggest that the first generation of aboriginal alcohol and drug
abuse workers were all taught the disease perspective.

Some First Nations alcohol abuse prevention workers and treatment
program personnel have begun to seriously explore or implement programs based on models of explanation and intervention that go well
beyond the basic conceptions of the disease model. Attempts are being
made to offer 'holistic' programming that attends to various physical
and psycho-social needs other than alcohol abuse. In addition, traditional elements have become a mainstay of most programming. Upon
closer inspection, however, many of these elements seem cosmetic,
politically correct 'add-ons' to conventional DCT programming. In a
phrase, the DCT still rules the therapeutic roost in 'Indian country.' In
the great majority of in-patient treatment programs operated by First
Nations, there is a focus on abstinence, the idea that problem drinking
is almost always a dependency best described as the 'disease of alcoholism.' The twelve steps tend to be integral to the program and AA is

considered an important referral. In fact, many First Nations AA chapters either meet at treatment centres or are facilitated by counsellors in the program.

In my telephone survey of treatment centre programs across Canada, informants in all regions described the community prevention workers in their area as tending to be recovered alcoholics and former or current participants in AA and/or clients of treatment programs based on the disease model. Confirming the findings of the General Review of NNADAP (Jock, 1998) these key informants in the treatment centres suggested that only a few of the prevention workers had paraprofessional training, and, to their knowledge, none had advanced training in addictions.

Many of the respondents to my telephone survey of treatment programs also suggested that all the prevention workers they knew seemed to be committed to the DCT. This came as no surprise. Worker after worker in the First Nations addictions field have indicated their commitment to the DCT, telling me, often quite assertively, that there is no such thing as problem drinking, just various stages of alcoholism. Many have said there is no such thing as 'social drinking,' at least for First Nations people; instead, most prevention workers I have had contact with claim that 'social drinking' is just an early stage of potential alcoholism, or an expression used by someone 'in denial.' First Nations addictions workers have also repeatedly told me in interviews, workshops, panel discussions, and in informal conversations that alcoholism is a chronic disease that cannot ever be wholly overcome, just suspended through total abstinence. Abstinence is seen to act like a safety on the trigger of a gun, the trigger being an analogy to a drink of an alcoholic beverage. In recent consultations in Saskatchewan with First Nations health workers regarding the proper and more extensive use of Methadone for opioid dependency treatment, the loudest voices of protest against the drug came from addictions workers who argued that the concept challenged the inviolable principle of abstinence in addictions intervention.

First Nations alcohol abuse workers have also frequently told me that aboriginal Canadians not only have a special 'weakness' for alcohol, they also have a tendency to act out their personal anger publicly when they are 'under the influence.' In short, most First Nations substance abuse prevention intervention workers are firmly committed to the idea that aboriginal Canadians simply should not drink because, if they do, trouble will ensue. Many have thus advocated 'sober reserves,' by which they mean implementing a zero-tolerance policy regarding the use of alcoholic beverages in homes and public events on reserves.

For many years, the DCT, right across North America, was 'the only game in town.'[3] For several decades in both Canada and the United States, public and private treatment program personnel and Alcoholics Anonymous have advocated the use of the disease model as an explanation of alcohol problems and the DCT as the sole basis for intervention in the problems associated with unwelcome drinking behaviours. Perhaps because of an initial lack of alternatives, the DCT and the Minnesota treatment arrangement were simply imported into programming dedicated to aboriginal peoples. First Nations programming has largely drawn its most fundamental principles from the body of beliefs and knowledge generated by the most popular self-help group advocates, theorists, and 'treatment' professionals serving a multicultural but primarily non-aboriginal clientele throughout North America.

'Health Transfer' and First Nations Addictions Programming

In its initial conception, NNADAP was viewed as an integrated, multi-tiered alcohol and drug abuse program. Conceptually, it was designed with a national policy-making and coordination capacity, regional coordination, policy development, and support provided through partnerships between Health Canada support units and regional First Nations support institutions, with front-line community prevention workers and treatment programs providing services 'on the ground.' Both prevention and treatment programs worked roughly according to certain guidelines standardized by Health Canada and under contribution agreements that were renegotiated annually. However, in the 1990s, the federal government offered First Nations the opportunity to self-administer and self-design community health services under 3–5 year service transfer agreements (Health Canada, 1999a).

The terms of these agreements are very general, based loosely on a one-line reference to plans prepared by a First Nation. While at the time of writing most treatment programs were not operating under transfer agreements, most alcohol and drug abuse program moneys were allo-

---

3 For an excellent summary of the history of problem drinking prevention and intervention ideas and approaches in the United States, see White (1998); for Canada, see Smart and Ogborne (1986).

cated directly to bands, the majority under long-term agreements. Thus the band administration now makes all significant decisions about who is hired and about the design of service provision. A band may decide not to provide direct services of this kind and use the funding for other legitimate health promotion services, continue with previous arrangements – which is most common – or revise the entire approach they had been taking in the past. While these new arrangements allow considerable room for creative new approaches, the federal health transfer initiative has made developing integrated regional or national programming very difficult at the community level. The counterbalance to this loss of central coordinating capacity in the alcohol and drug abuse area is the formation of the National Native Addictions Partnership Foundation (NNAPF), a national First Nations advocacy organization mandated to promote, advocate, and support the evidence-based, culturally sensitive upgrading and renewal of alcohol and drug abuse programming in the post-transfer era.

Challenges to the Disease Model

Despite the predominance of the DCT in alcohol and drug abuse treatment programs, there is an extensive literature and a highly vocal group of critics of the disease model; in fact, criticism of the disease model has become something of a flourishing school of critical thought, with some writers becoming famous not only in quiet academic circles but also in more public and far louder venues, inspiring heated reactions on radio and television talk shows. This criticism notwithstanding, the disease model survives in mainstream thinking and alcohol abuse treatment alongside or in opposition to more research-based approaches. As the American addictions theorist and historian William L. White (1998: 3) has noted: 'What is most remarkable about the "disease concept" of alcoholism ... is the concept's sheer survivability. This concept has survived more than 200 years of attacks from theologians, philosophers, reformers, psychiatrists, psychologists and sociologists, and yet continues to survive. This suggests that, as a people, we have both an individual and a collective need for this concept to be "true," regardless of its scientific status.'

The ease with which the disease model associates in the public mind, however spuriously, the stubborn problems of alcohol abuse with the hope of clean, efficient medical cures for diseases, may explain its continued popularity. Also, as White observes, contrasting the public and professional popularity of the disease model with its long questionable basis in evidence: 'This truth may be more metaphorical than scientific. Science is unlikely to destroy the popularity of the disease concept, but a better metaphor would' (1998: 330).

Within the occupations and services committed to alcohol abuse prevention and intervention, the 'cutting edge' of the field has for at least two decades distanced itself from the disease model. Several new, complementary evidence-based methodologies are now available in both prevention and intervention. Despite this significant shift away from the medical/disease model paradigm in mainstream alcohol prevention and intervention programming, among First Nations addictions workers and, not surprisingly, the clients exposed to their services, the principal elements of the disease model remain an integral and fundamental component of prevailing explanatory and treatment thinking. Much of that commitment originates in the fact that many if not most alcohol and drug abuse workers employed by First Nations see themselves as 'recovered alcoholics' who have successfully absorbed the 'life experience' of acute alcohol problems. They have acquired the 'wisdom' of recovery that can now be shared with other 'alcoholics.' Underpinning this understanding is a belief in certain invariant, essential elements of an apparently universally applicable healing process that can be shared.

Alcohol and drug abuse workers and other mental health professionals serving First Nations people must stand back and examine the very foundations of the thinking that guides the programs they operate. Despite the growth of alcohol abuse service coverage to the point where virtually all First Nations communities have a First Nations 'addictions program' and an 'alcohol and drug abuse prevention worker' to serve them, and despite having access to a network of more than fifty residential treatment centres across the country operated by First Nations organizations, careless drinking practices continue to be routinely implicated in many, if not most, of the population health problems that are significantly more common among First Nations peoples than among the general Canadian population. As we have seen, these problems include disproportionately high rates of homicide, suicide, family violence and other forms of interpersonal conflict, and of accidents, diabetes, respiratory infections, and various chronic illnesses related to inadequate self-care and dependant care.

It bears repeating that progress has been made on the First Nations alcohol abuse risk-reduction front. As indicated in the previous chapter, consistent quantitative evidence and considerable anecdotal data indicates that the proportion of First Nations abstainers has increased substantially. Several 'old timers' in the field have told me that frequent inebriation was once so commonplace that elected leaders and even alcohol abuse workers were often intoxicated or 'hung over' when participating in annual NNADAP conferences in the early days of the program. I have not witnessed any such intoxication at a NNADAP meeting for at least fifteen years. And as we have seen, more First Nations people than non-aboriginals now avoid the use of alcohol completely.

It will be argued below that, unfortunately, while 'treating' some problem drinkers with conventional approaches can provide a real service to those who meet the clinical criteria of 'alcohol-dependent,' the approach does not meet the needs of most aboriginal problem drinkers and may, in fact, be counter-productive for them.

Alcohol Abuse as a 'Social' Problem for First Nation Reserves

Intervention into the alcohol problems of First Nations depends heavily on *how the problems are defined.* If the causes are unclear and the interventions misguided or misplaced, the human tragedy of remarkably high levels of preventible mental health problems, injury, and death will continue unabated. The effectiveness of such interventions is truly a matter of life and death.

A careful review of the relevant research literature and the more thoughtful theoretical literature dedicated to the subject suggests that the disease concept is far too broadly used in diagnosis, and that it is far too narrow in the range of explanatory variables and strategic approaches it embraces.[4] In fact, as we shall see, the disease model undergirds many of the 'fictions' referred to in chapter 1. It will be argued that, rather than the outcome of a specific disease with a predictable series of secondary outcomes, alcohol problems exist along a continuum. Only a small percentage of the overall population fall onto the

---

4 In 2003, an e-mail communication transmitted by Sheila Lacroix, a librarian at the Centre for Addictions and Substance Abuse (CAMH) of Ontario (Toronto), suggested that, in recent years, the research and theoretical literature in the addictions field had moved beyond the disease model and now focuses on a plurality of factors. This is consistent with the more contemporary view that there are many causes of and paths to problem drinking and addictions, and many outcomes, a concept which is captured in the 'bio-psycho-social' model of addictions.

end of the continuum where acute and frequently arising life-threatening health risks are found.

Beyond the Disease Model: Alternative Perspectives and Social Control Strategies

Admittedly, the causes of alcohol abuse may be partially explained by factors of a biological nature (such as predispositional factors in the brain chemistry) or psychological nature (i.e., mental illness). However, the very fact that the frequency of the problem varies so widely over time among nations, within national populations, and among communities and ethnic and socio-economic groups makes it evident that the social determinants of problem drinking are primary in describing its aetiology.

Alcohol consumption styles as a social problem have essentially been described in two fundamental ways in the research literature. Scarpetti and Anderson (1989: 9) have described alcohol abuse as a 'primary social problem,' which means that the problem is itself a significant cause of additional social problems. There can be little doubt that excessive drinking and drunken behaviours are intimately linked with emotional and physical carnage and the grief that inevitably follows both. According to the other view, alcohol abuse, at least when it is an addiction, is essentially an outcome of underlying poor mental health status (Timpson et al., 1988; Potter-Effron, 1989). There is also extensive evidence that some kinds of alcohol-related destructive behaviour patterns are manifest in individuals with predisposing psychoses and personality disorders (Spotts and Schontz, 1982).

In short, alcohol abuse in First Nations sometimes acts as a primary social problem; at other times, it is a symptom of underlying mental health illness – just as it is in other ethnic populations. What makes alcohol abuse of special concern in First Nations is both its relative frequency and the rates at which drinking episodes translate into destructive outcomes in the form of injuries, both physical and emotional, violence, and death. It is the difference between the rates of these problems in First Nations and in Canadian society as a whole that makes the problem of particular interest and of special importance as a public policy concern.

Taken as a population health problem, alcohol abuse in First Nations must be considered in relation to the social forces affecting rates of occurrence, as well as the ideological orientation to alcohol use that arises in response to those broader forces. From the outset of the problematic use of alcohol by First Nations, those social forces originated in relations with Europeans. Historically and, in their contemporary context, the problem has been generated beyond, but has partially been maintained within, reserve communities. It is therefore essential to examine the alternative ways in which this imported social problem has been addressed in European and North American society generally.

When it first became popular in Britain, Europe, and North America, the disease model was particularly appealing to progressive health reformers and problem drinkers alike largely because of its apparent improvement over previous conceptions. Prior to the adoption of the disease model, drunken behaviours had been viewed simply as signs of immorality, slothfulness, and character weakness. At least in English-speaking societies, alcohol problems had long been considered as a *moral issue* alone. People who frequently drank to excess and publicly displayed their drunkenness were blamed for their behaviour and considered morally degenerate, lacking in self-discipline.

Responses to problem drinking and drunk and disorderly behaviour generally fit into historically specific social control doctrines. Those various doctrines have been translated into policies and programs designed to regulate the behaviour of the available labour supply, the economically disadvantaged, and the potentially rebellious. The aboriginal peoples of North America have not been the sole targets of such policies; peasants made landless in Europe during the period of enclosure, vagrants, and the unemployed and economically displaced and marginalized were also subjected to the often draconian sweep of such regulatory policies.[5] Many of these people shared the experience of dislocation engendered by the societal restructuring attending the large-scale reorganization of labour markets, land use, technological change, and concentrated capital accumulation, all of which, taken together, characterized the explosive development of capitalism from the seventeenth to the twenty-first centuries, a development beginning in western Europe, moving through its colonies in North America (and elsewhere), and subsequently evolving with the emergence of national societies in both Canada and the United States.

---

5 For an excellent review of historical studies of attitudes towards the poor and public reactions to their problems, see 'Shifting Attitudes,' in Bremner (1965).

It would be intellectually convenient if the different public reactions to social problems in Western society had moved forward historically in a clean, easily demarcated sequence. However, a reading of history suggests there is considerable overlap and even a combination of different ideas and approaches regarding appropriate social control strategies, whether the social concern is alcohol or any other problem that provokes a public reaction. Once established, intervention doctrines not only linger stubbornly as dominant influences, despite the attempts of reformers and innovators to dislodge them; they also continue influential long after they have been officially rejected and displaced by newer approaches. In fact, a case can be made that the influence of major social control strategies never fully disappears; they are reduced in influence but persist and overlap with other ideas. This tendency is reflected in policy statements and the high-blown words of policy makers and academics and, more readily, in the discussions of 'front-line' human service and public security workers and their clients, as well as in the wider body of popular beliefs.

In a short but insightful treatment of the subject, Richard Henshel (1976) attempts to describe the various doctrines and organized strategies that have been used historically to address social problems. Some of the doctrines he identifies, as well as others that have guided interventions in the problem of alcohol abuse, will be outlined below. While several of these doctrines and approaches to intervention have been officially discarded, in popular discussions they are still routinely cast as solutions to alcohol abuse.

In societies in which beverage alcohol is widely available, excessive drinking and drunken behaviour have probably always been looked at through moral lenses. While alcohol has long been valued for its presumed medicinal and mood-modifying effects, its excess use has been identified as a social problem in many periods and cultures. As Miller and Hester (1995) have noted, although the term 'alcoholic' was introduced in 1849 by Swedish physician Magnus Huss to refer to the adverse consequences of excessive drinking, the dangers of alcohol abuse have been known since the beginning of recorded history. As the same writers also observe, until recently, alcohol abuse was always understood as a natural consequence of bad personal choices.

Three corrective strategies reflect the ancient idea that immoral personal choices are the cause of alcohol abuse: the interventionist strategy of *reward and punishment*, the *denial of opportunity*, and *moral rejuvenation*. These approaches have been reflected in many cultures.

The Interventionist Strategy of Reward and Punishment

The simple belief that social control is best maintained by rewarding good behaviour and punishing bad behaviour has been a fundamental organizing principle of family and community life. In pre-historic societies (societies without a written language) and historic societies alike, rewards for exemplary behaviour have been handed out in the form of blessings from religious leaders, charity when you are 'down on your luck,' extra business for a trade, 'cushy jobs,' or other favours bestowed by the rich or politically powerful. For simply observing the norms and moral codes of a society, one is rewarded by being favoured with the protection of some form of security force, such as the police.

By contrast, punishment or retribution for unacceptable behaviour has probably been a part of the social control systems of virtually all societies. Running the gauntlet, being placed in stocks in a public square in medieval Europe, having a body part removed in Islamic or ancient pagan and Hebrew societies, hanging, electrocution, or various forms of imprisonment: all of these forms of punishment have been used at different times and in different cultures to avenge publicly perceived wrongdoing. The appeal of the principle behind this type of intervention is to the human sense of reciprocal justice and protection of the social fabric. A sense of fairness is signalled by the demand for a wrong avenged and the act of punishment invokes a collective fear, encouraging 'sober second thoughts' about engaging in similar deviant or antisocial behaviour.

The idea of balancing the damage of one party by reciprocating harm to the other is found in most cultures and reflected in the biblical saying 'An eye for an eye and a tooth for a tooth.' European society's 'skid rows,' vagrancy acts, workhouse placements, jailing, and other forms of marginalization were once understood as legitimate mechanisms for the punishment and segregation of the chronic alcohol abuser who displayed his or her drunkenness in public.

In medieval Britain, the precursor to the national society which, in subsequent centuries, expanded globally and established the (once) Dominion of Canada, concern about drunkenness focused solely on the poor. The issue arose in a religious context in which decisions had to be made about the use of charitable funds secured through tithing (church collections). It was assumed that those deserving of charity were those who displayed behaviours acceptable to the affluent and the aristocrats;

they were called the 'deserving poor' or the 'worthy poor.' Drunken behaviour was taken as a clear sign of being one of the 'unworthy poor' while sobriety was a sign of 'worthiness.' Those exhibiting drunken behaviours were punished through various means, including physical beatings and the withholding of food at times of destitution.[6]

Punishment for crimes against person or property committed when under the influence of alcohol remain very much a part of even the most advanced legal systems. However, it is also true that the argument that inebriation is in some cases a legal defence that can limit the severity of the penalty for the commission of a crime continues to be made before the Canadian courts.

Denial of Opportunity

One way to tackle a substance abuse problem is simply to reduce the supply of the consumable substance of concern. Strict prohibition laws were a part of the social control strategies directed against alcohol use by some aboriginal peoples of Meso-America (MacLeod, 1928: 28). Legal prohibition of the sale of alcoholic beverages, the interdiction of alcohol sales to Status Indians in Canada, and reserve bans on drinking or selling alcohol are obvious examples of the denial of opportunity, as are laws prohibiting the sale of alcohol or cigarettes to minors. While denial of opportunity is often an effective strategy for controlling the extent of a social problem, it rarely purges it entirely from a system and, when pursued to the extreme, it can result in new problems that emerge as a reaction to the problem for which the intervention was designed.

One well-known example of a social control policy misfiring was the spawning of a criminalized organization of liquor sales after the passage of prohibition laws in the United States during the 1920s. Another, more recent example, is the extensive cigarette smuggling across the Great Lakes from the United States to Canada following the deliberate inflation of cigarette prices through taxation to act as a cost-inhibitor of sales in the 1990s.

One of the most significant organizational influences on the strategy of foreclosing opportunities to acquire and consume alcoholic beverages came from the temperance movement. In its early years, the

---

6 Ibid.

movement emphasized the cautious and 'temperate' use of alcohol because its members believed it to be a hazardous substance – a drug which, when used excessively, tended to have harmful consequences (Miller and Hester, 1995: 2). Gradually, as its political influence grew, the movement became more confident and ambitious in its intentions, and its name could have been changed to the prohibition movement by the early 20th century. In the United States, the movement's thinking came to predominate until the repeal of prohibition in 1933 (Miller and Hester, 1995: 2).

The temperance movement was a significant social movement in Canadian history, with its members embracing various social causes in addition to alcohol abuse, such as male infidelity to their spouses, white slavery, and a lack of recreational and educational resources for women and the poor. Essentially an import from Britain and the United States, the temperance movement had its roots in fundamentalist churches, especially the Baptists and the Methodists, rather than the mainstream Roman Catholic and Anglican churches (Smart and Ogborne, 1986: chap.1). From the 1820s, the movement succeeded in its more than one hundred years of Canadian operation in converting a large part of the population to abstinence; it also convinced political leaders to introduce prohibition throughout the country.

Moral Rejuvenation

The idea of moral regeneration of a deviant or someone who, in the Christian tradition, has 'fallen from grace,' is an ancient, even prehistorical one. According to Henshel (1976), movements that encourage moral regeneration tend to arise in conditions of social and spiritual malaise – hence the growth of Christianity in the late Roman empire and the Ghost Dance on the North American Plains in the 1800s, the rise of the Native American Church in the twentieth century among aboriginal peoples in the south and west of the United States, and the emergence of the Cargo cults in Melanesia. These revitalist movements encourage a cleansing of ways that have corrupted individuals or societies and involve purification rituals and spiritual quests that can be quite elaborate. The reference to a 'higher power' and the confession before a group of embarrassing or shameful past behaviours in AA are clearly linked to the doctrine of moral regeneration. In non-religious cases, this approach is typically based on ideologies such as utopian social movements.

A major break with punitive doctrines occurred in the late 1700s in both Britain and British North America (Henshel, 1976: 10–11). Impetus for this new, less punitive, thinking derived primarily from the work of the Quakers and other religious reform organizations. The moral rejuvenation of legal offenders, including public inebriates, was called for, to be achieved by physical confinement to encourage 'meditation' and reflection about one's misbehaviour, discipline, strictly regimented days, and 'hard work' to help the prisoner to replace his or her 'idleness' with industry. Its intention may have been more benign than the punitive strategies of the past, but this correctional perspective took a great toll on those unfortunate enough to become its targets. Solitary confinement often had the effect of inducing severe mental and emotional stress and incapacitation in those being 'reformed' (Henshel, 1976: 11). During times of great economic stress, however, the severity of the conditions associated with confinement were often more relaxed. It was recognized that conditions beyond the control of the individual may have led to the individual's unemployment and distress, the latter sometimes being expressed through drunken behaviour.

The Interventionist Doctrine of Rehabilitation

The influence of the far more humane and hopeful interventionist doctrine of *rehabilitation* followed its more punitive predecessor. The idea of rehabilitation was based on the concept of 'salvaging' the soul errant (Henshel, 1976). In corrections and mental health, this began with the development of a system of asylums and the alteration of the names existing institutions. Youth detention facilities became 'reform schools;' adults who had committed minor criminal or major civil offences were similarly sentenced to incarceration in 'reformatories' or 'penitentiaries' (note the root word 'penitent') – and, finally, in 'rehabilitation centres.' As an even more sympathetic view of 'corrections' took hold, parole and probation were later added to the repertoire of legal interventions (Henshel, 1976: 11). While the changes were often made more in name than in practice, the rehabilitation perspective replaced moral reawakening as the ruling corrections and mental health ideology.

Perhaps impressed by the affluence, prestige, authority, and professional prominence of the physicians who 'treated' the physical health of the sick and injured, those whose work dealt instead with problems solely indicated by behavioural patterns turned to the medical model of curative interventions for organizational and strategic models of service delivery.[7] The new institutions developed as 'therapeutic communities' and counsellors and 'treatment professionals' sought to professionalize their knowledge base, much as the physicians had done, with their attendant university degrees, technical journals, and self-regulating associations.

The disease model was obviously not a great leap in thought or practice from the rehabilitation perspective, which had emphasized the social reshaping of the individual 'deviant' drinker. While the rehabilitation approach had moved intervention in the direction of the medical model of service organization, the subsequent treatment approach seemed to justify it, to make it a seemingly perfect fit. All that was required was the reframing of alcohol problems from deviance shaped by social pathology to a psychiatrically defined pathology defined in terms of psychological and physiological 'addiction,' perhaps with the addition of a truly medical cause, a *genetic predisposition*.

From a reformer and social critic's perspective, both the rehabilitation view and the disease models were significant, progressive advances over the view that drunkenness was simply a sign of moral weakness and a disinclination for work. Both fit neatly into the view that assistance with alcohol problems could be provided through residential institutions or day programs where 'patients' were 'treated' in a warm and comfortable respite setting by caring professionals. The theory that alcohol abuse problems are caused by factors independent of the will, character, or morality of the problem drinker was a welcome change from the older view which had blamed the individual with the problem and thereby justified immediate and harsh, punitive and degrading government interventions in the lives of the poor.

Explaining alcohol problems in disease terms was particularly appealing to therapists and social workers sympathetic to the needs of the habitual alcohol abuser. It represented an opportunity to recast intervention from a punishment orientation to one of assisted recovery. Stated colloquially, however, convincing a dubious public and resistant officialdom that behavioural excesses associated with recreational alcohol consumption were not to be blamed on the individual proved to be a 'tough sell.'

---

7 The literature on the professionalization of human service occupations is extensive. Three references that are especially useful in this regard are Wilensky and Lebeaux (1965); Etzioni (1969); and Toren (1972).

The Influence of Alcoholics Anonymous: Wedding Self-Help Groups and Spirituality to the DCT

The AA movement has been very influential in promoting the disease concept. With roots in the temperance movement of the nineteenth century and various social activist movements that have advocated prohibition, the organization was established in 1935 as a voluntary association among a handful of alcoholics. Its philosophical origins are reflected in its confessional style and 'salvation-from-sin' spirit. Originally, the movement reflected a bias against medicine's role in alcohol problems, because AA leaders did not believe physicians took abusive drinking seriously enough. However, realizing that medicine was rapidly becoming the gatekeeper of which health problems were acceptable as excuses for urgent intervention, the champions of AA campaigned to convince the medical profession that alcoholism was a disease. In doing so they made the conceptual leap from the 'alcohol-as-sin' metaphor to the disease model, neglecting to persistently underscore that a metaphor, no matter how adequate, remains a metaphor rather than the actual phenomenon.

As Stanton Peele has observed (1995: 119–26), in 1944, Marty Mann, an American publicist and early AA member, organized the National Committee for Education on Alcoholism (now the National Council on Alcoholism and Drug Dependence) as a public relations arm for the organization. She enlisted well-placed scientists and physicians to promote the disease model of alcoholism (later AA popularized its importance by enlisting public testimonials from famous entertainers and other public personalities). Without the collaboration with medicine, AA could not have enjoyed the enduring success that distinguishes it from earlier temperance groups.

Unfortunately, as Room (1983) has convincingly argued, the disease model presents problem drinking and alcoholism historically; further, rather than taking social and cultural variations into account, disease model advocates present it as a problem to which only some people are vulnerable, and a malady for which only some form of medically approved intervention can be expected to be effective. A social problem has thus become medicalized and dislocated from the social context in which it emerged.

Along with Canadian Martha Sanchez-Craig, formerly of the Addiction Research Foundation of Ontario, Harvard University's Stanton Peele and Archie Brodsky have been at the helm of a growing body of researchers, psychologists, counsellors, and social workers who have despaired at the muscular hold of the disease model over the addictions intervention community.[8] These researchers and writers remind us that AA has grown in its influence, even substantially widening the span of problems it defines as diseases and promises to cure. In this wider swath they describe, the critics correctly include a variety of 'spin-off' organizations targeted on various bad habits and addictions: Narcotics Anonymous (NA) for drug addicts; Al-Anon for spouses of alcoholics; Alateen for children of alcoholics; and Gamblers Anonymous (GA) for gamblers, as well as organizations for 'sexaholics' and 'shopaholics' (Sexaholics Anonymous and Shopaholics Anonymous). Discerning a material interest in this 'anonymous-organizations-for-every-bad-habit' trend, several commentators have suggested a 'cozy link' to counselling programs, hospitals, and treatment centres. In a personal comment to the author, Stanton Peele noted that, in the United States, the medical establishment has come to recognize the considerable financial and other advantages of piggybacking on the AA folk movement.

Reducing Risk Factors and Promoting Resilience:
The Psycho-Educational Alternative in Therapeutic Discourse

Another influence on my scepticism about the application of the disease/medical model to behavioural problems has been the suspicion by many social critics that policies and programs intended to help the disadvantaged have focused far too much on their weaknesses and limitations, and on the solutions of outside experts. To break the cycle of disadvantage, the critics have argued, factors that promote unhealthy outcomes must be identified and strategies mounted to reduce them, while the factors associated with empowerment amidst adversity should be emphasized in policy and programming. From this perspec-

---

8 Martha Sanchez-Craig, now retired, was a research scientist with Ontario's Addiction Research Foundation (ARF). She pioneered research into various types of alcoholic abuse, as well as skill-training techniques that could be used to assist problem drinkers to overcome their excess drinking habits by learning how to drink moderately. Sanchez-Craig also developed a well-known manual for training appropriately screened candidates in what has come to be called 'moderation management.' The program is called *Drinkwise* and is available through the Centre for Addictions and Mental Health (CAMH) in Toronto.

tive, emphasis in prevention must be given to programs that lower environmental risks and free up the latent strengths of people and their communities and to direct intervention programming that draws upon and enhances current assets and strengths. This perspective grew out of the work of Escalona (1982) and Werner and Smith (1982).

In order to explore the combined effects of prematurity and poor environmental circumstances on quality of life outcomes, Sibylle Escalona, a New York psychiatrist, collected extensive physiological and social-psychological data on a population she called 'babies at double hazard' (1982). Escalona identified a sample of infants who had been low-birthweight babies in the neonatal intensive care unit of the Albert Einstein College of Medicine in New York and monitored their health and social profiles from birth to age three and a half. She found the children who had been premature infants were far more vulnerable than full-term babies to damage resulting from environmental disadvantages, such as living in slum neighbourhoods in low-income families from marginal ethnic groups, and in poor housing conditions. Dr Escalona's work indicated that social class positioning acted as a buffer against the predictably damaging outcomes of environmental stresses.

The most well-known, path-breaking research into the positive outcomes of social and personal development factors for children trapped in environmentally adverse circumstances was contributed by clinical psychologists Emmy Werner and Ruth Smith (1982) conducted on the Hawaiian island of Kauai. Their study was able to track from birth to adulthood a remarkable 88 per cent of a sample of babies born in 1955. The ethnic and social spectrum of the sampled population was wide, encompassing Polynesian, Asian, and European descendants of many generations of islanders and a variety of social classes. More than half the sample were raised in families in which the mothers had completed high school and the fathers were low-income, unskilled, and semi-skilled workers, while others came from middle-class and professional families. Among other things, the study charted the relationship between physical disadvantages of a genetic nature and developmental outcomes over time as they varied with the stimulation, care, and stability of the nurturing family. They found that constitutional difficulties inherent in the child at birth were far more often overcome in stable, supportive families than in unstable families with stresses that limited their motivation for compensatory support.

The relationship between poor physical health or disabilities and mental health during childhood has consistently been shown to be a strong predictor of troubled outcomes. A background of social disadvantage during childhood is significantly more likely to be reflected in low educational completion levels, a lack of functional literacy, unemployment, legally defined child neglect, and other forms of conflict with the law.[9] Having caring parents and a stable family with a middle-class level of income provides a buffer against childhood vulnerability. Much of the available literature also suggests that even within families and community environments that reflect low socio-economic status, the outcomes for vulnerable children vary significantly. Specifically, parents with fundamental socio-economic disadvantages who somehow muster the resources to stimulate their children and provide ongoing, exceptionally caring support, even for those children with significant physical or mental disadvantages, can have a strong positive influence on the quality of life their children obtain as adults.

The 'resiliency' perspective has called the most fundamental assumptions of the 'pathological' or 'disease' model into question, encouraging us to be concerned about the self-fulfilling prophecy generated by its premises. Several writers have been influential in promoting this new emphasis in the intervention field, including Lisbeth B. Schorr, who has emphasized macro-level intervention (public policy) and community-based (mezzo-level) social programs targeted on mothers, infants, families, schools, and employment (1988). A variety of community-based programs delivered through the First Nations and Inuit Health Branch (FNIHB) of Health Canada have reflected this targeted, community-based programming strategy.

At the micro level of intervention, cognitive-behavioural and socio-cognitive psychology has encouraged personal skill development to solve practical problems of living rather than focusing on psycho-analytic and pharmacological treatments for people with mild to moderately disabling lifestyle and behavioural patterns. The psychiatrist Flach (1988) and Wolin and Wolin (1993), a physician and psychologist, respectively, have stressed resiliency as a theme in practical problem solving for psychological therapy, personal development, and general mental health enhancement.

---

9 The literature that catalogues these relationships is voluminous and I will not attempt to summarize it. Specific books that serve as useful references can, however, be mentioned, including: Schorr (1989); Townson (1999); Evans et al. (1992); Ross, Scott, and Kelly (1996); and Wilkins (1997).

The Harm Reduction Perspective

Yet another approach to problem drinking, referred to as the *harm reduction perspective*, is now playing a significant role in shifting the mainstream addictions treatment paradigm away from some of the basic assumptions of the disease model.

The harm reduction perspective has called into question the notion that people with social, cognitive, and behavioural problems must be motivated to change before they are appropriate candidates for therapeutic intervention. The disease/medical model and AA have long assumed that until a problem drinker admits to his or her 'alcoholism,' 'bottoms out,' and displays a robust motivation for change, s/he cannot be helped. While motivation is a critical element in any personal development strategy, advocates of harm reduction suggest that it is a far too simple and, ultimately, cruel approach to the needs of victims of what might be termed 'the biological or societal crap shoot.'

The harm reduction perspective suggests that the most vulnerable in society, such as homeless transients, sex-trade workers, chronic alcoholics, and drug addicts, should not be written off in public policy and programming service strategies because they do not meet the motivational expectations of service providers and self-help organizations. This perspective advocates the need for more protective care, care delivered, however, with a clear respect for the client, as reflected in a keen appreciation of his or her stage of motivation for change. The approach also challenges the insistence in the disease model that abstinence is the only goal, supporting instead the simultaneous intervention of pharmacological administrations, as well as psychological and social supports.

Social Reorganization: Beyond the Individual

The resiliency approach recognizes the potential strengths of the individual and, to some extent, even of the communities of the dispossessed. However, the emphasis always remains focused on interventions aimed directly at the individual, who serves as the focal point for strategies aimed solving social problems. A radically different response to mental illness generally and addictive and substance abuse behaviour specifically as social problems is reflected in what Henshel (1976) refers to as *social reorganization*. As that writer states: 'Far from regarding the acts of specific individuals as the source of the problem, its advocates tend to see these acts as symptoms only of a deeper flaw. Individuals are seen as victims of the system they live under, acting out what they are constrained to do by the impositions of a radically defective set of social arrangements' (14).

The literature that has recently given impetus to this focus in the mental health and addictions field derives from writers who have viewed therapy with suspicion, tracing its benefits to both an explicit and implicit alliance between the state and the professions and quasi-professions employed to provide human services.

Scepticism about the conceptual framing of 'mental health' difficulties as diseases when they are, at least arguably, social constructions imposed and negotiated by the individual has long been championed by Thomas Szasz (1961). An American psychiatrist with origins in Europe, Szasz has for decades argued that while mental 'illness' may on rare occasion be appropriately understood through metaphors describing a disease, it typically has nothing to do with neurobiological influences – and the metaphor itself should be employed infrequently, as it is often misused.

Psychologist Tana Dineen is another vocal critic of psychological interventions. Dineen has castigated many in her own profession by forcefully arguing that, all too often, the 'psychology industry' is based on false claims. She argues that counselling psychology has 'grown' its client base among large numbers of people whom it cannot help (1996). In too many cases, argues Dineen, clients would be better advised to sort out their own problems by utilizing their own resources and the advice of family and friends.

A more recent and professionally rigorous treatment of this matter has been provided in a publication by Allan V. Horwitz. A health policy analyst, Horwitz argues that the idea that mental illness is a disease is only applicable to a small number of serious psychological conditions (2002). He notes the striking acceleration in recent years in the rate of growth of conditions classified as psychiatric disorders, arguing that most of those now included are actually cultural constructions. Rather than benefiting those who are inappropriately classified as mentally ill, this expanded diagnostic inventory of disorders benefits various interest groups, including mental health researchers and clinicians, mental health advocacy groups, and prescriptive drug manufacturers. In support of this argument, Horwitz presents case studies of such conditions as hysteria, depression, and multiple personality disorder, arguing that such conditions are far better remedied with social interventions.

In fact, there is a growing body of writers critical of the entire notion of employing therapeutic methods as primary responses to social problems, at least to the extent that they are offered as alternatives to more fundamental preventive interventions that lie beyond the level of the individual. Thus, Chrisjohn and Young (1994) have taken issue with the attempts of therapists employed by governments to profile the difficulties experienced by First Nation adult 'survivors' of residential school abuse in psychological terms. Specifically, the two psychologists find dubious the concept of a 'residential school syndrome,' a phrase that was used for several years to cover such a wide variety of outcomes that the very concept lost its focus. The basic objection of Chrisjohn and Young is that treating victims of such abuse as candidates for psychological labelling in need of psychotherapeutic interventions is misguided. Such labelling and intervention, they argue, is often of questionable efficacy and, while it does little for the former school residents who were subjected to abuse, it serves to deflect attention from the true nature of the abuse itself. The residential school abuse is better seen for what it is: a crime that calls out for legal action and compensation for its victims.

Other critics of current poverty intervention policies have called for a fundamental reorganization of public welfare programs. The American social policy analyst Michael Sherraden (1991) has taken aim at the American approach (and, by extension, the Canadian and European approaches) to providing income security and promoting employment for the poor. He has argued that the efficacy of the income-based public welfare system in the United States has not been demonstrated and requires a fundamental overhaul. Sherraden calls for a new approach that includes income and assets, the latter in the form of adult education, support for one's self or one's children, housing down payments, access to equity to establish a small business, or retirement pensions. In *The Rise of the Therapeutic State* (1993), Andrew Polsky similarly argues that American welfare policies, rather than drawing the poor out of and up from their low-income and adverse social circumstances, have instead limited their personal autonomy and deflected a critical discourse on alternative, more egalitarian economic policies.

If the critics are correct that therapies and current public assistance programs cannot provide sound and effective assistance for problems rooted in poverty, why do the poor accept and cooperate with the approach? One answer is, of course, that choices are far more limited for the poor. Another answer given by the critics appears to rest on the accuracy of the Marxist concept of 'false consciousness,' which would suggest that the understanding the poor have of their own problems is distorted. Personal or group inadequacies, rather than the social structures and beliefs that define the nature of their current existence, are accepted as the primary source of problems. The poor come to believe that they are powerless to change the social system and that their personal fate is largely sealed by forces beyond their control. According to Herman and Chomsky (2002), the consent of the poor and powerless is given because their obedience is 'manufactured'; they are flooded with messages communicated through what amounts to a social control curriculum – a curriculum delivered by the formal education system and mass media, both of which are ultimately controlled by or working in the best interests of the affluent and powerful.

The critics further argue that the prevailing public policy orientation tends to reduce social problems to difficulties that can best be solved by individualized responses, often aided both by the 'helping professions' and income security programs.

John McKnight has argued that, on balance, interventions by the state and specialized professionals in the lives of the inner city and rural poor in the United States and Canada is more a curse than a blessing. He has argued that these outside influences tend to sap the self-determination of the residents, to undermine the informal and traditional institutional fabric of their communities, and to colonize their service provision rather than to enhance their communities and empower them as participants (1997: 117–27). In his writing, McKnight (1994; 1997; McKnight and Kretzman, 1993) has focused on re-empowering disadvantaged communities by drawing on their own internal strengths and reducing their dependency on outside 'experts.'

The common concern of these writers is that applying clinical labels, which in and of themselves may be of negative therapeutic benefit, subtly shifts the focus and blame from perpetrators to victims. The impression is left that the source of the problem and its solution resides wholly in the psyche of the victim or the slothful behaviour of a 'client group,' rather than with the perpetrators of the original abuse and their sponsors, the state and the elites whose influence tends to dominate the public policy agenda.

The alternative approach to social problems, that of social reorganization, calls for a reformist or a revolutionary response to social problems. The reformist approach emphasizes policies and programs that ameliorate the conditions which give rise to the concentration of social problems among the economically marginal. The revolutionary approach calls for the transformation of the socio-economic hierarchy that systemically and routinely distributes society's opportunities and benefits in an inequitable way.

4

Alcoholism as Pathology: The Reasoning and Allure of the Disease Perspective

According to the disease perspective, individuals with alcohol abuse problems are uniformly viewed as being chronically ill rather than bad or of weak character. This characterization has obvious appeal to individuals who have experienced significant alcohol-related problems. Having been subjected to the disapproval of the public and to punitive treatment by agencies of social control, for alcoholics and their sympathizers, being viewed as suffering from an affliction is preferable to being viewed and treated as a moral degenerate. The more sympathetic aspect of the model also has an obvious appeal to indigenous North American peoples weary of negative stereotypes and harsh judgments directed at them by individuals of non-aboriginal ethnicity.

The disease model originated in European and Euro–North American culture. It was welcomed by those concerned about alcohol abuse and addictions because it represented a break with the harshness of conventional views of the heavy drinker; it not only substituted sympathy and empathy for disgust and contempt, its advocates also claimed that it was scientifically grounded.

In the disease model, the problem drinker is an 'alcoholic.' As a person with an 'illness,' the alcoholic is viewed as victim of something beyond his or her control and thus a deserving object of compassion. Unlike the 'drunk,' the 'alcoholic,' a term forged in the public mind by advocates of the disease model, is considered to be someone who needs the care and concern of intimates and friends and the assistance of professional diagnosticians, treatment providers, and sympathetic support groups. In the disease model, the alcoholic is a person with a chronic disease for which there is no cure; instead, he or she must learn to completely avoid drinking beverage alcohol. The alcoholic's need to drink frequently and heavily is viewed as both the actual disease and the trigger for other behavioural problems. Allowed to play itself out, this reasoning offers a ready-made excuse for everything from public mischief and driving 'while under the influence' through wife battery and child neglect to even arson and murder.

Advocates of the disease model in its purest form hold that alcoholism is also a primary disease, which means that it exists separately from any other co-occurring illnesses, that it causes its own symptoms, and that it is not itself a symptom of some other disease. Most advocates of the disease model also believe that the disease of alcoholism has its roots in biology – specifically, in the distinctive, genetically determined chemistry of the alcoholic's brain. From this perspective, alcoholism is a primary and very significant social problem: it not only directly creates social-psychological impairment and health problems for large numbers in the general population, but its treatment and secondary consequences are very costly for society. The financial burden created by drunken comportment and the behaviour of alcoholics is enormous (Single et al., 1996), and it is associated with a variety of other secondary social problems. The most significant of those problems are those that victimize people other than the alcoholic, such as emotional abuse and neglect, violence- and accident-related injuries traceable to the impairment of the alcoholic. The expense to employers of alcoholics can also be substantial, in terms of costly mistakes on the job, employee days lost, and employee assistance plan program costs and benefit pay-outs.

The Disease Model and the Pathologizing of Problems of Living

The disease model fits readily within a larger conceptual framework that analytically shapes how deviance and mental illness are typically examined by many social and behavioural scientists. In that conceptual framework, the social problems concentrated among the poor and dispossessed are viewed as 'pathological,' unhealthy deviations from the norms of the larger society. For some sociologists, excessive drinking and its accompanying, destructive behaviours are a social concern because, in various ways, they are antagonistic to the normal functioning of families, communities, and societies.

The special temptation in sociology to view behavioural problems in pathological terms originates well back in the history of the discipline. Herbert Spencer, considered one of sociology's 'founding fathers,' wrote in the nineteenth century that the organic analogy, which equated society with a biological organism, allowed for the scientific study of the evolutionary growth stages of societies.[1] This analogy invites the examination of social problems in organic terms: a pattern of deviance is considered in terms of its threat to the organism as a whole (i.e., society) or to a subsystem of that organism (i.e., a community, minority group, subculture, or formal institution). Just as an organism may be invaded by a virus and its normal capacities threatened, so a deviant pattern of behaviour or a group antagonistic to society can threaten the normal functioning of society or a subsystem within it.

One indicator of this tendency to 'pathologize' problems of living is the inflation of both professional and popular vocabularies of human mental and behavioural disorder. A visit to your neighbourhood bookstore will expose you to a wealth of popular psychology literature replete with recently coined buzzwords for emotional, behavioural, and cognitive disorders. The championship belt for overstatement in this ever-expanding verbal wash of dysfunctional labelling must surely go to the American theologian and self-proclaimed family expert, John Bradshaw. In his once-syndicated television series, Bradshaw claimed that the vast majority of North American families were 'dysfunctional,' a claim which, phrased slightly differently, he reiterated in a book. Ninety-six per cent of all families, according to Bradshaw, were 'emotionally impaired' (1988). This penchant in 'pop psychology' for capturing socially irritating behaviours with diagnostic labels is more than matched by the certified professionals. As Allan V. Horwitz writes in his recent book on the subject, the standard diagnostic manual of psychiatric disorders (DSM-IV) has mushroomed in the past several decades. The manual now has nearly four hundred discrete categories in its classification of mental disorders (2002: 2). Reflecting on this fact, Horwitz comments:

---

1 Herbert Spencer (1820–1903) attempted to write a system of synthetic philosophy that would unify all sciences of the day. His publications on sociology included *Social Statics*, his first book, written in 1850; *Principles of Sociology* (1867); and *The Study of Sociology*, published in 1873. An excellent treatment of Spencer's sprawling thought is provided in chapter 3 of Timasheff (1967; first published in 1955). The organic analogy became a central component of much subsequent sociology and it is still very much a part of the discipline. While it has generally given way to systems theory, the metaphor in systems theory often better expresses a parallel between society and biological systems than other types of physical systems.

The culture of mental health that not so long ago was the province of a relatively small group of intellectuals and bohemians is now the everyday
reality of daytime talk shows, television series, popular magazines ... and
virtually all advice columnists. A huge cultural transformation in the construction of mental illness has occurred in a relatively short time. The broad
array of mental illnesses at the beginning of the twenty-first century has little resemblance to older stereotypes of madness that persisted throughout
most of human history ... many mental illnesses that are now taken for
granted as objective natural entities are recent creations. (2002: 4–5)

Despite the obvious irony, many sociologists, presumably students
of social causation, have themselves contributed in a major way to the
framing of explanations for social problems as individual or social
pathologies. In the latter case, the sociological tendency is to search for
the norms of subpopulations that make their members vary from the
standards of the majority in the wider society in ways that trouble
well-placed members of that majority.

The tendency in sociology to pathologize the problems of minority
groups; aboriginal peoples in industrial society; low-income, inner-city
areas of high unemployment; rebellious teens; and other marginalized
groupings is especially apparent in deviance theory. For those theorists who claim sympathy with deviant subcultures, a variety of deviant patterns are taken as a signal of need, a cry for help, an indication
that something must be changed *within* the community from which the
deviants come. The typical policy direction implied by the theoretical
output of these sociologists is that efforts must be directed at changing
the minority's pathological norms. Presumably, such intervention is
needed for the benefit of the members believed to be suffering from the
eccentric and unhealthy social norms characteristic of their community
(e.g., dysfunctional families or inadequate parents).

Students of social deviance who are less sympathetic with the deviancy of marginalized groups often examine the issue in metaphorical
terms, viewing the larger society as an organism and deviant subcultures within it as posing a sort of viral threat to the societal status quo.
Definitions of what is normal are assumed to be associated with a
broad, societywide consensus on what is and what is not acceptable
behaviour. The possibility that the chain of causation for social problems may begin with and be reinforced by social-systemic factors over
which deviants have little control, such as social disorganization associated with unemployment, community isolation, and poverty, is for-

gotten. In other words, it may be the society as a whole that is 'screwed up,' not its deviating minorities.

As Hagan (1977: 72) has observed, the fundamental question that these *consensus theories* ask is: *Why would anyone break the rules of life that nearly all of us accept – particularly when observing these rules may be a means of obtaining the things most of us value?* When deconstructed, this body of explanatory literature views geographically, ethnically, and socially concentrated social problems such as widespread alcohol abuse as individual or group adaptations to frustrated goals.

In keeping with this type of explanation, Dailey (1968) and others have described drinking in aboriginal communities as being consistent with the functions of vision quests, trances, dreams, and related rituals in many traditional North American cultures. Once adopted, beverage alcohol simply became another means of facilitating mind- and mood-altering experiences in a communal context. According to Dailey and others, drinking was, at least in these traditional contexts, a spiritual exercise which functioned in a positive way to provide novel physical and psychological sensations, to release inhibitions by providing a respite, a brief moratorium, on expressive control. Seen in this way, drunken comportment became a means of shoring up community by providing an outlet for the release of pent up, raw emotion. It allowed for the release of pressures that might otherwise rip the social fabric and destroy community. By allowing a 'time out' for interpersonal, emotional expression and irresponsible behaviour, group drinking enabled a return to a stoic social life. After the party, all is forgiven and community life returns to normal. While such drinking may have functioned to promote social integration prior to the pressures of enculturation and economic change associated with contact with Euro–North American society, Dailey (1968) noted that it became a primarily disruptive influence over time.

Other sociologists view concentrations of alcohol and drug abuse in specific population segments as the consequence of individually held but blocked aspirations for prized material possessions and participation in the more valued positions in the mainstream economy and society. Thus, in his classic formulation of social theory, Harvard sociologist Robert K. Merton (1957) argued that much of what is perceived as deviant behaviour is a product of the excessive pressures of the social class structure on all individuals in capitalist societies, including the disadvantaged. Society encourages standard types of achievement in terms of formal education, employment, material benefits, authority, power, and prestige, despite varying capacities for achievement. However, Merton argues, the affluence paraded before the public through advertising and the media and prized occupational positions in the economy are ultimately scarce. As a result, many are intensely frustrated by their own powerlessness, by their limited opportunities for advancement or their impoverished financial and social circumstances. While most conform, others accommodate their disappointment in deviant behaviour. Merton spelled out five alternative ways in which individuals adapt their available means to the ends (goals) set by society.

According to Merton, those who accept standardized cultural goals, and who have the personal, financial, and social resources to achieve them, tend to live in a relatively controlled fashion. While they may engage in relatively safe, low-risk, or 'white collar crime,' they rarely express themselves in acts of legal or social deviance that place them at risk of negative, informal social sanctions or conflict with the law. These people can most appropriately be referred to as following the path of *conformity*.

Those who accept society's valued goals but cannot achieve them because they lack the necessary material resources or supportive, high-prestige social networks to sponsor their efforts adopt a pattern of *innovation*: they exploit deviant means to achieve socially approved ends. Examples include cheating in school to pass, lying on production quota reports at work, or securing material possessions by relying on a 'black market.'

Another pattern of adaptation to blocked aspirations Merton labelled *ritualism*, an adaptation common to the lower middle class. After having forgone all expectations of successfully achieving prized societal goals, the ritualist abandons a strong commitment to lofty aspirations. Instead, s/he follows the rules automatically and without enthusiasm. The classic example of the ritualist is the low-level bureaucrat at the unemployment office who rigidly conveys the rules and completely depersonalizes interactions with applicants. The ritualist has lost ambition and is a cynic and a sceptic, given to providing colleagues and young neophytes in the workplace with such advice as, 'Play it safe.' 'Don't stick your neck out. I don't. You may not get very far but you won't lose your job.'

Another adaptative category Merton referred to as rebellion. Rebels demand a modification of goals and a revised, more accessible set of means for achieving them. They are the system changers, whether the object of change is to revolutionize the entire system or to create a more gratifying social subsystem.

Rebellion, and another adaptation identified as *retreatism*, might explain the type of problem drinking that many would view as being characteristic among First Nations people. According to Merton retreatism is the least common mode of adaptation to disadvantage. In this adaptation people engage in a wholesale withdrawal from society, often adopting their own subcultural values and norms. Such persons include homeless transients, skid-row dwellers, outcasts, alcoholics, and drug addicts.

While the retreatist adaptation might go far to explain the severely alcohol-dependent, middle-aged, homeless person of aboriginal ancestry typically seen on the skid rows of cities, or the extreme social outcast on a reserve, it does not explain most problem drinking among First Nations people. The survey data described in chapter 2 made it clear that high-volume, episodic drinking is the far more common pattern.

Some writers have viewed the substance use style of First Nations people as a political act, a gesture of joining together in symbolic resistance to white oppression. This approach is expressed in Merton's concept of a rebellious response to frustrated expectations. Seen from this perspective, substance abuse is not dysfunctional deviance, but rather represents one of two strategies. It reflects a selectively chosen, deviant lifestyle that essentially says, 'I'll (or we will) create rules which will, in large part, be antagonistic to and different from those of the larger society.' It may also be seen as an attempt to promote 'indigenous identity' by maintaining group solidarity in an assertive, even flamboyant way. Brody's study of First Nations people in a Canadian prairie city suggested that Status Indians migrate from the surrounding reserves and, together, create a community apart. He noted that skid-row contraculture exists in many cities and serves, among other things, to provide an enclave of acceptance in a world that tends to reject aboriginal people. While group sharing of beverage alcohol reinforces a sense of community, ultimately, Brody notes, the drinking itself becomes dysfunctional and the cold realities of homeless street life make for a very spare, and, I would add, an often mean-spirited community life (1977: 71).

Alcohol Dependency as Mental Illness: The Psychological Variant of the Disease View

Another variant of the disease model attributes alcohol problems to psychological causation, without being concerned about whether or not the problem has genetic origins. Two versions of the psychological approach have been most influential. One version holds that the reason why some people develop problems with their drinking tends to be related to the eccentric nature of their thought processes; another long-standing version considers alcoholism as a product of personality factors or, in other words, patterns of thought and behaviour that have been established as fundamental to the very character of an individual.

Alcohol Dependence as a Psychiatric Illness

One psychological approach describes the alcoholic as suffering from *alcohol dependence* and problem drinkers as having an *alcohol abuse* disorder. These terms are used in the American Psychiatric Association's standard disease classification and diagnostic reference book, the *Diagnostic and Statistical Manual of Mental Disorders,* the current version of which is more commonly known simply as 'DSM-IV' (1994). The manual cites nine symptoms of alcohol dependence, with at least three co-occurring symptoms necessary for inclusion in the disorder category. In abbreviated form, the symptoms include:

1 *Tolerance,* as defined by a marked need for increasing amounts of alcohol to achieve intoxication, while simultaneously experiencing a diminishing degree of intoxication as a result of drinking the same amount of alcohol.
2 *Withdrawal discomfort.* Withdrawal is uncomfortable and alcohol or a closely related substance is taken to relieve or avoid withdrawal symptoms.
3 *Consumption levels higher than intended.* Consumption amounts are often greater or the drinking episode is longer than intended. This exaggerated use is often taken as an inability to reduce or control use or the amount of use despite attempts to try and a recognition that one's use is excessive (or a desire for self-control but no actual attempts at such control).
4 *Persistent, frustrated efforts to quit.* A persistent but unsuccessful effort to quit is characteristic.
5 *Time spent obtaining alcoholic beverages.* A great deal of time is spent securing alcohol for consumption.
6 *Diminished quality of life.* Important social, occupational, or recreational activities are given up or their frequencies are reduced because of substance use.
7 *Continued use despite ill-effects.* Substance use is continued despite the dependent user's knowledge of the negative health effects of use.

The DSM-IV suggests that one or more of the following behaviours are indicative of an alcohol abuse problem, when the individual's behaviour has never met the criteria for alcohol dependence:

1 Recurrent alcohol abuse resulting in a failure to adequately perform primary role obligations, such as school work, caring for children, or paid employment;
2 Recurrent alcohol abuse in hazardous situations;
3 Recurrent substance-related legal problems; and
4 Continued substance abuse, despite significant related problems in one's personal life.

Further discussion of the psychological approach will be included in the subsequent text. However, it must be reiterated at this point in the narrative that, while the social status and influence of American psychiatry lends enormous international prestige to these definitions of alcohol problems, the basic notion that both mental illness and alcoholism are diseases has been challenged by a significant body of academic critics. Long in the forefront of this attack is Thomas Szasz, who has consistently argued that, while mental illness or alcohol problems may be understood as diseases in metaphorical terms, they should not be, as they all too often are, considered diseases in the literal sense (1991). Arguing that a disease is properly understood as a malfunction of physiology indicated by a lesion and traceable to a causal agent, Szasz argues that psychiatrists, members of allied professions, and the general public too frequently mistake the diagnoses of mental health problems for indicators of a brain disease. Szasz has argued with a compelling logic that few, if any, have satisfactorily challenged that, unlike an actual disease, psychiatric diagnoses do not point to anatomical or physiological lesions and they do not identify causal agents. Such diagnoses refer to human behaviours only as indicators. It therefore follows that they are not truly referring to diseases: 'No psychiatric diagnosis is, or can be, pathology driven; instead, all such diagnoses are driven by non-medical (economic, personal, legal, political, and social) factors or incentives' (Szasz, 1991: 1576).

Alcoholic Personality

More research and time has been spent in exploring the idea of an alcoholic or pre-alcoholic personality than has been devoted to almost any other area in the alcohol research field. Voluminous bookshelves are now filled with studies, yet no consistent personality pattern has been found. However, it is generally accepted that certain types of attitudes and behaviour patterns do develop after the onset of alcohol dependency. These include specific defences or learned tactics and strategies, including denial, minimization, projection, rationalization, grandiosity, and selective attention, all employed to manage discomforting emotions such as guilt, fear, anger, and anxiety (Wallace, 1985). Treatment counsellors typically notice in their clients a preoccupation with securing alcohol; they also notice cyclical thoughts about seeking help for the problem, which are then abandoned; avoidance of confrontation with the consequences; deception around drinking issues; low tolerance for frustration; and generalized, irresponsible behaviour in some or many areas of life. A tendency to be manipulative in order to secure alcohol or to facilitate social circumstances centred on drinking is also commonly observed.

There are also certain psychological characteristics which, when clustered, are described in psychiatry as 'disorders,' and these tend to co-occur with alcohol dependency. The research suggests that these co-occurring problems include not only neurotic and psychotic disorders but also personality disorders. While it is not known whether or not these disorders predispose an individual to alcohol problems, they do appear to raise risk levels for a variety of unhealthy and destructive behaviours. In their recent review of the relevant literature, Ordrica and Nace (1998) noted 'compelling evidence' in the early 1990s to indicate high rates of co-morbidity between alcoholism and other psychiatric disorders. Strong correlations were found between alcohol dependence and (1) dependence on other drugs; (2) generalized anxiety disorder; (3) phobic disorders including agoraphobia, simple phobia, social phobia, and agoraphobia with panic attacks; (4) panic disorder; (5) obsessive-compulsive disorder; (6) post-traumatic stress disorder; and (7) mood disorders. The Ordrica and Nace (1998) review also identified schizophrenia as a psychosis for which almost half of all treated patients also have significant alcohol or other drug problems.

Personality disorders occur more commonly among alcoholics than in both the general population (Drake and Vaillant, 1985) and the population of psychiatric patients (Koenigsberg et al., 1985). The most common personality disorder found among alcoholics in treatment is antisocial personality disorder, the second most common is borderline personality disorder (Ordrica and Nace, 1998).

The available data do not provide any clarity regarding the direction of the relationship between mental illness in general or specific mental illnesses and alcoholism. The best that can be said is that sometimes alcoholism precedes and may cause mental illness, while mental illness sometimes predisposes an individual to become alcoholic or eliminates the sensitivity to societal constraints that normally inhibits troublesome drinking patterns. It must also be stated that there is no evidence to support any different conclusion about the direction of the relationship between mental disorders and alcoholism in First Nations (Whitehead and Hayes, 1998).

The Genetic Variant: The Heart of the Disease Model

The third version of the disease model sees the cause of 'alcoholism' as lying in the genetic make-up of the 'alcoholic.' As a more extensive treatment of the disease model will be provided in the next chapter, a brief summary of the type of causal attribution in the genetically focused explanation of alcoholism will suffice for present purposes.

The recent research inspired by this view has focused on what is called *heritability* or, in other words, on genetic influences (inherited through the transmission of genes between the generations) on alcohol and drug dependence. While the great majority of alcoholics entering treatment programs have a history of alcoholism in their families of orientation, this fact alone does not support the conclusion that alcoholism is inherited. It could be an acquired trait predisposed through role modelling and triggered by peer group activity or some other environmental circumstance. In other words, alcoholism could be genetically transmitted or learned. Research on adoptive twin studies in which twins are separated at infancy has suggested that, while there is no single alcohol gene (or 'alcogene'), genetic factors may predispose an individual to alcoholism (Wallace, 1989).

Considerable research on the impact of one's biological constitution on the acquisition or reinforcement of alcoholism has centred on the brain. The brain is a virtual sea of chemicals and alcoholics may therefore differ from non-alcoholics in one or more of these neurochemicals. In recent years, much attention has been paid to the impact of low levels of serotonin, a chemical neurotransmitter that situates in the space between nerve cells in the brain (synapses) (Naranjo et al., 1984). Some alcoholics may have low levels of serotonin in their brains, and this deficiency may result in a predisposition to alcoholism.

Another direction in neurobiological research into the causes of alcoholism has involved exploring the impact of frequent alcohol ingestion on depleting normal levels of neurotransmitters, thus resulting in cravings and problems with such behaviour management functions as impulse control (Genazzani et al., 1983; Wallace, 1988).

Still other research suggests there may be different types of alcohol dependents and patterns of reaction to alcohol due to varying genetic influences (Cloninger, 1983). The heritibility of alcohol problems will be taken up in greater detail in the subsequent chapter.

5

Challenges to the Disease Model as an Explanation of Problem Drinking

Chapter 4 outlined a sociological group of explanations that shared the view that exceptional drinking problems among marginalized ethnic groups such as Canada's indigenous peoples were rooted in 'social pathology.' Conceptualizing society in metaphorical terms as a social organism, the sociologists in question tend to view high rates of substance abuse in a population subgroup as a sort of disease affecting a part of the body and threatening to spread to the larger society. The pathology is seen to lie in specific aspects of the distinctive group subculture that shapes the beliefs, values, and behaviour of the minority itself. The same chapter also described psychological explanations that treat excessive drinking as a behavioural outcome of an underlying mental illness. Finally, a biological framework that explains the alcohol problems of First Nations in terms of a genetic predisposition was examined. The latter approach has attracted the most adherents among alcohol and drug abuse workers, including those serving First Nations peoples. Issue will now be taken with each of the types of explanation identified.

The Problem with Consensus Theories in Sociology as Explanations of 'Social Pathologies'

Chapter 4 described explanations of social problems grounded in *consensus theory* – explanations that assume that the prevailing social order is normative and healthy, whereas deviance from the status quo, in the form of public drunkenness, drug addiction, or theft, is essentially considered to be unhealthy. This approach calls attention to the unhealthy nature of the individual or group that deviates from the norms of the social order.

Sociological explanations of the consensus variety *may* be applicable to the behaviour of some individual First Nations people, perhaps even to the behaviour of specific First Nations at certain points in the intersection of their lives with non-aboriginals. However, there is no evidence available to support the view that excessive drinking is either a formal or informal act of political resistance, nor is there evidence to suggest that it is a widespread, personal strategy of accommodation to frustrated goal achievement.

Consensus theorists assume that most of us agree about the rules we are expected to follow, and the things we hope to obtain. But anyone with the least familiarity with First Nations people and non-aboriginal Canada will recognize that there are substantial differences between the social and material aspirations of each, both historically and in the present. A consensus on achievement goals between most First Nations people and middle-class Canadians cannot be assumed, nor can we accept an explanation that sees the primary cause of problem drinking to be frustrated middle-class goal achievement.

John Horton, a sociologist who formally examined the fundamental assumptions behind the social pathology view of social deviance, described what he called the 'order vocabulary' that comprised this type of sociological explanation as follows:

> Order theories have in common an image of society as a system of action unified at the most general level by shared culture, by agreement on values (or at least on modes) of communication and political organization ... A key concept in the analysis of system problems (social problems, deviation, conflict) is anomie. Social problems both result from and promote anomie ... a system imbalance or social disorganization – a lack of or breakdown in social organization reflected in weakened social control ... inadequate socialization, etc. ... (and) ... in the failure of individuals to meet the maintenance needs of the social system ... Order theories imply consensual and adjustment definitions of social health and pathology, of conformity and deviation. (Horton, 1970: 608)

Horton goes on to observe that when prevailing standards of health are assumed to be the legitimate values of society at large, 'deviation is (conceived as) ... the opposite of social conformity and means the failure of individuals to perform their legitimate social roles; deviants are out of adjustment' (1966: 608).

The same writer notes that there is an alternative view which suggests that deviance is a product of a state of social organization in which the dominant society fails to provide the capacity for some segments of society and for some of its individuals to grow. Horton would find little argument with the statement in another text describing an alternative or *radical sociology* that demonstrates greater sympathy for the oppressed in a society, and, ultimately, offers a means of providing balance in a more comprehensive analysis. That statement clarifies the ways in which the false assumptions of consensus sociology can be reframed. It reads as follows: 'Radical sociology attempts to view society from the position of oppressed groups in society, such as the poor, the unemployed, blue collar workers ... minorities, and women. From this point of view it carefully analyzes all of the present institutions of our society [and asks] ... how these institutions – social, political, economic – evolved into their present forms. It asks who benefits from the present institutions ... [and] if a major change in society is both possible and necessary' (Sherman and Wood, 1979: 6).

Unless it can be proven that the value base of aboriginal and non-aboriginal peoples is wholly consistent, any consensus sociological explanation is flawed. First Nations people do share much in the way of knowledge, aspirations, and values with non-aboriginal people, thanks to the homogenizing influences of modern, mass society, with its common communications media and educational system. Yet there is evidence at every juncture that aboriginal peoples have been culturally, socially, politically, economically, and even legally isolated and marginalized from the larger society. As Buckley has written of the reserve system in western Canada: 'Throughout their long association with Canada, these people in the West have lived separately, actively excluded from white society in ways both large and small, by hostile teachers and co-workers, employers who won't hire them, and landlords who won't rent to them in the city ... It would be hard to explain why this separate world has been sustained over so many years ...' (1993: 22–3).

Rather than achieving its formal intention of assimilation, as Boldt has noted, the Canadian government's policy of reserve segregation has resulted in 'deculturation,' by which he means the destruction of traditional First Nations cultures in the absence of assimilation or cultural reconstruction. This loss of cultural traits, without an equivalent replenishment, has undermined the social order on reserves. As Boldt argues, high social problem rates, including problem drinking and violence, can be taken as indicators of the damage caused by this cultural vacuum (1993: 174).

One could therefore hardly assume as a given a fundamental value correspondence between aboriginal peoples and the larger society, in terms of either traditional values or the hybrid reserve or urban quasi-cultures that exist today. Few would claim that the material values of the larger society have been wholly adopted by aboriginal peoples. Few, if any, knowledgeable observers of Canadian and aboriginal peoples, for example, would argue that the emphasis on saving, the importance of private property, material acquisition, and capital accumulation emphasized in the larger society have been fully assimilated by aboriginal peoples. Despite a pervasive interest in both basic and luxury goods, any long-term acquaintance with First Nations people and their communities will reveal that aboriginal people simply do not assign the same degree of importance to material goods as do the majority of people in non-aboriginal communities, whether those goods be a specific house, a vehicle, or a CD player. Nor does the agriculturally and religiously based reverence for work found in the European and Asian groups in Canada appear to have been adopted with the same degree of intensity by most aboriginal peoples. The destruction and lack of contemporary replacement of traditional aboriginal economies and the conditions of mass unemployment have simply not created social conditions that nurture the overriding work ethic that serves in the larger society as a basis upon which to rate an individual's very social worth. Further, the external political regulation of reserve life and social assistance as a substitute for employment have encouraged attitudes of dependency rather than the interdependence required in a commercialized economy. On the basis of the discrepancy between the attachment of aboriginal and non-aboriginal peoples to these fundamental values alone, it is impossible to take seriously any explanation of problem drinking in First Nations as a social pathology rooted in the difficulties aboriginal people have in living according to the norms of North American society. For most aboriginal people in reserve communities, conforming to these norms is simply not possible.

A close examination of virtually every major federal government intervention into the affairs of Indian people, from social assistance through education, economic development programming, counselling, and alcohol and drug abuse intervention, has assumed a consensus that does not exist. This assumption is reflected in the longstanding policy of assimilation – a policy which assumes that, relative to the dominant culture, the host, aboriginal cultures are 'primitive' and that, when individuals resist assimilation through retreat into alcohol or drug dependency, or through the expression of individual rage, they are acting pathologically. Like skid-row subcultures, aboriginal problem drinking is viewed as a social pathology that must be 'cured' by intervening directly in the afflicted group's circumstances with programs to help that group to assimilate to the norms of the larger society. Yet if there is any message that aboriginal spokespersons have sent with clarity to the larger society, it is that First Nations people are not interested in cultural assimilation, but rather in economic integration and political partnerships.

The language of the order perspective assumes that the values of the larger society are superior and that social deviance, such as pervasive problem drinking, is a sort of 'cancer' that must be cured because it threatens the social health of the larger society. The constant fear of those who support the mainstream social order and its elites is that deviance from the norm might spread to and afflict the healthy core of society as a whole. This wrong-headed thinking has characterized much of the 'help' made available to aboriginal peoples, not only in alcohol abuse but in many other troublesome areas as well.

The most grievous error in sociological explanations rooted in the order perspective is that they overlook the possibility that the problems experienced by a marginal subgroup in a national society may lie within the dynamics of an imbalanced relationship with the dominant society. Stated differently, the problem may best be explained as the product of a troubled relationship with the larger society. The relationship between aboriginal people and Canadian society as a whole must be examined if any substantive explanation of disproportionate problem drinking rates in the former is to be offered. After all, on the lands that are now Canadian, not only did the problems associated with excessive drinking of alcoholic beverages not exist prior to contact with the European newcomers, the very act of drinking of such beverages was unknown.

The concensus perspective in sociology situates aboriginal problem drinking in either reactions to blocked frustration to assimilate or to a distinctive and maladaptive response to externally generated social change. Both approaches may explain some First Nations drinking problems, such as that of an individual who has been successfully socialized into mainstream values but is frustrated by his or her lack of opportunity. They may also explain the disproportionate numbers of aboriginal residents living in skid-row areas of cities (Beavis et al.,

1997). However, to cast the problem in these terms is of limited value. As a credible explanation of disproportionate rates of the First Nations drinking problems, such theories have little to offer. They are all too vulnerable to the perception that they are little more than a shameless means of defending the status quo and champion victim blamer of the type described so well by Ryan (1971).

The Problem with Pathology-Oriented Psychological and Psychiatric Explanations

To be sure, there are 'real' mental illnesses. Schizophrenia is an instance of a real disease: a condition caused by some abnormality of individual neurochemistry and precipitated in large measure by inherited biological vulnerabilities (Wynne et al., 1978; Beckham and Leber, 1985). When a person's dysfunctional behaviour is a result of a genetic defect, a nutritional deficit, or an infection or an injury, it is proper to speak of a disease. In contrast, when the primary evidence of eccentric or troublesome conditions is the person's behaviour, and especially when there is good evidence that the behaviour has been strongly influenced by social circumstances, characterization of the individual's actions as an illness is inappropriate and misguided.

But does real mental illness tend to trigger alcoholism, or is alcoholism more likely to trigger mental illness? As indicated in chapter 4, the available evidence, when objectively weighed, does not afford a confident answer to this question. The contradictory nature of the data suggests that mental illness and alcoholism can trigger the onset of each other, depending on variant causal circumstances. The far more important conclusion is that social environments characterized by high human stress levels have been consistently shown to increase the population rates of most mental illnesses. Populations that are geographically nested together and which have high unemployment rates, social assistance dependency, and low income tend to have high rates of mental illness. The burden of these social stressors in reserve communities is well known and, not surprisingly, rates of psychiatric disorders in First Nations are relatively high. The Working Group on Native Mental Health (1989) concluded that reserve communities consistently exhibit high rates of depression; hospitalization data for Manitoba indicate that the case rate for registered Indians was 1.7 times higher than the same rate for other Manitobans in 1986–7 (Whitehead and Hayes, 1998: 24) and the hospital separation rate for mental disorders in Saskatchewan for 1987–8 was 3.8 times higher than the rate for the provincial population as a whole (Health and Welfare Canada, 1991: 38).

While most psychologists are quick to admit that their field deals with psycho-social problems, their training often inclines them to reduce explanations of behavioural problems to psychological patterns of causation; in other words, they often 'psychologize' behaviour. Especially sensitized to what happens within people's minds or neurochemistry, psychologists and psychiatrists are often inclined to give social-environmental pressures and interpersonal dynamics short shrift (Dorpat, 1985). In particular, they are inclined to see interpersonal dynamics, such as hostile-aggressive acts associated with alcohol abuse, as an outcome of personality dilemmas.

Personality traits have traditionally been viewed as discrete qualities that are inherent in the individual. If a man tends to drink more than he intends to and more than what his intimates appreciate, a psychologist might assume that he has a disordered personality that predisposes him to inappropriate drinking comportment. Yet in recent decades there has been a growing awareness that psychological 'predispositions' are specific to a social context. Thus an honest woman will not be honest in all social contexts. Engaged in jury duty she may be passionate about the truth, but when she is describing her children's talents she may exaggerate or 'fib.' Similarly, when she is playing poker she may bluff and consider her deception a virtue rather than a vice. In short, social context is critical to a full explanation. Both psychological *and* sociological variables must be considered in explaining behavioural choices.

Specific references in the research literature to the types of personality profile that might predispose an individual to problem drinking include the observation by Tarter (1988) that the personality characteristics of the antisocial personality disorder and certain neurotic traits might increase the risk of alcohol abuse and subsequent addiction. Somewhat similar conclusions were drawn by Jenike (1989), who identifies a history of antisocial behaviour as being one factor that was useful in predicting which American servicemen returning from Vietnam who had used opiates would continue to use them.

There are, however, as many challengers as supporters of the view that there might be a causal relationship between the antisocial personality disorder and addiction. Some researchers point to the fact that there are no consistent psychometric patterns that reliably differentiate future alcohol dependent individuals from those who will not become dependent (Nathan, 1988). Similarly, there are no consistent psychometric measures that can predict who will be a 'sad,' a 'happy,' or a 'bad' drunk. Given the cultural norm that sanctions, in varying degrees alcohol use and even mild intoxication in celebration and passage rituals such as marriages, graduations, and funerals, as providing relief from the stresses of work and marriage, and during courting, casual love-making, routine recreation like card games, and socializing, it is hardly surprising that those with an antisocial orientation would transform normal social occasions into opportunities for excess, hostility, and decidedly antisocial expression. To be consistent with this reasoning would also require that we accept that an antisocial orientation would be a good predictor of antisocial behaviour generally, independently of whether or not the arena for antisocial expression involves alcohol use. As an example, in recent years, organizational psychologists have observed the existence and troubling consequences of psychopaths at senior levels of the workplace. Such individuals, who are presumably at high risk of alcohol dependence, are, typically, fully capable of avoiding alcohol use completely, and do not exhibit various characteristics considered typical of the antisocial personality. Instead, they reveal their antisocial behaviour through connivance, manipulation, cheating, lying, and ruthless treatment of peers, superiors, and underlings in their worksphere, if and when such behaviour is advantageous to them.

Some researchers have cast doubt on the relationship between the antisocial personality disorder and the risk of alcohol addiction. Nathan (1988) has argued that the characteristics of the so-called addictive personality found by earlier researchers might have been based on a misdiagnosis. In addition, as Miller (1995) has commented, more than fifty years of research have failed to distinguish a pattern of different personality traits between alcoholics and non-alcoholics.

The belief that certain personality characteristics 'cause' alcohol abuse and, in turn, 'control' the individual under the influence of alcohol, has been misused to exempt people entirely from responsibility for extremely harmful, even lethal, consequences of drunken behaviour. As Fingarette suggests, key 'gatekeepers' of individual freedom, such as judges, legislators, and bureaucrats, use the alcoholism label to clear their consciences, removing the intractable social problems caused by heavy drinkers from their agenda by compelling or persuading these difficult people, these 'alcoholics,' to go elsewhere – that is, to get 'treatment' (1988a).

However appropriate the terms *alcohol dependence* and *alcohol abuser* may be in referring to two common sets of distinguishable, problematic patterns of drinking, the fact that they involve significant adaptations of personality does not make either of them a 'disease,' no matter how tempted one is to invoke the analogy.

Abnormal Neurobiology *Can* Predispose an Individual to Alcohol Dependence

As noted above, there is now a growing body of research which, if not conclusive, suggests that alcohol dependence (addiction) is influenced by neurobiological factors rooted in genetic patterns that vary among individuals and families, although *not* with ethnic groups.

Results from adoptive studies have consistently demonstrated a substantial increase in the risk for alcoholism in the sons and daughters of alcoholics, even when these children are raised outside the alcoholic home and did not know their alcoholic parents (Goodwin et al., 1973; Cloninger, 1983; and Cloninger, Sigvardsson, and Bohman, 1988).

As indicated in chapter 4, considerable research on the impact of one's biological constitution on the acquisition or reinforcement of alcoholism has centred on the brain, and it is possible that alcoholics may differ from non-alcoholics in terms of their neurochemical make-up. For example, some alcoholics might have low levels of serotonin, a chemical neurotransmitter situated in the space between nerve cells in the brain (synapses) that results in reductions in human drinking (Naranjo et al., 1984). This deficiency may result in a predisposition to alcoholism, although the effects may only be linked to alcohol behaviour indirectly. Serotonin deficiencies have also been associated with poor impulse control, suicide, obsessive-compulsive disorder, obesity, and numerous other problems (Wallace, 1989: 328).

Kenneth Blum and his associates have studied naturally occurring substances in the brain that are similar to narcotics, in that they have pain-killing properties resembling those of morphine: these chemicals, which are synthesized in the body, are called endorphins and enkephalins ('endorphin' means 'inner morphine,' or morphine self-produced by the human). Blum and his associates argue that these chemicals play an important role in alcoholism. Studies of mice found a strikingly strong relationship between the amount the experimental animals drank and the level of enkephalins in the brain.

Others involved in neurobiological research into the causes of alcoholism have asked the question: 'Are alcoholics people who, through genetics or some physio-experiential process, develop deficiencies in these natural, morphine-like substances?' 'The jury is still out on this question, but both animal studies and human studies do suggest that such deficiencies are associated with high levels of alcohol consumption (Genazzani et al., 1983; and Wallace, 1988).

Another neurobiological interest in the research literature has centred on the possibility that people prone to alcoholism have characteristically low levels of a chemical extant in the brain called 'noradrenaline,' which is a stimulant (Borg et al., 1983). Individuals predisposed to alcoholism may be people who are emotionally flat and seeking the arousal effects associated with the early stages of a drinking episode. This contention is supported by research which shows declining noradrenaline levels in alcoholics after six months of recovery. Additional support for this hypothesis might also be provided by the fact that alcoholics who have become abstinent experience cravings for caffeine, nicotine, and sweets.

Other research suggests that alcoholics tend to have two abnormally functioning enzymes, monoamine oxidase and adenylate cyclase (Tabakoff et al., 1988). These enzymes are important to the overall operation of the brain because they are involved in critical information-processing events. Yet another line of inquiry has explored the possibility that frequent drinking itself results in the formation of new chemicals in the brain (Myers, 1985). Condensed products of the body's interaction with beverage alcohol called THIQs may result in an elevated attraction to alcohol.

Based on adoption studies, Cloninger et al. (1981) described two types of alcoholic: Type 1, a mostly environmentally influenced alcoholic, and Type 2, a male alcoholic who is often, normally, a moderate drinker but who is strongly influenced by genetic predisposition and who typically experiences legal problems in conjunction with drinking episodes. However, this dichotomy has been severely criticized by those who suggest that, once those subjects with co-occurring antisocial personality disorder are excluded, the differences disappear in the research (Irwin et al., 1990).

Several types of alcoholics have now been described in the literature. The *hyperarousal alcoholic* uses alcohol in search of sedation but experiences 'rebound stimulation,' a reaction to the discomforts experienced after the loss of the sedation. He or she pursues more alcohol to recapture the sedation and this becomes a persistent feature of his or her behaviour. The *anhedonic alcoholic* is normally characterized by a low level of arousal, finding little enjoyment in social intercourse, food, sex, or entertainment, and thus seeks the excitement associated with drinking episodes. This type of alcoholic may exhibit a deficiency in certain neurotransmitters. Yet another type is the *depressed alcoholic*, who seeks relief in alcohol or group drinking from feelings of sadness, loneliness, and limited self-esteem. Some researchers believe that problems with the actions of certain brain chemicals may also influence this type of alcohol consumption response. Finally, a *mixed type* of alcoholic has been described: a person who exhibits symptoms characteristic of the other three types of alcoholic. Problems with several neurotransmitter symptoms may be responsible for this type of alcoholism.

Critics of this 'typing' of different kinds of alcoholics have suggested that differences in alcoholic profiles may be better explained by factors that appear as early as childhood, such as hyperactivity or other behavioural disorders, and the severity of the alcoholism itself. In short, alcoholism may best be conceived to vary along a continuum of severity, rather than representing distinctly different and static categories of alcoholic.

In addition to the exploration of neurotransmitters, some researchers seeking the causes of alcoholism have examined abnormalities in electrical activity in the brain. Abnormalities in a specific brain wave called 'P-300' have been found repeatedly in recorded prints of electrical activity in the brains of both alcoholics and their children (Begleiter and Porjesz, 1988). The P-300 brain wave is believed to be linked to judgement, decision making, and impulsiveness. Gabrieli and colleagues found a predominance of fast brain waves (technically referred to as 'beta rhythms') in the young sons of alcoholics (1982).

The Addictive Wiring Must Be 'Plugged In' to Social and Psychological Processes

Heritability does seem to be one of several factors that might, in combination with other late-onset neurobiological factors associated with drug or alcohol use, social factors, and psychological factors, establish a causal chain leading to alcohol addiction. Some individuals and some families may be more genetically predisposed to alcohol dependency. Neurobiological factors resulting from the frequent interaction of alcohol with the normal brain chemistry may also, in some cases, encourage eccentric behaviour during intoxication and/or habitual drinking.

The reinforcement of dependency by physical constitution does not ensure the onset of alcohol dependency, however; the individual must be exposed to the drug and the use of the drug must be reinforced by either one or a combination of psychological and social factors. In part, this reasoning is supported by the fact that, in the absence of social learning, human beings are unable to acquire any significant behavioural strategies. Even the higher primates are utterly dependent on social learning to acquire such basic functions as procreative sex and mother/infant bonding. Similarly, many social and psychological factors are not of themselves sufficient to explain alcohol misuse.

Support for a 'Multifactorial View': At Least Two Factors Must Prevail

If the criticism of single causal models levelled by Lester and others is applicable to genetic theories, the same criticism holds for psychological and sociological theories: ignoring biological factors may result in the precluding of scientifically identified predispositional factors in large numbers of alcohol abusers. However, a fundamental contradiction lies behind all the research searching for that single physiological cause: unlike other problems referred to as 'diseases,' alcohol abuse and other drug addictions require the active participation of the victim. Unlike an infection, an addiction is not forced on an individual. In fact, the victim must go through a number of steps to become addicted, including the work and money required to secure the substance on a regular basis and all the social relations that must be reshaped because of the eccentric behaviours associated directly with the drinking. As Doweiko (1990: 196) observes with irony, 'If it took as much time and energy to "catch" a cold, pneumonia, or cancer, it is doubtful that "any" of us would ever be sick a day in our lives!' What explanatory model is then supported? And how should the various types of behavioural problems linked to alcohol use best be understood?

The Bio-Psycho-Social Perspective

The most sophisticated thinking about the causes and behavioural correlates of problem drinking suggests that, while some people may have an inherited disposition to slow alcohol metabolization or other physiological effects, this disposition requires the active choices of the individual with that predisposition before any problem is manifest. Problems arise from either an interaction of psychological and social factors or the interaction of such factors with biological (genetic) factors. Genetics may both predispose an individual to alcoholism or reinforce alcoholism as a result of neurochemical interactions arising from the extended effects of alcohol on a person's brain chemistry. The bio-psycho-social approach assumes that there is a need for a more appropriate model than the traditional disease model, which depends on the logic of straightforward cause and effect (Brennan, 1990).

Brennan argues that it is inappropriate to use a linear causal model of explanation (i.e., a model which associates alcohol dependence with single factors) because it is impossible to separate alcoholism from the context in which it occurs. No one variable, including alcohol itself, is sufficient to cause problem drinking or alcohol dependence. Brennan argues that only a theory that accepts interaction between various factors with various degrees of influence can be scientifically acceptable. For example, Brennan accepts the evidence that a genetic factor may contribute to alcoholism for some people but believes that evidence also exists for the involvement of learned behaviour and for the influence of social factors. In short, the issue is not a question of nature versus nurture but rather to what degree and in what manner each factor contributes along with all the other subsystems. In summarizing what we might refer to as 'the state of the addictions treatment science and art,' William L. White has noted a shift away from the disease model, which was based on the distinctive predisposing genetic and related psychological vulnerability to alcoholism. The disease model, as codified during the mid-twentieth Century, is increasingly being supplanted by 'multiple pathway models' (1998: 288).

According to the *bio-psycho-social perspective*, each of these factors – sociological, psychological, and biological variables – may be more or less critical for different persons at different points in time and in different settings. Further, an understanding of each factor is necessary for an accurate assessment of an individual's condition. Advocates present this perspective not only as a useful description of alcoholism, but also as a clinically significant model with therapeutic validity. Essentially, they are arguing that, if a given individual's problems are identified as being a function of the interaction of physiological, psychological, and social variables, then it would seem reasonable that the assessment process should consider each of these areas. It would also follow that the primary therapeutic interventions should be directed at the areas of greatest influence and disruption.

There are surely a variety of factors that contribute to the alcohol problems of an individual. However, to determine that a particular population group is more vulnerable to influence than others, we must prove that there are specific causal variables directly linked to risk levels. We must ask ourselves: Does a population (or population subgroup) characterized by a high problem drinking rate also exhibit an exceptional biological (i.e., genetic) predisposition to alcohol use and dependency, a widespread psychological predisposition to alcohol problems, or cultural inclinations or social influences which influence alcohol abuse in exceptional ways? Or does the population of interest exhibit relatively high frequencies of all of these?

Alcohol Misuse Problems on a Continuum

In treatment, for many people, the 'disease' concept may have provided a useful way of engaging in and developing a commitment to a structured recovery plan. However, a review of the research literature forces us to conclude that, for the majority, the disease model is probably irrelevant. For still others, it may act as a deterrent to self-help or, if used, may well prove to be more harmful than helpful in its consequences.

For the majority of individuals with drinking patterns that are either episodic or simply too frequent and which, while not reflecting severe dependence, are still in some way troublesome, pressure from professional (and non-professional) helpers to accept the alcoholic label may result in more mischief than assistance however good the intentions of the counsellor. If an individual can learn responsible drinking behaviour and learn to control excessive consumption and antisocial behaviour, why subject that person to an elaborate and, to many people, humiliating process by which individuals are labelled as 'alcoholics forever,' intimate confessionals are demanded, total abstinence is deemed essential, and self-help group involvement is considered requisite?

The sheer volume of drinkers who are not addicted but who experience significant problems with alcohol – and who can be classified as *psychoactive substance abusers* by psychiatrists – suggests that intermittent binge-drinking episodes leading to intoxication represent a far more significant problem for society than the problem of alcohol dependence. Acknowledgment of this latter point is extremely important because, at present, far greater intervention expenditures are allocated to treatment based on the medical model and the disease concept than to alternative, more appropriate, prevention and treatment programs in Canada generally, and in First Nation communities in particular.

By ignoring individual differences, use of a single diagnosis of alcohol problems (i.e., 'alcoholism') is more likely to interfere with effective treatment planning than to promote it. Such a simplistic approach to assessment also lessens the potential effectiveness of treatment. For example, it would discourage such intervention in treatment when early intervention might be extremely effective in preventing the further development of the problem. An either/or diagnosis will tend to lead to a generalized profile which, at worst, does nothing to produce a natural history of the disorder and attaches a deviant label to the client. That label can itself serve to aggravate the problem; at best, it meets only the needs of individuals with serious, chronic, long-standing substance abuse disorders.

A Plausible Continuum of Potential Substance Abuse Problems

Instead of conceptualizing alcohol problems in terms of a disease / non-disease or dependency / non-dependency dichotomy, individual patterns of alcohol abuse are best understood as falling along a continuum that ranges from non-problematic to extremely problematic. In agreement with this approach, one writer (Vaillant, 1983) describes six categories that would lie along such a continuum, insisting that, while these categories may mark stages on a line of progression from lighter to heavier abuse problems, there is nothing inevitable about this sequence. Vaillant 'guesstimates' that perhaps 10–15 per cent of drinkers reach a stage of heavy use associated with moderate life problems, and it is quite possible that 50 per cent either return to asymptomatic (controlled) drinking or achieve stable abstinence. The same researcher suggests that, in a small number of such cases, alcohol abuse can persist intermittently for decades with minor morbidity and even become milder with time (1983: 309).

One of the most reasonable ways to conceptualize a full continuum of possible service responses is to think of a continuum of substance abuse problems that an individual might experience. Such a continuum is conceptualized graphically and described in figure 5.1. The question following from this continuum is: Are prevention and intervention resources being allocated in an efficient way, given the numbers of people falling into the various categories of need and the potential costs to society associated with each category?

Public resources are scarce and alcohol problems must compete with other legitimate citizen claims on public goods. Yet alcohol problems

Figure 5.1 A continuum of substance abuse

No risk -- Extreme risk

0	1	3	4	5	6
Non-use	Moderate, infrequent non-problematic use	Frequent use; managed behaviour	Chronic, heavy use; moderate health, personal & interpersonal problems	Infrequent, but volatile, episodic use, often accompanied by bizarre, high-risk behaviours & individuals with strong physiological reactions to alcohol such as those with allergies or with a health disorder that contra-indicates alcohol ingestion	Acute dependence, with life-threatening health problems and practical & interpersonal problems

are both widespread and of enormous consequence for the emotional, social and even economic health of the first peoples. The quality, effectiveness, range of coverage, and efficiency of substance abuse prevention and intervention services are therefore extremely important aspects of public health policy aimed at overall community development.

The idea that alcohol problems fall along a continuum rather than constituting a single disease entity with a specific profile of characteristics, or a problem that develops through specific, predictable stages, has been advocated by several writers (Brower, et al., 1991; Peele, Brodsky, and Arnold, Brodsky, 1991; Doweiko, 1993), all of whom have been influenced by George Vaillant's research. Vaillant (1983) found considerable fluctuation in the consumption of alcohol by individuals over the course of their lives. Thus, rather than simply progressing smoothly from occasional drinking to addiction, a rare social drinker might go through a period of frequent, abusive drinking, followed by a period of no drinking, and then return to a period of moderate drinking. The patterns were extremely varied, and a continuum allows us to capture, through classification, these various patterns and intensities. However, it must be recognized the continuum represents progressive degrees of intensity, not a graduated line that depicts a sequentially intensifying alcohol abuse course that will predictably be followed unless treatment occurs.

An appropriate continuum describes a range of drinking styles that runs from non-use through low-risk social drinking to high risk and acute dependence. In terms of services needs, the non-user may be the target of prevention messages, tailored to their level of use and the probability that they may, at least on occasion, drink to the point of intoxication. Chronic, heavy users, and those with dangerous psychological, neurological, or physiological reactions to alcohol, including a genetic tendency to addiction, can benefit greatly from interventions aimed at either complete sobriety or clearly established drinking limits, depending on the specific personality and circumstantial profile of the individual. Finally, the individual who is acutely dependent is essentially following a potentially suicidal behavioural trajectory. Such individuals can benefit from pro-active outreach, intensive intervention, sometimes pharmacological support, personal support through relapse prevention programs, and self-help groups.

In large populations, it must be understood that a wide diversity of psychological, social, and allergenic responses can occur, including variation in the pace of alcohol metabolization.

Addictive Potential Is 'in the Normal Wiring' of the Human Animal

The disease model of alcohol problems assumes that the problem of abusive drinking is necessarily one of *addiction*, and that addiction is a phenomenon that is in some way extraordinary. Yet we can all be addicts and, to some degree, probably most of us are addicted to something – that is, if addiction is viewed as a habit that we derive pleasure from or use to stave off pain and we find that, even when we realize it is against our best long-term interests, we choose to indulge our short-term pleasures. The normalcy of addictive potential has often been lost in professional discussions of the issue, but recent thinking on the subject reminds us just how ordinary that potential is.

In a useful summary published in the lay person's psychology serial *Psychology Today* (September 1994), Joann Ellison Rodgers described the scientific rethinking of the basis of addictive behaviours, noting that 'scientists have learned that every animal, from ancient hagfish to reptiles, rodents, and humans, shares the same basic "reward" circuits in the brain, circuits that all turn on when in contact with addictive substances or during pleasurable acts such as eating or orgasm.' The conclusion to be drawn from this research, according to Rodgers and many of the leading substance abuse researchers, is that 'addictive behaviours are normal, a natural part of our "wiring." If they weren't or if they were rare, nature would not have let the capacity to be addicted evolve, and stick around in every living creature.'

Recent thinking in the addictions field suggests that the human brain has evolved a reward system, just as it has evolved a pain system, and that reward system ensures that the human species carries out its essential functions – the functions of eating, drinking, and having sex and of relieving pain and anxiety – in order to survive. Everyone engages in these types of behaviours and they are strongly reinforced by our brain circuitry. Most people learn to balance their responses to their survival needs. As a consequence of various intervening factors, imbalances can occur, however; this leaves one or a small number of forms of gratification in a 'compensatory mode': the individual becomes preoccupied with certain types of immediate gratification.

A Practical Understanding of Addiction

As I have argued, addiction should not be viewed as an all-or-nothing ailment that an individual either has or does not have. Addiction problems occur along a continuum.

The Range of Plausible Social and Psychological Factors Contributing to Alcohol Addiction

In addition to neurobiological factors affecting the acquisition of alcohol addiction, a range of social and psychological factors beyond genetics can influence both alcohol dependence and alcohol abuse generally. These include:

- *Disordered, self-defeating thought patterns, low self-esteem and low perceptions of self-competence.* Such problems can reduce an individual's willingness or ability to resist peer pressure to drink or take drugs (Beck et al., 1993; and Ellis et al., 1988).
- *Previous alcohol experience.* Familiarity with the experience of using a particular drug is an important determinant of a drug's effects. Initially, the experimental use of alcohol often produces an immediate and excessive 'drunk,' whereas the same amount, taken after many bouts of 'learning' to drink, is likely to have a milder intoxicating influence. At least in part, tolerance to drugs is a learned response (McKim, 1986).
- *Expectations.* A user's expectations about a drug's effects, which are partly conditioned by the experience of use itself, can have a strong influence on the effects of a drug. A user's expectations can also be derived from friends' accounts, education, the mass media, and professional descriptions. Placebo studies using interactive materials provide clear information on the effects of expectations. Controlled studies show that expectations of a drinking experience are strongly associated with the account of the experience during and after intoxication. For example, Gottleib and colleagues (1987) found that, in a treatment experiment, addicted smokers given gum identified as having nicotine in its composition reported fewer withdrawal symptoms when abstaining from cigarettes, whether the gum actually contained nicotine or was simply a placebo. Brown et al. (1980) attempted to determine common expectations of people in North America for alcohol. Their research indicated that their subjects expected alcohol to enhance life experiences, including heightening sexual pleasure, improving social interactions by opening up and encouraging communications, and making them feel better physically. Brown et al. (1980) also found that moderate use of alcohol would increase their subjects' assertiveness and reduce social tensions. A large number of studies have reported that behavioural changes occur in people who believe they have consumed alcohol

but actually have not (Sumner and Parker, 1995: 24). Apparently, when people have learned that drinking causes increased sociability, they tend to become more sociable when they drink; when they learn that they will become aggressive, they take this belief into the drinking episode and act accordingly.

- *Mood*. The mood that a drinker – or even user of other drugs – brings to the process of use also has an influence on his or her tolerance level and other effects of the substance. According to a well-known principle often called 'Wilder's Law of Initial Value' (Leavitt, 1982), a drug cannot make a user exceed his or her capabilities behaviourally, emotionally, or cognitively. Further, the 'Law' states that a drug's effects depend on the user's pre-use state; that is, the further one is from one's maximum, the greater the potential effect. In other words, if you are already highly stimulated, a stimulant will have relatively little effect or even a numbing effect on you. If you are fatigued, however, the same dose of the same drug can have considerable impact. A practical application of Wilder's Law is found in the use of methylphenidate, a stimulant, in controlling hyperkinesis in children. The stimulant acts to *destimulate* the hyper-activity.

- *Modelling*. Through modelling and other forms of *social learning* and reinforcement, human beings learn drinking comportment and they can acquire temperate behaviours or 'acting up' behaviours, depending on the learning and the norms of the milieu in which their drinking occurs. Parental behaviour is the biggest single influence on the long-term behaviour of children. While problem drinking cannot be blamed solely on the parents of the problem drinker, parental attitudes and behaviour do create expectations and values about drinking, and depending on the degree of identification with the parental drinkers, the child is more likely to follow in their footsteps. Critics ask of social learning theorists: What about the negative reinforcement of job loss, guilt, ostracism, emotional upset, and psychological deterioration? Shouldn't such experience act to encourage aversive association with the substance causing the problem? This incongruity is explained by the principle of delayed reinforcement. The morning after a hangover, social punishment will not be effective because it is delayed. Further, if the stressors are great, the immediate relief offered by substance use will be more likely to be heeded, thus causing new stress which will, in turn, lead to more substance abuse (Tarter and Schneider, 1976).

- *Unstable and alcoholic homes during childhood*. Angry reactions to neglectful parents whose negligence is related to alcohol abuse may also result in alcohol problems for the affected children. Many observers have argued that the most likely causes of problem drinking lie in the effects of family instability. In the summary by Stanton and Todd (1982) of characteristics that separate drug-abusing families from other seriously dysfunctional families, a higher frequency of multigenerational chemical dependency, especially alcohol abuse, is characteristic, as is a propensity for other addictive behaviours, such as smoking and gambling. It is estimated that more than 50 per cent of alcoholics have a history of alcoholism in their family of orientation (Miller, 1998: 269).

- *Social location.* The symbolic definition given to a physical environment both constrains and facilitates various behaviours (Sumner and Parker, 1995). An activity undertaken at a religious function while people are under the influence of alcohol is likely to result in very different behaviour than one occurring in a 'tough bar.'
- *Peer group influence.* It is also true that the peer group can contribute significantly to an individual's choice to abuse alcohol or other drugs. Peer relationships have a significant effect on the initiation, development, and maintenance of substance abuse. In fact, the strong relationship between a person's substance abuse and the substance abuse of his or her friends and acquaintances is the most consistent and reproducible finding in the literature (Jessor and Jessor, 1977). This is particularly true for adolescence, but it is also true during adulthood. People often model themselves after their peers or the leadership among their peers. Susceptibility to peer influence is associated with involvement in peer-related activities that include substance abuse and with the degree of social attachment to peers rather than parents (Kandel, 1978). This modelling will often involve the development of both attitudes and behaviour which mimic the model. Alcohol has a range of socially ascribed meanings associated with it: it signifies being 'older' to young people; being masculine; being sexual; being violent – all of which might merge with a young person's desire to be accepted. The influence of peers on drinking behaviour is not confined to close friends. Research has shown that some occupations routinely create relatively more circumstances for and/or pressures for alcohol consumption.
- *Marital status.* Married persons of both sexes and all age groups tend to have fewer alcohol problems than the unmarried, divorced, and separated (Smart and Ogborne, 1986: 90).
- *Urban/rural differences.* Data from the Canada Health Survey indicate

that Canadians who live in large urban centres drink more often
than those who live in smaller cities or rural areas. Those who drink
every day are twice as likely to live in communities of more than 1
million people than in communities of less than 100,000 (McConnell,
1981).

- *The social shaping of expectations.* The individual's expectations play a
  significant role in how she or he will interpret the effects of normal
  doses of alcohol (Brown et al., 1990). Their alcohol experience of adolescents and adults who drink will be shaped not only by the pharmacological effects of alcohol but also by their expectations of what
  the alcohol will do, and these expectations vary by several social
  variables. For example, males are more likely than females to expect
  that alcohol will result in a decrease in their anxiety, make them
  more aggressive, and enhance their sexual arousal (S.A. Brown,
  1990; E.D. Brown et al., 1987). Females are more likely than males to
  anticipate pleasurable changes from moderate drinking (Brown et
  al., 1980). There is also evidence that alcohol abuse among adolescents is associated with the expectations adolescents have of the
  pleasurable or un-pleasurable effects of alcohol. Brown, Creamer,
  and Stetson (1987) found that adolescents who abuse alcohol are
  more likely to anticipate a positive experience when they drink,
  whereas those who do not abuse alcohol are less likely to anticipate
  drinking experiences that are positive.
- *The impact of nationality and culture.* In North America, alcohol use is
  limited legally and restricted to licensed premises. Not surprisingly,
  many young people feel that drinking alcohol is a major route to
  becoming adult. In France and Italy, drinking is a normal part of
  growing up, with few restrictions. The result is that drinking comportment is relatively civil, but health problems associated with frequent use are great. In North America, the reverse is true: alcohol
  consumption is associated with antisocial behaviours.

Historically, the use and understanding of the value of alcohol has
changed dramatically over time, even in Western society. Despite the
well-known history of the Temperance movement, it is often forgotten
that, until that movement, in Britain and colonial America – both north
and south of the forty-ninth parallel – the use of alcohol was widespread, widely accepted, and in many ways promoted by the clergy
(Smart and Ogborne, 1986: chap. 1). In the seventeenth and eighteenth
centuries, 'New World' colonists believed alcohol to be healthier than

water. According to William L. White, 'What is striking about early colonial history is the utter pervasiveness of alcohol ... consumed throughout the day by men, women and children and integrated into nearly every ritual of social and political discourse. Alcohol was the "Good Creature of God" – a blessing used to bring cheer, relieve sorrow, and nurse the sick' (1998: 1). Puritan preachers sometimes extolled the benefits of alcohol from the pulpit, and George Washington plied voters with liquor during election campaigns. In British North America, men of prestige tended to be heavy imbibers, and at major festivals and events, including community building bees, a supply of wine, spirits, or beer was expected and heavy drinking was often common (Smart and Ogborne, 1986). While there were no doubt instances of drunkenness that offended and led to calamity, drunkenness itself was not perceived as a special problem in early colonial times.

There are also substantial differences in drinking patterns among ethnic groups in a single society. While aboriginal Canadians have dis-proportionately large numbers of problem drinkers, some ethnic groups exhibit very few alcohol-related problems. A Vancouver study found only two cases of drunk driving and one case of alcohol abuse involving Chinese Canadians, although there were more than 50,000 Chinese Canadians in that city at the time (Lin and Lin, 1982). Smart and Ogborne (1986) review the literature on alcohol and ethnicity, noting that, while Irish Canadians are overrepresented in treatment populations, Jewish people appear to be underrepresented. The same writers note that certain Protestant denominations, particularly those of fundamentalist persuasion, are opposed to alcohol use and expect abstinence of their membership, as do Hindus and Muslims, and that, among the devout of their congregations, this opposition appears to be effective.

As these data suggest, various socially and psychologically deter-mined sets of rules, motivations, and expectations about the effects of alcohol and appropriate drinking styles in various social contexts tend to either shape the nature of the behaviour that occurs during drinking episodes or to proscribe its use altogether. As will be subsequently argued, so powerful are these influences that even some of our assump-tions about drinking as the cause of antisocial and criminal behaviour are directly called into question by the research.

6

An Unhealthy Relationship: The Profession of Medicine and Alcohol Abuse Treatment

The emphasis on troublesome alcohol use as a pathological problem or disease has come to be associated with what has been called the *medical model* of curative health intervention. Emphasizing the role of expert interventionists, the model places responsibility for the treatment of 'diseased' substance abusers in the hands of physicians, psychologists, social workers, and trained 'chemical dependency' workers, all of whom counsel and provide support for complete abstinence. The treatment for this unavoidable illness is to create the psychological and social conditions and refusal skills to resist alcohol consumption. In his examination of the subject, Yalisove (1997) argues that medicine played a key role in originating the 'disease concept of treatment,' and in both North America and Europe, advocacy of the DCT actually did begin with physicians. Unfortunately, the DCT has been mismatched with the normal, clinical criteria for medical intervention.

Dr Benjamin Rush, a physician and prominent citizen of the new U.S. Republic, first proposed the 'disease concept' of alcoholism in a pamphlet written in 1785 entitled *An Inquiry into the Effects of Ardent Spirits upon the Human Body and Mind, with an Account of the Means of Preventing and of the Remedies for Curing Them.* Rush came to be known as the 'Father of the temperance movement.' He believed that hard liquor posed a problem for public health because it was addictive and he recommended avoiding it entirely. Rush's prominence did much to elevate concerns about liquor. A friend of Benjamin Franklin and Thomas Jefferson, Rush was one of the men who signed the Declaration of Independence. It should be noted that his concern about hard liquor did not extend to wine and beer, which Rush apparently took to be drinks of common use not exploited extensively for their potential as vehicles to achieve drunkenness.

Shortly after, a Scottish physician, Dr Thomas Trotter of Edinburgh (White, 1998: 1–4), published an essay entitled *On Drunkenness*, in which he referred to drunkenness as a 'disease of the mind' that caused bodily disorders. Unlike Rush, Trotter encouraged those afflicted with this disease to avoid not only hard liquor but also beer and wine (Milam and Ketcham, 1983). However, the Church of England did not appreciate Trotter's view, warning its parishioners that considering drunkenness as being caused by disease, relieved the individual of moral responsibility for making appropriate drinking choices.

It was also, as we have seen, a physician who first used the term 'alcoholism': the Swedish doctor, Magnus Huss, employed it in his professional writing about alcohol problems. However, the term did not take for a time, at least in North America, where a chronic drunkard was referred to as an 'inebriate.' One of the first professional publications in North America specializing in research into alcohol problems was the short-lived quarterly, the *Journal of Inebriety* (Yalisove, 1997).

Despite the early sponsorship of the disease view by physicians it was, ironically, the most famous, spiritually oriented, 'self-help' movement of modern times, Alcoholics Anonymous, that was most effective in promoting the belief that alcohol abuse patterns reflected a diseased state. According to Yalisove, 'AA is a spiritual self-help fellowship based on the 12 steps and the 12 Traditions, promising "recovery" from the "malady" of alcoholism ... Its principles are spiritual and not scientific' (1997: 469).

The disease explanation was spread by the growth of AA as an organization, as well as by the popularization of E.M. Jellinek's *The Disease Concept of Alcoholism* (1960), in which the author suggested that there were five types of alcoholism:

- *alpha* – psychological dependence on alcohol, with no physical dependence,
- *beta* – heavy drinking, resulting in physical damage, but no dependence,
- *gamma* – as described above, physical dependence, with loss of control when drinking,
- *delta* – inability to abstain for even short periods, and
- *epsilon* – long periods of abstinence combined with bouts of binges.

Only selective aspects of the Jellinek model have been accepted by disease model adherents, and Jellinek himself believed that only the gamma and delta versions, which manifested as physical dependence, qualified as a genuine disease. As Ogilvie notes, there has been no corroborative evidence to prove the reality of these different types of alcoholism, and the typology has generally been abandoned in medical science (2001). The idea that the alcoholic eventually develops overwhelming cravings and that he or she becomes 'out of control' when drinking, and fear of the discomforts of withdrawal, have each been viewed, consistently, as true markers of alcoholism. Further, it has persistently been argued by Jellinek's followers that alcoholism is a uniformly *progressive* disease that gradually and inevitably works its way through various, predictable stages.

The Jellinek alcoholism typology and subsequent diagnostic and assessment tools long dominated the treatment of people with alcohol problems and the Jellinek formulation remains a powerful influence. The fact that it emerged professionally within medicine gave the disease model a high level of public legitimacy. It should also be noted that the influence of medicine has prevailed well beyond the simplicity of the original Jellinek conceptions of alcoholism.

Like medicine, alcohol intervention focuses on the individual and provides diagnoses, assessments, prognoses, and treatment through individual consultations and through in-patient treatment programs administered in hospitals and quasi-hospitals, or institutional residential centres. But should it?

The medicalizing of the public understanding of alcohol problems did have the advantage of emphasizing the seriousness of alcoholism as a health problem and the importance of science in identifying causes and seeking solutions. However, the very prestige of medicine creates a diagnostic imperialism in relation to any health problem that it addresses. This is an especially troubling effect in fields in which medicine can make no claims to superiority over other fields of inquiry and remedial practice. This problem is most profoundly manifested in areas such as environmental health, psychological (or 'mental') health, and social health.

The questionable quality of the influence of the medical model of health care in the treatment of problem drinking begins with the fact that Jellinek's description of the different types of alcoholism or the predictable, progressive character of alcohol problems has never been scientifically validated. In fact, the Jellinek model and the notion of progressive stages have essentially been invalidated by science and largely ignored for many years.

Let us consider some of the most salient concerns that have or might legitimately be raised about medicine's acceptance of the DCT.

1. Failure to Distinguish Degrees of Dependence

The DCT is based on the capacity to identity those who presumablably have the disease of alcoholism, as indicated by physical dependence or in some cases, psychological dependence. However, there is really no accepted way to objectively distinguish between psychological and physical dependence or between loss of control and inability to abstain. When put to the task, the 'experts' cannot clearly maintain these basic distinctions, thus seriously undermining scientific confidence in the disease model.

2. Lack of Accepted DCT Definitions and Assessment Measures

There are also various criticisms that suggest that the DCT simply does not fit the criteria required for addressing an illness according to the scientific standards expected of medicine. The scientific basis to the disease theory is weak. The original Jellinek study of 1946 used an unrepresentative, self-selected sample of ninety-eight already indoctrinated AA members in an attempts to validate the disease model (see Mendelson and Mello, 1985: 346–7).

To date, the scientific research that would normally be used to work up the type of full profile of a real disease expected in medicine has not been conducted. To satisfy scientific medical standards, the DCT should include theories strongly supported by genetic studies (Murray et al., 1983), endocrinology (Smith, 1982), studies of brain dysfunctions (McEvoy, 1982), and biochemistry (Tewari and Carson, 1982). While research at the infancy stage has been undertaken in each of these areas, the medical/disease model was institutionalized as a convention long before such research began.

3. Lack of Proof of a Single Disease Entity

The questionable assumption that there is a single entity called 'alcoholism' has encouraged an inappropriate search for a single cause – and, perhaps, an expensive and futile misappropriation of health care funding. Taken as single factor theories, genetic theories of alcoholism have been criticized by several researchers. David Lester, a biochemist at the Center of Alcohol Studies, Rutgers University, argues that the factual support for the view that heritability is the primary cause of alcohol dependency is weak. He argues that the trend towards genetic explanations is primarily a victory for ideology over careful scientific methodology and solid evidence (Lester, 1988). Lester argues that what is needed prior to any consensus on the primacy of single factors (or clustered factors) is a profile of the etiology of alcoholism based on a prospective longitudinal study. Such a study would embrace assessments of probability mechanisms from the biological to the sociocultural – and, Lester argues, no such profile has been generated in the research. Such a holistic approach would, of necessity, reject what he refers to as a 'simplistic and reductionist search for a single cause.'

Rather than being based on science, the disease model is grounded in a relatively simplistic set of hypotheses based on impressionistic accounts. Each of these hypotheses assume that alcoholism and drug dependence are primary, progressive, chronic, and relapsing diseases.

4. The Non-Confidence Expressed by the Opposition to the DCT

The DCT in alcohol intervention is now routinely attacked with a vigour reminiscent of the attack that the disease advocates themselves once made on those who held alcoholism to be a character flaw. The DCT thus by no means has the confidence of the scientific community as a whole. Unfortunately, DCT clients are often not informed about the debate concerning the treatment assumptions and methods used in specific programs.

5. The Non-Scientific Influence of AA on the DCT

The close relationship between the 'recovery movement' and the practitioners of the DCT creates great potential for the encroachment of faith on scientific objectivity. As Yarislove has noted (1997), the promotion of the disease-based explanation and the medical approach to intervention was driven as much or more by spiritually committed advocates of Alcoholics Anonymous as by physicians and scientists.

In his study of the DCT, Yalisove found that, with the exception of out-patient clinics, alcoholism treatment programming in the United

States had its origins in early, informal AA treatment (1997: 469–76). He argues that AA facilities, detoxification units, and state mental hospitals all had their roots in AA and, further, that DCT is essentially a structured and didactic presentation of AA principles, with some additional treatment elements, including the confrontation group. Some writers have gone so far as to equate AA with a 'religious cult.' Like any cult, it provides lonely and often troubled individuals with a sense of community. It also uses the powerful influence of a tightly knit organization and membership pressure to convert new recruits to its basic ideology and promotes inclusion in the group at the expense of the autonomy of the self of each member. Finally, it reacts defensively and critically to criticism and has all the sociological elements of a cult, including what amounts to persuasion strategies that are similar to 'brainwashing,' (Schaler, 1995). Galanter (1989) has similarly compared AA meetings to Unification Church (i.e., the 'Moonies') workshops, in which expressions of difference from the group's model of treatment are 'subtly or expressly discouraged.'

Galanter, a widely respected contributer to the addictions literature, uses the example of controlled drinking to illustrate his point. Controlled drinking or 'moderation management' has been proven effective for a significant minority of treatment program clients. Even prior to 1980, researchers had identified nearly eighty studies which indicated that controlled drinking was a stable treatment outcome for alcoholism program clients. These studies reported observed rates of normal drinking, resumed after a period of successful treatment for diagnosed alcoholism, for between 2 and 32 per cent of graduated program participants studied (Heather and Robertson, 1997). Despite these findings, Galanter notes that controlled drinking is wholly unacceptable to AA and the option is therefore 'anathema to active members'; it is rarely discussed, and discouraged when the matter is raised at meetings.

Another addictions researcher has commented that AA members seek a relationship with the supernatural and, in this way, diminish their personal sense of mastery over their own addictions and everyday lives. Essentially, AA tells the newcomer that his or her life is unmanageable and that it is ridiculous to try to manage it without the help of treatment professionals and/or AA (Sadler, 1977). The same writer further notes that powerlessness must be conceded in AA; this admission and the supportive interaction of AA chapter meetings and sponsors are substituted for training in empowerment skills – the thinking and social behaviour that enables the avoidance of excessive drinking.

Until recently, modern alcohol intervention approaches have been given shape and implemented in a manner in which the ideal of scientific scepticism has been compromised. Partially due to their impassioned commitment to the cause of alcoholism prevention and a curious integration of the model with spirituality, AA and overzealous advocates of the disease model have established a relatively closed system of prevention and treatment. By contrast, an open system of knowledge building based on continuously changing scientific evidence is the ideal of medicine and any other science-based profession allied to it, such as counselling psychology and addictions therapy.

6. An Unworthy Imitation

Another problem with the influence of the medical model of occupational organization on alcohol abuse intervention is that intervention specialists cannot make the same claim to expertise as physicians. Physicians are given special authority to assist the sick by virtue of the scientific basis of their understanding of health problems and their hard-earned and well-tested technical skill. While alcohol programming might typically be delivered by treatment personnel in hospital-like settings, there is no clear concensus on the nature of the problem itself. The standard for therapist qualifications is far lower than what is expected of physicians, and there is no integrated, self-regulatory machinery comparable to a college of physicians and surgeons. The establishment of such a body is the standard organizational marker of public acceptance of a consulting occupation's professional credibility. Self-regulation is essentially a special occupational exemption from the full authority of the state. The warrant for that exemption is the argument that the public tends to be incapable of objectively judging the knowledge base or skills of a full-fledged professional because only through extensive and difficult formal studies, and intensive, supervised apprenticeship, can a person gain the advanced knowledge and complex skills needed to practice in fields which, if badly handled, can have grave consequences for clients or patients (Johnson, 1972; Carr-Saunders and Wilson, 1933; Etzioni, 1969; and Freidson, 1970). That knowledge and skill base is certified by a state-authorized process. It is on this basis that special legislation is passed to grant professional colleges (e.g., self-governing organizations in a specialized occupation) the right and authority to monitor the quality, and discipline the infractions, of any of their own members. Stated differently, in varying degrees, health professionals have been successful in securing a quasi-state monopoly over their own domains and no occupational group has been more successful in securing a degree of independence in practice than physicians. Such organizational and legal status grants not only special authority but also prestige and status. Both the rigorous demands of study placed on new recruits and the limited supply of new recruits to a profession are assured by the monopoly over self-regulation held by the professional colleges.

The professional model of occupational organization established by medicine has been the envy of many occupations, although few have succeeded as well in gaining a special status. The model has obviously been a very attractive one, if only for the full professional status in society and the financial rewards it ensures. However, at its best, the professional model is anchored in its members' special knowledge and skills, and in the case of medicine and counselling, the basis of that knowledge is empirical evidence rather than metaphysical thought. Yet the influence of AA assured that, throughout North America, it was 'recovery' from alcoholism and a period of post-abstinence sobriety, and not a professional education, that served as the most important basis for recruiting employees in the alcohol intervention field. While gradually the pressure has increased for addictions workers to acquire specialized academic credentials, the disease model came to infuse and serve as the basis for training programs and lingered 'on the ground,' at the point of service delivery. Openness to new ideas such as controlled drinking or, for many, even the bio-psycho-social model of addiction, has been viewed as heresy. In short, as it played out as an influence on the practice of alcohol abuse intervention, the medical model merely served as an influence for granting a modicum of professional prestige to a non-professional group of workers.

Another problem with the influence of medicine is that its very emphasis moves it out of the political sphere to the private sphere and away from the sphere of social change towards the realm of individually focused therapy. The social problem of widespread alcohol abuse is for all intents and purposes converted from a macro- and mezzo-system problem to a micro-system problem. In the process, alcohol abuse is redefined almost exclusively as a private matter between a 'client' or 'patient' and professional interveners rather than as a political issue.

By assuming a physiological cause, the emphasis of the medical/disease model of addressing alcohol problems shifts the issue away from sociological factors, despite the fact that they are statistically indicated as having profound significance. This approach is in clear contravention of the more recent emphasis in public health, which has moved beyond an exclusive emphasis on bio-medical approaches. The more recent emphasis has been given to population health strategies, the practice of community health development, and returning primary health care responsibility to individuals, families, communities and policy makers.

At this point, no-one seems to be really clear as to what the addictive disorders actually are. In a presentation to a Treaty 6 addictions forum in Edmonton on 6 and 7 November 1995 in which I participated as a speaker, psychiatrist and social critic Thomas Szasz concluded that alcoholism is simply a 'bad habit.' While, admittedly, bad habits should be overcome, this does not make them a disease. With uncanny foresight, Szasz's writings have predicted for over three decades that, if we choose to call bad habits diseases, there is no limit to what we may consider a disease.

While the cutting edge of contemporary health promotion theory has come to understand that conditions and preventive intervention strategies dwarf individualized medical interventions as positive determinants of health, intervention in alcohol problems remains focused on treating individuals as if they had a disease, despite the fact that they can only legitimately be described as having a disease in metaphorical terms.

By placing so much emphasis on the treatment of the alcohol dependent, the vast majority of problem drinkers who are not alcoholics (or alcohol dependent) are simply ignored or driven from seeking help because, for very rational reasons, and not because they are 'in denial,' they want to avoid the lifetime stigma of the alcohol-dependent label. While much of the intervention system is now in the process of changing, from a public policy perspective, the cultural lag between the knowledge base of best practices in the alcohol problem prevention field and prevailing practice is clearly problematic.

7. Lack of Treatment Tiering

Another unacceptable disparity between the DCT and the standards of medicine is a lack of treatment tiering. It is now commonly held that good medicine involves individually tailored treatment that matches the distinctive nature and intensity of the patient's needs. Yet this type of treatment tiering is simply not a part of the DCT, which is largely centred on the Minnesota model of standardized therapy.

Lack of treatment tiering in alcohol intervention programs following the medical/disease model is especially troubling. A valid medical intervention should be organized around the severity of a presented disease, tiering the intervention according to some criteria to determine the matching of intensity with severity or to recovery potential. However, treatment for alcohol problems influenced by the disease model was standardized rather than tiered. By focusing on alcoholism as a single disease entity, individuals with various problems are mistakenly treated as if they all have the same problems and require the same type of therapeutic assistance. In general, whether in AA or inpatient treatment programs, a standardized, 'boiler-plate' approach to 'recovery' is the only treatment available. Yet there are a wide variety of addictive and alcohol abuse problems and an equally wide variation in the quantity, quality, and type of psychological, social, and economic resources that individuals may have available to them in their attempts to overcome their problem. The highly respected problem drinking researchers Linda and Mark Sobell (1993: 149) have observed that, in its lack of treatment tiering, the alcohol field is nearly unique.

8. Lack of Informed Consent

Finally, the DCT has often been criticized for not requiring, and frequently not even encouraging, informed consent in many treatment situations. This is a clear violation of medical ethics. Informed consent is a legal concept that determines if a patient has knowingly consented to care. It is also an ethical relationship between a patient and a service provider grounded in the expectation that the patient acts intentionally, with understanding, and without controlling influences.

The principle of *informed consent* is often not honoured in the alcohol intervention field. In fact, some writers have been very vocal in arguing that alcohol treatment referrals by employers and courts are a frequent, often unchallenged, violation of human rights (Schaler, 2000: chap. 12). Coercion, not consent, frequently dictate an individual's path to treatment for alcohol problems. Judges routinely make AA and in-patient 'alcoholism treatment' standard conditions of probation and parole orders, and drunk driving courses, which often include instruction in the disease model, counselling, and group therapy, are typically required as part of a sentence for driving while intoxicated.

A growing number of employers, sports teams (both professional and amateur), and schools are attempting to introduce drug-testing programs and require treatment as a condition of employment for those reputed to have such a problem. The growth of Employee and Family Assistance Programs (EFAPs) in industry, which tend to offer alcoholism treatment as a condition of employment continuance, can be seen in part as a welcome and humane addition to the modern workplace. However, the emergence of EFAP as a standard feature of the workplace in large corporations and government may also be an indicator that, in the guise of a helping hand, greater employer intrusion in the human rights of employees is becoming acceptable practice.

The research appears to discourage the use of AA for those coerced into attending meetings by courts (Glaser and Ogborne, 1982; Peele, 1989; Peele, Brodsky, and Arnold, 1991). Those who are sentenced to jail or placed under a probation order for drunk driving have better subsequent driving records (fewer accidents and fewer arrests) than those 'sentenced' to participation in treatment programs in which AA plays a central role (Peele, 1989).

9. Lack of Scientifically Demonstrated Effectiveness

A hallmark of a legitimate medical intervention is a rigorously investigated, reliable, and valid body of evidence that demonstrates its comparative effectiveness. However, as my review of the literature in other sections of this book indicates, neither the bio-medical model of intervention nor participation in Alcoholics Anonymous have been shown by research to be more effective than other interventions. In fact, alcohol addiction may be overcome as often or more frequently in the absence of either form of assistance (Vaillant, 1983). The measured effectiveness of treatment should be the most crucial criterion of a medical intervention, but medical model interventions for alcoholism have in general been very disappointing. The approaches usually taken in programming efforts in Canada and the United States involve intensive inpatient care in which an individual is assumed to have a disease called 'alcoholism' and is treated according to a standard set of individual and group counselling methods. The individual 'in treatment' is expected to divulge his or her intimate thoughts and to admit to having an uncontrollable dependence on alcohol. S/he is also expected to watch educational films and videos and to listen to guest speakers talk about the disease of alcoholism. Unfortunately, when careful reviews of effective treatment have been conducted, it becomes evident that the approaches grounded in the medical/disease model and centred on intensive, in-patient treatment, simply do not work very well. Very rarely are inter-vention methods used that have been shown to be effective in refereed, summary reviews of the literature on best practices (see Miller et al., 1995: 12–44).

Referring to standardized interventions based on the disease model, in the 1995 version of their ongoing evaluation of standard treatment practice, Miller and Hester conclude: 'The negative correlation between scientific evidence and application in standard practice remains strik-ing, and could hardly be larger if one intentionally constructed treat-ment programs from those approaches with the *least* evidence of efficacy' (1995: 33).

The effectiveness of AA has never been clearly demonstrated; indeed, to the extent that it has been adequately investigated scientifically, the results have been mixed and in some studies very disappointing. While AA is considered by many treatment professionals to be the most important component of an problem drinker's recovery program, a growing number are either far more cautious or openly critical in their appraisal (Ogborne and Glaser, 1985). Some researchers warn that any positive shift towards abstinence that is statistically associated with entry into an AA program might be more the result of the participant's decision to make a vigorous attempt to overcome his or her problem and a commitment to ongoing abstinence. There is some American evi-dence that would suggest that the relapse rate among AA members may be almost as high, or even as high, as it is for the 'recovered' problem drinking population as a whole (Alibrandi, 1978).

Admittedly, only a limited number of scientifically credible research studies have attempted to measure the effectiveness of AA. The princi-ple of anonymity, which is obviously fundamental to the AA approach, has made frequent research into effectiveness very difficult. Typically, access to participants is very difficult, but there have been three con-trolled studies of AA.

A study by Ditman and colleagues (1967) of 'alcohol addicts' assigned by courts to no treatment (probation only), treatment in a clinic, or to AA found that those assigned to probation in which no treatment was demanded did better than those assigned to either AA or an inpatient treatment program on rearrest outcomes.

In another study, Brandsma, Maultsby, and Welsh (1980) recruited subjects primarily from the court system and randomly assigned them to AA, insight therapy, professionally delivered rational behaviour therapy, or to a control group in which participants could make their own arrangements for treatment. The study results showed AA had the highest drop-out rate of the four groups (68 per cent versus 57 per cent for the other groups) and AA subjects showed the least improvement of the three *treated* groups. AA subjects were also more likely to have binged when questioned at a three-month follow-up interval. It should be noted that both of these studies can be faulted on the grounds that AA principles encourage voluntary participation and so this group may not be representative of the AA population as a whole. It should also be remembered, however, that AA is very much a part of a court referral system for drunkenness violators that extends across North America.

A third controlled study by Miller and Hester (1980) found no difference in outcome for AA and a comparison group of alcohol-abusing methadone maintenance patients.

While there is a need for further research, it would appear that AA is not effective for many subgroups of problem drinkers (Ogborne and Glaser, 1985). Instead, AA may actually be most effective with a specific subset of drinkers: white males over the age of forty years who are relatively stable socially, who are physically dependent on alcohol and prone to guilt, and who are the first born or only child (Ogborne and Glaser, 1985).

10. Lack of Cost Effectiveness

Brodsky (1995) argues that, while *cost-effectiveness* is not intrinsically a medical issue, it must be a major consideration in any credible health program or social service program, whether in the private or the public sector. Cost-effectiveness must also be regarded as an increasingly important consideration at a time when fiscal policies are preoccupied with deficit reduction and debt recovery. Yet cost-effectiveness has not been demonstrated for DCT, the medicalized approach to addictions.

Critics have raised a variety of serious issues concerning the influence of a medicalized view of alcoholism. The critics argue that Western medicine has been developed specifically to address biological and biophysical problems and these are problems that are typically quite different from those experienced in the psychological, spiritual and social realm. Critics argue that, while addictions may have a biological component that is partially responsive to medications, dietary improvements and an exercise regimen, ultimately overcoming such problems involves modified thinking patterns and reconstructed social relations. The latter, most significant aspects of the therapeutic process is not a 'patient role,' it is a life-enhancement and persued development rule, which is, ultimately, an approach to healthy living, not to overcoming sickness under the tutelege of an expert.

Ethicists are uncomfortable with the message sent both to society and to the problem drinker by the medical/disease model. Specifically, they are unhappy with the fact that individuals with a record of violent or other antisocial behaviour or self-destructive habits, such as repeated drunkenness, are treated as if they suffered from a disease rather than held to account for their actions. The concern is that a problem that is at least partially one of personal and social responsibility is converted into a problem that is viewed as requiring professional intervention and the application of an illness label. Taken to its logical conclusion, when such an approach is in play, the violent drunk whose behaviour causes emotional discomfort for others, injuries, or even death, comes to share equal status as victim with the individuals on the receiving end of his hostile behaviour.

The concept of a disease may at times serve as an excellent analogy for assisting people in understanding the psychological and social challenges confronting them. The organization of counselling intervention as a dyadic, professional-to-client, consulting relationship and the use of in-patient, residential treatment programming also has much to offer clients with specific types of problems, especially acute dependency. However, for many problem drinkers, the disease model has too often been taken literally at the point of intervention; it has been inappropriately applied to all people who have problems associated with drinking. In turn, this literal interpretation of alcohol problems as a disease has invited a specific kind of response, namely, the patient/consultant 'helping relationship' in which one person is sick and the other is the professional healer. Critics of the disease/medical model are concerned with the 'slippery slope' effect that can result from the literal acceptance of the disease metaphor. The risk is that those struggling with bad drinking habits and antisocial or self-destructive behaviours associated with drinking episodes find it very expedient to shift not only blame but responsibility to another party. When the substance abuser has run out of unfortunate background circumstances or a parent to blame, the professional is often waiting with not only a scapegoat (a disease classification) but also a willingness to share a major part of the responsibility for solving the problem. The weighty influence of the medical (or, perhaps, better stated, 'quasi-medical') intervention model can have the effect of establishing dependencies. As a consequence, typical marching orders in textbooks assigned to undergraduate students of these disciplines instruct future human service workers to avoid encouraging dependencies with clients.

Factors Sustaining the Disease Concept of Treatment

Despite the abundant evidence pointing to an alternative view of alcoholism, many factors in the alcohol and drug abuse self-help and public policy and programming environment contribute to the continued dominance of the disease model. One such factor is the ongoing commitment of AA to that model. The power of AA in the field of alcohol recovery is undeniable. The influence of the specialized occupational cultures in the United States on their counterparts in Canada is also a factor.

Despite decades of robust criticism and scientific evidence discrediting the medical/disease model, the model is defended by its advocates with an almost cultlike rigidity. A client who refuses to concede alcohol dependency is likely to be described as being 'in denial,' whether or not s/he has accurately self-assessed his or her circumstances. Professional critics who challenge the model in public are viewed as dangerous and ignorant dissenters who, if they really understood alcoholism, would realize that it is obviously a disease.

The self-interests of treatment professionals in the United States also play a highly influential role in sustaining the disease model, and the dominant sway of the American addiction professions establishment over their Canadian counterparts is well recognized. The high costs and considerable profit potential in privately funded health care in the United States have combined with high insurance costs to press health care providers into group practices in which economies of scale in funding and premiums for group insurance payments can be realized. The health management organization (HMO) thus rules the administration of most health care in the United States.

To defray the high costs of private medicine individuals, businesses, and employer groups participate in HMOs and, through them, secure group insurance. For these organizations to realize the goals of their membership, they must negotiate a legitimate list of insurable health problems and insurable rates with insurance companies. It is therefore in the interest of the insurance companies to delimit coverage of any health problem that may be of a questionable nature, such as the false physical symptoms of a hypochondriac or a worker who is trying to get paid for time away from work at the insurance company's expense. To prevent questionable illnesses from being bootlegged into the 'grey areas' of insurance coverage, the HMOs and insurance companies stick rigidly to relatively narrow definitions of health problems. In matters that are considered to be primarily of a mental health nature, the definitions of the American Psychiatric Association's DSM-IV are used. It has typically been the decision of the insurance companies that, unless an individual is an 'alcoholic' (suffers from the alcohol dependency syndrome) s/he does not qualify for reimbursement and time off or treatment. To ensure that they are paid, addictions workers must attempt to tailor their services to meet the needs of those who fit the medically defined categories (which, as often as not, are actually behavioural and mental categories defined in DSM-IV). Often the exercise reminds them of fitting square pegs into round holes. Consequently, while it was on the wane for several years in the face of challenges from its critics, the medical model re-emerged as a major impetus in the field in the United States – and, given the influence of the United States on Canadian professional culture, the disease medical model has been sustained on this side of the border as well. As part of the larger Canadian addictions intervention environment, First Nations in Canada have themselves supported the use of this highly questionable model.

The tendency for advocates of the disease model to spurn revisionist thinking in the problem drinking intervention field may be at least partially explained by political and economic forces. As one writer has argued, in the United States, the disease model has become 'big politics' and 'big business' (Fingarette, 1988b: 64). It now forms the basis of a massive 'treatment' industry, into which billions of dollars are invested. Thus the medical model has taken on a life of its own, invading various other areas of troublesome human conduct and embracing these behaviours within the disease framework.

There is an unfortunate tendency in science and the applied scientific professions to overprotect an explanatory model once it has been accepted and to discourage open debate, and this tendency is clearly in evidence in the alcohol abuse prevention and intervention field. In the United States, it is reinforced by the fact that the 'treatment industry' has become a multi-billion dollar business which depends on a continuous flow of clientele to treatment professionals and therapy programs.

Some Further Thoughts on Personal Choice

The most controversial issue in the substance abuse field concerns the degree of personal responsibility to be assumed by the problem drinker. Advocates of the disease model legitimately fear a return to previous unsympathetic and punitive methods of dealing with alcoholics. The idea that severely troubled people should turn to physicians or counsellors for assistance with their problems is, in compassionate terms, far better than treating them with contempt and punishing them. Yet there is a clear difference between being troubled and being incapable of making moral choices. Even subject to unspeakable extremes of pain, many prisoners of war have refused to share secrets when tortured. Yet one of the most influential contributions of the disease concept of substance abuse has been its insistence that the addicted individual should not be held responsible for his or her dependence. Critics have been concerned that this assumption of blamelessness might serve to encourage feelings of powerlessness and therefore be counter productive in the recovery and personal problem-solving process undertaken by the problem drinker. As Marlatt and Gordon (1985) have argued, the greatest strength of the disease model is the fact that it absolves the addict of personal responsibility for the problem behaviour; ironically, this may also be one of its major shortcomings. It is essential that problem drinkers believe they are capable of identifying their problems, that they learn about their own thoughts and behaviour that trigger drinking episodes, and that they acquire skills for overcoming them. To the extent that the disease model and AA discourage personal empowerment, they perform a mischief. This is a tricky subject, for there is much that is valuable for both the alcoholic and the problem drinker in the caring support of AA and the therapeutic communities organized in treatment centres. But ultimately, the message must be that the individual in treatment is in charge of the therapeutic and relapse prevention processes. Unlike in physical medicine, no surgery or pill can cure problem drinking.

Prevalent messages in alcohol abuse counselling may actually undermine the sense of personal power needed by recovering problem drinkers to cope with the stresses that contribute to problem drinking. For example, a study by Kobasa (1979) examined factors that differentiated between people who became ill and those who stayed well in situations characterized by similar stressors. She found that those who stayed well displayed a *hardiness* defined by four major characteristics: a vigorous orientation to the environment; a sense of meaningfulness; a strong commitment to self; and an internal locus of control. Simply put, Kobassa's research suggested that those most able to cope with the same stress were those with the strongest belief in their own abilities to meet the challenges placed on them by their environment. Further evidence for this view was found in a study by Lazarus (1980), who identified differences between people who see potential stressors as threats to their well-being and those more capable of coping with the stresses of both everyday life and disruptive events, viewing them as significant frustrations but also challenges to be overcome by 'drawing upon existing or acquirable skills' (48).

7

From Myth to Reification:
The Firewater Complex

As a reference to the drinking troubles of the first peoples of this continent, the term 'firewater' first appeared in the North American literature in the nineteenth century (Dailey, 1967). However, the view that 'Indians' had a special weakness and fallibility to impairment and an intrinsic penchant for behavioural excesses when drinking dated as far back as the seventeenth century (MacAndrew and Edgerton, 1969).

There is now a concensus in the relevant research literature that, prior to contact with Europeans, no indigenous cultural group in the land area within what is now Canada had developed the process of preparing alcohol (Smart and Ogborne, 1986). Yet once contact occurred, there are many reports of 'Indian' interest in European alcohol. Those reports trace to the first trade between host peoples and Europeans in Canada, the latter including the French explorers, adventurers, and traders and the scattering of European settlers who toughed out the winters on lands once occupied solely by indigenous North Americans.

Trade between the French *coureurs de bois* and indigenous peoples occurred as exchanges of blankets, guns, and beads for harvested furs sold into the European market (Smart and Ogborne, 1986). The French traders made long canoe trips inland for the purposes of trade with various aboriginal groups. The fact that a primary interest of the indigenous traders in the fur trade was French brandy has been documented by several researchers (Heath, 1982; Ray, 1974; Rich, 1967). The historical record indicates regional variation in the style of European alcohol use by First Nations immediately after contact, but there is extensive evidence suggesting that it was often very troublesome. The impression that the indigenous peoples of North America could not hold their liquor was so strong that both the Canadian and American governments eventually imposed long-lasting prohibitions on the sale of alcoholic beverages to them.

Summarizing the standard impression gleaned from early reports of indigenous alcohol use, Smart and Ogborne write: 'From a very early time, Indians showed a great love for alcohol, a desire to get drunk on every occasion and a tendency toward violence afterward' (1986). The comment is supported by a number of records indicating a special First Nations attraction to European beverage alcohol and the accompaniment of its consumption with drunkenness and violence.

A seventeenth-century reference includes an observation by Father Chretien LeClerq regarding the violent, injurious, and irresponsible behaviour of the Mi'kmaq of Gaspé while intoxicated. LeClerq wrote of 'Lewdness, adulteries, incest and several other crimes ... [and] ... injuries, quarrels, homicides, murders, patricides (all)... the sad consequences of the trade in brandy' (cited in MacAndrew and Edgerton, 1969: 101). An anonymous memorandum, apparently written in 1693, describes the drinking behaviour of the Indians of Nova Scotia as lacking moderation and leading to 'extremities of fury and cruelty ... They slaughter one another ... murder ... disfigure their faces ... burn and cripple in their scuffles.[1] Similar historical references describe orgiastic, cruel, and violent behaviour during and after the drinking episodes of indigenous North American tribes and bands, including bands in the Great Lakes region (Parkman, 1885) and other parts of eastern Canada and among the Cree (Eastman, 1915).

The Firewater Theory

Lacking an anthropological concept of culture, the Europeans in early contact with North America's indigenous peoples, perhaps inevitably, viewed the troublesome response of the host peoples to be a racial trait – and this has been viewed by some scholars as the context in which the 'firewater theory' originated (see Dailey, 1967). It is true that there was no genetic theory to inform the views of the early European explorers

---

1 This quotation is taken from *Collection de Manuscripts contenant lettres, memoires, et autres documents histroiques relatifs a la nouvelle* (1883), 4 vols. (Quebec: Impremeric à Cote, souse les auspices de la legislature de Quebec) 1: 541, cited in MacAndrew and Edgerton (1969: 101).

and traders. However, given the religious conviction that racial differences were pre-ordained, and racial mixing unnatural and sacrilegious, it is reasonable to assume that the Europeans would have taken the antisocial comportment characteristic of aboriginal drinking to be a function of their distinctive biological constitution.

While the firewater theory, according to which the 'North American Indian' is 'constitutionally incapable' of reasonably managing the use of liquor dates back to the early days of interaction with Europeans (MacAndrew and Edgerton, 1969), the essence of that theory survives to this day. It is my opinion, informed by more than two decades of active contact with First Nations, that the firewater theory currently prevails in popular opinion and even in most problem drinking therapy programs operated by and for First Nations people on reserves. Further, the firewater theory has become a part of a persistent cultural construct that has been modified and expanded over time. As both a cluster of beliefs and a set of actual drinking norms, this construct has, in effect, acquired a life of its own, becoming an independent cause of destructive substance abuse patterns and an obstacle to personal and community self-determination and resiliency.

Scientific Prestige: The Influence of the Disease Model on the Firewater Theory

One of the great attractions of the disease model is that it is allegedly grounded in science. In the modern era in Western society, science wed to technology has frequently been referred to as the 'new religion,' in that it has replaced organized churches and their scriptures as the most convincing guide to human understanding of the complexities of life. Whether this analogy is credible or not, there undoubtedly is a tendency in Western societies to take the findings of science as the most legitimate knowledge claims. At least from the time that E.M. Jellinek published his first formulation of it, the disease model of alcoholism has been considered a scientific explanation of alcohol problems. Framed in scientific language and purported by its adherents to be grounded empirical research, the disease model of alcoholism became the most prominent technical and popular explanation for habitual behavioural problems in which alcohol is implicated.

The disease model also came to bolster the firewater theory, breathing new life into and sustaining it long after reason would suggest that it should have died. The reasoning goes something like this: when disproportionate numbers of First Nations people are classified as alcoholics, they must, as a people or 'race,' have a predisposition to alcoholism. Thus the firewater theory is, in effect, the disease model of alcoholism projected onto people of aboriginal North American ancestry, and, at least in Canada, it is sustained most forcefully within reserve communities.

For many addictions professionals and academics, such thinking is a relic of the past and misguided. However, this is very much a minority view, and the disease model retains a powerful influence on First Nation views of addictions. Its influence is especially powerful within First Nations and on the people providing substance abuse services to them.

The Attraction and Commitment to Disease Model Logic in First Nations

Over the past decade and a half, key informants actively situated on the front lines of First Nations alcohol abuse intervention efforts have indicated to me that addictions workers have a special, even an emotional, commitment to the disease model. It has been explained to me that the disease concept, once grasped, was wholeheartedly embraced by First Nations people as a positive alternative to the 'victim-blaming,' moralistic, and superior opinions of white people regarding aboriginal alcohol problems.

Undoubtedly, as First Nations increasingly subject to critical scrutiny the social problem-solving methods imposed on them by outsiders, the disease model will lose its grip on the occupational scripts of the addictions and substance abuse establishment serving them. The current struggle for self-determination and the attempt to overcome the dependency associated with decades of neo-colonial administration by the Department of Indian Affairs (now Indian and Northern Affairs, Canada [INAC]) will gradually render the disease concept less and less acceptable. However, so welcome has the disease perspective been to a people whose self-esteem was devastated by earlier views that its defenders can be expected to cling stubbornly to the model for years to come.

The Firewater Theory Rejected: A Review of the Literature

Is there a 'racial disposition' to alcohol addiction and to the troubled drinking styles characteristic of First Nations people. Stated differently, do First Nations people, as a population, have a special genetic predisposition to alcohol dependency and high risk behaviours when under the influence of alcohol?

The race concept has been employed as a research variable in biological and behavioural studies examining group variations in alcohol problems. In North America, there has long been an interest in determining whether or not there is a biological basis for the popular stereotype of the 'drunken Indian.' Admittedly, that characterization has been powerfully reinforced in public perception by extremely high rates of arrest, conviction, and incarceration of indigenous people for behaviour in which alcohol is implicated.

Relevant Biological Research

Despite some well-known studies, a careful review and analysis of the research literature indicates that there is little evidence that aboriginal people in Canada have something unique in their biological make-up that makes them especially sensitive to the reactive effects of beverage alcohol.

Compared with the Caucasian population, lower rates of alcoholism and alcohol abuse have been well documented among people of Asian ancestry in North America. While many Asians drink, even to the point of intoxication, their drinking comportment is typically controlled. A report of a study by sociologist Milton Barnett in New York's Chinatown observed that residents of that community drink, at times becoming intoxicated, but intoxication and alcohol dependence is extremely rare (Barnett, 1955). Barnett goes on to note that the children of the Asian community in New York that he studied were essentially taught how to drink. As part of their learning, they were taught a set of values that promoted relatively well-mannered drinking behaviour. Drunken behaviour in the community invited ridicule and social ostracism if it occurred repeatedly. As noted above, a Vancouver study of its 50,000 Chinese residents found that the police had recorded only one case of alcohol abuse and two cases of impaired driving (Lin and Lin, 1982).

At least part of the explanation for this more controlled Asian drinking comportment may lie in several studies that have shown a greater Asian bio-physical sensitivity to alcohol. A review of that literature by Arthur K. Chan (1986) indicated that the primary manifestations of this sensitivity include a highly visible facial flushing in 47–85 per cent of

Asians, compared with 3–29 per cent of Caucasians. The research Chan reviewed also indicated that this facial flushing was accompanied by other objective and subjective symptoms of discomfort, including headaches or nausea. Chan reported that some studies have suggested that elevated acetaldehyde levels, plausibly responsible for the flushing, may result from a higher than normal production of acetaldehyde dehydrodgenase (ALDH). However, Chan's review refers to several studies that indicate that there is actually a stronger base of support for the hypothesis that the Asian tendency to facial flushing, nausea, and painful and lengthy hangovers is a function of a slower than normal metabolism of acetaldehyde. This condition appears to be genetic and arises in people who have inherited an inefficient version of a liver enzyme that is important to the body's capacity to break down alcohol.

Hypothetically, let us assume that those aboriginal people who have no bloodlines traceable to non-aboriginals share with Asians a tendency, as a population, to slower metabolization of alcohol and therefore experience longer discomfort associated with hangovers, and greater blood vessel dilation, than other ethnic groups. They also share a consequent 'flushing reaction' visible in the facial and ear lobe areas. If people of purely aboriginal origin did share these physiological reactions with the Asians, it would be more reasonable to assume that they too would have an aversion to alcohol rather than a special attraction to it.

One of the studies intended to test the contention that Amerindians had a special physiologically based susceptibility to alcohol dependency and extremes of impairment was entitled *Ethanol Metabolism in Various Ethnic Groups* (Fenna, et al. 1971). It studied the effects of intravenously administered alcohol on Canadian 'Whites,' 'Indians,' and 'Eskimos [sic]' in Edmonton, Alberta. After measuring blood alcohol levels and individual metabolism rates with a breathalyzer, individual scores were averaged for each of the groups and compared. The researchers found that, while each group required comparable amounts of alcohol to achieve intoxication (as measured by blood alcohol levels), compared to their 'white' co-subjects, the Natives metabolized alcohol at a significantly slower rate.

While a number of criticisms have been made of the Fenna research, two are most convincing in the challenge they posed for the study. The first salient criticism questions the way the experimental groups were selected. Fisher (1987: 85), an anthropologist, challenged the value of the results on the grounds that the study did not identify any specific genetic traits or differences in genetic traits between the three study groups, nor did it compare the genetic representativeness of any of the three groups to their presumed 'parent' population groupings. Hence, it cannot reasonably be assumed that the study group traits can be generalized to the population groups from which they are supposed to be derived.

Fisher also noted that both the white and the Inuit groups studied by Fenna et al. had far more light drinkers than the Indian group and the Indian group had far more heavy drinkers than the others. Thus the study actually compared one group of heavy drinkers to two groups of moderate drinkers, rather than three biologically differentiated 'racial' groups. And in comparing different group averages, rather than the total variance within each group, the methodology used in the Fenna et al. study does not meet the basic statistical criteria for determining significant differences.

Fisher also took issue with the assumed racial homogeneity of these study groups. He noted that Fenna and colleagues selected all but a few of their subjects in a large urban centre, and he argued that there is no way of determining the genetic mixture represented in that sample of Indians. There were similar problems with the Inuit subjects. The Inuit in the sample were drawn from a hospital in Edmonton and a hospital in Inuvik. The Inuvik hospital serves a population in the Mackenzie Delta that has been disrupted for over 150 years by Arctic whaling operations, and this may have resulted in the extensive interbreeding of Caucasian and indigenous people. Fisher therefore concluded, 'One cannot say that twenty-one Eskimos and twenty-seven Indians are a representative sample of some naturally occurring indigenous populations' (1987: 86).

A study of Eastern Crees by Wolff (1973: 194) likewise reported that these subjects reacted in a physiologically distinct way to alcohol ingestion. Even more often than the Asian subjects after whom the reaction has been named, the Crees displayed the 'Asian flush.' Wolff also found that his Cree subjects reported more symptoms of intoxication than would normally be expected for the amount of alcohol ingested.

Despite Wolff's conclusion, subsequent studies and further analysis have served to dispel the genetic argument.

One well-known study comparing the rates of ethanol metabolism for an aboriginal ethnic group with two other ethnic groups, all considered 'races,' virtually reversed the findings of the Fenna research. Reed, Kalant, Gibbins, Kapur, and Rankin (1976: 852) studied 102 Chinese, Caucasian, and Ojibwa subjects, recording observations after giving them a controlled amount of food and a single glass of an alcoholic beverage. In sharp contrast to the Fenna *et al.* study and Wolff's findings, the Reed et al. study found the Ojibwa to have significantly *higher* rates of ethanol metabolism than the Caucasian and Chinese groups (1976: 854).

It should be noted that some of the fundamental flaws in the Fenna study were repeated in the Reed et al. study. Most significant was the fact that the Reed study did not demonstrate that its samples had enough in common with the 'parent' populations they are supposed to represent. Therefore, any generalizations from the study could not be of major scientific interest. But it remains noteworthy that Reed and his colleagues concluded that variation in alcohol metabolism among the groups commonly viewed as races is no greater than the variation within racial groups.

Three decades ago, Joy Leland, the American anthropologist, conducted a comprehensive review and analysis of the research relevant to the firewater theory. Her review considered studies completed up to the first half of the 1970s (1976). Leland's monograph, aptly entitled *Firewater Myths*, found no evidence for the popular idea that Indians had an 'inordinate craving for liquor' or that they necessarily lost control over their drinking when they imbibed (1976).

Leland compared Native drinking-related behaviours to the 'alcoholic traits' in the Jellinek taxonomy of alcoholism types, and found no close fit. Nor did she find evidence supporting the argument of some investigators that alcohol addiction occurs less frequently among aboriginal North Americans than in the general population.

When attempts have been made to fit common Indian drinking into Jellinek's 'species' of alcoholism, the efforts have failed. As we have seen, Jellinek described two types of 'addictive alcoholism,' which he referred to as *gamma* (bout drinking) and *delta* (steady drinking). He also recognized a type of alcoholism that he referred to as *epsilon*, periodic, often explosive drinking, which some have thought to represent an extension in degree of the *gamma* category. As Joy Leland stated in her book, 'At first glance, this brief reference to *epsilon* sounds as though it might be pertinent to Indian drinking, which certainly seems "explosive" in most accounts cited so far' (1976: 55). Leland also noted that Jellinek did not flesh out the category and did not make it clear if such a drinking style was addictive. She goes on to note that R.C. Dailey, an anthropologist who was a close associate of Jellinek at the

Addiction Research Foundation in Ontario, suggested referring to Native American drinking patterns as 'Zeta' – a unique pattern of use in which drinking is periodic and explosive, but not necessarily addictive. The fact that the Zeta drinking pattern was so destructive convinced Dailey that it was indeed a distinctive form of alcoholism. Yet while this pattern may be more pronounced among problem drinkers in First Nations, the notion that a distinctive, racially based, genetic trait causes it is not supported by the evidence. It accounts for only some, not all, of the styles of drinking among first peoples. Admittedly, the so-called Zeta pattern is prevalent among aboriginal problem drinkers. However, it does not equate closely with the more common view of alcoholism as an addiction, nor does it conform to the stages model of progressive alcoholism. Finally, the Zeta pattern does not conform to the psychiatric definition of alcoholism.

Based on the data presented in chapter 2 and the discussion above, it is apparent that most problem drinkers among First Nations people in Saskatchewan and Canada cannot be readily categorized as 'alcoholics' or appropriately fitted into the psychiatric category of the Alcohol Dependency Syndrome (ADS). Indigenous Canadian people do tend to be high-risk drinkers; in other words, if they drink, they are far more likely than other Canadians to experience drinking episodes in which they commit acts which harm themselves, other people, or valuable property. However, the available research evidence does not support the contention that First Nations people are predisposed to alcohol dependency (alcoholism). There is also no convincing evidence that they are genetically prone to alcohol problems or that they are necessarily problem drinkers if they do drink.

The most recent direct attempt to test the firewater myth came in a study of alcohol sensitivity among eighteen- to twenty-five-year-old male subjects. The forty subjects lived in a community in the southwestern United States and had varying degrees of Native American (Mission) Indian lineage. The study involved testing for subjective and physiological measures of intoxication before and after the ingestion of a placebo and 0.85 ml/kg of alcohol in physically healthy male subjects (Garcia-Andrade, Wall, and Bhlers, 1997). Subjective measures were self-reports of feelings; objective measures included blood pressure, plasma cortisol level, and pulse rate. The overall effects of the alcohol ingestion on those with more than 50 per cent Native American ancestry were compared with the effects on those with less than 50 per cent aboriginal ancestry. The results indicated that those with less aboriginal ancestry were more physiologically and subjectively sensitive to the effects of alcohol. The authors concluded that their results clearly contradict the firewater myth.

The most salient conclusion to be drawn from this evidence is that aboriginal people should be more likely to avoid alcohol than to be drawn to its use. Thus, the explanation for exceptional problem drinking rates for First Nations people must lie with variables that distinguish environmental influences differentiating the social realities of Asians from those of First Nations people.

'Race': A Scientifically Discarded Concept

It should be also be recognized, however, that the racial studies of differences in alcohol metabolization are themselves flawed by the very use of the concept of 'race' as a variable of study. While remaining in common use and perhaps possessing some limited value as a superficial physical discriminator, the term has largely been rejected as a useful analytical concept by scientists.

It was actually a nineteenth-century European preoccupation with unitary explanations of human variation that first drew attention to the concept of race as a significant distinguishing characteristic of subgroups of the human species. The idea was inspired by the differences observed in the form of superficial physical traits. In pursuit of global trade objectives, Westerners saw these superficial traits when they encountered people from different regions of the globe. The race concept sorted human groups into a finite number of categories, distinguished from each other on the basis of specific characteristics (Banton, 1987). In conformity with the ethnocentric world-view inherent in the European imperialism of the time, these categories were often used to sort peoples into a hierarchy of superiority-inferiority. The West identified the race concept with science, despite the long-standing cultural biases that it reflected.

The supposed authority of these pseudo-scientific classifications of races accentuated group differences, making them appear more comprehensive and unalterable than they actually were (Stocking, 1968). Subsequent study of racial differences has shown that, as an independent variable according to which interesting predictions of human group variation can be predicted, race is of little if any use. Almost all variations of interest have been shown to be as wide within so-called race groupings as among individuals in different race groupings. In fact, many social scientists have attacked the concept as being a far better mask for socio-economic exploitation than a useful scientific variable.

The problem with the race concept is that, as a measurement category, it cannot usefully differentiate individuals of different ethnic backgrounds from one another. The most damaging evidence against the use of race as an independent or dependent variable in scientific studies is the finding that the physiological variation within each of the so-called human races is far greater than the variation between the races. When studying the classically defined racial groupings, the Harvard geneticist Richard Lewontin (1972) found that membership in such a group accounted for only 6.3 per cent of human differences on various traits, while between 67.4 and 90.7 per cent of human variability could be accounted for within these populations. The author concluded, 'Human racial classification is of no social value [and has] ... virtually no genetic or taxonomic significance ... no justification can be offered for its continuance' (397). Stated succinctly, when biases are removed, the fact of being Mongoloid, Caucasian, Negroid, or North American Indigenes, provides virtually nothing of scientific value in terms of predicting physiological, psychological, or social behaviour patterns. From a genetic standpoint, what separates a 'Caucasian' North American from an Inuit or an African Bantu is little more than what separates that individual from another North American Caucasian.

Justifiably, some scholars are passionately opposed to the application of the race concept to the study of human affairs (Miles, 1982). Critics of the use of race as a variable in the scientific study of human beings argue that not only is there no validity to the idea that race is germane to the study of human diversity, but that distinct and discrete categories of racially pure people, an idea which is the cornerstone of racial classification, does not exist because of the extent of cross-breeding that has occurred through migration and intermarriage. This process has resulted in the extensive mixing of ethnic groups often considered distinct races.

The Social Roots of Troubled Drinking: The 'More Teetotallers, More Problem Drinkers' Paradox

Despite the almost fixated search for an 'alcogene' (a gene to explain alcoholism) apparent in the research literature – and, presumably, the desire for a 'magic pill' cure that would follow upon such a genetic discovery – the far more profound impact of social variation in problem drinking virtually screams out for more analytical and policy-oriented attention. Such is the influence of the medical/disease model on the way researchers, professional interventionists, politicians, and the public at large.

Consider the fact that drinking problems vary substantially by ethnic group. Repeatedly the relevant research indicates that the Slavs, the Irish, and aboriginal North Americans are at high risk of assuming problem drinking behaviour patterns. In North America, Italians, Jews, Greeks, and Asians have very low percentages of problem drinkers in their populations. George Vaillant found that Irish Americans are seven times as likely as Italians to become alcoholics (1983). Behind this comparison are culturally imported drinking norms, not genetics. A large bookshelf of academic research and computed statistics in government reports have made it apparent that coming from a difficult family background or having a parent who role models problem drinking increases the likelihood of a child developing drinking problems at adolescence and during adulthood. Being nurtured in a more emotionally and psychologically comforting environment is a powerful prophylactic against careless drinking.

Comparing white college students to inner-city, working-class subjects in Boston over forty years, Vaillant found that the working-class subjects were three times as likely as those in the college group to become alcoholics (1983). There is also extensive research that shows that, in the United States, African Americans and Hispanics become alcoholics far more often than whites (Peele, Brodsky, and Arnold, 1991). First Nations and aboriginal peoples in the United States, Australia, and New Zealand also all have high alcohol problem rates in comparison with the larger populations of the societies in which they are embedded as ethnic and national minorities (Saggers and Gray, 1998). In each of these instances, social marginality and a lack of economic integration beg to be identified as the factors that explain most of the differential rates.

What is especially interesting is the *more teetotaller, more drunks* paradox apparent in some of the ethnic groups in which problem drinking rates are high. Thus George Vaillant found not only that Irish Americans had more drinking problems than Italian Americans, but they were also more likely to be non-drinkers or, in the vernacular, 'teetotallers.' Vaillant explained it this way: 'Irish culture see[s] the use of alcohol in terms of black or white, good or evil, drunkenness or complete abstinence, while in Italian culture it is the distinction between moderate drinking and drunkenness that is most important' (1983: 187). By contrast to many other ethnic groups, especially those who describe alcohol in pejorative terms ('demon rum,' etc.), Greeks, Italians, and Jews introduce children to wine, beer, or spirits early, as part of common and special religious rituals, and it is not presented as a special, emotionally charged substance. Just as you are taught to limit your food intake to reasonable portions (except on special family occasions, when flattering the hostess is essential), you are taught to limit your beverage consumption.

As I have shown in chapter 2, this same paradox characterizes the First Nations drinking culture in Canada. First Nations communities tend to have more abstainers than the Canadian population as a whole, but they also have more problem drinkers and probably more alcoholics. Drinking is assumed to have an enormous attraction in First Nation communities but, at root, it is considered a dark and evil enterprise, a mischief, and a mature adult should forsake it entirely. Ultimately, drink is viewed as a 'bad' thing; a 'good' person does not drink. The approach to drinking is a culturewide example of the 'all or nothing' thinking that cognitive-behavioural therapists so frequently warn us against. I have noticed that, as gambling has emerged in recent years as a recreation of choice in First Nations, especially among former problem drinkers and alcoholics, the same all-or-nothing, bad/good perspective has come to define perceptions of gambling. Thus, I have frequently been told by health workers that a leader has been seen at a casino, and that professional workers and leaders should steer people away from gambling through role modelling. Apparently, it is assumed that simply by partaking in gaming activity, one is displaying a gambling problem. But there is no necessary connection between the two: being seen at a doctor's office with some frequency should not lead an observer to conclude that you are a doctor, or even that you are gravely ill.

The 'Indian Binge': The Problem Drinking Norm in First Nations

As the data in chapter 2 have indicated, First Nations styles of drinking include disproportionately high rates of conscious abstinence; alcohol dependency (or 'alcoholism,' as many would have it); disproportionately high rates of high-risk alcohol use, typically expressed in binges rather than as a regular, ongoing activity; and moderate, controlled drinking characteristic of professional and administrative community leaders.

The services in place to address alcohol problems in First Nations are focused almost wholly on the alcohol 'addict' or 'alcoholic.' Unfortunately, the majority of alcohol problems and its tragic correlates – crime, vehicle accidents, fires, family violence, homicide, and suicide in which drunken behaviour is implicated – arise from episodes of social interaction involving ordinary First Nations people who are not alcohol dependent. While alcoholism may be well covered by service interventions, the core of the problem drinking, as a social problem, remains intact and undisturbed.

The problem drinking pattern that is most troublesome, if only because it involves the most people – including most youth and young adults – and therefore responsible for the greatest health, social, and economic costs, is the drinking episode conducted in a social setting. This drinking pattern is so common in First Nations that some anthropologists have developed theories to explain it. Thus Hallowell (1955) explained binge drinking and some of its behavioural excesses as a release from the normal reserve and control characteristic of traditional indigenous cultures. Many accounts have described Indians as being polite, shy, non-aggressive people who become transformed when drinking. Drinking is then explained as analogous to a 'safety valve,' functioning as a means of release, a response to an otherwise repressed need for emotional expression.

Indian drinking has also been described as being similar to 'frontier drinking' and 'skid-row drinking,' a style in which large amounts are consumed in order to get drunk. Such drinking takes place at specific 'Indian bars' or 'party houses.' These drinking episodes often become extended for more than one day, and they end when the money runs out. As Smart and Ogborne suggest, this binge-drinking style 'also tends to be social drinking and to be accompanied by loud and boisterous behaviour' (1986: 106).

The Anthropological Evidence: Were the Norms of Pre-Contact First Nations Cultures Significant Determinants of Post-Contact Alcohol Use Patterns?

Was there something about the traditional cultures of First Nations that would predict the alcohol problems they developed after contact with the Europeans? As noted above, many of the indigenous peoples first exposed to beverage alcohol in the early European contact years adopted alcohol and engaged in destructive drinking behaviour almost immediately. However, there is also substantial evidence that the initial reaction of indigenous peoples to European alcohol varied considerably.

In his article on Indians of the Northwest Coast, published in 1942, F.W. Howay noted that the indigenous peoples of that area of Canada were first introduced to beverage alcohol by traders. They were initially repulsed by the liquor, and their first reaction was to spit it out. It took the concerted efforts of the traders to teach the Indians to drink to the point of drunkenness.

The willingness of a cultural group to adopt a new cultural product or activity, and the pace of the adoption, will depend upon receptivity factors intrinsic to the host culture. The most comprehensive compendium of the variation in the reception of indigenous peoples to the beverage alcohol of European colonizers is included in the widely respected work of McAndrew and Edgerton (1969). Those writers note that, from coast to coast, many, perhaps most of the indigenous peoples of North America, resisted the adoption of European alcoholic beverages during the first years of their encounters with Europeans. This conclusion is supported by several other writers (Dailey, 1967: 45–9; Jilekaal, 1974; Carpenter, 1989), including the historian Paul Philips. In his study of the fur trade Philips noted, 'The use of alcohol in the Indian trade developed slowly. The Indians were unwilling to use it at first, but the White traders persisted in offering it to them' (Philips, 1961).

The balance of available data suggests that not only was there considerable variation in the immediate receptiveness of Native Americans in what is now Canada to European beverage alcohol, there was also variation in the speed of its adoption. This variation is of immediate interest to us. It serves to negate the argument that either the genetic make-up of First Nations people, or the configuration of their cultures, or both, were intrinsically and uniformly receptive and behaviourally sensitive to alcohol consumption, as expressed through careless or antisocial actions.

As MacAndrew and Edgerton have concluded, there are two ways in which people respond to alcohol. In the first instance, their sensorimotor skills are impaired, albeit at different blood alcohol levels, by the consumption of alcohol (1969). The second response is culturally defined. While the first response is fairly uniform and is associated with alcohol toxicity, the second, cultural, response refers to behaviour influenced by local norms, or 'comportment.' Stated another way, how people 'comport themselves' while drinking is culturally defined and socially learned (MacAndrew and Edgerton, 1969). How do we know?

The answer is, quite simply, that the behaviour accompanying drinking episodes varies extensively by cultures, as it did with aboriginal peoples in North America when their cultures were still intact.

There has been very little evidence to support the view that people with First Nations ancestry, as a distinctive population, have a genetic predisposition to problematic alcohol consumption behaviours, such as unusual physical reactivity and physiologically based alcohol dependency. The limited evidence that has shown variation has generally been inconclusive or contradictory and marred by a lack of demonstrated representativeness and flawed usage of the concept of 'race.' The cultural version of the firewater theory is also undermined by evidence of the variation of receptiveness to alcohol across indigenous cultures.

The Rise of the Firewater Complex

Despite the lack of evidence in support of the firewater theory, its basic tenets persist in a far more expansive version and are now deeply embedded in a more elaborate cultural construct that can best be referred to as the 'firewater complex.' The firewater complex includes a set of beverage alcohol consumption and comportment norms in First Nations. Like the Americans' right to gun use, soccer hooliganism among working-class youth in Britain, or the significance of the sacred cow to Hindus, the 'firewater complex' in First Nations is an 'integrated and patterned set of culture traits' (Theodorson and Theodorson, 1969: 98) that has become deeply embedded. That complex has persisted over time and has been 'reified' as an accepted 'fact of life' for First Nations people socialized in reserve cultures.

In their influential essay on the sociology of knowledge, 'reification' is described by Peter Berger and Thomas Luckmann as 'the apprehension of the products of human activities as if they were something other than human products – such as facts of nature, results of cosmic laws or manifestations of divine will' (1967: 89). Reification involves treating an abstraction as if it were real; as such, its reasoning rests on a basic error of logic. Reification can and often does refer to an actual behavioural phenomena that may be more frequent in a specific population. However, that phenomena is not a constant; it is of human origin and can be unseated. Its persistence is in part due to the fact that people believe in it uncritically, accepting it without question as part of reality.

The firewater complex is not only a set of beliefs about the vulnerability to alcohol of First Nations people, it also includes a set of infor-

Figure 7.1 The firewater complex: A schematic representation

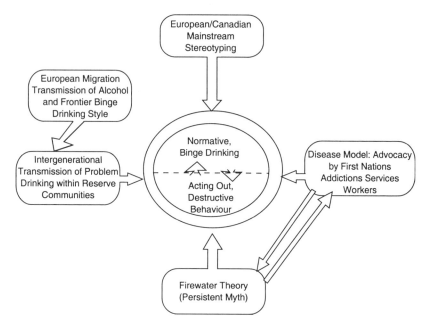

mal beliefs that guide the drinking pattern of socially disaffected band members, implicitly justify drunken episodes, and serve as an excuse for drunken comportment. The legitimation of that complex has been further elaborated and reinforced by an adherence to the disease model of alcoholism in alcohol abuse treatment programs serving First Nations. The firewater complex sustains the firewater theory as a popular belief and belief in the disease model among alcohol abuse workers in reserve communities and treatment centres dedicated to First Nations.

Inherent in the firewater complex is the belief that aboriginal Canadians are constitutionally (genetically) incapable of moderation in the amount of alcohol they consume in drinking episodes. Drinking, moreover, is seen as a social activity, typically carried out in venues devoted wholly to group drinking. It also tends to be carried out through binges, rather than as persistent, ongoing, addictive drinking. The firewater complex also includes the popular belief that 'Indian drinking' is inevitably associated with extreme impairment and irresponsible and antisocial behaviour. The assumption is that, once a drinking episode has begun, indigenous North Americans lose their capacity to regulate their drinking behaviour, including the amount they drink, as well as other behaviours during the episode. Colloquially stated, Indian drinking tends to quickly get 'out of control,' a concept which is consistent with conventional notions of alcoholic behaviour described in the disease model of alcoholism.

Beyond Alcohol Abuse: The Firewater Complex as an Overarching Influence on First Nations Social Problem Solving

What is often not understood is the more insidious way that the disease model and its expression in the firewater complex is implicated in the generalized self-image and local norms of reserve communities. Even those who have long dismissed the disease model as an appropriate explanation of First Nations problem drinking have often missed the larger implications of the durability of the firewater complex.

The firewater complex has not only weighed heavily as an influence on community understanding about alcohol abuse, it has also influenced the entire approach to explaining and seeking solutions to high rates of unhealthy and destructive behavioural patterns in reserve communities. Social problems in First Nations have come to be viewed as chronic pathologies that demand intervention in the form of programs based on a series of therapeutic engagements and personal healing experiences. Rather than encouraging and facilitating personal and community empowerment, this generalized style of explanation and problem solving promotes a sense of dependency and disability.

The thinking behind the firewater complex has been extended to assist in the explanation of many other social problems on reserves, including co-dependency, gambling, family violence, anxiety, depression, anger, and rage. Even various effects of the personal legacy of residential school abuse, assumed to be indicated by various forms of dysfunction, are now treated as 'syndromes' that can be corrected with therapies (Supernault, 1995; Chrisjohn and Young, 1994). The use of such concepts as 'toxic parents' and 'dysfunctional families,' employed with reckless abandon in the 'pop psychology' industry, are probably the best examples of the tendency of advocates of psychological approaches to social problems to inflate the coverage of their ever-expanding dictionary of disorders beyond their valid application. And pop psychology has been very influential in First Nations communities, thanks to the influx of a virtual army of partially trained counsellors and self-appointed healers to give workshops and occupy mental health therapy positions.[2] Admittedly, some of this influx has mixed well and responsibly with traditional healing concepts, and has stimulated a personal healing movement that has been and will, hopefully, long continue to be a valuable and fundamental part of personal and community development in First Nations. Yet the looseness of some of the terminology, the expectations associated with it, and the context in which it is used to inform dialogue leaves much to be desired.

Consider the example of 'co-dependency,' a useful term when employed by credible family therapists. Used appropriately, it refers to the tendency of family systems to adapt to the behavioural problems of a troubled member; as an unintended consequence, this accommodation enables and reinforces the undesirable behaviour pattern rather than discouraging it. By denying, excusing, or shielding the troubled behaviour of an alcoholic, family members often inadvertently avoid the fundamental problem solving needed. For example, by 'picking up the slack' for responsibilities unmet by the alcoholic, the alcoholism itself is inadvertently sustained. Further, these adaptive roles have their own rewards, such as tacitly promoting a spouse or even an older child to a more elevated family status. However, co-dependency has been inflated beyond recognition by some pop psychologists, who now define it as an independent disorder.

Arguing that there is great mischief in much of the expanded use of the co-dependency concept in what they call the 'recovery movement,' Katz and Liu (1991) have examined the values, goals, methods, leadership, and overall philosophy of this movement. They argue that true recovery is much different from what they consider the conformity and dependency cloaked in what they describe as the 'guise of recovery.'

Katz and Liu argue that the recovery movement is overwhelmingly influenced by AA philosophy, which demands that problem drinkers

---

2 In the 1990s, the First Nation and Inuit Health Branch of Health Canada and the Aboriginal Healing Foundation began to provide relatively flexible funding for mental health therapy services and workshops and workshop series to address various human relations and personal development issues from addictions through family dysfunction to residential school abuse. While there is some screening of mental health therapists, it is not uncommon for counsellors with a single university degree and less than a year of supervised counselling experience to be providing services or presenting workshops.

are helpless to control their 'disease;' they need treatment and lifelong participation in AA because their disorder is lifelong. The same authors also argue that the premises of co-dependency result in labelling people, whether identifying them as adult children, addicts, victims, diseased, powerless, or needy, and this 'intensifies feelings of insecurity and low self-worth' (1991: 41). Katz and Liu promote an alternative form of self-help that avoids labelling, encourages individual choices and self-reliance, facilitates personal empowerment, and shifts the focus of problem solving from the 'it' (disease) to the 'I' (self).

Further insight into the recovery movement thinking that has been incorporated into the firewater complex is provided by Wendy Kaminer in her wryly entitled book, *I'm Dysfunctional, You're Dysfunctional* (1993). The book is essentially a commentary on the ideology of the recovery movement and its impact on North American culture and the people seeking to overcome personal problems. Kaminer argues that the recovery movement encourages what she calls 'invalidism,' which tends to disempower people with its repetitive message that we are all weak, diseased, and helpless (1993: 25). She situates the movement in a long line of personal development movements, from the Puritans to AA and the 'co-dependency movement.' Kaminer argues that each of these movements encourage surrender of the personal will to a system or a higher power that demands unqualified acceptance of an expert's advice (1993: 40). It is part of a long tradition in which 'order and obedience' to technique are virtues and 'respect for complexities and uncertainties are signs of failure, if not sin' (152). The author argues that the most fundamental flaw in the recovery movement is an ideology which places both the blame for problems and the solution outside of the self, thereby obscuring personal responsibility and accountability.

Such sloppy theoretical thinking is characteristic of a significant part of the recovery movement. It has been nurtured, legitimized, and reinforced since the late 1980s by a burgeoning self-help literature, personal development workshops, and a host of popular radio and television talk shows, all abuzz with the new vocabulary of personal healing. The danger inherent in this situation was illustrated for me in a review of an alcohol and drug abuse treatment centre in western Canada in which socio-drama techniques were employed as a part of an anger-management ritual. Despite the riskiness of this type of therapeutic technique and the fact that a careful review of the relevant literature would have discouraged the practice, and regardless of the staff's lack of specialized training in confrontational socio-dramatic methods, the centre encouraged clients to expel their memories of anger by smashing a punching bag with a baseball bat. One of the clients, without any notice to program staff, abruptly dropped out of the program, presumably after finding the emotional discomfort of confrontational techniques too much to bear. Tragically, the client who exited apparently used a baseball bat to assault a former female intimate.

It must be acknowledged that the idea of bringing personal troubles out into the open and discussing them publicly has been a welcome development. The focus on the impact of family systems on the behavioural outcome of children must also be considered an important contribution to civic discourse. However, the basic message conveyed by the recovery movement emphasizes the personal rather than the social nature of such problems. It also emphasizes the need for expert assistance with problem solving, whether those experts come in the form of treatment professionals, healers, or recoverees who participate in self-help groups.

Unfortunately, the excesses of the recovery movement have been grafted onto the main ideational stem of the firewater complex. With some adaptation to First Nations culture, the recovery movement has been imported with a vengeance into the entire style of approaching community health problems by the technical and elected leadership in First Nations reserve communities. Based on a rough synthesis of a thick file of personally recorded vignettes, the set of characteristics listed below typify the formal and informal response by elected leaders and human service workers in First Nations communities to a health problem or social concern.

Current Normative Orientation Social Problem-Solving in First Nations

1 Attribution of blame for public health and social problems. There is a tendency to almost automatically attribute the causes of all social problems in First Nations communities to external forces, typically with reference to historic events situated in interactions with white settler society or to current legislation, program or cultural trends. The disease model is essentially extended to describe the pathogenic transmission of public health and social problems from non-aboriginal society to inside First Nations reserve communities. Not only European alcohol but the bullying of women by men, commercial gambling, illicit drugs, AIDS, promiscuous sexuality and youth violence learned from movies, television, and electronic games, gang activity, and disrespect for parents and Elders: all these problems are viewed, metaphorically, as virus-like, foreign cultural invaders, transmitted from white (typically urban) culture to typically rural, reserve communities. These influences are seen as long term and overwhelming, with the family, the individual, and the community leadership having little capacity to mediate them in a favourable way. The temptation of this metaphorical thinking is understandable, originating as it does in a knowledge of the actual historical record. However, in a fundamental way it also assumes and reinforces a sense of powerlessness and it can thus serve as a self-defeating prophecy. This singular blame attribution, however, completely ignores external and internal social class differences, treating all levels of reserve society in a unitary, blame-free fashion, and all levels of non-aboriginal society as being equally responsible for causing reserve problems. The rather obvious fact that most non-aboriginal people are also concerned about alcohol and drug problems, about violence and its inducements by the media, and gang activity, and that they also legitimately view themselves and their children more as potential victims of these problems than as causal agents, is simply ignored.

2 *Assumption of locus responsibility for external provision of resources to solve basic community problems.* Typically, it is assumed in First Nations reserve communities that the primary responsibility for the provision of resources to solve basic community problems lies wholly with the federal government or non-aboriginal society generally. While it is true that the federal government does have specific historic trusteeship and treaty obligations to assist First Nations in addressing a variety of social problems, the scope of such presumed external responsibility is all-encompassing. A gang problem or a group solvent abuse crisis typically inspires calls from reserve members or leadership for the provision of new program resources, even if the community already has a large education staff, an alcohol and drug abuse worker, a mental health worker, and special program funds to address youth needs. If there is a housing shortage, it is automatically assumed that the solution lies entirely in the hands of government funding sources, with no personal or family equity being factored in as part of the equation. Emergency response (ER) services are typically provided through formal arrangements with nearby towns because, despite the fact that agreements are often in place that demand an emergency response service capacity on the reserve, the ER teams have not been established.

3 *Type of solutions to be provided.* Rather than a combination of personal, familial, and voluntary mutual aid supports with publicly supported professional and technical services, expected solutions are, typically, of an exclusively professional or technical nature. Just as solutions to alcohol abuse call for full-time addictions workers, so mental health services by trained psychologists or counsellors are also sought. Even Elders and Traditional Healers now typically expect cash payment, and many Healers present themselves as specialists who deserve to be accorded the same pay and authority as a professional regulated by a full-fledged professional association, despite the lack of any form of collegial or state monitoring.

4 *Expectations regarding solutions to public health and social problems.* There is a sense of hopelessness and fatalism about the nature of social problems in reserve communities. Like the chronic nature of alcoholism described in the disease model, there is an assumption that, so long as white society exists as an overwhelming influence, while many current social problems may be reduced to a manageable level, they will never completely go away.

5 *Level of assumed local accountability.* It is assumed in reserve communities that reserve leadership cannot be expected to be fully accountable to either their membership or funding agencies for their administrative actions. The history of oppression and impoverishment that First Nations have experienced has not allowed for the full development of local administrative and professional capacities in many communities. Thus, it is often assumed by band councils that accountability demands should be lowered to respond to the distinct nature of reserves. Often entire health plans that constitute the core of a community health services agreement, including job descriptions and long- and short-term goals, are not followed. Staff are often unaware of their own job descriptions and do not have a policy and procedures manual to guide their work, nor do they have regular supervisory sessions – even though job descriptions have been included in the community health plans, a policy and procedures manual and adequate professional supervision are primary goals stated in the plans, and the plan itself is the primary reference document for the administration and delivery agreement.

6 *Assumption of liability.* Much the way the disease model and the firewater complex tend to distance the problem drinker from responsibility for his or her own drinking behaviour, so the assumption of liability by local leadership is simply not wholly accepted. This is made especially apparent in hiring decisions, in which family or political loyalties

and local employment goals often, perhaps typically, supersede the hiring of the most qualified technical and professional candidates for vacant positions.

Each of the characteristics described is understandable, given the history of oppression, disruptive social change, and insensitive and at times downright stupid policies that aboriginal peoples have experienced through interactions with and colonization from non-aboriginal governments. However, taken to their extreme, these characteristics are also the antithesis of the self-determination that is professed by First Nations leaders to be the beacon of contemporary aboriginal politics. Such characteristics also reflect a collective sense of permanent victimization, of perpetual malaise, and of being wholly dependent on the compensation of the oppressor for solving local problems.

Undoubtedly, there are distinct therapeutic advantages to providing troubled people with advice, good counsel, and necessary social supports. There are also important reasons to secure external support for communities that have suffered long-term socio-economic underdevelopment. Yet we must also recognize the potentially destructive secondary consequences of labelling an individual, group, or community as being 'prone to' a psychological or cultural malaise.[3] Unfortunately, if victims are convinced that the solutions lie only in change assisted by professional helpers or other, organized 'self-helpers,' a profound mischief may be the outcome. The result can be that victims have confidence in their own personal capacity to manage their own affairs diminished. Paradoxically, a repetitive victimization-dependency-victimization cycle can be completed through this process: dependents

---

3 Indeed, there is an entire theoretical school of sociology that explains deviant behaviour in terms of the societal assignment of labels to behaviour patterns rather than to anything intrinsically deviant. For a summary discussion of these ideas, see Schur (1971). 'Labelling theorists' argue that, independent of the fact or fiction behind a person's alleged deviance, the consequences for those labelled deviant can be devastating. Thus, to be labelled a poor student by teachers can reinforce poor performance, and singling out a child as a 'bad kid' rather than a kid who committed a bad act can transform the child's self-concept in negative ways, virtually creating a role that the child feels obligated to fill. Family therapists have shown us how deviant roles are systemically generated in family systems in order to focus the family's energies away from more fundamental problems that are believed to be beyond the family's capacity to solve.

with problems are convinced by ostensible helpers that they are victims who must therefore rely on others (often including the ostensible helpers) to solve their problems. Rationalized as compensatory help to redress past injustices, that compensation becomes institutionalized, an integral part of the very economy and social structure of the community. In short, dependency becomes permanently institutionalized. The victims adapt to and become comfortable with their dependency and lose faith in their capacity for independence, justifying and becoming firmly committed to their dependent status on the grounds that they have been victimized.

It is argued that one of the basic assumptions of the firewater complex is that the distinctive and healthy nature of First Nations people and their communities has been and is persistently disrupted by the intrusion of foreign (European and Euro-Canadian) elements into their communities. This disruption is condemned and commonly viewed as the source of all aboriginal social problems. In the process the metaphor of the germ theory of disease becomes all-encompassing, in essence, the metaphor suggests that traditional indigenous societies became an unprotected host, lacking a natural immunity to cultural elements originating in outside (European and Canadian) sources through transmission processes imposed upon them via political, legal, administrative, economic, educational, religious, and mass media arrangements. Obviously, the objective, historical relations between the invading and host cultures in North America have provided ample reason to accept this analogy. However, it must also be recognized that, like any analogy, it has its limits. The analogy cannot explain everything and it is not usefully assumed to be a constant. Circumstances change over time, as do the fortunes of individuals and groups. Much has improved in recent decades in the social and economic circumstances of First Nations, from material wealth to life expectancy, and the power of the metaphor has thus weakened over time. It cannot appropriately serve as the perpetual basis for understanding the problems afflicting First Nations communities. Yet in my experience the reasoning behind the firewater theory has become the dominant way of thinking about current social and health problems, as well as their causal origin. The metaphor, which assumes victimization and externally situated solutions, has crystallized into a permanent aspect of the firewater complex.

In the cluster of norms and beliefs that constitute the expanded version of the firewater myth, virtually all significant social problems and health problems are seen to be imported from white society rather than locally generated. As noted above, on First Nations reserves in Canada, everything from alcohol and drug problems to aggressive gender relations are typically blamed on the influences of the 'whites' and their institutions. The whites and their 'decadent culture' are seen as persistently threatening to corrupt an otherwise innocent people. Consequently, the solution almost always lies almost wholly with the federal government's trusteeship for Indian affairs. It is a curious and unsettling view that seems to imply that a group's oppressor can also be relied upon to be its liberator.

The paternalism of federal dealings with First Nations has no doubt created this sense of dependency and externalized blame, and the federal government must be partially held accountable for helping First Nations in their effort to overcome it. School curriculums, the role modelling of sports heroes, junk food, or the pornography or violence conveyed through the film, magazine, book, and electronic media industries – all are viewed in reserve communities as 'white man's diseases' that persistently eat away at the purity of the First Nation person and culture. A discussion of AIDS at a reserve health workshop, or the sex trade, which has successfully lured a disproportionate number of aboriginal teens into its embrace, will almost inevitably turn to the blaming of outside forces and the need for more expert programs and services while, at the same time, calling for a return to some of the old ways of living or healing.

A significant flaw in this thinking is the crude reverse racism that it reflects. It is not modernism, capitalism, globalization, or particular industries to which blame is attributed for the exceptional social problems of First Nations. Nor is the social-systemic nature of the reserve system blamed; in fact, the reserves are defended adamantly by band leaders as homelands that must prevail as the seat of band authority and the focus of development. Instead, the 'white man,' 'white society,' or the federal government are almost always identified as the devil behind the destructive cultural intrusions that invade the reserves. In all of this, little distinction is made between the real perpetrators and those who are simply victims with much in common with aboriginal people. A broad-brush stroke of blame is painted over both irresponsible corporate directors and unsympathetic politicians and those who are seriously and demonstrably concerned about and victimized by the same influences as those which cause great concern among aboriginal people. Ordinary, struggling workers and parents of non-aboriginal ancestry are placed on the same plane as the big shareholders and managers of corporations that produce and sell such potentially corrupting products as violent Hollywood movies, fatty hamburgers, cigarettes, or alcohol. It is also my experience that, in First Nations communities, there is now a widespread and firmly held belief that the federal government and local service providers have ultimate responsibility for addressing chronic social problems such as alcohol abuse.

Just as many believe that the physician has the capacity to cure one's every ailment, the understanding on reserves of how to overcome personal problems has been colonized by the idea of expert 'treatment.' Thus, an addictions treatment program rather than the problem drinker or drug addict becomes wholly responsible for solving a personal substance abuse problem; a housing shortage or renovation need can only be solved with a social housing program provided without any kind of personal investment; and, rather than families and local mutual aid networks, social services, police services, child welfare authorities, and school personnel are expected to be able, independently, to intervene expertly to solve every basic problem of living.

While it is true that a dependence on experts and agencies to solve personal and family problems is characteristic of modernism itself, in First Nations communities, this dependence and the attitudes and beliefs that lie behind it are extreme and, ultimately, crippling for First Nations.

No amount of federal government policy change or external, visiting, federally funded expertise can, of itself, transform the nature of social problems and dependency in First Nations. To truly overcome the disproportionate levels of social problems, the false consciousness reflected in the firewater complex that is now so pervasive in First Nations communities must be overcome. In its place a consciousness dominated by self-determination, self-management, and interdependence with the larger society must established.

As a cultural construct, the firewater complex is, in effect, the heart of a community belief system that inadvertently legitimizes and enables an abiding paternalism on the part of the federal government. Despite lip service being paid to the idea of self-determination, the 'Indian problem' fundamentally remains defined by the federal government in the most pessimistic fashion. Examined with a focus on objective conditions rather than the platitudes of official pronouncements, that policy assumes that, because assimilation has not worked, the best that can be done is to meet basic obligations for reserve residents by providing a reasonable array of local community services and an exceptional level of services focused on addressing social problems. Development policies are rooted in the cynical idea of 'warehousing' unemployed aboriginal people on reserves which, for the most part, allows but a very short opportunity horizon for generating significant, short-, intermediate- or long-term economic development potential.

It is true that public and private discussions of social problems and health problems in non-aboriginal communities also focus much of their attention on causal forces that lie well beyond the corrective capacity of the individual, community, region, or even nation. Yet contained within those discussions is a selective identification of institutional victimizers, such as particular industries or businesses within a specific industry, as well as a demand for change that includes popular and representative advocacy. In other words, the appeal for change cuts across ethnic lines and thus often speaks to and arouses common interests.

It is my experience that the reserve system and federal policies have so profoundly separated First Nations people that discussions at community health meetings on a reserve tend to be insular. They yield a kind of omnibus blame against non-aboriginal society rather than finding common cause with some non-aboriginal interests and identifying specific policies, institutions, or business interests that are working for and against the interests of reserves. In not discriminating between supportive and non-supportive interests, band leaders are failing to separate the powerful from the powerless. They also fail to enjoin non-aboriginal victims to rally in common cause with aboriginal people. In this way, enormous political leverage is lost and a great abundance of potential partnerships and strategic alliances are not secured. Yet the benefits potentially available from working cooperatively with non-aboriginal, non-governmental community service organizations, organized labour, government institutions, and business are enormous. With almost prototypical consistency, the conventional, far more insular approach is to call on reserve, tribal council, and intertribal leadership to demand corrective responses in the form of policies, programs, or resources to address any and all social problems. With a few rare and notable exceptions, approaches taken on reserves to address an emerging social problem both attribute the cause and identify the resources and even the types of solutions required as lying wholly with the federal government.

This unfortunate state of dependency on federal resources and initiatives has obviously originated in separatist-oriented federal policies, and in the cultural disruption and economic dislocation caused by an insensitive and short-sighted historic approach to assimilation. Those who suggest that aboriginal peoples in Canada have been exposed to a cultural holocaust are not far off the mark: the sense of local powerlessness associated with the culture-destroying impact of European settlement and federal Indian policy is easily appreciated. And there is a broad consensus among researchers that the disparities and social problems experienced by aboriginal peoples throughout the world are the product of a combination of formidable sociocultural intrusion by larger, more technologically advanced societies (Saggers and Gray, 1998). However, a familiarity with the literature on aboriginal peoples and other oppressed minorities also makes it clear that optimism is warranted. Specific cultural and economic development strategies can make a significant difference in overcoming socio-economic underdevelopment and reducing the rate of social problems in communities experiencing severe adversity.[4] Rather than fixating on weaknesses and strengths, community leaders and members, as well as individuals on their own behalf, can learn about and emphasize the strengths and the resiliency factors in their communities that promote healthy growth and effective economic development.

Some of these resiliency factors are situated in the persistence of traditional social structures and cultural loyalty. Kunitz and Levy (1994; 2000) and Levy and Kunitz (1971; 1974) used longitudinal data, including suicide rates, to compare various Plains, Southwest, and Plateau tribes on several dimensions of social stability and community health. These writers have argued against the validity of sweeping 'social disintegration' theories to account for observed intertribal differences in the rate of social problems. They have argued that those tribes which were highly integrated socially and politically, and which kept more of their traditional social structures intact, have had fewer social prob-

---

4 The subject of appropriate economic development strategy is far too complex to review extensively at this point. However, a discussion of the factors that promote development and reduce social problem risks (including alcohol abuse) is taken up at various points below. In addition to the Saggers and Gray reference identified in the text, the problem of social problem intervention specific to First Nations is directly addressed in Whitehead and Hayes (1998). A consideration of variations in approaches to and relative success in economic development is presented in the Harvard Project in the United States, reported by Cornell and Kalt (1992). A comprehensive discussion of factors contributing to social change is provided in Sztomka (1993).

lems, as measured by such 'hard' statistical indicators as lower suicide rates, than those that were loosely organized and less traditional.

It must also be recognized that aboriginal/non-aboriginal disparities are not static; much has improved in recent decades. By virtually any yardstick, the opportunities now available even to the poorest communities in post-industrial societies are enormous – and as Waldram, Herring, and Young (1995) have stated, aboriginal development levels, as measured by standard international health indicators, are now well above their former 'Third World' levels. An unparalleled abundance of cultural resources (consider the world inventory of cross-cultural library holdings and Internet stores alone) is now available to virtually all communities in Western nation states, with Canada's abundance rivalling all of the most advanced countries affiliated in the Organization for Economic Co-operation and Development (OECD). Educational, nutritional, economic, and technological tools far outweigh any cultural inventory available to traditional hunting and gathering, horticultural, fishing, or agricultural societies.

The most dramatic example of the potential for positive development and change is found in measures of population health. The decline in infant mortality and increase in life expectancy in recent decades in aboriginal Canada has been striking (Waldram, Herring, and Young, 1995: 66–8). Most First Nations were formerly hunting and gathering societies, in which life expectancy tends to hover around a maximum of thirty years, yet aboriginal life expectancy is now well over seventy years and fast approaching parity with the Canadian average.[5] Much of this improvement is associated with improved nutrition, modernized, safer parenting practices, better housing, stable incomes, and increased formal education. The challenge is to set realistic goals and organize the cultural, political, educational, and economic means to achieve them. It is true that population losses were overwhelming during the years of

---

5 A bibliographic review of Native American demography by Johansson (1982) is cited in Young (1994). Johansson cited a skeletal-based estimate for a life expectancy of approximately twenty-three years among pre-contact Native Americans, a figure which is comparable to most basic hunting and gathering societies around the world. Young further cites the similarity of that figure to an Inuit life expectancy of twenty-nine years between 1941 and 1950. Since that time, an increase in Inuit life expectancy has been so striking that its rate of acceleration may mark an historical record. The rate of population increase for First Nations over the past half-century has also been extremely high.

early contact, as a result of the importation from Europe of such diseases as smallpox. However, if not immediately, then at some point in the near future, aboriginal people should recognize that, on balance, even basic population growth will have to be counted as a benefit of population interaction with Europeans and participation in a more multicultural society. This is not to suggest that First Nations people should be beholden to the carriers of imported culture. What it does mean is that modernism, an openness to the cultures of the world, and advanced technologies have become available as normal outcomes of global interactions of many kinds – and those potential benefits are rightfully available to First Nations people, as they are to all other Canadians.

As a growing body of social and environmental criticism and a flourishing activist movement has justifiably warned us, there is much to be disdained and repelled in globalization. It is true that the globalization process is often driven by ethnocentric motives and destructive greed, and it is often tempting to view globalization as merely a code word for American economic imperialism. However, there can be enormous benefits to the internationalization of cultures and commerce, and aboriginal people, as much as any other ethno-cultural group, have every right – and various degrees of opportunity – to place it at their own disposal and exploit it to their own benefit.

Another insidious element of the firewater complex is the general attitude so commonly expressed in First Nations that, so long as non-aboriginals dominate the lands of their ancestors, alcohol problems and a series of other social problems are unlikely to disappear. This fatalistic, self-defeating attitude is no doubt a product of the colonization process, but it must be overcome for healthy personal and community development to occur. Just as 'alcoholism' is assumed to be chronic, so are the abiding social problems that generate disproportionate rates of family violence, suicide, homicide, and accidental deaths in First Nations, reserve communities. This view is accompanied by the idea that, as individuals and as communities within the oppressed circumstances of reserve society, First Nations people are unable to overcome externally caused problems. Again, such a perspective flies in the face of the data that shows significant variation in the circumstances of First Nations.

8

Violence and the Firewater Complex

The expectation of drunken comportment as a fundamental, even inevitable, aspect of First Nations drinking patterns is a central element of the firewater complex, and one of its most fundamentally destructive features. As repeatedly noted above, it is widely believed that alcohol dissolves the inhibitions which constrain irrational, antisocial, and violent behaviour during sobriety and that those predisposed to impairment are therefore more likely to be violent. Thus, it is often argued, even in courts of law, that the physical process of alcohol consumption is the cause of much of the interpersonal violence and careless behaviour associated with the extremely high rates of physical and mental injury in aboriginal populations. This chapter challenges those assumptions.

Mortality linked to alcohol impairment is significantly higher for aboriginal people compared to the general Canadian population. A Saskatchewan study found aboriginal deaths associated with alcohol impairment to be 43.7 per 100,000 people compared with 23.6 for the general Canadian population (Fiddler, 1985). Another study of alcohol use among the Registered Indian population for the years 1985–7 was based on injury and poisoning data from Health Canada's Medical Services Branch database. The study found that 38 per cent of homicide perpetrators were impaired by alcohol consumption at the time they committed the murder (Szabo, 1990). It is amply documented that First Nations people in Canada have substantially higher death rates associated with suicide, injury, and poisoning. Suicide rates in First Nations are at least 2.5 times as high as the rate for the rest of Canadians (Mao, Moloughney, and Semenciw, 1992). Given the significance of the drinking and violence issue for First Nations peoples, it is important to single it out for special consideration.

There has long been scepticism in some research quarters about whether a strong correlation between drinking and violence reflects a direct causal relationship. The question is, does the exceptional violence and antisocial (and antiself) behaviour associated with alcohol intoxication result solely from alcohol impairment, or does such destructive behaviour require other influences before it materializes?

Discarding the 'Out of Control' Notion

It is essential that we first consider the evidence that weighs in on the notion that the drinking of alcoholic beverages inevitably leads the problem drinker to poor judgment and loss of control over his or her behaviour. This idea is a crucial element in the 'alcoholism-is-a-disease' perspective.

As noted above, numerous studies of clinically defined alcoholics indicate that, after treatment or a self-motivated determination to control drinking, many such subjects were able to moderate the number of drinks they consume during a drinking episode. As long ago as 1962, Davies, reporting from data gathered from a long-term follow-up study, observed that seven of ninety-three recovered male alcoholics had overcome their alcoholism by adopting a normal drinking pattern. The former alcoholic subjects had learned to moderate their consumption in order to avoid intoxication.

Findings similar to Davies's results were reported by Kendall (1965), who conducted research amid the controversy that followed Davies's study. It should be noted that neither Davies nor Kendall found any relationship between the ability of alcoholics to control their drinking and any specific physiological characteristics.

In 1971, a test in which five chronic alcohol dependents were subjected to environmental rewards if they refrained from excessive drinking was given to hospitalized subjects categorized as 'gamma alcoholics' (Cohen et al., 1971) (in the Jellinek formulation, a gamma alcoholic characteristically loses control when drinking). The subjects in the Cohen et al. study were all in various stages of withdrawal, after being admitted to the hospital through the emergency ward. For five consecutive weeks, all subjects were provided with a supply of alcohol and given the freedom to drink as much beverage alcohol as they wanted, up to a limit of twenty-four ounces of 95-proof ethanol alcohol during the week. On weekends they were not allowed to drink. However, the subjects were also given the alternative of better living conditions in the hospital if they cut down on their drinking. The research found that many of the alcoholics moderated their drinking when they had the opportunity to secure a more pleasant living environment. The experimenters then cut back on the improved conditions for selected patients. When the improved living arrangements were withdrawn, the alcoholic subjects returned to their excessive drinking. The researchers concluded that the loss of control was not inevitable for alcoholics after their first drink, even when the amount available equalled or exceeded what might have been available to them outside of the experimental situation (Cohen, et al. 1971: 441).

A study by Sobell, Sobell, and Christelman (1972) concluded that the loss-of-control theory was more a belief taught to alcoholics by addictions professionals than a hypothesis supported by evidence. They also suggested that such a belief may itself have a significant influence on the behaviour of alcoholics. Stated in other terms, it may be a self-fulfilling prophecy.

To test the belief that alcoholics have an invariable attraction and a uniform lack of resistance to alcohol, Gottheil et al. (1972; 1973) provided alcoholic subjects with a constant supply. Contradicting the claim that alcoholics have cravings that make alcohol irresistible and lose control after taking their first drinks, the researchers found a wide range of responses, including heavy drinking and then stopping, moderate drinking, daily variation in alcohol intake, and abstinent days followed by drinking days. Gottheil et al. observed no powerful withdrawal effects in those subjects who stopped drinking daily during the experiment.

Mello and Mendelson (1972) challenged the idea that alcoholics cannot plan their drinking pattern because they are 'out of control.' They made alcohol readily available to alcoholic subjects and then observed how those subjects approached its use. Mello and Mendelson found that alcoholics often bought and stockpiled alcohol in order to drink in the future; however, their stockpiling occurred when they were abstaining in order to recover from a binge. None of the subjects drank all of the alcohol available, nor did they try to drink to the point of unconsciousness. The authors concluded that no empirical support had been provided for the notion that 'once drinking starts, it proceeds autonomously' (Mello and Mendelson, 1972: 159–69).

The out-of-control characterization of alcoholics is also challenged in the more recent work of Catherine Ortner and her colleagues, psychologists at Queen's University in Kingston (Ortner, MacDonald, and Olmstead, 2003: 151–6). The study divided seventy-six male undergraduate students into three groups: one sober, one intoxicated, and a control group that was given a placebo (drinks flavoured with alcohol but not in sufficient amount to induce intoxication as measured by blood alcohol level [BAL]). The research team wanted to find out if, compared to the sober group and the control group, the inebriated group would favour immediate rewards over more delayed gratification. They were investigating the prediction, asserted by what is referred to as 'alcohol myopia theory,' that as alcohol levels increase, so does cognitive impulsivity and the tendency to make choices reflecting immediate rather than deferred gratification. Ortner and her colleagues tested their hypothesis by offering all groups fifteen dollars immediately after the experimental session, or double that amount later. Surprising the researchers, members of the sober group were more likely to choose the immediate cash reward over the more substantial delayed reward than either the intoxicated group or the control group. In addition, the researchers found that blood alcohol level was actually inversely related to the choice of immediate gratification among the subjects. The authors therefore concluded that, contrary to common assumptions, alcohol intoxication is associated with more cautious decision making, at least in some circumstances.

The Relationship between Alcohol and Violence

The most comprehensive research review of studies examining the relationship between alcohol abuse and violence was conducted by a British research team (Sumner and Parker, 1995). In addition to various other findings, Sumner and Parker found no convincing evidence from biological research to support the view that alcohol unleashes some preexisting aggressive or sexual impulse. They also found that the available research indicates that, while alcohol is a powerful drug, its affect on the brain, the central nervous system as a whole, and on hormonal systems – all of which play an important role in regulating human behaviour – are not well understood. What *is* known is that no one neurotransmission system functions as a locus of aggression. The authors of the review make the point that, in any case, it is at least questionable that something as complex as crime, or highly selective acts of violence such as a pattern of violence specifically directed against a spouse, could be singularly explained by variations in individual physiological reactions to alcohol or other psychoactive substance ingestion.

There may indeed be pharmacological consequences of alcohol that are relevant to the commission of crimes. As an example, the effects of alcohol on thinking processes can reduce our ability to 'read' situations and the behaviour of others; it can also impair our ability to respond in socially appropriate ways. We might therefore be more likely, under the influence of alcohol, to get into arguments that have the potential to escalate into violence. There is no empirical evidence to support this view, however, and the fact remains that most people who drink, even to excess, do not go on to commit crimes.

There may also be hangover effects which lead to violence. The irritability associated with withdrawal from alcohol's effects may indeed increase the possibility of violent outcomes in social interactions. Workers in drug treatment programs are familiar with irritable, hostile, and occasionally aggressive clients in withdrawal.

According to Goldstein (1990), prostitutes using heroin often explain robbing and/or assaulting 'johns' in terms of the withdrawal experience. In Goldstein's studies, female prostitutes reported that if they were feeling 'sick' (i.e., experiencing withdrawal symptoms), they would be too irritable to engage in verbal conning and would thus resort to violence or robbery. While irritability and the experience of low frustration tolerance may contribute significantly to an individual with a hangover making a violent choice, the actual choice itself must still be made. To lose sight of this fact is to lose sight of one of the most essential qualities of being human. The hungover prostitute, rather than resorting to assault or robbery, could instead simply be more verbally aggressive in her demands or take her frustration out through other means after the 'trick' is turned. Basic logical inference tells us that various factors other than primitive, neurological command responses to irritability might have contributed, such as economic considerations, background learning, the influences of peers (e.g., the persuasions of other prostitutes and, perhaps, pimps), and personality characteristics. One or a combination of these factors might affect the choices of action confronting the prostitute who selected the criminal course. Of itself, alcohol (or other drug) withdrawal does not dictate specific choices of action, although the discomfort sometimes felt during and after impairment may have some influence on which choice is ultimately made.

A 'Risk-Taking' Lifestyle

As Sumner and Parker admit in their review and critical analysis of the relevant literature, there does appear to be such a thing as a 'risk-taking lifestyle,' which tends to couple drinking to excess with various kinds of crime. Some youth subcultures are characterized by this life-style. The causal connection does not appear to be the link between crime and alcohol, however, but between the peer culture, the charac-teristics of a social milieu, and the crime. The correlates of age, gender, socio-economic class, and oppressed minority status reveal an over-arching causal connection with crime that occurs quite separately from the use or non-use of alcohol. In some high-crime neighbourhoods in North America, alcohol has an extremely weak association with the commission of crimes, although drugs are often implicated. In these areas, narcotics or other 'street' drugs of choice typically outpace alco-hol in terms of their popularity and they have been incorporated as a major trade item in the local underground economy.

Drinking, Violence, and Indigenous North Americans at the Time of First Contact with Europeans

It should also be recalled that, in their seminal review of the historical and anthropological record, MacAndrew and Edgerton (1969) found considerable variation in the reactions to beverage alcohol among aboriginal peoples during the years in which they adopted European beverage alcohol consumption. History does not support the view that drinking and violence in First Nations are innately connected.

While members of some indigenous North American societies appear to have quickly exhibited drunken comportment and violent behaviours as a normative adaptation to beverage alcohol use, others displayed no such behaviours. For example, a ship's dinner party involving three Indians was described in the following statement by Captain George Vancouver: 'After dinner they did not make the least scruple of partaking of our repast with such wine and liquors as were offered to them; though they drank very sparingly seeming to be well aware of their powerful effect' (Howay, 1942). Further, as various his-torians and anthropological accounts have indicated, the extent to which aboriginal North American cultures exhibited destructive alco-hol use patterns during the early years of contact varied according to their previous use or non-use of alcohol and whether or not they had already established alcohol control norms. Those who had used alcohol prior to European contact exhibited more moderate behavioural pat-terns as part of and after drinking rituals. Mexican Indian societies had a long tradition of alcohol use prior to contact with the Europeans, but they also had a well-established set of control norms (Wax, 1971). What this and other evidence suggests is that destructive, drunken comportment and violent behaviour is not intrinsic to aboriginal people as individuals, as a single, multicultural population, or as specific cultures.

Alcohol as an Excuse for Socially Unacceptable Behaviour

Alcohol is not only a drug of leisure in Western society; it is also characteristically used as part of scheduled 'time out' events in which people are relieved of the routine obligations of work and other toils of everyday life. Alcohol also has important symbolic functions: it is used in rituals such as weddings, birth rites (e.g., christenings), communion and mass, wakes, adult birthdays, and celebrations such as Oktoberfests and the like. Beverage alcohol thus has powerful, positive associations with pleasureful social activities.

As Sumner and Parker remind us, alcohol is also attributed with a great deal of power in common belief systems in Western cultures. It is widely believed to disinhibit behaviour and to act as a symbolic key, opening the door to a social space in which the rules for normal behaviour are, within limits, temporarily relaxed. This belief makes it possible for alcohol to be used as an excuse for unacceptable behaviour. Thus the role of alcohol in crime is often a rationalization, after the fact, of the commission of the untoward act. The belief that alcohol impairment is a cause of misbehaviour is so strong, according to Sumner's research-grounded argument, that under some conditions the behavioural changes that people believe are due to alcohol impairment can be induced with the substitution of a placebo.

Research dedicated to examining the relationship between alcohol consumption and crime must highlight the importance of the role of social beliefs – not only beliefs about the effects of alcohol, but beliefs about how one should behave after drinking.

The research indicates that there is substantial international and intranational variation (reflecting ethnic, age, gender, and socio-economic differences in a population) in the social rules governing 'drunken comportment.' It also suggests that heated arguments, public disorder, and brawling in and around licensed premises might be more fully explained if other situational factors are included. Other than the pharmacological effects on the aggression of a drinker, a variety of influencing factors might prompt violence. These factors include the nature of the particular set of beliefs about masculinity and femininity adhered to by the drinker, the rules of comportment that prevail in the setting, the people sharing the drinking episode, the expectations drinkers have of their cohorts' behaviour, and their beliefs regarding the effects of alcohol.

A thorough review of each of the biological, psychological, and sociological approaches to research all suggest that the effects of alcohol are to some extent dependent upon the immediate context in which it is consumed. Violence and disorder are less likely to occur in premises that are comfortable and clean, where food is available, and which have friendly staff and skilled management than they are on premises with the opposite characteristics.

Logical inference from the existing data would strongly suggest that beliefs about the impact of alcohol impairment produce a 'self-fulfilling prophecy' effect. Independently of the psychopharmacological influence of the drug on cognition and behaviour, the belief that alcohol has a violence-predisposing influence acts as a powerful source of motivation and, indeed, as a sufficient cause to trigger a violent action. At least one writer inspires a parallel with beliefs about barbiturates. Aware that barbiturates are reputed to stimulate aggression (they are sometimes referred to as 'gorilla pills' by users), although that reputation is probably not deserved, the individual user may act out irresponsibly or violently he has learned (Goldstein, 1990: 27).

Some alcohol and drug-taking might be used purposively because the user, familiar with its anticipated effects, perceives it as facilitating the perpetration of violence or other forms of criminal acts. Thus, based on beliefs about the impact of specific drugs on mood, drugs are often taken selectively. Tranquillizers and marijuana are often used to 'calm nerves' (i.e., control nervousness), where alcohol and other drugs are consumed to give courage.

Similarly, users may want to engage in a violent act but be deterred by scruples, and they may therefore ingest alcohol in order to feel freed from the constraints of morality – assuming that the alcohol/brain interaction shrinks moral constraints. The violent behaviour is then explained by the expedient claim 'The drug drove me to it.' In brief, drinking provides a convenient excuse – and one that can be arranged in advance. The same process has also become a significant legal stratagem, with lawyers capitalizing on alcohol impairment as an argument against their client's alleged malicious intent.

More recent research on the impact of alcohol impairment on judgment further calls the legitimacy of alcohol as an excuse for destructive behaviour into question. We are reminded of the research published recently in the journal *Studies on Alcoholism*, which suggests that people who drink too much, mess up, and then blame their irresponsible behaviour on alcohol need to find a new excuse (Ortner et al., 2003). This study, as we have seen, suggests that alcohol may make people more cautious in their decisions rather than impulsive. The important conclusion to be drawn is that, despite the conventional wisdom that alcohol impairment necessarily leads to recklessness and poor judgment, drunkenness and rash decisions do not necessarily coincide.

None of this research indicates that alcohol consumption, after a certain quantity has been ingested, does not lead to intoxication and more limited intellectual capacity while 'under the influence.' What it does suggest is that, whether at our most coherent or when we are impaired by too much alcohol, our capacity for assessing and choosing between right or wrong, and for acting responsibly or carelessly, remains with us. Alcohol consumption is a weak excuse for foolish behaviour.

Whether or not drunkenness is an appropriate legal defence for criminal acts is an issue that has plagued ethicists, addictions researchers and theorists, legal philosophers, and the courts. In a review of the scientific basis of this legal defence, referred to in law as the 'legal state of automatism,' Harold Kalant concludes that the defence essentially rests on a reference to the scientific evidence. He further concludes that, on this basis, the defence is weak (Kalant, 1996). Available research evidence shows that (1) during a 'blackout' neither the body nor the brain function adequately to coordinate a premeditated crime, and (2) in instances in which there is a neurobiological predisposition to automatism, such as epilepsy, alcohol is only a trigger for the onset of that condition. While finding that, in high doses, some drugs known as 'dissociative anaesthetics' can induce a legal state of automatism, alcoholism cannot (Kalant, 1996: 645–6). While Kalant admits that severe alcohol intoxication does impair judgment in assessing external events and responding to them, he argues that this is more accurately regarded as a self-provoked condition of temporary brain malfunction than as automatism.

There is great advantage to be gained from recognizing the fact that addictive habits and destructive behaviours associated with alcohol use are learned behaviours, influenced and even triggered by social milieu variables but ultimately subject to personal choices. With this view, rather than assuming that addictions are products of chronic disease, there is great hope for prevention, intervention, and relapse prevention programming. Prevention programming can be based on the manipulation of environmental (milieu) variables that encourage substance abuse and addictions. Intervention can be based on the learning of substitute or replacement behaviours for alcohol triggers and on reconstructing factors in the immediate social milieu. Relapse prevention programming can be similarly arranged.

Contemporary Aboriginal Drinking Styles and Violent Behaviours

Does the research literature inventoried by Sumner and Parker and others apply to aboriginal people? Admittedly, no studies in the review explicitly focused on aboriginal people – at least not to my knowledge. However, the research did draw upon most if not all well-known empirical studies of genuine scientific merit that considered the alcohol impairment–violence connection and found that, on balance, the connection was mediated by other factors rather than simply reflecting a cause-effect relationship between heavy drinking and violence. Obviously, an aboriginal study would be of value. But unless there is some unique, unalterable genetic basis for the high aboriginal Canadian problem drinking rates, a possibility that the available research has essentially dismissed, we are left with the same conclusion as Sumner and Parker reached in their research review. Just as non-aboriginal problem drinking styles originate in non-genetic factors, including sociological, cultural, and attitudinal factors, so must the drinking styles of aboriginal people, including the tendency towards violence.

A high-risk drinking style has taken on the patterning of a cultural trait, at least among young aboriginal people, and it has been in existence for several generations. Three phrases that I have heard repeated many times in slight variations, stand out as indicators of this style:

- 'Man, when we drink, we drink as if there is no tomorrow!'
- 'Us Indians, man, when we drink, we drink until we're drunk and deadly!'
- 'When we drink, we drink crazy. We want something we go after it. Someone's in the way, they better move or they might get hurt!'

9

Explanations of Problem Drinking in First Nations That Fall 'Outside the Pathology Box'

The people of Canada's First Nations share their troubled experience of alcohol use with other North American indigenous peoples. Based on a review of the literature on First Nations (and 'Native North American') problem drinking, explanations that assume pathology on the part of indigenous peoples have been rejected. Explanations according to which First Nations alcohol problems are an outcome of internal social dysfunction or underdevelopment, a socially deviant, 'unhealthy' pattern of responses to frustrations in meeting the goals set by the larger society, a widespread psychological disorder, or a genetically based disease have been dismissed. After first considering those explanations which legitimately fall outside the 'pathology paradigm' in this chapter, we will turn to a multifactoral explanation centred on social change, social organization, and a socially constructed cognitive orientation.

The Positive Functions of First Nations Drinking Patterns

Let us now turn to those explanations that characterize aboriginal drinking styles as having positive social functions rather than being simply 'dysfunctional.'

Explanation Type 1: Aboriginal Drinking Is Personal Relief from the Expressive and Introspective Constraints of Traditional Cultures

One attempted explanation for the preference among aboriginal Canadians for 'binge' drinking and its associated behavioural excesses suggests that aboriginal drinking behaviour offers an escape from cultural norms. For a population that generally encourages introversion, quietness, control, and a lack of extravagant expression, the ritualized, emotional excess associated with extended drinking episodes provides a much-needed 'time out' (Hallowell, 1955). From this perspective, alcohol use offers a psychological and social respite from the emotional containment that is typical and normally expected of First Nations people in the routines of their everyday lives. Drinking is thus viewed as a process in which social animation is increased (MacAndrew and Edgerton, 1969).

In a similar vein, Ferguson (1971) argues that drinking became a substitute for Shamanism in the Western Arctic, and an outlet for individualistic behaviour in otherwise conforming, tightly knit, small arctic communities.

Some versions of this theoretical slant see alcohol consumption not simply as offering emotional relief from a spare and stoic social life, but as an opportunity for an imaginative, mind-altering adventure otherwise unavailable. They argue that alcohol and other mind-altering substances serve as liberating mental lubricants. An intriguing variant of the hallucinogenic thesis regarding aboriginal alcohol use patterns is offered by anthropologists who have observed that Native North American peoples tend to place a higher value on altered states of consciousness than most other North Americans (Price, 1978). Alcohol may therefore be valued for its capacity to facilitate such experiences and indigenous drinkers are seen to be trying to change their perceptions of reality. What makes this view intriguing, albeit merely speculative, are early observations that indigenous North Americans, when still living in their traditional state, would sometimes pool resources, including alcohol, to make it possible for at least one of them to become intoxicated while the others watched. In fact, some indigenous North American religions may provide motivation for intoxication. Opiate use – the 'peyote ritual' – is a central ritual in the Native American Church, an institution which draws on the traditions of the American southwest. Salish traditions in the northwest maintain that during altered states of consciousness, or 'dream quests,' people can communicate with the supernatural. Alcoholic delirium may thus be looked upon as a sign of contact with the supernatural.

Some theorists have speculated that alcohol has been incorporated into a much older tradition within aboriginal North American cultures of using mood-modifying substances as vehicles for introspection. Psychedelic drugs, opiates, and marijuana have been used in many traditional cultures, including some aboriginal cultures on other continents, and alcohol came to serve the same function.

There may be some truth in these cultural explanations which view alcohol as a lubricant for social intercourse and/or imaginative thinking. However, a similar argument can be made for a wide variety of cultures in which drinking or drugs are used for similar purposes, but which are not noted for such a destructive, high-risk drinking style. Many Asian cultures are considered to be extremely conformist and repressive in terms of controlling emotional expression, but troubled drinking has not become a characteristic social problem. Similarly, some subcultures have been created by people who consciously adopted drug-associated practices and then later abandoned their use of drugs. The 1950s 'beatniks' and the 'hippies' of the 1960s and 1970s immediately come to mind. Explanations centred on the use of mind-altering substances in a single indigenous culture make no mention of any spread of such practices between indigenous cultures, so generalizations from to Native American cultures as a whole cannot be made. The peyote rituals of the Native American Church provide an example of people from a number of aboriginal cultures adopting a mind-altering drug as part of their ceremonial and expressive spirituality, but this example cannot be generalized because it has not taken root in many First Nations cultures, especially in Canada.

Explanation Type 2: Lack of Appropriate Social Controls Cause Disproportionate Aboriginal Drinking Problems

The influence of cultural and value differences on troubled Native North American drinking styles was investigated by Flores (1985–6). The researcher began with the premise that those indigenous North American cultures which have poorly defined norms of appropriate drinking usually have abnormally high alcoholism rates and that group-specific cultural values play an important part in the way individuals drink. Flores intended to identify value differences between Native Americans and Anglos and to determine their relationship with alcoholism and recovery. The study provided evidence indicating that Native American values can indeed be defined and measured and, when they are, some of them are distinctly different from Anglo values. Value differences, moreover, did have some influence on the variation in the frequencies of problem drinking. However, the Flores study does not help to explain the fact that, compared with North American norms, even those indigenous societies which had a pre-contact history of alcohol use eventually came to display disproportionately high levels of problem drinking – even if those levels were somewhat lower than the rates found in North American indigenous populations that did not use alcohol prior to European contact.

It remains the case that several researchers have conducted credible studies which have suggested that alcohol abuse and related social health problems have been positively affected by social integration and cultural continuity with the past (Levy and Kunitz, 1971 and 1974; Kunitz and Levy, 1994 and 2000; and Chandler, 2001). Taylor's work on peasant Indian communities in Mexico (1979) indicates that, despite considerable disruption by the Spanish colonialists, the traditional village stayed in tact and traditional alcohol use norms (they drank pulque) that forbade interpersonal violence during drinking episodes were likewise retained, although externally directed hostilities (occasional violence against outsiders) found widespread expression.

Explanation Type 3: First Peoples Drinking Styles Contributing to Social Cohesion

Several writers have argued that substance use patterns in First Nations may represent positive social reactions to the negative consequences of being overwhelmed by the European colonization of their indigenous homelands and communities. Adolescents between the ages of thirteen and seventeen years old in First Nations for example, may once have had traditional means of establishing contact and maintaining group cohesion; substance use now serves this purpose, because traditional social norms have disappeared. Binge drinking, drug abuse and even gang activity may function as a 'rite of passage,' providing a substitute for traditional vision quests and other rites testing and marking the transition from childhood to adulthood (Thatcher, 2000a).

Heath (1964), in reviewing ethnographic studies of alcohol use, identified a substantial number of studies indicating that alcohol in some ways contributed to social cohesion and that group drinking symbolized group unity. MacAndrew and Edgerton (1969) made a similar observation about the Tarahumara Indians of Northern Mexico.

Assessment of Culturally Based Lines of Explanations Not Cast in Pathological Terms

The several cultural explanations described immediately above may have some validity in explaining *some* of the problem drinking styles of aboriginal individuals; they may even help to explain certain patterns of drinking in specific groups of First Nations people (or Native American people in the United States). However, there is no evidence to suggest that any of these explanations alone or together convincingly explain most of the extremely high *rates* of aboriginal North American problem drinking. Nor do these cultural explanations offer any leads to explaining the dramatic decline in recent years in the overall proportion of aboriginal drinkers to non-drinking aboriginals. The explanations cited may also be flawed because they tend to exaggerate the extent to which traditional culture affects alcohol problems, despite the overwhelming dislocation of culture that has attended and continues to attend the imposition of White settler society on First peoples, and the ongoing, rapid rate of technological and social change that is part of that imposition. They also fail to write human subjectivity into the equation. Human beings, aboriginal as well as non-aboriginal, have the capacity to make choices, as do the leaders of communities; these cultural explanations err in their implication that individuals and, indeed, individuals forming communities, are completely culture bound. Individuals and, by extension, community leaders and opinion makers, are reduced to reactive agents incapable of redefining the terms on which they interact: they are essentially seen as responding automatically to external persuasions and social forces rather than as fully human actors capable of making choices, of negotiating and affecting outcomes. Human beings are not completely determined products of their cultures and the social forces impacting on them. To be human is to be actively involved in the construction, deconstruction, and reconstruction of one's own cognition, behavioural limits, and social roles and, as part of groups, in the range and nature of what aspects of culture should and will prevail in a given social context. In other words, to be human is to be engaged in the process of personal and social construction. The social self is both the subject and object of cultural interactions. It is true that the choices offered to individuals and groups in the human family are often fixed by nature and social structures. However, what makes us human is that we make, break, and remake our own personal identities and influence, in at least some small way, the structure of the group relations we engage in through a constant process of social interaction and exploration. Destructive drinking patterns, like any other human actions, can be the product of uncritical or passive responses to situational and social pressures or of dynamic cognitive and behavioural choice-making. One's history is a unique, personally negotiated production process. To ignore that process in an explanation of cross-cultural variance in drinking styles is simply unsupportable.

It is also true that the choices confronting the individual vary enormously, as do the choices confronting groups of people, whether formed as a family, an economic enterprise, a community, or a society. Careful studies of human resilience show that just as most people are overcome by extreme adversity, many confront it and learn to thrive, overcoming adversity itself (For a discussion of the literature, see, for example, Flach, 1988; and Wolin and Wolin, 1993). The challenge for the student of population health is to determine what the impact of variations in choices available to groups on variations in rates of illness and social problems.

Explanation Type 4: Linking Problem Drinking to Dysfunctional Family Systems Produced by Imposed Social Change

Another recurrent theme in the literature is that drinking excesses and associated antisocial behaviour patterns are learned in dysfunctional aboriginal family systems, which have been devastated by generations of systematic disruption by assimilationist interventions. The argument generally holds that the separation of large numbers of parents and children through both the residential school system and child welfare practices acted to break the link that provided continuity between the generations, deskilling the childrearing function in families and, by debasing aboriginal cultures, inadvertently schooling aboriginal students in disrespect for parents, community Elders, ordinary band members, and traditional cultures.

This argument is surely a very compelling one. Many of the cognitive, emotional, and social problems of aboriginal children and, later, of course, adults, may well be linked to dysfunctional aboriginal family systems. The quality of aboriginal childrearing has been weakened in recent years by the growth of lone parenthood, the absence of permanent father figures, and the poverty associated with the unemployment typical of maternally managed households in which social assistance is the only form of income. However, assertion of a direct causal linkage of alcoholism or problem drinking to residential schooling would require some form of proof that residential school instruction or extra-curricular activities encouraged drinking, and no one has even suggested such a possibility. Alternatively, a comparison of problem drinking outcomes between day school attendees and residential school participants would have to be made, and a search of the available research to date has not indicated that such a study exists. Any linkage between high rates of First Nations problem drinking and residential schooling (or child welfare apprehension) remains speculative, given the testimonial nature of virtually all the relevant research on the subject. Further, some research and much anecdotal evidence has described positive residential school experience. Unfortunately, there has been a reductionist tendency in recent attempts to explain First Nations socialization ills in terms of the rupture in the parent/child relationship caused specifically by the residential school experience.

The displacement of the adult male economic role and the family dependency that followed from that experience probably did much more to create family dysfunction than did residential schooling – and that displacement can be traced to the entirety of Canadian national development policy as it has impacted on the economic participation of First Nations. That reality, however, is often lost in the tendency to blame specific institutions, such as the residential school system or the 'child welfare scoop' of the 1960s. At different moments in recent history, such institutions have been blamed for virtually every unhappy outcome of post-contact aboriginal life.

A book by Maureen Lux (2001), covering the 1880 to 1940 period on the Canadian Plains, forces us to put the residential schools into perspective. Describing residential schools as underfunded and inadequate, and even as centres for the spread of epidemic diseases, she argues that it was the economics behind the epidemics and other problems, more than the nature of residential schooling itself, that caused the most severe social problems experienced by indigenous, reserve-based populations. Poverty, Lux claims, was the real culprit, and that poverty was reflected in the underfunding of the residential school system.

Treatment of the residential school issue has largely resembled the disease concept of treatment to problem drinking in First Nations. Despite a lack of careful research linking the residential school experience to specific, negative quality of life outcomes, and in the absence of any empirical outcome comparison with day school participation, residential school abuse has been named as a problem with a wide range of consequences. It has been referred to as a 'syndrome' by a variety of mental health counsellors and aboriginal spokespersons. Finally, residential schooling became a rallying call for redress, and, in large part, the response to the problem has centred on therapy, although a cash settlement process for individual claims of abuse is also in place. While there was much about the residential school program that was problematic, arguably, the preoccupation with residential school abuse has partially served to deter the focus of First Nations leadership from the larger economic and macro-social sphere of under development determinants and more effective social change strategies.

Employing the concept of a psychological syndrome to cover simple participation in the residential school program surely does a disservice to those who were emotionally, physically, or sexually abused. It also medicalizes a social problem and exaggerates the stature of that problem within the overall context of European-aboriginal interaction.

What can be assumed from the scientific literature is that the frequency of both inadequate parenting and dysfunctional family systems is significantly greater in aboriginal populations than in the Canadian population as a whole. It would only be consistent with the research literature to suggest that aboriginal children are at higher risk of maltreatment if they come from families in which alcohol abuse is characteristic of parental behaviour, and because alcohol abuse is more widespread in aboriginal populations. It follows that aboriginal children are at greater risk of neglect and abuse than Canadian children generally. A direct, positive relationship has been consistently demonstrated in research examining the relationship between victimization through child maltreatment and substance abuse exhibited in adolescence and young adulthood. That victimization has occurred both among day school attendees and residential school participants.

Some commentators have suggested that Native American teenage substance use may primarily be a response to situational stress associated with parental alcohol abuse and family dysfunction. Therapists refer to this strategy as 'self-medication' to escape from or soothe the associated emotional pain. This explanation, which looks to dysfunctional family norms and parental alcohol abuse as precipitants of problem drinking in early life, is very compelling: it coincides with the experience of far too many aboriginal young people. An especially interesting aspect of this explanation is the cyclical, intergenerational effect of alcohol abuse, in which the problem drinking of one generation leads to the problem drinking of the next. In their study of drinking patterns among different selected tribes in the United States, Weisner, Weibel-Orlando, and Long (1984) interpreted drinking behaviour modelled by the family of origin as socialization and role modelling that produce an adult drinker. Their data indicated that participants with 50 per cent

Indian ancestry (i.e., individuals 'with a foot in each world') drink more than those with either less or more Indian ancestry. The researchers argued that the relationship between Indian ancestry and drinking level is more suggestive of an acculturation stress than a direct genetic effect, without ruling out individual family differences in genetic predisposition. Weisner and his colleagues also found that while the drinking level and style may be unique in some respects among Indians and, in turn, influenced by cultural heritage, the overall differences in drinking levels and the lifetime drinking patterns in the Indian sample parallel findings on drinking in the general American population (drinking is heavier among younger people; men in every ethnic group drink more at each stage of life than women; and there is some tendency for the drinking pattern modelled in the family of origin to be reproduced in the next generation). Although they did find differences in drinking level by tribe (reflecting the influence of tribal culture and values), Weisner and colleagues concluded that sex, age, the models of drinking behaviour provided by the family of origin and psychological stress best predict drinking level (Weisner,Wiebel-Orlando, and Long 1984).

The relative disrepair of the aboriginal family system surely contributes to high aboriginal drinking rates. However, aboriginal family systems do not exist in a vacuum; they occupy a social space that has experienced various unwelcome intrusions and which lacks many of the most essential, supportive conditions required to link that system to the wider society and economy.

Explanation Type 5: Aboriginal Problem Drinking as the Fulfilment of Expectations Contained in a Stigmatic Label

A final and especially compelling explanation of aboriginal problem drinking rates argues that a powerful, self-fulfilling prophecy may be at work in influencing drinking behaviour patterns among First Nations. A 'drunken Indian' stereotype has long characterized non-aboriginal opinions of First Nations people. Beauvais and LaBoueff (1985), speaking to the experience of indigenous peoples of North America generally, observe that there is a long-standing belief that most 'Indians' are alcoholic. When this belief becomes pervasive enough, aboriginal people themselves begin to believe the stereotype; this results in turn in a belief in the inevitability of alcoholism and in a sense of fatalism. Consequently, argue Beauvais and LaBoueff, out of shame, Native American children may not want to identify themselves as 'Indian.' Denial of their heritage and its traditions may be very stressful and it may lead to a greater vulnerability to excessive alcohol use.

It is very difficult to link stigmatic labelling to specific, long-term behavioural outcomes. There is evidence to suggest that negative labelling has some short-term impact on the quality of life and educational and behavioural success of individuals and sub-groups within a national population. Even the statistical average of IQ scores and academic performance of students can be dramatically enhanced for short durations when teachers' perceptions of the intellectual promise of students formerly labelled as low achievers are elevated (see Rosenthal and Jacobson, 1968). Admittedly, there is no clear evidence to suggest that social problems experienced by individuals over extended periods are necessarily *caused* solely by normative public perceptions of minority characteristics. However, the labelling hypothesis is particularly interesting as an explanation of how self-image is constructed, and how opportunities for mainstream social participation have been foreclosed for aboriginal people, beginning in their formal schooling years, because of negative self-image development. It is also of special interest as an explanation of some of the factors that may reinforce long-term substance abuse patterns. A comment cited in a book by Helen Buckley by Oscar Lathlin, once the chief of a First Nation band near The Pas, Manitoba, is noteworthy in this regard: 'Indians have come to accept the negative views that whites have of them. Tell a child all his life and by 16 he thinks that to be an Indian is to be on welfare, in jail or drunk. That's the programming the Department [of Indian Affairs] has done for Indian people (Buckley, 1993: 140).'[1]

Summary

Analysis of previous, competing explanations of exceptional aboriginal problem drinking rates would suggest that family dysfunction may well be the most direct, immediate cause of these rates. However, that dysfunction has been caused by family disruption associated with socio-economic change. The labelling thesis offers some interesting leads but is, of itself, probably insufficient to explain problem drinking

---

1 Buckley was citing a *Winnipeg Free Press* article in the 14 October 1988 edition of the paper.

rates in First Nations. A full explanation of high problem drinking rates on reserves requires both a social-structural explanation and an explanation of the particular norms and attitudes that emerge from social organizational factors and which, in turn, come to act independently as causes of problem drinking.

10

The Genesis of Alcohol Abuse Norms in First Nation Reserve Communities: An Explanatory Outline

The explanatory alternatives to the pathological paradigm described in chapter 9 all bear kernels of truth. Each one may explain part of the variation between aboriginal and non-aboriginal problem drinking rates. However, taken separately, these alternative explanations are far too limited in their capacity to explain the emergence and persistence, to date, of the firewater complex. As described in previous chapters, that 'complex' encompasses a set of beliefs, assumptions, and behaviour patterns associated with the troubling aspects of the drinking experience of First Nations people living on or socialized within a reserve social structure and culture in Canada.

The firewater complex comprises a number of elements, including the fact that First Nations people tend to believe they have a special sensitivity to alcohol, and that drinking alcoholic beverages is typically associated with the goal of intoxication. In turn, intoxication is pursued, in effect, to release an inner, mischievous, adventurous, outspoken, unafraid, and often belligerent inner voice to guide drinking behaviour. In effect, aboriginal problem drinkers believe that self-control is lost (or, in psychoanalytic terms, the *ego* loses command) and concern about the regard of others or conventional values is diminished (or, in psychoanalytic terms, *superego* strength is weakened), leaving one's most fundamental desires to take command. In psychoanalytic terms, the *id* takes control – and, unfortunately, that id is often a very angry and troublesome master.

The firewater complex also assumes that non-aboriginal people believe that 'Indians' have exceptional vulnerability to and trouble with drinking as a result of a genetic anomaly or lack of cultural sophistication. This view of First Nations people is given its most negative expression in the meaning keyed by the ethnic stereotype of the 'drunken Indian.' The existence of this stereotype may have far-reaching implications for attitudes towards and the reception given to aboriginal people by those in important gate-keeper roles, such as educators, police, landlords, merchants, taxi-drivers, and the like.

The widespread belief that aboriginal drinkers will inevitably abuse the use of alcohol also serves as a common excuse for irresponsible, immoral, or highly destructive behaviour. This understanding has been reinforced by the understanding of alcoholism provided by the adherents to the disease model of alcoholism working in self-help groups and as prevention and treatment workers.

The challenge before us is not simply to describe the genesis of the firewater complex, but to explain the problem drinking that is at its core.

Some of the explanations advanced in the previous chapter trivialize the fact that alcohol abuse is implicated in a wide range of personal and interpersonal carnage in aboriginal populations. Aboriginal problem drinking may have been partially influenced by hallucinogenic traditions in First Nations, and it may also be a rebellious gesture, an ineffective act of political resistance by some very powerless people, but neither possibility contributes much to a full understanding of exceptional problem drinking rates in First Nations. The breakdown of the traditional aboriginal family system, negative role-modelling, and the isolating and reinforcing influences of stigmatic labelling offer far more compelling leads in explaining the firewater complex. However, all of these aspects of the causal field are situated in a social and economic context which, by the very nature of societal dynamics, has been subject to change over time. What is required is a historically grounded, sociological analysis of the common experience of First Nations in absorbing and adapting health-damaging beverage alcohol consumption styles into their social lives. Such an explanation should also identify those factors that have reinforced and sustained the continuance of that destructive drinking comportment. The burden of this chapter is to provide such an explanation.

With other indigenous host populations throughout the world, Canada's First Nations share a history of dramatic economic, cultural, and social upheaval. These various societies share the experience of being encompassed by foreign, expansionist economies with settlement policies that have isolated and typically marginalized their members. A dual legacy of impoverished social conditions – relative to invading cultures – and disproportionately high levels of substance abuse are common to these displaced indigenous societies. The conclusion is therefore forced upon us that there is a complex causal connection between destructive substance abuse patterns and the disruptive social change and disadvantages suffered by aboriginal people who have been marginalized by incoming, expansionist societies. Alcohol abuse and high alcoholism rates in the aboriginal outposts of Russia have long been reported in the press, and academic studies have documented similar problems in the aboriginal populations of Australia and New Zealand (Saggers and Gray, 1998).

What is missing is a gathering together and sequential ordering of the factors that have manifested and now sustain the firewater complex. In my opinion, because a common consensus on the conditions that have given rise to and currently sustain problem drinking has never been reached, policy and programming have been seriously flawed. Interventions have either been of a trial-and-error type, or they have simply emulated and partially adapted mainstream approaches. Lacking a clearly defined understanding of primary causal influences, policy and programming have been misguided and coverage limited. Tragically, an effective strategy for reducing the risks and harms of alcohol use in reserve communities has therefore been stifled.

In what follows, an attempt is made to provide a more systematic and comprehensive explanation of the emergence and durability of the firewater complex. This explanation will be presented as a set of interconnected propositions, accompanied by reference to additional evidence or research findings already described in the text.

Explaining the Genesis and Endurance of Problem Drinking in First Nations: A Series of Interconnected Propositions

1. Addictions and substance abuse yield short-term pleasures

All human beings are biologically predisposed to seek pleasure and to avoid pain. Alcohol and several other psycho-active substances, when ingested and accompanied by specific expectations about mood change, are effective means of providing pleasure and escaping pain within a relatively brief period of time. However, the impairment of human cognition brought about by their excessive use, the immediate risks of extreme impairment, and the cumulative effects of excessive dosages over time tend to produce injurious consequences. These consequences may be of a social, psychological, or physical nature, and they may be of short- or long-term duration. Many people will take health-damaging doses of alcohol or other drugs as long as the immediate pleasure derived from doing so is perceived to outweigh the disadvantages that tend to arrive at a later date.

2. As a population, First Nations people are not 'genetically driven' to alcohol abuse

On the basis of genetics alone, First Nations people as a population are no more given to alcohol temptations or intoxication and aberrant behaviours associated with drunkenness than other human groups. Some First Nations individuals and groups *may* tend to metabolize their alcohol more slowly than average, and they may therefore be more likely to be intoxicated or discomforted (i.e., 'hung over') for a longer period of time. They may also be at greater-than-average risk of engaging in inappropriate behaviours related to their alcohol use for a more extended period after the completion of a drinking bout. However, the evidence with respect to whether or not there is an ethnically distinctive alcohol ingestion effect for aboriginal North Americans is at best contradictory. Most experts have accepted that there is insufficient evidence to prove a genetic difference. Yet the point is now academic; it is difficult, if not impossible, for researchers to determine whether there is a distinctive, genetically based group reaction to alcohol among indigenous peoples because the bloodlines of aboriginal people cannot readily be determined. The outcome of unmapped interbreeding with non-aboriginals has made such sorting virtually impossible. The individual to whom the colloquial label 'pure Cree' (or Saulteaux, Mohawk, etc.) can be applied with accuracy is fast becoming a statistical rarity in the populations of First Nations.

Even if there were a distinctive profile of effects of alcohol ingestion on indigenous North American peoples, individual volition, situational pressures, and sociocultural influences will ultimately determine whether or not a given aboriginal individual actually indulges in excessive drinking or destructive personal comportment during or after alcohol use. Further, even if it could be shown that aboriginals did have a group-based genetic reaction, as we have seen, the normative Asian reaction to alcohol has been to avoid excessive drinking. This cultural reaction to a physiological trait is what would be expected: a physiologically aversive reaction to beverage alcohol in an ethnic group could hardly explain a culturally based attraction to the same substance.

3. *In Canada, drinking patterns in aboriginal communities were learned – originally from non-aboriginal people – and, through a 'self-fulfilling prophecy,' they are reinforced by internalization of non-aboriginal 'drunken Indian stereotyping.'*

As MacAndrew and Edgerton (1969) observe in their well-received book on aboriginal drinking, there are two aspects to the ways in which people respond to alcohol. The first of these is the bio-physiological impairment that alcohol causes, including the diminution of sensorimotor skills. This type of impairment is relatively standard and directly associated with intoxication. However, the second response to alcohol impairment is the way in which people behave or 'comport themselves' during and after drinking episodes. Drinking behaviours are contextual and transmitted through social learning, and drinking comportment is a socially constructed phenomenon. First Nations people in Canada were first exposed to alcoholic beverages by and learned their drinking styles from contact with people associated with the European commercial and settlement frontier. The indigenous people of Canada had no positive role models of their own to encourage moderation and sobriety.

As MacAndrew and Edgerton (1969) have noted, some descriptions of the drinking comportment of early traders were at least as lurid as those describing the behaviour associated with the drinking episodes of indigenous North Americans. The authors quote Daniel Harmon, an early trader, who worked and travelled among the French Canadian fur traders in the early part of the second half of the eighteenth century. Harmon stated: 'Of all the people in the world, I think the Canadians, when drunk, are the most disagreeable; for excessive drinking generally causes them to quarrel and fight, among themselves. Indeed, I had rather have fifty drunken Indians in fort than five drunken Canadians' (MacAndrew and Edgerton, 1969: 143–4). Dailey (1967) similarly cites a statement in the *Jesuit Relations* about the French soldiers stationed at Michilmackinac, which described their drinking behaviour as almost always leading to quarrelling, fighting furiously with each other, and grabbing their guns to try to kill each other.

After colonization and settlement, the drinking behaviour of First Nations people came to be viewed as deviant and dangerous to the maintenance of (non-aboriginal) order, especially in frontier communities. But many First Nations people in Canada originally learned their excessive 'acting out' drinking styles from whisky traders of European ancestry, who encouraged their impairment to gain advantage in trading transactions. Traders manipulated indigenous peoples to enter into exchanges for goods, while modelling excessive and aggressive alcohol use (MacAndrew and Edgerton, 1969). Through modelling, the uninhibited drunken behaviour of young, white, male (and only male) explorers, traders, convicts, loggers, oil drillers, military personnel, miners, and the like, intoxicating and reckless drinking styles were transmitted to pre-reserve and reserve communities. During their lonely leisure hours, these (generally) young Caucasian men, who shared their drinking with aboriginals, were unhampered by the behavioural restraints of family monitoring and the constraints and demands for sobriety dictated by the social norms of their home communities. It was from these socially unattached 'teachers' of alcohol use that people of the First Nations in Canada first learned their drinking styles. This learned drinking may have been reinforced by a legacy of traditional ceremonial and drug-induced states of mind alteration intended as hyper-expressive healing rituals and bonding activities which functioned to create group solidarity in the band or tribe.

As Duran and Duran (1995: 104) observe, the labelling of aboriginal drinking behaviour as deviant became a convenient rationale for further regulating the behaviour of indigenous peoples through such mechanisms as prohibition. While, as groups, First Nations people may have learned their drinking comportment from Europeans, subsequent generations learned their drinking style from individuals within their communities: drunken comportment has been a recycled cultural phenomenon on First Nations reserves. However, problem drinking has also been an accommodative response to non-aboriginal stereotyping. As Beauvais and LaBoueff (1985) have suggested, there is a long-standing public belief that most Indians are alcoholics. When this belief became sufficiently pervasive, Indian people themselves came to believe the stereotype, and internalized a belief in the inevitability of alcoholism in the Indian population. The upshot is that, if they drink, aboriginal people expect to become intoxicated and if they drink on a regular basis, to be alcoholics.

4. Distinctive intracultural influences that preceded European dominance probably influenced drinking practices in First Nations

Certain aspects of pre–European contact indigenous cultures themselves have arguably influenced the destructive character of contemporary First Nations drinking styles. As discussed earlier, some aboriginal populations in the Americas, especially those residing in what is now Mexico and Central America, had drinking traditions of their own prior to European contact and had developed normative behavioural frameworks to guide and limit the excesses of drinking comportment. To achieve a state of euphoria, the Aztecs used pulque, an alcoholic beverage made from the fermented juice of the Agave plant (also called the maguey) enhanced with peyote, a narcotic derived from a cactus (Driver, 1969). In several city states, the Aztecs implemented strict prohibition laws to control drunkenness in certain contexts, and the penalty of death applied for second offences (MacLeod, 1928).

The traditions of cultural adaptation to the challenging topography and extremes of the North American climate must also have been influential. Coping with the extremities of weather and hunting for food with primitive weapons, faced with the dangers of wild animals and the risks of intertribal warfare, aboriginal peoples tended to encourage a stoic reserve in everyday comportment. But they also had 'time-out' ceremonies in which the rules of comportment were relaxed and frustrations could be acted out. Verbal abuse, sexual promiscuity, and playful fighting that sometimes became violent were not uncommon. This type of event, onto which beverage alcohol consumption was later grafted, may have independently contributed to the socially destructive outcomes of social gatherings. The merging of the two may have compounded the destructive nature of these problems.

Another norm among indigenous peoples in what is now Canada was the collective sharing of community bounty, whether from the hunt or in festive or ceremonial feasts. Collective drinking, in the form of binges, may simply have been absorbed into institutionalized sharing practices.

The pre-contact 'principal of non-interference' in the affairs of other individuals and families certainly survives today. The late psychiatrist Clare Brant once declared that this ethic was among the 'most important' of the prescriptive ideals guiding the behaviour of First Nations people (Whitehead and Hayes, 1998: 85–6). This norm, which influences childrearing and responses to family members, friends, and neighbours acting out in troubling ways, also influences the reaction of community members to mental health and addictions issues. Specifically, the principle of non-interference is a community sanction against the application of informal controls on unwise drinking choices.

5. *The history of real and perceived health and cultural threats to First Nations posed by Euro-Canadian society has led to a belief in the inevitability of high rates of social problems in reserve communities.*

European observers of indigenous North Americans at the time of contact and during its early years regarded 'Indians' with a curious mix of respect and disrespect, fear and awe, sympathy and contempt. From afar, some Enlightenment philosophers of Europe regarded the 'Indian' as a 'noble savage' who, left untouched by the 'advanced' cultures, would continue to live a life of relative innocence, cooperation, and primitive luxury.[1] In more recent years, the view that indigenous cultures were universally healthy prior to European contact has become an article of faith at health service meetings and health conferences held by and for First Nations people. This romanticization of the past and its theme of innocence lost has been integrated into the politico-historic narrative of First Nations, at least as espoused by many First Nations leaders and polemicists.

---

1 Such seventeenth-century thinkers as Thomas Hobbes regarded life in indigenous North America as savage, brutish, and short, protected only by the most primitive and tenuous of social contracts that occasionally prevented a seething, almost always ready, war of all against all from erupting. Many of the European Enlightenment philosophers of the eighteenth century and journalists of the nineteenth century, however, regarded North and South American Indians as exemplary of humankind in its pure and innocent, precivilized form. The French Enlightenment philosopher Jean Jacques Rousseau coined the phrase 'noble savage,' but he was just one of many who challenged the negative view of Indians. To these writers, indigenous North Americans represented humankind in an unspoiled 'state of nature.' Both the romantic version and the unsympathetic view suffered from simplicity and reductionism. Just as pre-ancient Europeans had done, and as most if not all societies continue to do today, aboriginal North Americans had fought among themselves and with other tribes. They also suffered from various injuries and diseases and their life expectancy was probably less than half what it is today in North America. Pre-Columbian life was not a bed of roses. Further, aboriginals were contact sources for certain pathogens and unhealthy practices. American indigenes were the source of mosquito-transmitted yellow fever, which travelled to Europe from North America, and the cancers caused around the world today by smoking tobacco originated in the crops of pre-Columbian South America. But it was the Europeans who exported these diseases back to Britain and Europe, not the indigenous North Americans – and it is clear that there was no parallel in Europe to the death rates and population devastation from disease experienced by the indigenous peoples of North America.

It is probable that what assured the survival of such a perspective more than anything else was the reaction to the high mortality rates and illnesses experienced by First Nations during the early years of their interaction with Europeans. Smallpox, measles, and tuberculosis are examples of major imported epidemics that killed and in various ways devastated huge percentages of aboriginal populations because they had no natural immunity to them. As one historian writes: 'The sight of destruction caused among the Indians by disease did in fact have an unpleasant effect on native psychology; it led to hatred (promoting irritation and war) of the whites who, the natives frequently realized, were the sources of the new diseases, and it led to social reactions of despair ...' (MacLeod, 1928: 50). The danger posed by immigrant communicable diseases for populations with insufficient immune protection must have been burnt permanently into the collective consciousness of First Nations people. The devastation of alcohol abuse further encouraged this sense that European lifestyles posed an extreme threat to aboriginal health and well-being. This sense of vulnerability to European intrusions has proven a lasting influence in determining which explanations of public health and social problems are considered socially acceptable and which are not in First Nations.

Take, for example, the similarity of attitudes towards such leisure-time pursuits as gambling, commercial sex, and delinquent and criminal gang activity. While all of these are ostensibly pleasurable activities, they are also, when indulged in to excess, potentially harmful. How an individual engages in these activities is a matter of choice, even if the choices made are influenced by social and psychological factors. Yet at virtually every meeting I have attended as a community health consultant in which discussion of these specific issues took place, it was noted, by concensus, that the cause of these problems in reserve communities is the invasive, non-aboriginal culture outside the reserve – and that the solution therefore required special programming with the assistance of external expertise, and provided as compensation, to overcome the problem. This dual attitude of blame and corrective demand is surely understandable, even to the least sympathetic observer of things aboriginal. However, there is also something insidious in the process itself, and in its outcome. Rather than encouraging personal, familial, and community responsibility for tackling a social problem, it deflects that responsibility. Ideological accommodation to the experience of colonization triumphs, and no effort is made to move beyond past grievances and take ownership of future solutions. This attitude has become entrenched in the discourse of health clinics and band offices, and it does little to encourage the moderation and self-management of drinking problems. Many First Nations people believe that alcohol problems and related social problems will persist in reserve communities as long as non-aboriginal people dominate society.

6. *The organization of 'Indian Affairs' through 'total institutions' and 'semi-total institutions' has socially segregated First Nations, encouraged dependency, and fostered a contraculture.*

The history of First Nations interaction with Euro-Canadian society also includes several experiences, externally initiated and orchestrated, that colonized and segregated First Nations people within a custodial and semi-custodial framework, and that reality has nourished the persistence of the firewater complex. Early colonization and segregation nourished a contraculture within First Nations reserves, a sense of a divided 'us' and 'them,' the former being aboriginal reserve residents, and the latter the surrounding communities specifically and mainstream society more generally. Early conflict and ongoing incidents of interpersonal confrontation, competition for scarce resources through active lobbying, protests, demonstrations, legal challenges, and the like, and occasional open conflicts, have nourished a contracultural reaction of First Nations members to Canadian society as a whole. As Lewis Coser, sociology's pre-eminent conflict theorist, once argued, patterned group conflict serves to establish, reaffirm, and maintain the identity and boundary lines between societies and between groups within society (1956: 38). Unfortunately, these 'patterned enmities' and 'reciprocal antagonisms' also tend to conserve social divisions and existing stratification systems, thus 'preventing the gradual disappearance of boundaries between the subgroups of a social system' (38).

The *reserve community system* itself, with its economic isolation and limited job and business opportunities, and the cultural isolation it created, has been the primary nexus through which many of the influences on the persistence of the firewater complex were born and have thrived. After studying the reserve life of an Ontario band in the late 1950s, the anthropologist R.W. Dunning described a community that did not truly function as a society, that survived through government transfer payments and thus as a fully dependent collection of people; in short, government policies were perpetuating a 'caste like position' in Canadian society for First Nations people (1959; 1964). Dunning described reserves he studied as settlements in which there was no transmission of culture and only minimal norms to guide behaviour. He painted a picture of despair in which people depended on social assistance for their livelihood and on the Department of Indian Affairs to make their basic community decisions (Dunning, 1964). Dunning also described widespread psychological disorders and extensive interpersonal violence and alcohol abuse. His reports, which link the loss of traditional social structure and culture with alcohol problems and violence, is clearly supported by the research of Kunitz and Levy and Chandler described above.

In the early years of reserve organization, especially in the west, the reserve system, in loose approximation, resembled what social psychologist Erving Goffman referred to as 'total institutions' (1961). Goffman defined a total institution as an organization and facility that inhibits a specific group of people from regular contact with the larger society and schedules and makes basic life decisions for those people through the exercise of authority by an administrative staff. Examples of total institutions include prisons, boarding schools, mental institutions, and the military.

Members of a total institution collectively develop an informal subculture designed to promote their own separate interests from the administrators who govern them. Often, those who have spent lengthy periods of time living in such an environment retain a sense of separateness and group identity with their formerly confined peers when they leave, and they often form a 'contraculture' – a subculture that is adhered to by members with a separate identify and which in specific ways defines itself by contrast and stands in opposition to the culture of mainstream society (Theodorson and Theodorson [1969: 76], with a reference to the definitional work of sociologist Milton Yinger). Deviant drinking behaviour is an integral part of the contracultural lifestyle of many marginal populations.

The impact of life in total institutions on several generations of First Nations people must be profound. Such experiences include the reserve system itself, which was effectively organized for decades by the Department of Indian Affairs. A majority, a substantial proportion of First Nations people were also raised in residential schools from a young age. These too were total institutions; residents were subject to the daily discipline of set meal and bed times, prayer, schooling, and recreational scheduling by teachers and administrators. Language use, clothing, and religion were likewise controlled.

Many first Nations men were also active participants in the world great wars and thus experienced the regimentation of army life. Other institutions that have had the grip of a total institution on disproportionate numbers of First Nations people include sanitoriums for tuberculosis patients (Lux, 2001: chap. 5), the group homes associated with the 'child welfare scoop' of the 1970s (Johnston, 1983), and both juvenile and adult correctional institutions. Lengthy exposure of a population to so many highly regulative habitats can do little to promote independence and what psychologists refer to as an 'internal locus of control' rather than an 'external locus of control.' Being socially conditioned to routinely accept the discipline of people regarded as unwelcome outsiders must stifle adult autonomy and responsibility and encourage rebelliousness and irresponsible behaviour when away from the purview of one's social 'keepers.'

The imposed *education system*, at least until the 1960s, was geared, with great insensitivity, to assimilation. The curriculum and many teachers characterized the ancestry of First Nations people as 'pagan,' 'savage,' and 'primitive' (J.P. Miller, 1997). This cultural degradation process must have left an imprint on First Nations children, a toxic residue which, at least occasionally, made 'going Indian' a phrase that came to refer, both inside and outside First Nations, to acting wild and uncivilized and, when possible, drunken, a temptation. It does not take a profound psychological imagination to see how such a self-concept might, in times of stress and frustration with the intrusions of 'white society,' encourage a drinking binge as a rebellious antidote.

The exposure of First Nations people to imposed institutional life has involved a fundamental disjuncture: a combination of loosely structured community life on reserves, in which discipline is absemt and most major life decisions are made by overseers, and highly regulated time spent in custodial and semi-custodial institutions. This contradicting experience has surely encouraged the breakdown of local norms and internal social controls, a condition described by sociologists as 'anomie.' Anomie is equated with disproportionately high levels of retreatist behaviour patterns, typically earmarked by social problems, including alcohol and drug abuse (Merton, 1957).

The most insidious aspect of living for a lengthy period in a total (or 'quasi-total) institution stems from the fact that independence of thought tends to be discouraged rather than encouraged – and independent decisions about a moderate approach to drinking alcohol or using other drugs are indeed discouraged in communities in which peer groups tend to apply pressure in support of abusive alcohol use.

7. *Community social disintegration has resulted in a loss of traditional social controls, which has weakened the internal capacity of reserve communities to regulate antisocial drinking.*

As Duran and Duran (1995) have observed, colonization and the establishment of the reserve system resulted in the weakening of the traditional systems of social control in First Nations. In fact, May (1982) has asserted that the vulnerability of Native American populations to alcohol problems is associated with the degree of social disintegration experienced by a community. Data supporting this contention are found in other sections of this text, suggesting that indigenous populations which had historically used beverage alcohol, and therefore had a social control framework in place, were not devastated by the introduction of European alcohol beverages. Further, the important work of Chandler (2001) on comparisons of aboriginal youth suicide rates and an examination of homicide rates by Levy and Kunitz among the Southwest and Plateau Indians in the United States support the notion that social problems are mitigated by social integration, as reinforced by continuity with the past or by the emergence of revivalist movements such as the Native American Church. As Duran and Duran state: 'Tribes with high traditional integration and low acculturation stress experience much lower levels of alcohol- and drug-related problems than tribes with high acculturation stress and low traditional integration' (1995: 105).

Suggesting that this correlation of social integration with moderate alcohol use, especially social integration based on cultural continuity, is a key element of substance abuse risk reduction strategies in aboriginal communities, Duran and Duran point to the widely known example of Alkali Lake in British Columbia. In that community, comprised of Shushwap Indian residents, alcoholism and problem drinking had had an impact on almost every adult, as well as many youth and children. By revitalizing traditional culture and in part inventing a local approach, the Shushwap mobilized a 'community culture that no longer tolerated alcoholism' (Guillory, Willie, and Duran, 1988: 30). The now widely celebrated outcome was to reduce alcohol dependency from 95 to 5 per cent. As Duran and Duran stress, the fact that tribal leaders assumed their legitimate authority to govern proved to be an important aspect of the solution (1995: 105).

8. *The displacement of traditional, associative arrangements by imposed bureaucratic and professionalized service systems virtually froze locally conceived community building.*

The failure to immediately establish the operations of reserve communities through the active participation of local people created what we might refer to as generative conditions for problem drinking and other social problems. The social philosopher Ivan Illich (1971; 1976) has criticized the imposition of First World education and health care on Third World peoples because, in his view, local and personal responsibility for health care and the education of children withers in less developed societies (LDSs) with the importation of more specialized service technologies. The people of the host society gradually become dependent upon the 'solutions' of government policy makers and health advisers with specialized expertise. However, with their highly sophisticated but often very specialized knowledge, those experts are really only capable of providing a limited response to such basic needs as health care or education. Illich's abiding concern has been that the Third World has lost much of its vital community self-determination and independent economic capacity through an ever-increasing dependence on professionals whose knowledge is attuned to the needs of an advanced industrial culture rather than to local needs in an LDS.

Taking his cue from Illich, the American community organizer, John McKnight, has written extensively about the creation of a similar dependency on externalized bureaucratic decision making and expert authority among formerly self-sustaining neighbourhoods in North America (1997). He has been especially concerned about the destructive effects on low-income, high unemployment inner-city neighbourhoods and remote rural communities. While recognizing that there are many local effects which are distinctive to each community, McKnight concludes that remain four negative effects of external, public intervention remain, which he believes could be described as universal and inevitable. Anyone familiar with reserve settlements will recognize that McKnight's description of community disempowerment captures the dissipation of the very concept of community on First Nation reserves.

According to McKnight, *by focusing upon a person's deficiencies*, on his or her weaknesses, troubles, faults, or 'brokenness' rather than on his or her capacities, *external interventions serve to degrade that individual's self-concept*. As McKnight comments: 'We know that if one surrounds any individual with messages and experiences that are always saying to them, what's important about you is what's wrong with you, that will have a powerful, powerful, depressing, disillusioning and degrading effect upon that person' (1994: 4).

The second negative side effect relates to a community's economy – and to what McKnight calls the individual's personal economy. He argues that disadvantaged communities confronting the routine dynamics of capitalism tend to experience what he refers to as a *disemployment of the community and personal economy*. McKnight's basic point is that every time a service intervention is chosen as a response to a human personal or social problem, a fundamental *economic* decision is actually made. 'Every time, in fact,' he argues, 'you decide to buy a service professional you are *de facto* deciding not to buy something else, including income for people whose primary problem may be lack of income' (1994: 4). The net result of this process is that the allocation of a substantial amount of public investment in the poor is diverted to professionals rather than to the poor, whose primary problem is lack of income.

The third effect concerns the impact that decisions to draw upon professional or external public interventions have on the capacity of local associations, leadership, and membership to solve local problems. Referring to this process as *disabling local capacity*, McKnight argues that each time a community's leaders say that they need more services, more agencies, more systems, more outreach contributed by outside experts, a decision is being made that the community's existing informal networks, associations, leadership, and capacities are inadequate to solve the problem. A community's powers are diminished by investing in exogenous approaches that displace local efforts.

Finally, McKnight argues that *an entire system of specialized services can be more harmful than beneficial to a community*. A series of interventions to consolidate and replace pre-existing systems for doing things can be calamitous for a community. The older systems might actually have worked better than all the new systems, taken in aggregate.

McKnight's concern is that the inevitable consequence of implementing modern social services, professional interventions, and governmental services in previously self-sustaining communities is that the original capabilities that comprised the very fabric of community are destroyed in the process. He refers to these externally contrived

technical services as 'systems' and to the displaced traditional arrangements as 'associations.' He suggests that the knowledge vested in government agencies and professionals displaces the historic knowledge
of the community and, as a result, personal, family and community
confidence withers in the face of professional mystique. McKnight
argues that, eventually, communities lose or forget how to perform the
vital functions which originally brought them together and sustained
them as communities. And this loss, McKnight argues, extends right
down to the level of the family. His most fundamental solution is to
redirect moneys from externally imposed systems back to the associations within the community.

McKnight provides a compelling conceptual description of how the
informal and formal problem-solving structures of traditional First
Nations have been undermined by external interventions. His proffered
solution, however, has a fundamental flaw in terms of its relevance to
First Nations. Traditional community structures have been undermined
for so long in First Nations that little is left. There is nothing mysterious
about this state of affairs. Economic anthropologists, perhaps beginning
with Karl Marx, have shown that the cultural superstructure of a society
rests on an economic base and must adapt to the requirements of that
base. When the traditional economic livelihood of a society is disrupted,
the belief systems and non-economic institutional arrangements also
collapse, gradually leaving but vestiges of their original configurations.
Further, many of the problems confronting reserve communities
demand technical knowledge and modern service systems. To ignore
this fact is to invite enormous losses on a variety of cultural, social, economic and administrative fronts that few First Nations people would
find acceptable.

Current transfer policies that are shifting funds from the federal
government directly to First Nations reserves are essentially heeding
McKnight's advice. Often, however, because local capacities are not sufficiently strong to administer and adequately deliver services, the transfer process results in a regression in the quality of services and very little
if any revival and rebuilding of traditional structures.

Referring to a perceived breakdown of family support for children,
and challenging McKnight's idea of setting off systems and associations
as opposing potentials within community, Urie Bronfenbrenner has
written that, 'Desirable as such an economic reorientation may be, it
rests on the assumption that the local groups and individuals will have
the knowledge, know-how and motivation to use the newly acquired
financial resources in ways that will in fact be effective in reducing, let

alone reversing ... social disarray' (1997: 124). Bronfenbrenner quite sensibly calls instead for a reorganization and interconnection of what McKnight calls 'systems' and 'associations' to serve their mutual advantage (Bronfenbrennew, 1997: 124). In the reserve context, community development would mean either creating or reviving structures with roots in the past and integrating and coordinating them with modern service system approaches delivered by highly qualified professionals and technicians. Too often, second-rate service in First Nations communities has been justified on the basis of the argument that local hiring is a must, even if basic qualifications cannot be met.

9. *Accommodation to lengthy prohibition reinforced binge drinking in First Nations.*

A patterned reaction to *targeted prohibition*, another external imposition on First Nations, may also have contributed to the persistence of substance abuse. In Canada, First Nations people were prohibited from drinking (Smart and Ogborne, 1986) until the early 1960s, and they would have to obtain alcohol illegally. Status Indians would drink rapidly in order to avoid confiscation of the liquor and arrest by the police.

During the prohibition period, First Nations adults would obtain their liquor from bootleggers or acquire it in the form of diluted alcohol concentrates. Occasionally they would be allowed into roughneck bars, and sometimes police simply looked the other way. Other times, the source was a raucous house party 'hosted' by someone who had obtained booze from a bootlegger. Some writers have speculated that the rapid, high-volume consumption became a habit over the course of the prohibition years – a habit that crystallized into a drinking style that perpetuated the 'drinking until the drink is gone' aspect of the firewater complex.

10. *First Nations people were essentially bypassed by Confederation and the 'National Policy,' which was based on the pro-active development of a national workforce and a capital formation process that relied upon immigrants.*

Canada's nation-building efforts in the latter half of the nineteenth century, and throughout the first half of the twentieth century, were framed by the so-called National Policy. That policy included railroad building that sought to unite the country 'from sea to sea,' settlement of the west, a protective tariff system designed to promote central Canadian manufacturing, and a strategy to develop an immigrant labour force. Unfortunately, rather than as significant partners in Confederation, First Nations people were generally viewed as groups with rights to lands that had to be brought into Canadian jurisdiction. While economic integration and even the assimilation of aboriginal people was a long-term goal, the most substantial 'Indian' elements of the National Policy were the western treaties and settlement, both aimed at ensuring rapid and orderly land settlement and access to primary resources, such as cereal grains, subsurface minerals, timber, and fish. The interests of First Nations people were viewed as secondary to the challenges of central Canadian business development, the desire for conflict-free, orderly capital accumulation throughout 'British North America,' and the pivotal need for the development of resource extraction and new consumer markets on the 'frontier' (Davis, 1971).

With a development schedule prompted by the realities of closing British and American opportunities, the Canadian government simply developed a reserve system to deal with surface land rights matters, an assimilation strategy geared to promote off-reserve migration over the long term, and a subsurface mineral rights policy that essentially overlooked the interests of First Nations. This exclusion of aboriginal people from the core elements of the National Policy has turned out to be perhaps the single greatest failure of Canadian public policy. Rather than fully involve aboriginal people in the country's development, nation building and capital formation after the second half of the nineteenth century relied almost wholly on imported, European labour and protected national businesses.

The inevitable outcome of this strategy was the ideological and institutional ethnic domination of the white settler society in Canada – a domination expressed in terms of population size, political and socio-economic organization, and cultural hegemony. While aboriginal peoples hosted Europeans during the exploration era and served as economic partners in the fur trade, their immediate economic value in the capitalist labour market dwindled and virtually died as agricultural settlement, mineral extraction, and industrial development emerged as the key development sectors in British North America. The peoples of First Nations were expected to gradually become involved in the new economy, aided by what eventually could be seen as a fundamentally contradictory policy of basic employment skills training, cultural assimilation, and reserve isolation rather than an ambitious, carefully paced policy of labour force development, resource sharing, and economic partnerships.

The approach of the Canadian government to its 'Indian affairs' lacked vision, commitment and, ultimately, an ambition worthy of the country's larger development framework. The emerging country of Canada failed to pro-actively share with aboriginal peoples the management or production functions of the emergent resource and industrially based economy. The alternative of carefully husbanding and giving priority to the development of an indigenous workforce and a collective share of business opportunities was never given serious attention.

An especially insightful analysis of this failure of government is documented in Sarah Carter's *Lost Harvests* (1990), which describes how the early successes of First Nations' reserve communities in prairie agriculture were negated by misguided government policies and unsympathetic locals and speculators far more interested in securing agricultural land than in giving Indian farming communities sufficient room to grow. Other studies have depicted a similar evolution in other geographic-cultural areas, and many are yet to be written. They can be expected to tell a tale of economic exclusion coupled with expectations of cultural assimilation – an obviously impossible duality.

Throughout the twentieth century, the traditional aboriginal workforce was de-skilled and not effectively drawn into either the country's modernizing labour force or the mainstream capital formation process. The grim outcome has been a redundant labour force unattached to the mainstream economy. As the Canadian economy followed the modernization process, all citizens, including aboriginals, became increasingly dependent upon rapidly advancing labour-substitutive technology and market-oriented activities. The outcome of this process had profound effects for aboriginals. Not integrated into the new production system, they gradually lost their traditional skills, becoming impoverished dependents on government income transfers for personal income and community services. The subsistence-based skills of hunting and gathering, horticultural skills and the domestic skills of food preparation, lodging and apparel making of First Nations came to be seen as outdated, and irrelevant and were almost wholly displaced by work or income supports that related more readily to the cash economy and its offerings of prepackaged foods; factory-made, low-priced clothing; semi-manufactured housing; highly efficient machines and tools; and a cornucopia of luxury goods. The skills and activities in the household economy disappeared, a process hastened by the separation of children from parents through boarding school stays. In general, traditional male roles – that once were organized to apply to basic economic and security needs – were eliminated and not replaced. These roles declined dramatically in importance as dependence on cash purchases for work equipment, shelter, food, transportation, and recreational goods increased. Traditional occupations were thus deskilled with under-utilization and devalued because of their lack of fit with the commercial economy. Many, perhaps the majority of First Nations people, are a stranded population, 'warehoused' on reserves or, if they have left the reserves, confined within the low-income areas of inner cities.

11. *Male economic role displacement in First Nations communities has encouraged addictive habits as relief from boredom, and violence-related drunken comportment as compensation for male status anxiety.*

With the loss of his role as warrior and hunter, horticulturalist or fisher, the First Nation adult male was displaced and family role relations were thrown into confusion. With their survival no longer linked to the productive output of their male members, the reserves gradually developed a socio-economic reality of social assistance dependency, economic isolation, and a relative lack of interdependence with neighbouring communities.

The separation of consumption from production, and the destruction of the traditional aboriginal economic role relations in many, perhaps most First Nation communities, strained the aboriginal family system to the breaking point. Bound by the limited range of educational and occupational options available on the reserve, the First Nations male and the family he was expected to support economically became increasingly dependent on social assistance after it was introduced to reserves in the late 1950s. Loss of the male economic role was accompanied by a fundamental change in personal pride and authority in the family and community affairs. Elders point wistfully to the voluntarism in their communities prior to the transition to social assistance dependency, and shake their heads in disgust at the difficulties of soliciting any type of unpaid participation in community affairs today.

Over time, reserve life and male family heads adapted to the reality of normative unemployment, while local cultures developed around social assistance incomes and cash transfers to the community administration for all other local services. The reserve populations came to expend consumer dollars in neighbouring towns and cities but otherwise contributed little beyond menial and occasional labour to enhance the value of their own local, on-reserve economies. Despite their contribution as consumers to the economy of the areas in which they nestled, reserve populations came to exist in a strange and unique form of cultural isolation. In dozens of workshops attended by this writer, both women and men have suggested that male unemployment causes stresses in families that often lead to conflict and violence. This role displacement has perhaps contributed to a high level of aggression and violence between males during emotionally charged, disinhibited drinking binges. The aggression might partially be explained as a compensatory, shame-based adjustment to the status anxiety associated with the spousal conflict and family violence, both of which may nourish drunkenness, which often leads in turn to more family violence because of the excuse provided by the firewater complex. The violence and its after effects are thus reproduced in a vicious, circular manner through the generations.

12. First Nations female problem drinking as a sociological 'folie à deux'

Descriptions of problem drinking in North American indigenous communities during early contact and early post-contact periods typically focused on men. In fact, even today, the attention paid in the relevant research to the subject of gender differences in aboriginal drinking styles has been very limited. Yet my own impressions, gained from direct observation and synthesized from the comments of key informants in community health studies, indicate that on-reserve women who drink alcoholic beverages are also far more likely to become problem drinkers than non-aboriginal female Canadians.

Joy Leland (1976: 16–17) commented several decades ago that conclusions about aboriginal problem drinkers have largely been generalized from observations made and studies undertaken by Europeans who focused exclusively on aboriginal males. Leland also noted that sex differences in drinking norms appear to exist in most cultures: as a rule, women drink less than men. Yet even E.M. Jellinek's typology of alcoholics, developed in the latge 1940s and early 1950s, was based primarily on male data (1976: 17).

Despite the inappropriate, speculative basis on which assumptions about aboriginal female in drinking have been made, there is evidence that, at least the second half of the twentieth century, aboriginal female problem drinking has been much more common than it is among non-aboriginal women. While much lower than those of aboriginal males in study populations, statistical estimates of aboriginal female problem drinking rates in the twentieth century were typically higher than rates for non-aboriginal females. Young (1994: 200–1) notes that on many of the psychological and physical illness conditions associated with alcohol abuse identified in the coded disorders listed in the International Classification of Diseases (ICD), both male and female 'Natives' in the North American population are excessively afflicted compared with their non-native counterparts.

A study of the observations of friendship centre personnel across Canada, which, among other things, examined substance abuse as a health problem, suggested that 96 per cent of all aboriginal clients using the centres had a substance abuse problem, and most of those with such problems included alcohol abuse (National Association of Friendship Centres, 1985). While friendship centres are typically located in urban or semi-urban sites, the very nature of their programs tends to draw a dispropriationate number of recent migrants from reserves who are making an adjustment to urban life, as well as temporary visitors from reserve locations. The exceptionally high rates of substance abuse cannot be generalized to the First Nations reserve population as a whole, but they are instructive regarding the gender difference issue. The friendship centre personnel are obviously in close contact with a large number of female clients who have alcohol problems. The bias in the estimates may be an artifact of inflation based on the exceptional concerns of the centre administrators or a reflection of the type of clientele coming to the centres. The same study indicated that friendship centre personnel estimate that 76 per cent of pregnant women and 77 per cent of single women who participate in their programs have a substance abuse problem (1985). It is noteworthy that the percentage estimated for substance abusers among the clientele of single women using friendship centre programs is the same as the percentage estimated for the unemployed male clients of the centres.

Another indicator of the fact that problem drinking is widespread among First Nations women is the repeated concern about drinking during pregnancy expressed by physicians and community health workers when asked in key informant interviews that I have conducted in reserve communities. Concern about female drinking during pregnancy has been observed for many years in reserve communities;

in fact, a focus on limiting such drinking as a means of preventing fetal alcohol syndrome disorder (FASD) has been a central feature of community health education programming on reserves for two decades. Community health studies based on self-reports I have conducted have also consistently shown disproportionately high rates of heavy drinking as a feature of First Nations female drinking patterns. Again, those rates tend to be substantially lower than the male rates.

Thus, while the study of female drinking practices in First Nations constitutes a significant gap in the research, a familiarity with contemporary accounts of female drinking among reserve females provides some basis for generalization. It appears that, at least in what is now Canada, the drinking style of Europeans visiting what was to them an 'uncivilized frontier' was adopted by First Nations men involved in meetings, gatherings, and commercial trade with European males. The social, binge-drinking style that was absorbed into First Nations culture from that early interaction with the Europeans may have remained a largely male pursuit as long as indigenous males were actively engaged in traditional economic roles. In those cultures in which the men hunted or fished in groups away from the women, the Elders, and the children of the community, alcohol use was an exclusively male indulgence; in many cases it may even have functioned, like other natural intoxicants, as an important male bonding ritual. However, the destruction of traditional economic roles and the lack of successful reconstitution within the Euro-Canadian society that enveloped the First Nations, destroyed significant aspects of the traditional divisiion of labour that had structured distinctive male and female roles in indigenous communities.

Once the traditional male economic role on reserves began to disintegrate, replaced first by unskilled, seasonal employment, and later by welfare dependency, alcohol problems became a family affair. Shkilnyk's study (1985) of Grassy Narrows in northern Ontario in the 1960s and beyond indicates that, once the trap line no longer comprised the primary source of income for families and the male spent most of his time in the community, alcohol problems increased substantially. As unemployment became the most common economic state of the First Nations male, a variety of social problems escalated, including family violence and adult alcoholism and alcohol abuse. Shkilnyk reported that, in 1978, a community survey of Grassy Narrows indicated that, while 70 per cent of the adult males could be counted as either 'heavy drinkers' or 'very heavy drinkers close to addiction,' 62 per cent of females could be similarly classified. In the younger age groups, specifically fifteen to nineteen years and twenty to twenty-nine years, female problem drinkers actually outnumbered the males (Shkilnyk, 1978: 22).

At least in the latter half of the twentieth century, the drinking party for First Nations people, whether held on a reserve, a residence in a city, or in public drinking establishments, gradually became very much a 'mixed' affair; in fact, such venues became essential meeting grounds for entertainment purposes and for establishing friendships and intimate relationships. Partially in self-defence against the coercive elements of male behaviour during and after drinking episodes, and partly to socialize in an enjoyable fashion within their own social network, women were drawn into much the same reckless drinking style as men.

It is my experience in western Canada that, today, in small towns near reserves and in the 'Indian bars' in cities, one often witnesses an equivalent ratio of female and male patrons. Professional colleagues of mine report similar impressions in cities throughout the country that have bars frequented by aboriginals.

Female problem drinking within the First Nations population thus reflects a sort of 'sociological folie à deux'; it is a combined product of sharing social binge-drinking episodes with males and reacting defensively to the negative personal and familial impact of male drinking. 'Folie à deux' is a psychiatic term used to refer to a particular form of induced psychotic disorder, in which the delusional thinking and dysfunctional behaviour of a dominant personality is assumed, absorbed as it were, into the psyche and behavioural patterns of a second party in close, ongoing contact with the dominant party (Kaplan and Sadock, 1991). When I refer to a 'sociological folie à deux' I am, with admitted conceptual imprecision, borrowing and adapting the psychiatric concept and directing its application to an entire set of relations between genders. It appears that exceptional problem drinking rates among First Nation males were transferred to the female population through close association with the males.

13. *Disproportionate numbers of First Nations people have not acquired sufficient 'stakes in sobriety' to enter the career track trajectory that normatively shapes the life cycle of non-aboriginal Canadians and the aboriginal economic elite.*

In mainstream Canadian society, the high-risk drinking styles of youth normally give way to low-risk drinking and binge drinking episodes decrease in frequency as opportunities are opened up and material and social rewards and obligations expand. This status curve functions to motivate and at the same time limit the time available for the average Canadian to engage in problem drinking; it is society's normal buffer against long-term excess drinking and drunken comportment. A tragic consequence of the economic history of aboriginal peoples in Confederation has been that this normative career trajectory does not come into play for the majority of people in First Nations reserve communities.

Both traditional and market economies provide a complex and many-faceted system of incentives for individual members to participate actively in the development and management of the basic institutions through which community affairs operate. Participation in the operation of these institutions also serves to create the personal empowerment and normative social control structure that provides the basis for social order in the community. Reserve communities are characterized by neither traditional, subsistence production nor market economies; instead, they have been developed and managed as dependent client mini-states by neo-colonial federal government administrations. This situation offers few incentives for the individual to acquire the type of cognitive and behavioural mind-set that encourages what psychologists refer to as *self-efficacy* (Bandura, 1982). Yet it is this very psychological characteristic that problem drinking researchers suggest is the key to preventing and overcoming problem drinking patterns, as well as the key to avoiding relapse. Self-efficacy is the personal belief that one is primarily in control of one's own behaviour. This self-control includes fending off the temptation to take too many drinks in the face of social pressures and situational cues.

It is normative in North America for abusive drinking comportment to decline with the obligations and rewards that expand with age: society offers the individual an increasing set of sobriety incentives, or 'stakes in conformity.' Excessive drinking leading to impairment and, to varying degrees, risk-taking lifestyles in which alcohol is implicated, is normal for young North Americans of all races, with greater indulgence being sanctioned socially for males. This does not mean that such a norm is applauded, or that it is necessarily a statistical norm (i.e., that the majority of youth and young adults are problem drinkers). It only repeats the common observation that such behaviour is *expected* and, except for its more serious criminal excesses, quickly forgotten and forgiven as 'part of being young.'

It is also normative for excessive drinking and reckless, antisocial drinking behaviour to decline with age. The principal factor influencing the normative decline of problem drinking among Canadians and Americans is the expansion until retirement age of role obligations, rights, and financial rewards associated with an *upward social status curve* that begins early in adolescence and drops off dramatically for most at retirement. This curve inclines upward according to the heightening of role authority and the expansion of the absolute number of role positions available to the individual in the social structure. The available system of obligations and rewards, including increased income and the acquisition of material possessions, especially private home ownership, associated with a social career on this status curve involves a substantial investment of ego, time, and money and results in significant returns of material benefits and pride. These benefits serve as a prophylactic against the continuation throughout life of high-risk drinking and other self-destructive and antisocial deviant behaviours that invite negative social sanctions. The concept of 'stakes in sobriety' is a variation of American sociologist Jackson Toby's concept of 'stakes in conformity' (1957).

Toby notes that, in North America, an upper-class white Anglo-Saxon Protestant schoolchild is heavily favoured to have a high stake in conformity. Why? If that child comes from a 'good family,' lives in a 'respectable' neighbourhood, has teachers who like him or her, and gets good marks in school, moving easily from grade to grade, s/he is acquiring a reasonable basis for anticipating future achievements. Expecting to complete college and to take up a professional, technical, or business career, s/he has everything to look forward to. If that child applied the same energies to delinquency and experimenting with solvents, drugs, and alcohol, s/he would risk not only the ego-flattering rewards that s/he is currently receiving, but his or her future prospects as well.

It is often argued that the development of high stakes in conformity is not entirely related to social class or ethnicity. Jews and Asians, for example, despite their marginality at the point of initial immigration and the overt prejudice they have faced in North America and Europe, have fared extremely well in terms of educational performance, professional employment, and business. However, unlike the people of Canada's First Nations, Asian and Jewish populations lived in agricultural, semi-industrial, or industrial societies and many were already specialists in crafts, certain businesses, and trade and had a history of the demanding work ethic associated with those occupations.

As Toby observes, in the case of the Jews, social ascent was also rooted in generations of religious learning. In the New World, this faith was simply transferred to the educational system; thus a commitment to conformity paid off in the form of occupational advancement. It is also important to note that the European economy was fuelled by both a formal educational system originally linked to the church and the Protestant ethic, which grounded the pursuit of material goods through business and employment in a set of religious values. European, Jewish, and Asian cultures had also produced mutual aid concepts adapted to the needs of agricultural, village, and industrial economies. Through extended family networks and formalized voluntary associations, church activities and group insurance arrangements, these newcomers were able to protect themselves against the vicissitudes of cyclical economic activity ('boom and bust') and the strong ethnic prejudices of the mainstream white settler society largely drawn from Northern Europe and dominated by immigrants from the British Isles.

People in reserve communities, in contrast, have never entirely embraced formal education as a highly ranked local priority. Much like their attitudes towards the police, community attitudes towards schooling in First Nation communities is often marked by bipolar attitudes, with need and acceptance at one extreme and suspicion and rejection at the other. The revelations of sexual, physical, and emotional abuse in residential schools has done little to encourage First Nations people to embrace education as a cultural priority. This is a significant buttress to inebriety: the relevant research literature presents a relatively consistent correlation between level of completed formal education and sober lifestyles.

In summary, as figure 10.1 depicts, the disproportionate frequency of destructive behaviours and habits associated with drinking beliefs among First Nations peoples can best be explained by the interaction of historic causal and contemporary sustaining factors.

Summary

This chapter has argued that, in mainstream Canadian society, the youthful pleasures and functions of alcohol excess and its associated uninhibited behaviours are normally phased out as adults secure a place on and, over time, ascend, a social status curve in which material and social rewards reduce the opportunities and motivation for high-

Figure 10.1 Upward social status curve: Schematic depiction of how normative role expansion crowds out problem drinking and creates stakes in sobriety

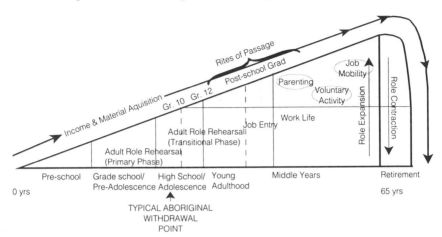

risk drinking. That curve is plotted in a rising time line synchronized with education and age; it rises and then declines with the approach of one's senior years. Historical and socio-political realities have tended to exclude the majority of First Nations people from that normative social status trajectory. Thus the barriers to continued alcohol abuse that deflect adults in mainstream society from long-term problem drinking do not exist for disproportionate numbers of aboriginal people. Consequently, the problem drinking patterns of youth all too often crystallize into a long-term 'Indian drinking style' that abides through middle age. The firewater complex, a reified entity, makes that style seem inevitable; the disease model is now part of that reification.

11

Governmental and Community Reinforcement of the Firewater Complex

I have argued in preceding chapters that the generative conditions for exceptional rates of alcohol abuse in First Nations grew out of a specific pattern of interaction with early European explorers, traders, and workers and the limited purposes, modest ambitions, lack of enthusiasm, and flawed efforts of the federal government to establish effective economic integration and development policies with First Nations. High alcohol abuse rates have been one of several troubling outcomes of the colonialism of the French and British and, later, the neo-colonialism of the Canadian state (neo-colonialism is a term used to signify a continuing legacy of colonialism, typically with governance and service delivery functions delegated to local leadership by a colonizing, external leadership).

Oppressive conditions expressed as social problems are not static; they wither, are sustained, or increase in response to ongoing social pressures. The needs and intentions of superordinating groups can change over time, and rare is the case in which a person, a group, or a society is simply a victim of the oppression or exploitation of others. The motivations, interests, and negotiating capacities of the oppressed are also dynamic, changing in place and time. It has been the error of much social theory guided by progressive intent to treat the oppressed simply as passive receptors of social influences, to consider their behaviour only as a dependent variable, subject to the shifting of external, causal factors: the intelligence, creativity, even foibles and weaknesses of their subjectivity is thus lost. In the reality of human affairs, victims relate intersubjectively with perpetrators; they engage actively with their victimizers in conceptualizing, resisting, challenging, succumbing, accommodating, and in various other ways viewing and objectively shaping the nature of their own oppression. In the case of an entire group of victims, internal divisions often arise as a result of alliances formed by local power-brokers with oppressors, especially when these alliances yield substantial benefits for the power-brokers.

This chapter sets out to determine whether other social forces currently sustain the firewater complex in reserve communities. Challenging the opinion that no one benefits in sustaining the firewater complex, an attempt is made to identify factors both external and internal to reserve communities that reinforce the firewater complex in the limited sense of its meaning, namely, a problematic, drinking culture. The broader implications of the firewater complex are also examined, and further attention is given to the argument that the complex has encouraged an entire way of thinking about and responding collectively to social problems in First Nations.

As described above, in its limited form the firewater complex is a tacitly accepted, emotionally charged drinking style engaged in by First Nations people who have been socialized in reserve cultures. That style is reinforced by the firewater myth which assumes, erroneously, that First Nations people are constitutionally predisposed to alcohol cravings, incapable of moderate consumption, and especially given to impulsive, often destructive behaviour during bouts of intoxication. Further, that same fatalistic belief functions to excuse the destructive impacts of the misbehaviour of First Nations people during and immediately after bouts of intoxication.

The broader meaning of the firewater complex involves the overextension of the disease metaphor; it refers to the tendency to assume First Nations people must be treated as being distinctive and virtually powerless in their vulnerability to a steady stream of cultural intrusions from the larger society. This broader meaning leads, ironically, to a demand for therapeutic solutions imported from the same external source of cultural intrusions. Inadvertently, the solutions demanded are targeted on purportedly personal and pathological troubles requiring external intervention rather than on personal empowerment and social change. Understood in this broader context, the firewater complex encourages a problem-solving stance that views First Nations people as victims only, incapable of self-directed change.

First Nations people on reserves have become economically and socially stranded, frozen in a sort of development warp through what some writers have referred to as the 'deviancy-processing' industry (see Spitzer, 1975; Thatcher, 1986). That 'industry' emphasizes the social control of economically marginal populations and short-term fiscal savings rather than adequate developmental investments in the participation of marginalized people in advanced sectors of economic activity. For First Nations, substantial investment is needed to support a comprehensive and consistent macro-policy of multifaceted educational support, assisted economic development, resource sharing, and generous and active economic partnerships with various sectors of mainstream society.

Protectionist Public Policy Sustains the Discredited Firewater Theory

Even a cursory examination of federal policy towards First Nations reveals a fundamental paternalism, an expectation of inferiority rather than capacity. Originally, the design of Canada's national policy was exploitative, focused on setting First Nations aside as an obstacle to modernization. Once that initial goal was achieved, the newly established federal government's policy towards 'Indians' came to reflect an institutionalized, ethnocentric sense of stewardship. In relation to alcohol abuse issues, that attitude has been reflected in protectionist policies. As we have seen, until the early 1960s, Status Indians were prohibited from drinking by law. After the late 1970s, programming to provide direct services was implemented that, again, assumed that First Nations people were especially vulnerable to alcohol. In keeping with the mainstream influences in the addictions field of the time, it was also assumed, uncritically, that large numbers of First Nations people were 'alcoholics.' Influenced by the disease concept of treatment, the prevailing approach to alcoholism in treatment programs assumed that the problem was caused by a genetic predisposition, even though the scrutiny of science had discredited that very notion. Mounting evidence was showing that alcoholism was largely attributable to learning and contextual factors, even if genetic predisposition was a risk factor. By recruiting personnel schooled in Alcoholics Anonymous views and the disease model for prevention and treatment positions in First Nations, the genetic suppositions of the firewater theory were inadvertently reactivated. The firewater myth was thus resuscitated and, with little opposition, became entrenched in the alcohol services provided to reserve residents.

Permanent Clients Rather Than Economic Partners

Rather than being full partners in the Canadian economy, greatly disproportionate numbers of socially and economically dislocated First

Nations people have instead become, by default, a population of 'permanent clients.' The majority of First Nations people have in various ways become dependent for basic income and fundamental problem solving on what the American political scientist Andrew Polsky (1993) has referred to as 'social personnel:' social workers, probation officers, parole officers, psychologists, and alcohol treatment program personnel who perform surveillance and therapeutic roles.

As I have stated elsewhere (Thatcher, 1986), when an explanation of aboriginal deviancy is pursued in response to questions about the positive functions of such deviance, one must ask, who benefits? When the problem is cast in these terms, there are some very real ways in which aboriginal deviance offers functional support to specific beneficiaries of the economic organization of the status quo.

> The application of deviant labels to a [marginal] group by official agencies of social control ... has the consequence of discrediting any claims that group might make for a larger share of the material and social benefits of the society. The discrediting of the relevant subgroups is accomplished through the development and general dissemination of reputedly 'scientific' explanations of the different types of deviancy found in the marginal population and the deviancy of other ethnic or nationality groups. The social science community creates the relevant labels, computes the deviancy rates and puts the signature of academic repute on those theories which explain minority group deviancy as originating with the minority group itself rather than from within the larger sociopolitical system ... A residual effect of deviancy-processing is that members of the problem population, having been exposed to the same mass communication system as the general population, tend to internalize a negative self-concept. (Thatcher, 1986: 287–8)

Instead of gaining occupational titles, a vastly disproportionate number of First Nations members have been officially stamped with such disreputable labels as 'violent offender,' 'negligent parent,' and 'alcoholic.' These labels potentially transform them into likely candidates for admission to correctional, mental health, and alcohol and drug abuse treatment programs. In the past decade and a half, the DCT for alcohol problems has been substantially expanded to address a variety of social problems. Linguistically enhanced by a growing body of new labels for ill-health, the firewater complex is now supported by an extensive glossary of disorders. These chronic pathologies demand the intervention of therapists, counsellors and even Traditional Healers. Not only alcohol abuse but also 'co-dependency,' gambling, family violence, anxiety and depression related to social conditions, anger, rage, and 'lateral violence' (too much gossip) cry out for therapeutic intervention, and even the personal legacy of residential school abuse is described as a 'syndrome' that can be corrected with therapies that assume the 'dysfunctionality' of the person or his or her family system.

Of course, personal and family problems often need or can at least benefit from counselling intervention, intervention requires diagnosis, and diagnosis demands clinical labelling, so we must live with the labelling process: as the saying goes, it is a 'necessary evil.' Those who remind us of the need for diagnostic labelling suggest that the potentially destructive by-products of labelling an individual or a group as being 'prone to' a genetic, psychological, or cultural malaise are usually justified by the person's pressing need for good advice and intensive therapy. Admittedly, there are often times when the assistance of good counsel is priceless. Unfortunately, all too often, a profound mischief is committed: the labelling process convinces not only officialdom and public opinion but the victims of social conditions themselves that the solutions to social problems lie primarily in a normalizing process assisted by professional helpers or other organized 'self-helpers.' In my opinion this entire understanding and approach to problem solving has resulted in a significant reduction in the self-esteem, self-confidence, and social competence of many if not a majority of reserve residents.

As described in the previous chapter, the key attribute of a socially and personally healthy human being is captured in the concept of 'self-efficacy' (Bandura, 1982), an attribute which informed observers of reserve communities consistently report to be in substantial deficit. Self-efficacy refers to a confident belief in a personal ability to make effective, autonomous choices in most of the important areas of basic living. A therapeutic orientation that assumes pathology, damage, and victimization as the most fundamental attribute of an entire community of people can work to undermine rather than enhance that confidence.

Therapeutic approaches to social problems, if dominant, are essentially a contradiction in terms: they offer individualized solutions to socially generated problems that require social intervention. Yet this is the major thrust in the alcohol abuse and mental health programming serving First Nations people on reserves. Paradoxically, the dominance of the therapeutic approach to this social problem completes a victimization-dependency-victimization cycle. Dependents with significant problems are convinced by ostensible helpers that they are victims who must therefore rely on others (often including the ostensible helpers) to help them overcome their victimization, inadvertently making them more dependent. The victims adapt to and become comfortable with their dependency and gradually lose confidence in their own capacity for achieving the standard of independence and social and economic fulfilment that is prized in the larger society. The victims adapt to and do not seek to transcend their dependency; in fact, they come to defend their dependent status on the grounds that they have been wronged in the past, thus becoming locked into perpetual dependency, relative poverty, and marginal status in the larger society.

Every bit as insidious as the undermining of the self-efficacy of an impoverished population at the personal level is the shift in thinking that takes place at the policy development level as a result of this therapeutic emphasis in social problem solving. By emphasizing personal problem solving aimed at behavioural normalization, governments, community leaders, and even community members are relieved of the challenge to change the very social conditions that originally nourished and continue to nourish the creation and growth of social problems. Even if the immediate problems are solved and the interventions work, they are only curative; they do not address the larger, systemic factors that produce high social problem rates. The dilemma is easily understood via the example of an automobile manufacturer who honours the warrantee requirements of its sales agreements and, upon demand, pays for its service affiliates to fix a flaw in the steering of all car owners who come forward for repairs, but refuses to change the manufacturing process that caused the flaw. The result is that, while some of the cars that needed repair get fixed, more flawed vehicles follow behind as outputs from the production line. Some of the problems are rectified at the individual unit level, but collective or systemic problems are ignored, despite their much more significant impact.

Admittedly, there have been various governmental attempts since the late 1960s to right the wrongs of past injustices. A variety of new programs, vast increases in dedicated expenditures, and a formal apology for residential school abuse must be credited as legitimate attempts to compensate for the historic inattention and lack of commitment to the needs of First Nations demonstrated by Canada's governing and economic elites. However, to enlist a tired cliché, these policies and programs have been too little, too late.

Since Confederation, federal expenditure allocations mushroomed, especially in recent decades. A review of Canada's public accounts reveals that, in 1882, the entire federal budget for 'Indian' allocations was approximately $1 million; in 1966, the combined band support funding paid out through Indian and Northern Affairs Canada (INAC) and Health and Welfare Canada's Medical Services Branch funding was $80 million, while current spending is approximately $6.5 billion annually – and that does not include extensive provincial expenditures paid out in support of First Nations. Taking inflation into account, real spending per capita on First Nations people rose from $7,289 in 1991 to $8,479 in 2002 (Milke, 2002). Yet fundamental structural impediments to mainstream workforce and business participation remain. The entire support system focuses primarily on reserves and a geographically fixed, non-mobile labour force, despite the fact that, on most reserves, employment needs far exceed local demands and well over half of First Nations people now live off-reserve. It is as if reserve populations are being paid a guaranteed annual income as 'hush money' to restrict their demands for improvements that lie 'outside the box.' That box is virtually owned and maintained by the existing federal 'Indian Affairs' action paradigm that assumes as a given that the continuance of national obligations to First Nations is largely restricted to providing services to residential tracts on reserve settlements, despite the fact that very few of these reserves have the potential for economic viability.

Routinely destructive, highly dependent behaviour patterns, of which addictions represent one type, thrive in social conditions in which individual responsibility and local control have been evacuated through the coercive relocation of power and authority to the hands of external agencies. This is not a condition unique to aboriginal communities in Canada; it is characteristic of minority populations whose lands have been colonized, whose economic functions have been displaced by competing labour pools or more advanced, labour-substitutive technologies, and whose basic social institutions have come to be regulated by the governments of the colonizing classes. As Saggers and Gray (1998) have observed, the alcohol abuse patterns characteristic of Canada's first peoples are remarkably similar to those of the Maoris of New Zealand and Aborigines of Australia. So critical to indigenous substance misuse patterns is the link between current patterns of leadership functioning, social hierarchy, and the selection of addictions program personnel that the entire subject demands an extended analysis, which this chapter is intended to provide.

The Reserve System as a Social Control Infrastructure for the Segregation and Therapeutic Colonization of First Nations

The social and economic segregation of most reserve communities from the mainstream economy and the deprivation characteristic of the reserves themselves has created for First Nations people a sense of profound distance from Canadian society. Reserve residents tend to view themselves as living in communities that are unique and socially distant from the settlements of their non-aboriginal neighbours. The reserve reality exists as 'another solitude,' separate from neighbouring, non-aboriginal communities and society at large. This other solitude is comprised of culturally marginalized populations bereft of the economic foundations of their own original lifestyles yet not assimilated to the Euro-Canadian cultural mainstream. Residents tend to live out their lives on reserves not sufficiently large or geographically situated to the type of exchange relationship with the market economy that could even potentially support them.

As dramatic altercations in recent years between provincial and Canadian law enforcement agencies and First Nations people at the communities of Kahnawake, Kanasatake, in 1990[1] and later, at Ipperwash and Burnt Church, have illustrated, a militant, contracultural response lurks just beneath the surface in many First Nations communities. From a state perspective, that potential for rebellion calls for a strategy that will ensure a sufficient level of social order to allow the routine operations of the mainstream economy, polity, and society as a whole to function without major disruption. The federal solution has been to select reserve populations as the primary target of a massive, multidimensional social control policy. The pillars of that policy are a welfare system that virtually operates as a guaranteed annual income system, a social housing

---

1 In March 1990, Mohawk residents and allied First Nations people, all of whom referred to themselves as 'Warriors,' erected a barricade at Kanasatake, near Oka, Quebec, in protest against the commercial development of lands they claimed were their own. The protest turned into an armed stand-off between the Kanasatake Warriors and the police, and a wave of protests by aboriginal people and their supporters took place across the country. The Mercier Bridge, a vital link to Montreal for tens of thousands of daily commuters from Chateaugay, was closed as an act of support by members of the nearby Mohawk reserve of Kahanawake. Hostilities escalated and riots ensued. While the protesters surrendered on 26 September of the same year, the Mohawks had clearly and widely publicized their claims that they were a sovereign nation.

program, fully supported physical infrastructure, and a repetitive out-
lay of program funding aimed at developing community-based, 'culturally sensitive' approaches to helping 'dysfunctional' individuals and
families to 'normalize.' Sizeable band administration funding gener-
ously supports a local economic, political, and administrative elite and
provides governments with a convenient system of single-table bargain-
ing with individual reserves and with groups of reserves joined in tribal
councils and other forms of federation. The allocations to reserves provide the most obvious proof of this paradox. An examination of much of
the programming in recent decades reveals that, with the exception of
land entitlement settlement moneys, expenditures on social assistance,
basic community services, and therapeutic assistance dwarf economic
development investment efforts that link community development
efforts to the realities of the wider economy and society. Apparently
there is simply more public pressure, both non-aboriginal and aboriginal, on the federal government to emphasize a social control approach
centred on the maintenance of reserves than to take a more challenging,
creative, and aggressive approach to economic integration.

The reserve system was originally conceived as an 'incubator' for the
economic integration of First Nations.[2] Paradoxically it has instead
become both a symbol of the failure of Canada's 'Indian policy' and a
solution to containing at least a significant number of First Nations
people within an institutionalized environment that pacifies the residents by meeting basic needs. Unfortunately, that same reserve system
condemns reserve residents to what amounts to guaranteed, multigenerational poverty. Compared with statistical norms for Canadians, off-
reserve band members do not thrive – at least according to commonly
accepted quality of life indicators. However, for at least two decades,
off-reserve band members fare better than their on-reserve counterparts on such measures as education and employment.

The shape and administration of the basic institutional life of First
Nations has been based upon external decision making for so long that

---

2 Buckley (1993) argues that western reserves were settled as part of a larger assimilation policy, 'originally envisaged as a staging ground' for that strategy (11). The
  reserve concept, at first glance, seems reasonable enough. Buckley notes that reserves
  were supposed to serve as an incubator for protecting and preparing a people for
  entering the cultural and economic mainstream of the emerging society. But as Buckley's book suggests, an inadequate and often weak and faltering commitment led to
  highly detrimental outcomes for the western reserve residents.

ordinary band members have become habituated to it. They have come to accept as normal an extreme psychological and social powerlessness in relation to both their personal affairs and the management of their communities.

It is true that the gradual transfer of local administrative authority from the federal government to First Nations government councils has accelerated in recent years. Services and programs such as schools, housing maintenance and construction, health services, alcohol and drug abuse counselling, and the maintenance of roads, garbage collection, water supplies, and sewage have all been transferred to local or joint band administration structures. Yet these are 'programs,' each provided, like social assistance, in response to the needs of people who are presumed not to have the ability to secure any of these services on their own. And of course the cruel irony is the nature of the truth behind this presumption: on the limited, marginal lands that most reserves occupy, there are few alternatives to government transfers mediated by a local power elite. Indicators of the profound dependency witnessed by this writer in approximately two decades of active involvement in community health studies on reserves include the following:

- Social assistance rather than employment is the primary source of income for the majority of First Nations families. But social assistance is increasingly understood as constituting a treaty right rather than a form of temporary relief from unemployment when jobs cannot be found.
- The lack of economic incentives to husband and protect local resources leads to some bizarre outcomes. Thus, local fire trucks on many reserves are often housed in unlocked garages, are not maintained, and are often vandalized. While formal, multiyear health service transfer agreements have demanded emergency response plans, many reserve communities that have signed the agreements have never developed such plans. Emergency response planning requires specific, certified training for volunteers. In non-aboriginal communities, if a certified ERP capacity cannot be formally demonstrated, insurance rates go sky high, insurance eventually lapses, and local tax rates spiral. Citizens and local leaders consequently make sure an ERP capacity is in place. On many reserves, there is no equivalent incentive and thus there is no ERP capacity.
- Independently owned houses are almost non-existent on most

reserves. Because band governments rather than individual residents own reserve houses, band members have no way of acquiring what is typically the most significant personal, convertible asset of most non-aboriginal Canadians. There is little to motivate responsible maintenance of such property, and reserve homes tend to have approximately half the life span of the average non-reserve home. While the quality of housing has gradually improved in First Nations communities over the years, largely owing to better, more hardy construction, the general level of householder upkeep on most reserves remains visibly poor. Renovation is currently believed to be the responsibility of the band administration rather than the householder, while the supply of housing is believed to be wholly the responsibility of the federal government, provided in the form of band loan programs run by Canada Mortgage and Housing Corporation or grants from INAC. Band members play virtually no role in the construction of their own housing and have come to see housing as a right, independent of personal investment. When housing issues are discussed, the option of private construction is no longer a serious consideration: new housing means new government funding for materials and labour.

- Independently owned businesses are rare on reserves, with most people securing almost all of their food, clothing, shelter, and recreation needs from off-reserve vendors, and very few band businesses have been successfully developed. Only the larger reserves and reserves close to cities or in possession of a rich natural resource have been able to establish and sustain band-owned or band partnership-based businesses.
- Voluntarism is normally considered an essential building block of a healthy community. While mutual aid between friends and families remains extensive in reserve communities, formally organized voluntary activities have become so rare that many band observers indicate that, unless the reserve administration pays people to facilitate or host community activities, the activities simply will not occur. Even AA meetings are not sustained on many reserves unless a paid worker acts as facilitator – a development which contradicts the fundamental self-help principle of the organization. Elders, band staff, and band leaders frequently complain that voluntarism is virtually a forgotten practice. The turnout for band meetings is embarrassingly small, unless there is a key issue involving a matter of personal, material interest to members. At important meetings band staff are

often ordered to attend to create the illusion of participation, and most or all of the participants in community health workshops are frequently band staff rather than the general band membership. Some leaders resort to paying band members to attend at band meetings, and it has become the norm in many reserve communities to pay members for participation on committees that would be considered voluntary activities off-reserve. Community health workers from many communities have complained during interviews that members of band councils and community committees virtually demand payment for every meeting they attend, regardless of whether they contribute a single word to the proceedings. Elders are now routinely paid for their participation in community affairs and often that participation involves nothing more than attendance or a prayer offered at the outset – and despite the fact that paying for such blessings is considered a sacrilege by many traditionalists. When there is no payment for committees, band leaders complain that there is no participation. In recent years, this norm has sometimes extended to staff, who are often paid amounts over and above salary reimbursement during work time for their committee work, even though that work is often a simple extension of their job, or even written into their job descriptions.

- When significant problems among youth arise, from teen pregnancies to gang violence, band members almost automatically tend to view solutions as lying primarily with the police, health professionals, the schools, outside experts, and the chief and council. Personal responsibility and initiative, parental obligation to dependent adolescents, family action, and voluntary community organization are not considered. A tragic example of this attribution of blame and allocation of ameliorative responsibility to external agency is the problem of underage sex-trade workers. The typical lack of remedial response to this issue from reserve administrations indicates that the issue is regarded as a family rather than a community problem, or a problem of off-reserve, urban agencies rather than a matter requiring band services and band leadership, even if the teens have an ongoing attachment, however erratic, to a reserve family.
- On many reserves, the most basic maintenance of plumbing, garbage stands, or roadways across land allotments to houses is considered by many residents to be the sole responsibility of band maintenance staff rather than their own. I have listened to numerous complaints from disgruntled maintenance staff about residents who

refuse even to unplug a toilet or hire a commercial plumber to clean up a sewer back-up if a reserve maintenance worker is not available.

• Reserve residents tend to overuse medical services, turning to physicians even for very minor ailments. In some communities I studied, annual physician service utilization is over 95 per cent of the population fifteen years and over. Admittedly, this level of consultation with physicians might be an indicator of a healthy, preventive approach to medical care utilization. Unfortunately, the physicians I interviewed in community health surveys have consistently suggested that such consultations are rarely for preventive purposes. Key informant surveys regularly indicate that, compared to the non-aboriginal population, preventive consultations such as regular check-ups for children and adults and early dental examinations for children are relatively infrequent among reserve health care clients. Acute care dominates physician and physician-referred health care services in First Nations. Emergency services to treat the results of accidents or person-to-person injuries, acute hospital care for chronic and life-threatening diseases, medications to relieve emotional pain: these are the disproportionately allocated services rendered by health care workers serving First Nations. This type of physician use is an indicator that, at least in personal and health care, reserve populations tend to be exceptionally governed by an external locus of control, a strong indicator of unhealthy dependency. Community surveys consistently indicate that any health service that must be paid for out of pocket is typically spurned by First Nations people. The federal government reimburses Status Indians for the costs of all services covered under Medicare by provincial governments; this includes not only physician consultations and procedures but also services directly linked to medical referrals, such as physiotherapy, drugs, and the provision of eyeglasses and prosthetic devices. However, personally chosen rather than physician-referred services, such as chiropractic adjustments; health-related activities or materials such as personal exercise programs; nutritional aids such as megavitamin supplements; and naturopathic remedies tend not to feature in the health product consumption in First Nations. Various observers of reserve life have told me that if a health-promoting service or a product has to be paid for out of pocket, reserve residents will rarely even consider it.

Cumulatively, this evidence of dependency points to the fact that the economic role of far too many First Nations adults in the Canadian economy has been reduced to that of simply a *public service consumer*. In place of the fully productive economic roles that were characteristic of traditional lifestyles, a role vacuum has been created.

Private production of goods and services through the type of businesses and non-profit community organizations typical of local economies surrounding reserves is virtually absent or very modestly developed on most reserves. As discussed above, the most significant factor contributing to this situation was the failure of federal 'Indian' policies throughout the first half of the twentieth century to secure the long-term participation of First Nations people in primary production, such as modern agriculture and mineral extraction. As the Canadian economy developed and became increasingly industrialized and urbanized, the lack of access of most reserves to urban centres and manufacturing and service industry work sites left First Nation males on reserves dependent upon a casual, seasonal labour market in the area surrounding the reserves. (The central Canadian reserves close to major metropolitan centres and oil-rich centres were exceptions, of course.) As the twentieth century moved through its first quarter and into its middle years, the mechanization of agriculture and logging and the shift to trades-based mining resulted in the virtual elimination of demand for unskilled, aboriginal labour. Education, language, and skill deficits were the primary obstacles, but racial discrimination was also often a significant impediment to both rural and urban employment for First Nations people.

In effect, social assistance became the primary economic strategy for addressing reserve unemployment in the 1950s. The introduction of the welfare system on reserves in those years, and of the needs-based eligibility system in the late 1960s as part of the Canada Assistance Plan, resulted in massive dependency. Previously, the more rigorously tested means-assessed welfare approach for unemployed employables had exerted greater demands for reserve residents to pursue work opportunities. Welfare payments simply surpassed the limited incomes that could be gained through the application of the traditional skill sets or menial contemporary skills possessed by the males of First Nations and the incentive to follow any traditional pursuits or casual labour consequently disappeared. Tragically, long-term and multi generational dependency became the common remedy for high levels of reserve unemployment. Welfare was no longer relief; it provided a steady income. The shared participation in ownership, jobs, and profits from agriculture and natural resource production that was no doubt envisioned by the First Nations leaders who signed the treaties was never pursued with sufficient commitment by federal politicians. Consequently, the foundation was created for a system which, once created, reinforced dependency on externally generated income, authorities, and technical expertise rather than serving to truly empower communities.

The social reforms of the post-1960s era did result in the continuous expansion of on-reserve infrastructure improvement and public service programs that responded, however modestly, to virtually all basic needs. Yet the reserves are typically situated at much too great a distance from centres of economic activity sufficiently robust to permit a market-oriented development strategy. Development strategies broadly targeted on the real opportunities in the wider economy were and are fundamental to success. Thus the only basis for establishing a system of significant economic development incentives responsive to real market conditions has been largely ignored; instead, on-reserve development of housing and community services has been the primary focus of reserve development expenditures. The result has been nothing less than a socio-economic catastrophe.

It might be countered that the administrative transfers currently heralded as the 'slow but sure march towards self-government' signal a reversal of the neo-colonial, paternalistic relationship that for so long defined the interface between the federal government and First Nations. However, many observers who are part of or close to First Nation communities firmly believe that, unless far more ambitious capacity-building processes accompany these administrative transfers, the outcomes will best be described as a substitution of brown (or 'brownish red') local faces for white faces in the administration of the same 'programs' that keep reserves operating as client mini-states – an outcome that is clearly undesirable!

First Nations people are not alone in their fate. North American society appears to have created a permanent social rung comprised of those who live in geographic and social locations characterized by low incomes, multigenerational unemployment, permanent welfare dependence and a cluster of unpleasant social problems, coercive social relationships, extensive juvenile gang activity, and widespread personal addictions. Living as virtual outcasts at the margins of a society in which the gap between the affluent and the poor is widening, First Nations people tend to share the fate of a growing number of North Americans who have been redundant to the labour needs of the market economy for more than one generation. The economic displacement of millions of unskilled, semi-skilled, and skill-outmoded workers through technological change and the transfer of labour demand to lower wage countries has resulted in the creation of an enormous welfare class, typically drawn from the 'visible minorities' (Wilson, 1987; Kazemipur and Halli, 2000).

The Role of the 'Firewater Complex' in the Maintenance of the On-/Off-Reserve Divide in the Reserve Class Structure

How is the social organization of the reserve system implicated in the social control of the people victimized by the socio-economic marginalization process described above? Several writers have encouraged a critical examination of the establishment of a social class structure on reserves and the implications of that structure for community development and population health. Satzewich and Wotherspoon (1993), Loughran (1990), and Hull (2001) have separately argued that social class structuration has become a critical dynamic in aboriginal affairs. Thus, Loughran has argued that reserve economies are dominated by a 'social welfare mode of production' built around the securing of government funds and their allocation within the reserve to provide for basic necessities for the reserve inhabitants (1990). In Loughran's view, the political and managerial class have virtual ownership of the means of production through their control of the main economic flows.

Boldt has observed that, traditionally, First Nations leaders were servants of their people (1993: 120). However, under the administration and political structures imposed on the First Nations by the Department of Indian and Northern Affairs and Northern Development, local leadership was essentially assigned governance and administrative authorities and responsibilities. At least partly growing out of the original 'leading families' selected by Indian agents to act as 'role models for assimilation,' an elite class has been created that forms a recruitment pool for band government positions. Those who were selected were socialized into the values, principles, and norms consistent with those of DIAND officials. Political and economic favouritism was given to specific families who were willing to ally with the government. By channelling essential goods and services to bands through their leading families, non-aboriginal Canadian officials were able to subvert resistant, traditional leadership and create a social foundation for a more compliant reserve local elite.

The imposition of semi-colonial administrative systems on First Nation communities was also a major influence in transforming traditional leadership into a ruling class system in band and tribal communities. When the government began to hire local people to perform clerical and paraprofessional functions, they tended to recruit from among the leading families and their descendants. It can be convincingly argued that a local class structure grew up around this system. A strong case can also be made for the view that at the apex of local reserve power structures is a 'comprador' elite, a group which receives special powers, authorities, and benefits by acting in ways that are primarily consistent with the needs of external economic interests rather than local interests.

Using Manitoba data, Jeremy Hull (2001) has described a social class structure in reserve populations that extends off-reserve and into cities. Hull interprets his data to suggest that a 'new class' of elected leaders and senior administrators constitute a permanent political and economic elite on reserves. According to Hull, the class structure also includes a small social class comprising business owners and self-employed workers, a working class, and a class that consists of non-participants in the workforce (Hull, 2001). The non-participants living on reserves are significantly less likely to be employed than the non-participant class off-reserve.

The new class is also firmly committed to the maintenance of development policies focused almost exclusively on the reserves, which is not surprising, given that the reserves are targeted as recipients of the vast majority of INAC funding. The folly in this approach is suggested by the fact that, as long ago as 1981, the advantages of urban residency for aboriginal people in such indicators as education was striking and it was apparent that off-reserve Status Indians were faring far better than their on-reserve counterparts. By 1986, the percentage of off-reserve residents with at least a completed high school education was almost double that of on-reserve residents (Whitehead and Hayes, 1998: 95). Off-reserve employment and family income figures were also significantly better than on-reserve figures that same year (see Frideres, 1993: 159–71). According to the 1996 census, 30.6 per cent of off-reserve aboriginals fifteen years and over had some post-secondary education, compared with only 24 per cent of on-reserve residents. According to the same census count, 39.6 per cent of on-reserve residents fifteen years and older were unemployed, compared to 27.1 per cent of those living off-reserve.[3] When, in 1991, the social assistance dependency figure for on-reserve Indians was 41.5 per cent, the same figure for off-reserve Indians was 24.8 per cent (Royal Commission, 1996: 212).

While the powers of this new class are delegated by the federal government, the decision making of at least the chief and council and family and social networks that administer reserves encompasses many of the decisions normally made by the municipal, provincial, and federal levels of Canadian government. The delegated powers to the band councils are thus hardly insignificant.

Band officials have the authority to determine who does and who does not qualify for band housing and a variety of other material benefits, including band jobs, service contracts, membership on boards providing ample travel expenses and honorariums, and funding for post-secondary education. Given the economic dependency on federal cash transfers of most reserves, and the fact that those transfers are not sufficient to provide all band members with the benefits of all program categories, band officials exercise very substantial control over the allocation of basic resources.

Boldt (1993) has made the point that, in those bands once officially considered 'advanced,' local ruling elites have tended to achieve and sustain their privileged status through semi-privatized land holdings. Even in bands without advanced status, a long-standing system of providing 'certificates of possession' to certain leading families created a basis for continued social status. In part, these families have translated their land holdings into political-administrative power, which they have used to protect their land holdings and to ensure that their network of kin secure the greatest benefits in the form of housing, housing renovation, public sector jobs, business contracts, and post-secondary education (Boldt, 1993: 120–32). While elections often turn over the council incumbents, and sometimes small groups or even the entirety of positions on a band council change, real opposition to the reserve elite is relatively rare.

The rewards of the elected segment of reserve leadership are not small. Salary levels have mushroomed in recent years, with many chiefs now often earning more than either mayors of major cities or

---

3 These figures are rounded. They are computed from a CD-ROM purchased from Statistics Canada entitled the *Dimension Series: Portrait of Aboriginal Population in Canada*, based on the 1996 Canada Census.

provincial cabinet ministers, when their income tax advantages are factored in. Information secured from INAC records under the Access to Information Act by the Canadian Taxpayer's Federation indicate that, when the taxation that would normally reduce salaries is added to the salaries that reserve chiefs obtain, the range of annual remuneration runs from a low of $39,443 to $88,369 (Milke, 2002). Some bands have recorded enormous annual salaries for chiefs and band councillors. One report indicated that the chief of the Horse Lake Band in Alberta, with a population of 360 at the time, had a take-home pay of $439,425 in 2001 and two band councillors made just $15,000 less that same year.

Travel expense claims are another source of considerable income for many leaders of First Nations, as many sit on several other band committees and receive honorariums when they attend over and above the basic income from their band support allocation. Chiefs, and sometimes councillors, also sit on tribal councils and some of their committees, regional organizations, and the Assembly of First Nations. Per diems are typically paid for most of these meetings, despite the fact that they usually take place while chiefs and councillors are already being paid what amounts to a salary by their own bands, and travel expenses are usually paid as well. The salaries of chiefs and some councillors are often doubled by these other activities, even though there is frequently little expectation or practice of reporting on the contents and outcomes of meetings to administrative employees or to their general band membership. Technical staff typically undertake the actual research and report preparation for the chiefs and councillors, and they too must therefore be paid.

Not uncommon in recent years are newspaper accounts of protesting reserve residents who have discovered chiefs, councillors, or their extended family members having been paid enormous expense payments for sitting on casino boards, businesses, or as land entitlement trustees. One of the more extravagant cases concerned the former chief and council of the 800-member Saulteaux First Nation near North Battleford, Saskatchewan, who spent $600,000, which was, in that year, more than the entire travel budget for the cabinet of the provincial government, in which the reserve is located (Truscott, 1999). A Toronto *Globe and Mail* report (Cheney, 1998) described in shocking detail how the extremes of the class system played on the Samson Cree Reserve in Alberta. The story was summarized with the heading: 'The money pit:

an Indian band's story. Taxpayers pour millions of dollars into the Samson Cree Reserve. That's good for the well-connected few. But most people live in abject poverty.'

One indicator of the extent to which the governance and administrative elite constitutes a distinctive class is their sheer numbers. An attempt to compare the electoral representation of a Canadian city (Regina) with the leadership numbers of Canada's off-reserve population estimated that First Nations leadership exceeded Regina's fifty-fold. While Regina, with a population of 202,000 people, had thirty-eight elected officials in 2001, including members of Parliament and the provincial legislature, city council, and two school boards, First Nations had an elected leadership of 3,800 strong for a population of 368,556 (Milke, 2002). Stated as ratios, First Nations governance includes one politician per ninety-seven people, while Regina has a politician-to-citizen ratio of 1 to 5,316.

Key informant surveys on reserves have frequently indicated to this writer that contracts for refuse collection, water delivery, and school buses on many reserves are routinely awarded on the basis of family ties rather than a cost-effectiveness comparison. In fact, elected leaders or their spouses will often dominate the driving positions for the local fleet of band transportation vehicles, usually including school buses and medical taxis. In resource-rich bands, substantial businesses such as oil and gas servicing companies that are controlled by the band often turn over with a change of chief and council.

It is clear that substantial power does flow to the top of the class system on reserves; in fact, the reserve elite has so much delegated authority that its members can deny basic human rights to residents who are out of favour with the leading families. Anderssen (1998) has described the notorious example of the resource-rich Sawridge Band's chief and council, who have provided housing on the reserve exclusively to twenty-six direct descendants of one man. They refused to expand the housing inventory to include those outside the family group they favour, and at the time of Andersen's written coverage there were two hundred band members who could not live on the reserve. It was also estimated that the leading family on that reserve controls business assets valued at $85 million (Anderssen, 1998).

Community health studies conducted in reserve communities consistently reveal that substantial numbers of band members believe that hiring choices are typically made on what sociologists call 'particularistic'[4] grounds. Specifically, band members believe that family members and political supporters of current band councils are favoured when it comes to housing allocations, housing renovations, post-secondary education funding, jobs with the band administration, and even consistency of home care service provision. The most socially distant reserve residents and political outsiders are often left without the most basic support. Many believe that band elections essentially revolve around kin alliances and negotiations centred almost entirely on securing scare resources as post-election benefits. While this interpretation may be an exaggeration, there is little doubt that family and personal benefit acquisition is a key to election choices and to post-election policy and resource allocation decisions.

First Nations leadership drawn from the economic elite has obviously not created the class division that places them at the helm of localized power structures. However, the gap in ongoing benefits between them and the majority, especially the most marginalized families, is enormous, and increasingly hard to ignore. While benefits accruing to the elite are substantial, the majority of reserve residents are condemned to long-term welfare dependency and intergenerational poverty. In the conceptual vocabulary of sociologists, a forceful argument can be made that the preservation and even bolstering of the current system is 'functional' for the First Nations reserve elite. For the sociologist, 'function' refers to 'the consequences of the existence or operation of a unit (a custom, attitude, institution, etc.) for the other units in a (social, cultural, or personality) system or for the system as a whole' (Theodorson and Theodorson, 1969: 165). A structural unit of a social system can be viewed as functioning to support the maintenance of the system as a whole.

---

4 The term 'particularistic' refers to the emphasis placed in a community or society on making important choices in human relations on the basis of local preferences tied to tradition, loyalties, sentiments, or some other aspect of the pre-established relations between people. The alternative is an orientation that defines relations between people on the basis of 'universalistic' standards of quality, quantity, or ethical principles. Thus, in hiring recruits to new jobs, a particularistic choice would select candidates on the basis of family ties, friendship, or even congeniality. A universalistic choice would hire according to the fit of the candidate with formally established criteria that describe the qualifications and skill set needed to perform a job. The 'universalism-particularism' pattern variable is one of the dichotomous choices in social behaviour described by the Harvard sociologist Talcott Parsons (1951).

To say that a local social stratification system is functional for the local social elite is not to say that the members of that elite are especially conscious of this fact, or even that they support the concept in principle. Many elite members may never have thought about the fact that their personal interests are being far better served than those of the membership majority, or that their interests are served at the expense of their fellow band members.

It is my personal experience that most elected First Nations leaders take their jobs very seriously – and those jobs primarily involve promoting local improvements by advocating, negotiating, and in other ways transacting business with external agencies, primarily but not exclusively with the federal government. The primary object of the work of reserve leadership is to secure more and better public infrastructure and services for reserve residents. In working with the leaders of other reserves, through joint affiliations such as tribal councils, First Nations leaders actively seek to promote the interests of their membership by establishing a parallel system of services under organized self-government formations. In all of these endeavours, it would only be fair to suggest that most First Nations leaders typically exercise their duties with good intentions, determination, and resolve. However, the question remains, is the overall lot of the majority of band members best achieved by the current organization of First Nations? And that answer must be no.

A leadership advocating continuous enhancement of local services on settlement lands that are typically far too meagre in size and too limited in potential agricultural, mineral, or urban industrial production capacity to support local populations hardly serves the interests of the majority of band and tribal members. The process of transaction for more local services and programs carries with it activities both intriguing and rewarding – from sitting in negotiations with top government leaders to frequent travel and envious expense accounts – and it does secure new school buildings, health clinics, and better roads on reserves. It does little, however, to create sustainable local economies. The result is that while the few benefit substantially and the creature comforts of residents and access to modern services are marginally enhanced, the majority, unless they have left the reserve for urban centres, are lulled into adapting to an expectation of permanent unemployment and social assistance dependence. As an antipoverty formula, the current approach is doomed to failure because there is obviously an upper limit to what public opinion will allow the federal government to provide in the way of community building in the absence of any significant local contribution to wealth creation.

It is true that many individual instances of progress are made through partnerships between First Nations leaders, governments, and business in settlement areas where there are significant primary resources to tap. However, the majority of reserves do not have economies that can sustain more than a small fraction of their membership. Rare is the government official or First Nation leader who is willing to publicly address the fact that the economic base of most reserve communities is simply not viable, and that reserve-centred development investments are doomed to failure. For the current generation of First Nations leaders, maintenance of the reserve system and a reserve-oriented development focus is a fundamental article of faith.

In response to a variety of federal funding initiatives organized through an allocation program referred to as the 'Community Based Funding Package,' it has been common in recent years for reserve leadership to give primary emphasis to addressing social problems through health education, mental health counselling and traditional healing, child health promotion services, and alcohol and drug abuse prevention and treatment. The recent emphasis has been on 'healing' the 'dysfunctional' individual and family and helping problem drinkers recover from their 'disease' of 'alcoholism' or other 'addictions.' The far more challenging macro-level and mezzo-level issues of changing the reserve-centred First Nations state of participation in the Canadian economy and society are not a priority. In these circumstances, it is in the interests of local leadership and the elite social classes on the reserves for the majority of band members to demand what they can most easily secure. Instead of criticizing local leadership for not stimulating economic development or job creation, band members demand services that heal the 'lost child,' 'inner warrior,' or the 'disease of alcoholism.' The reserve leadership has been legitimated almost exclusively as a broker of income security and other social transfers, and as an advocate and administrator of individualized, therapeutic responses to social problems.

Band Members as 'Co-Conspirators' in the Manufacture and Maintenance of Their Own Dependency and Deviant Status

The oppressed majority of First Nations reserve residents have themselves played a critical role in reinforcing and maintaining their own dependency and unhealthy lifestyles. Aboriginal problem drinkers have tended to inadvertently conspire with the 'deviancy processing' system. They have actively played out the self-defeating prophecy embedded in their collective self-expectations by seeking periodic escape in binge drinking and other mood-modifying substances. This passively acceptant stance functions to enable the avoidance of confrontation with the more fundamental issues in their lives, including their poverty, limited education, lack of economic skills, unemployment, and the damage they have caused themselves and other people during and after drinking episodes. Confronting the pain of unresolved emotional issues is very difficult, and the challenges of adult life are daunting. When self-confidence has been stifled by the toxic messages of parents, systemic racism, and bigotry projected from the wider society, and by the disease/pathology paradigm, the pain relief and euphoric pleasures of substance abuse are very attractive short-term antidotes.

It must be recognized that, even in the absence of negative, repressive messages, the commitment and discipline required to complete a formal post-secondary education, responsibly secure and maintain employment, and to raise and provide adequate material and emotional nurture for family dependents is a formidable burden – as is the challenge of effectively contributing to the stewardship of organized community activities in a voluntary capacity. Taken together, these various responsibilities require a sober lifestyle. By contrast, the 'booze party' or 'narcotic fix' provide an immediate opportunity for socializing, a way of escaping the emotional pain of personal troubles and memories of childhood difficulties, and an outlet for unfettered emotional expression. The attractiveness of inebriation is often forgotten by alcohol and drug abuse educators: it is undoubtedly often fun, exciting, rewarding, and pleasurable, and it provides a social lubricant for shy or reserved people in numerous celebrative events and gatherings.

By accepting the disease model as an explanation and, in fact, as an *excuse* for their antisocial behaviour, aboriginal problem drinkers are able to avoid the significant challenges of personal empowerment and self-control. Personal acceptance of the disease concept appeases guilt and offers a ready-made rationalization for bad habits and destructive behaviours and their often long-lasting consequences. Unfortunately, refusing to confront one's own actions may be more likely to sustain alcohol abuse and destructive behaviour patterns than to assist the abuser in overcoming his or her more fundamental problems. In the world of the problem drinker, the belief that alcohol is to blame for various events and for the limits to one's quality of life is tantamount to a generalized, fatalistic belief in one's self as an inevitable loser. As an increasing amount of research on addictions is indicating, constructive personal development, enhanced self-efficacy, and constructive social action are the keys to sobriety (Peele, Brodsky, and Arnold, 1991; Meyers and Smith, 1995). The very fact of attempting to secure an education and employment, working, establishing a sober and supportive network of friends and acquaintances, working rationally and lovingly through spousal conflicts, fulfilling family obligations, enjoying wholesome recreational activities, and contributing, altruistically, to community affairs are the best antidotes to addiction and destructive lifestyles. Admittedly, this focus on the conspiracy of victims in undermining their own potential may be criticized as simply another example of 'victim-bashing.' Yet in First Nations, as in all stratified societies, oppression is reinforced by passive acceptance and false consciousness and, for significant progress to occur, changes of belief and attitudes and popular social action by the oppressed must occur.

Another aspect of the false consciousness impacting on drinking comportment in First Nations is the transmutation of the traditional male warrior construct from its original moorings in the economic culture of hunting and intertribal defence to a sort of contemporary 'macho' style of human interaction (Supernault, 1995). In an especially thoughtful analysis, Duran and Duran (1995) have argued that the Native American male lives with an understanding that his community has been colonized by conquerors who surround him, while his role as warrior has been eliminated. The persistent, aggravating presence of the conquerors is a constant reminder of colonization and the loss of his traditional role. Lacking the wherewithal to challenge the conquerors, the Native American male represses his anger and rage, which is diverted, with the disinhibiting aid of alcohol, and finds expression in fights or spousal abuse. Duran and Duran write 'alcohol has served as a medicine that keeps this rage within some type of boundary ... Alcohol ... removes impulse control and allows for venting of the rage. In order for the cathecting outward of the warrior, the rage is vented on the family. Generations have elapsed during which the lamentations of women and children haunt the landscape in what appears to be the stillness of reservations across the country' (1995: 37).

Such an interpretation of the drunken comportment of aboriginal males may simply provide an excuse for perpetrators of violence. However, it does partially explain a grievous problem in First Nations that cries out for special attention and amelioration. The legacy of the male role of warrior and the frustration and repressed anger stemming from the lack of role substitution in contemporary Canada is surely implicated not only in much of the family violence on reserves but also in the combative outcomes at house parties and in barrooms. According to many of my First Nations acquaintances, an 'Indian bar' is not only one that is especially welcoming to aboriginal people, it is also a bar associated with drunken behaviour, fights, and tragic outcomes. While the reserve elite may have found appropriate substitutes for traditional roles, the majority of unemployed male adults have not.

The 'macho' ethic is a largely unexplored aspect of Canadian aboriginal studies, yet its comprehension and transformation may be an important key to the social development of First Nations. Binge drinking episodes have been described to me by some aboriginal observers as a socially acceptable context in which the shame of the 'lost warrior status' can be acted out in physical, person-to-person combat. While some have viewed this pattern as a reaction to male status anxiety, others have seen it simply as a means of working up one's courage to fight a feared opponent. It is at least tempting to view the widespread interest in recent years of First Nations adolescents in violent youth gangs and participation in gang conflicts as an attempt to regain this warrior status through collective empowerment and combative expression. Organized gangs in Manitoba have long had a significant influence on aboriginal youth and they are a major factor in the informal organization of that province's jails. A recent report of the Federation of Saskatchewan Indian Nations (FSIN) described the growth of aboriginal gangs in the province as a problem of 'epidemic' scale.[5] The FSIN findings were supported by a report of the Criminal Intelligence Service Canada (CISC) released to the public at approximately the same time.[6]

A reluctance to overstep the boundaries of what is properly one's own, private concern has also made it difficult to create effective social control norms regarding beverage alcohol on reserves. The principle of

---

5 The FSIN report was summarized in the 22 August 2003 edition of Regina's daily newspaper, the *Leader-Post*. In consultations conducted as part of the report's preparation, the FSIN-appointed panel heard former gang members talk of initiation rituals for new recruits that included beatings, sexual assault, and crimes against property.

6 The CIS-Canada study was described by reporter James Wood in the 23 August 2003 edition of the *Leader-Post* of Regina.

non-interference in First Nations is not simply a norm; it is a more, and a sensitive and complex subject (Whitehead and Hayes, 1998: 86–8). This principle discourages intervention in the lives of other individuals, even those of one's own children after their early childhood. 'Minding one's own business' is traditional in Anglo-Saxon and many other cultures. Among First Nations, however, there is an abiding concern with the maintenance of personal freedom by avoiding interference with the choices of individuals, unless those choices are clearly harmful to oneself. Unfortunately, this norm is most effectively situated in traditional hunting and gathering cultures, and, to a lesser extent, in small-scale horticultural, agricultural, and fishing societies and family farming cultures. While prevalent in mainstream society today, it is a principle that demands formal limitations in order to ensure the personal safety of the weak, dependent, and mentally troubled.

It must also be recognized that the principle of non-interference is a family-centred norm that exists in virtually all societies. Family formations often fuse for economic and collective security purposes into communities and nations. After such fusion, much of the authority and responsibility that was once exclusively assigned to the domain of the family is subject to the social and legal constraints ceded to the larger body politic. To avoid that secession is to reject the riches of social development that accompany the transition from the dominance of families to the dominance of community and national societies as a mode of organizing social life.

Traditionally, Elders in First Nations performed a critical role as educators, socializers, and moral advisers of both children and adults. Today, the role of the Elder has been diminished, both within the family and without, and the role of providing informal advice and close supervision is less clearly defined. Many families do not have an Elder in their nuclear or immediate extended family domain, and community determination of who is and who is not an Elder is often unclear. Further, many of the traditional controls on behaviour that threatened the health of the traditional aboriginal community are no longer in place. As a result, family units themselves together with friends and neighbours, as well as formal community agencies, must now play a more active role in providing children and troubled adults with guidance and support. Unfortunately, the concept of non-interference often leads to a 'looking the other way' when early advice and helpful intervention might prevent the intensification of a personal problem such as alcohol abuse.

Friends and family can often be far more effective than professionals in assisting people with alcohol problems to address those problems and manage their behaviours in more constructive ways. This fact has been recognized in family therapy and even in many healing circles organized in First Nations. In these group contexts, family, friends, and community influentials listen to problems, help identify contributing factors, and assist in arriving at a solution. After the fact, they encourage and support the solution process.

The Vested Interests of Alcohol and Drug Abuse Program Boards and Personnel

The National Native Alcohol and Drug Abuse Program (NNADAP) was shaped in the late 1970s and over the 1980s it crystallized into a relatively standardized and enduring program throughout the country. While many reserves now operate under service transfer agreements, most have maintained the same addictions worker role in their community health service units. These workers have done much to challenge and reduce alcohol abuse in reserve communities. Unfortunately, over time, members of the treatment centre oversight bodies and the treatment centre and prevention project workforce have themselves developed a vested interest in prevailing outmoded explanations and approaches to addressing problem drinking and alcohol dependence on reserves. First Nations health workers that I have talked to from locations dotting the entire length and breadth of the country agree with my observation that addictions workers, most of whom are schooled in the disease concept of treatment, are reluctant to change their ideas about alcohol abuse and the appropriate solutions to it. Threatened and fearful of the changes demanded by new knowledge and a more complex and demanding set of problems in the addictions field, these 'foot soldiers' in the war against problem drinking and drug abuse on reserves have become a major source of resistance to program upgrading and change.

To understand the nature of this resistance, one must understand the genesis and program content of the current network of prevention programs and treatment centres that serve reserve communities.

Genesis of NNADAP and Its Personnel

When, in the mid- to late 1970s, Health Canada, in partnership with First Nations, began to mount a strategy aimed at reducing alcohol abuse on reserves, they did not have the qualified personnel required to execute a comprehensive national program. Social workers and bachelor's degree–level psychologists with non-aboriginal backgrounds working in the mental health field might have been recruited, but the cultural gulf between First Nations people and non-aboriginals was very wide at the time, and there was an understandable preference for hiring local, aboriginal people. Alcohol and drug studies as a specialized field, moreover, was in its very early stages. As a result, there were almost no obvious candidates for prevention and treatment programs serving First Nations. Similar to program recruitment efforts in North America more broadly, (Regional Advisory Board 2000; White, 1998: 273–4), a stop-gap human resource development strategy was adopted in NNADAP to populate emerging counselling and community prevention positions.

Discussion of building a workforce for alcohol intervention in the academic literature in Canada is rare and it appears to be almost non-existent regarding First Nations services specifically. However, my familiarity with that growth suggests that William L. White's discussion of the subject stateside is helpful, as there are obvious parallels. According to White (1998: 273), when in the 1970s there was an 'explosive growth' of alcohol intervention programs in the United States, a shortage of qualified staff was the primary obstacle to recruitment. White notes that there was very little formal training available that focused specifically on alcohol problems, and counsellors who claimed to have specialized knowledge and skills in addictions and alcohol abuse problems were almost non-existent. The solution was to recruit Alcoholics Anonymous members who had demonstrated sobriety for several years.

In the minds of the policy makers and, of course, AA advocates, who better to provide services to alcoholics than former alcoholics who had successfully recovered, demonstrated lengthy abstinence, and made a positive contribution to the recovery of others through participation in AA self-help groups? In the absence of a formally trained labour force, treatment programs modelled after the Minnesota concept therefore recruited 'recovered alcoholics' as both counsellors and managers. Both in the United States and Canada, in alcohol abuse outreach jobs and in counselling positions in treatment centres, it became standard practice to recruit recovered alcoholics with strong AA backgrounds. Recruits were also screened on the basis of certain exhibited traits, such as warmth, flexibility, humour, creativity, self-motivation, and discipline, rather than on the basis of formal qualifications acquired through professional training (White, 1998). The same general approach was adopted in First Nations programming in Canada.

Under the influence of AA and the disease model of alcoholism, the NNADAP selected former alcoholics from reserves who had been sober after a treatment process (including AA) and had demonstrated an ability to operate 'prevention projects' to service their own band members. Being a member of a First Nation was also expected of most recruits to the emerging network of treatment centres across Canada established in the late 1970s and throughout the 1980s.

While people with social work degrees and various human service certificates were preferred as counsellors in treatment centres, there was generally no such preference in NNADAP when it came to recruiting prevention program workers. Prevention workers were expected to provide alcohol and drug abuse education in the communities, initiate prevention projects, provide basic, lay counselling, and refer and provide pre-care and aftercare services to clients targeted for inpatient treatment. Based on my attendance at First Nations addictions and community health meetings of various kinds over two decades, it is apparent that, for many years, the formal criteria for hiring both prevention and treatment workers combined recovery from alcohol problems, a specified period of sobriety (usually at least two years), and legal status as a person of recognized Indian ancestry. Formal qualification as a community organizer, health educator, or alcohol and drug abuse specialist was rarely a requirement for prevention jobs, and professional training in general counselling or substance abuse counselling was rarely a requisite for assuming treatment centre positions. Early in the life of NNADAP program development, stringent hiring criteria would have been virtually impossible if First Nations also wanted to hire people from their own communities.

The Influence of the 'Minnesota Model'

In establishing their approach to in-patient treatment, the federal government and First Nations looked to the programming being undertaken by the alcoholism commissions recently established by the provincial governments. The commissions themselves were heavily influenced by the approach taken in the United States, where AA and the Minnesota model of inpatient treatment was considered to reflect a 'state of the art' approach to rehabilitation from 'inebriety.'

The Minnesota model, as we have seen, accepted the disease concept of alcoholism and the Jellinek 'stages' of addiction as a standardized explanation of alcoholism. As a remedial response, the therapeutic design, steeped in AA thinking, was to provide in-patient substance abuse rehabilitation ('rehab') in centres providing a twenty-eight–thirty-five-day treatment program (Doweiko, 1993: 317–19). The Minnesota model has often been described as 'residential milieu therapy for "alcoholism."' Other components of this model include the goal of complete abstinence, twelve step programs, the support of AA or other 'anonymous' self-help programs modelled after AA, the use of group therapy, and the heavy involvement of 'recovering' counsellors (Cook and Cook, 1988).

The Minnesota model combines individual and group counselling with lectures aimed at helping clients understand alcohol dependency as a chronic disease. The organization of treatment is also influenced by the notion of a 'therapeutic community,' in which the participants in treatment played an active role in the therapeutic process. Clients were 'in recovery,' a term which metaphorically described the process of healing from a physical disease or injury. The model virtually became the template for NNADAP treatment programs across the country, although, from the outset, philosophical ideas shared through Elder narratives and cleansing and other healing rituals were added to many of the programs.

The Controversy Surrounding Paraprofessional Addictions Program Personnel

From the very outset, the trend of hiring recovered alcoholics who lacked formal addictions and substance abuse counsellor training to work in treatment programs attracted controversy and challenge. Concern about the efficacy of the practice was highlighted in a debate between two psychiatrists, Dr Henry Krystal and Dr Robert Moore, published in article form in the *Quarterly Journal of Alcohol Studies* in 1963. The debate was framed in answer to the question: 'Who is qualified to treat the alcoholic?' Reasonable arguments were presented from both sides, both in the journal debate and in the field generally. However, in mainstream addictions and substance abuse treatment circles, clear, albeit temporary, settlement of the issue would not come for a few years.

That temporary settlement was achieved with the work of psychologists Carl Rogers (1965; 1969) and Truax and Carkhuff (1967), each of whom argued that the competence of counsellors in any field could be identified with specific qualities and skills and that those skills could be learned through focused training in specific competencies. These psychologists and others who joined the chorus all argued that the critical qualities needed to form a sound 'counselling relationship' included genuineness; the ability to engender trust; empathy; and an unconditionally accepting, respectful, non-judgmental attitude towards the client. The list of skills was longer, including the mastery of such basic techniques as questioning, encouraging identification of the source of problems, careful listening, paraphrasing, summarizing, and reframing negative or emotionally harmful ways of thinking about problems.

The conclusions of Rogers and Truax and Carkhuff are supported by highly reputable research which has consistently found that the therapist's demeanour and style of counselling is a significant factor in determining treatment outcomes. Thus, Najavits and Weiss (1994) have noted a consistent finding in the relevant research that treatment outcomes improve when therapists have strong interpersonal skills such as an 'ability to forge a therapeutic alliance' with clients. Consistent with Najavits and Weiss, Hester (1994), in a study of behavioural self-control strategies (BSCTs), found that alcoholism clients seen by therapists with low levels of empathy fared worse than those in self-directed groups, while clients seen by therapists with high levels of empathy did better than those in self-directed groups. Miller, Taylor, and West (1980) and Sanchez-Craig, Spivak, and Davila (1991) found that neither experience nor training in and of themselves are strong predictors of positive client outcomes. Further, these psychologists and others have argued that the basic elements of an effective counselling relationship were not necessarily present in the styles of professional psychologists or psychiatrists or absent in ordinary people or untrained counsellors. Sometimes a part of one's demeanour, and often not, the critical qualities and skills of an effective counsellor could be acquired and improved with training and practice. However, it was also recognized that the individual performing in counselling and community roles would have to develop a critical capacity and an increasing base of empirical and theoretical knowledge to respond to the increasingly complex nature of addictions and addiction-generating milieux. These latter needs were the very factors that distinguish a professional worker. To meet these needs, professional training would increasingly become a prerequisite for employment in the alcohol abuse field, and such professionalization is now occurring throughout North America. This understanding broke the stalemate initiated by the debate over whether or not individuals lacking university degrees or technical certificates in counselling should be hired in treatment programs. Yes, suggested the research, personal suitability of recruits to such work should be examined, regardless of professional qualifications. The extent to which they exhibited the attributes of a good counsellor and knew and used good 'helping skills' should be tested and enhanced through training if their screening indicated they were lacking in some dimensions. However, the literature also strongly advocates the view that professional training should gradually become a prerequisite. Professional education is necessary in order for addictions workers to gain a sufficiently broad knowledge base for practice and the theoretical sophistication to critically assess ongoing developments in the field.

In the 1970s and early 1980s, untrained 'indigenous non-professionals' were hired from the ranks of agency client groups to serve as professional aides and to perform basic assistance roles in other health and human service fields. Yet in most of these specially designated positions, recruits required an orientation that included information, knowledge, and some skills specific to their respective service areas. To meet this need, both the federal and provincial governments undertook a variety of programs aimed at ensuring basic knowledge and skill levels among the non-professionals hired to work in front-line human service positions, including addictions counselling. Gradually, these qualifications became steeper as national certification programs were established, in mainstream addictions programming, one-two-year technical certificates from community colleges and polytechnical institutes were expected of new recruits and, gradually, professional degrees were preferred, in part due to the influence of professional associations.

There has been a major thrust towards professionalization in the substance abuse field, largely as a response to the emerging reconstitution of the intervention field. The field is now being redeveloped in response to several influences:

1 The disease model is gradually being displaced by a multiple-pathway, bio-psycho-social model of addictions and problem drinking, and the belief in the superiority of AA's effectiveness has coincidentally been challenged on empirical grounds. Thus, newer, more sophisticated intervention approaches are being developed and a

deeper and more comprehensive understanding of the field is being expected of prevention educators and intervention personnel.

2 The alcohol and drug prevention field generally is becoming far more complex, both in terms of the types of abused substances available from criminally manufactured and distributed substances or through the illegal diversion of prescription drugs, and in terms of the various treatment modalities available. Service cost rationalization is now a much greater pressure than it was when alcohol and drug programs were established in the 1970s and 1980s, and proof of the effectiveness of diagnostic and treatment methods is increasingly required. Best practices are now expected to guide programming and those best practices are changing more rapidly, as more is learned from basic and applied research. Programs must be ready to adapt and change and boards, operational managers, and staff must be able to rely on fully professional workers who keep abreast of the field and are committed in thought and practice to continuing professional education.

3 While the Minnesota model long dominated the intervention field, a much more varied system of services has developed in recent years. Compared to fifteen years ago, most Canadian provinces have addiction and substance abuse services that attend to a much fuller continuum of care, give greater emphasis to prevention and out-patient care than to the in-patient model, provide various lengths of stay for those who require residential care, and emphasize customized intervention tailored to the distinctive needs of individual clients rather than the template curriculum offered through the Minnesota-modelled program (Health Canada, 1999b).

The Sluggish March to Program Upgrading and Professionalization in First Nations Addictions Services

Elevating First Nations addictions programming to the standards of mainstream programming has also been on the First Nations community health service agenda for many years. In addition, professionalization has always been a part of the discourse in and about NNADAP. In fact, the original conception of NNADAP included the goal of having professional addictions counsellors available on reserves (Jock, 1998: 5). In practice, this element of the program never materialized.

A reading of several reports indicates that the process of program upgrading and professionalization of NNADAP and band programming not directly connected to NNADAP has been much slower than what has occurred outside of First Nations. Key reference documents include a report by the Addictions Research Foundation (1989), the General Review of NNADAP (Jock, 1998), and the comprehensive literature review prepared for the Regional Advisory Board to NNADAP in Saskatchewan (2000), together with various reports referenced in that document.

A survey of NNADAP community workers, conducted as part of the *General Review of NNADAP* (Jock, 1998), an evaluation of national scope, provides the following profile of a 'typical' NNADAP worker in reserve communities throughout Canada:

- Some elementary or secondary schooling (grades one to twelve) is the most frequent level of completed, formal education (exclusive of addictions training).
- When prevention workers do have training credentials, the vast majority are certificate programs directly associated with the addictions field.
- The vast majority of NNADAP community workers work on a full-time basis; a relatively small minority work on a part-time basis.
- The *average* pay range for NNADAP community workers is $20,000 to $25,000 per year, although many receive considerably less and some significantly more. These rates are in keeping with workers with similar job assignments in the public sector but outside of NNADAP, extensive formal training has typically become a requirement of employment. While regional and national First Nations addictions and substance abuse organizations have been encouraging employment skill upgrading for several years, current qualification levels appear to remain far below mainstream standards.
- Staff turnover rates were viewed as being a problem for the program. On average, the length of service is over five years.

Change has come very slowly to First Nations addictions programming.

In the initial NNADAP design, the treatment centres were envisioned as having at least one formally trained chemical dependency worker or counsellor supervising treatment. An informal survey of First Nations treatment centres across Canada conducted in preparation for this book in August and September 2003 indicates that, while most centres now have at least one trained counsellor on staff, supervision by a person with a master's degree, often considered a minimal requisite for professional supervision, is a rare exception, not the rule.

Why has the program and professional upgrading process in First Nations been such a slow one? One answer frequently provided by key informants acting in consulting support positions to First Nations or NNADAP is that the federal government has not been willing to make upgrading a requirement of funding. This view is supported by the fact that there are no mandatory requirements of any kind for addictions programming under the multiyear community health service agreements offered to First Nation administrations in the late 1980s.

Another possible answer lies in the frequently heard complaint of NNADAP workers and treatment program managers that professional staff are hard to secure because funding is inadequate. This complaint is valid to the extent that salaries for alcohol and drug abuse workers are typically very low, compared with human service positions in other fields. However, a comparative examination of addictions worker pay scales and expected salary levels would suggest that NNADAP positions are funded at industry averages but educational qualifications in NNADAP are well below industry averages.

A more plausible explanation for the lethargic pace of NNADAP program and staff upgrading lies in the degree to which resistance is coming from entrenched treatment centre management boards and reserve prevention workers whose knowledge and skills are not in keeping with current needs. The words of one key informant with lengthy working knowledge of NNADAP reflected the sentiments and impressions expressed by many others about many of the existing boards: 'The treatment board members are mostly "old school" and other than some idea that alcoholism is a disease, they don't really have much to contribute to a board in the alcoholism field.' Many have indicated that, because board members are often on limited and fixed incomes, they cling to their roles tenaciously, and do not want to yield them to boards with more knowledgeable members who have much more to contribute.

Most board members are selected by chiefs and band councils, many of whom have confronted their own problem drinking with the assistance of AA or treatment programs oriented to the disease model. Many key informants in close contact with addictions programming for First Nations believe that an inadequate system of creating management boards in treatment centres has become entrenched. These key informants argue that the beneficiaries of that hiring process have acquired a strong stake in the status quo. The reality of this vested interest is that First Nations people experiencing alcohol problems are the losers – and, despite the growing levels of abstinence, problem drinking and the mentality and social conditions that nourish it continue to have a profoundly negative impact on the health and well-being of First Nations.

Further, many treatment program staff themselves, community members and health staff consulted in the preparation of this book, indicated that hiring in treatment centres may be swayed as much by leadership preferences and a belief in the special helping abilities of recovered alcoholics as they are by strong professional credentials. Such an approach is obviously a significant obstacle to program upgrading.

Key informants from First Nations elected councils and reserve health staff have frequently suggested to me that the prevention workers hired in reserve communities also tend to be from what many refer to as the 'old school,' by which they mean recovered alcoholics loyal to the disease model and lacking a complete high school education. The most prevalent opinion is that those workers who had formal training obtained it through short orientation programs, short course training of at most ten months' duration, in curriculum dedicated solely to training local aboriginal people in basic addictions counselling centred on the disease model.

The anti-drinking messages conveyed by the community program have surely contributed in a significant way to the increase in recent decades of the number of people leading abstinent lifestyles on reserves, and even to reducing the amount of drinking per episode in Status Indian communities. Yet NNADAP personnel and other addictions workers can only take some of the credit. Increased education levels and the advent of a variety of social and community development programs that have improved material and social conditions on reserves must have played a major role in lowering the percentage of drinkers in Native communities. An 'addictions shift' from alcohol abuse to other drugs, gambling, or relationship addictions may also have contributed to the reduction in the number of drinkers on reserves – an opinion that has been a standard explanation of reduced drinking when the explanations have been canvassed or community health studies I have conducted on reserves.

While NNADAP and other addictions workers have undoubtedly accomplished much in reserve communities in terms of promoting sobriety, the fact is that there are far better intervention models available than the Disease Concept of Treatment but the DCT remains the predominant approach to addictions programming in First Nations. Most critically, it is also a fact that NNADAP's community and intensive intervention services remain focused on the alcohol-dependent client to the exclusion of all other client needs. The entire system is organized on the assumption that the target of all prevention and treatment programming is the alcohol-dependent individual rather than other problem drinkers, despite the fact that the latter group is much larger. Both intervention and prevention services remain relatively underdeveloped for such client categories as

- binge drinkers,
- individuals with substance abuse problems rooted in and sustained by their families and acquaintanceship networks rather than in any predisposition to alcohol use,
- women (and sometimes men) who use drink only to function in abusive relationships involving frequent drunken episodes initiated by their partners,
- adults who do not, cannot, or should not accept a self-definition as alcohol-dependents,
- at-risk youth in need of specialized prevention programming, and
- at-risk youth who cannot relate to the conventional NNADAP worker because of a wide generation gap.

It must be emphasized that many community health workers and many enlightened First Nations leaders, advisers, researchers, evaluators, and government staff have been working diligently at promoting the upgrading of staff knowledge and skill levels and to redefine and update programming approaches. However, all too often they have been met with silence or a wall of resistance. Not surprisingly, much of that resistance has come from the 'old guard' of NNADAP workers and community leaders who are reluctant to dislodge a hiring process so strategically linked to the larger political decision-making process. By the accounts of a large number of key informants interviewed as part of my program evaluation work with First Nations, local hiring of prevention workers is often, perhaps typically, a *highly* politicized process. A pool of far more capable recruits is urgently required, as is enhanced training in specialized skills. Meanwhile, the firewater complex is being perpetuated by First Nations workers themselves, as is the ideol-

ogy of the powerless victim, ever in need of more healing and therapeutic support.

Despite the fact that most alcohol-related problems in First Nations
are associated with occasional but excessive or binge drinking comportment, alcohol abuse programming continues to be focused almost
singularly on alcohol-dependents. The tragedy is that this type of programming, which is, in effect, 'the only game in town,' has little to
offer the binge drinker who legitimately rejects the required self-cate-
gorization of 'alcoholic.

As argued in previous chapters of this book, not only are appropriate services not available because of the emphasis on the disease/med-
ical model, but the firewater complex that it perpetuates is profoundly
implicated in the dependent thinking styles that are so self-defeating
for first peoples.

In fairness, there is much that is hopeful in the trends occurring in
First Nations alcohol abuse policy and programming front in Canada –
and many plausible changes that can be made. It is to such change that
Part Two of this book will turn.

**Winds of Change: Holistic Health and Community Revitalization as
a Post-Colonial Addictions Prevention Strategy**

Despite the resistance in the current First Nations alcohol abuse prevention and intervention workforce, significant, progressive forces
have emerged within it, as well as in external program advocacy bodies
pressing towards a paradigm shift. Evidence of this change is apparent
in policy direction being encouraged by some federal program officials
with FNIHB. More important, it is being advanced by some of the most
passionately committed, articulate and educated aboriginal treatment
professionals, who confidently integrate traditional values and principles with contemporary methodologies. It is also being encouraged by
the National Native Addictions Partnership Foundation and, gradually
it is emerging in the curriculum development process in treatment centres, which has placed a holistic conception of health and multifaceted
skill training alongside counselling, social group work, and education
grounded in the disease model in treatment centres. Unfortunately, the
contradictions between the convential view and the emerging view are
sharp and desperately require resolution.

According to our telephone survey of NNADAP treatment centres across Canada, multifaceted programming is now in place in the majority of centres, although, admittedly, in almost all of them the disease model and AA philosophy remain a fundamental, and typically dominant influence. Yet the signs of progress can be found in many corners.

For four years, such organizations as the Regional Advisory Board to NNADAP in Saskatchewan have been pressing for program reconfiguration that gives far greater emphasis to building a stronger, more coordinated and interconnected system of services. The goals of that proposed change include the improvement of both effectiveness and efficiency, and the promotion and adoption of more contemporary, evidence-based practices. Community-based and out-patient counselling, the upgrading of intervention methodologies, and the adaptation of counselling to the individual needs of clients, rather than the boilerplate approach offered in conventional programming, are now being encouraged. As stated above most NNADAP treatment centres across the country are now offering multidimensional treatment in addition to DCT. Thus life skills training, the use of ceremony to solidify pro-sobriety values, the advice of Elders, anger management, communication skill development, and talking circles are all becoming mainstays of treatment programming. Unfortunately, much of this approach is contradicted by the assumptions of the disease model – and the treatment that does exist is focused on alcohol dependence (or other drug addiction), while binge drinking, and occasional but high-risk use of illicit drugs the most significant substance abuse problem in First Nations, is largely ignored.

Progress is being made on many fronts, but it has been very slow. Employment positions in most reserves are precious commodities, and the choice of allocating secure employment positions in a reserve administration is something that band councils tend to guard jealously. Electoral supporters, family members and, at times, potential political opponents, all have dibs on the local alcohol and drug abuse prevention worker position – and often their interests are given higher priority than training. The outcome of this fact is that the goal of uniformly upgrading staff positions across a First Nation health region is a difficult, and perhaps in the short run, even impossible challenge. Under both annual contribution agreements and multiyear 'transfer agreements' with the federal government, band councils and treatment centre boards administering services are not required to make technical qualifications for NNADAP prevention or treatment centre positions mandatory.[7]

An effort to promote professional upgrading of addictions programming has also been championed at the national level by the National Native Addictions Partnership Foundation (NNAPF). This national body, formed to encourage the implementation of the recommendations of the national review of the program in 1998, is giving major emphasis to personnel upgrading, improved information management, program certification, and other strategies aimed at upgrading and enhancing both community-based programs and treatment centres with best practice methodologies. This is a welcome development and desperately deserves federal government support.

The boards and treatment directors of the Youth Solvent Abuse Treatment Centres (YSATC) program have also been an important voice for change in the addictions and substance abuse field. Established in the late 1990s in response to the public outcry following youth solvent abuse crises in remote communities, the YSATCs are a federally funded initiative operated by First Nations. The program has established a network of eight regional solvent abuse treatment programs, each with a national intake policy. All centres either have or are developing a substantial outreach capacity and capacity-building strategy to assist communities with the development of their own youth-oriented crisis prevention and intervention programs. From the outset, the YSACs have made a concerted effort to systematically integrate a traditional understanding of balanced, holistic healing with contemporary, evi-

---

7 Through FNIHB, Health Canada provides funding for services to bands, tribal councils, and organizations formed by a band, tribal council, or unaffiliated group of bands to provide community health services, including prevention services and treatment services, under one-year contribution agreements or three-to-five-year 'integrated service agreements' or 'health transfer agreements.' In all of these agreements, some aspects of services have been defined as mandatory, including nursing and communicable disease prevention and control, but addictions services are not. The decision not to make mental health and addictions services mandatory was ostensibly intended to recognize local desires for self-management. However, funding such services under separate agreements with every band makes it very difficult to provide coordinating and program development functions in an effective and cost-efficient manner. In Saskatchewan, almost fifteen years of attempts to develop a strategy that would significantly upgrade regional programming in keeping with best practice goals has been frustrated by an apparent reluctance on the part of chiefs to relinquish any decision making for local programs to supra band organizations.

dence-based treatment and community organization approaches into their helping strategies. These solvent abuse centres have been more richly endowed financially than NNADAP centres and they were established more recently than NNADAP, at a time when the empirical knowledge base of addictions programming had improved and there was a more confident sense of First Nations health promotion principles. The solvent abuse centre leadership, with access to enhanced funding was able to draw upon a more qualified human resource pool than NNADAP.

It remains the case that, in substance abuse and addictions programming on many, probably most, reserves in Canada, change from the DCT model has been very slow. Most program managers and intervention personnel stubbornly retain their commitment to the disease model and do not have the educational background to move beyond the twelve-step, abstinence-only approach. Further, few of them are versed in more contemporary cognitive-behavioural and social coping skill approaches. Feelings of inadequacy combine with fear of job loss to make for an extremely resistant workforce.

The type of community revitalization required to mount a significant challenge to problem drinking and widespread addictive behaviour patterns among first peoples is to be found in traditional indigenous philosophies of well-being, more realistic economic development strategies, and contemporary community health development strategies targeted on both prevention and intervention. As a member of the Akwasasne First Nation stated in a submission to the Royal Commission on Aboriginal Peoples, 'A holistic approach that encompasses emotional, mental, physical, spiritual, social, cultural and sexual attitudes will need to be developed. Historically and culturally we, as aboriginal people, are one with nature and is elements. It only makes sense to approach health care with a view towards community-based health care in the development and implementation of programs and services' (R-CAP consultations: The Pas MB. 92-05-19 62. Chief Flett. PG 70-1).

In their report on health issues (RCAP, 1996: 3: 220), the commissioners overseeing the Royal Commission on Aboriginal Peoples wrote that they saw a 'powerful resonance' between the findings of bio-medical research and traditional aboriginal philosophies of health promotion. They note that traditional aboriginal health principles are now being confirmed by bio-medical researchers. A formal statement to RCAP by Penny Ericson, dean of the Faculty of Nursing at the University of New Brunswick, commenting as a spokesperson for the Canadian Association of University Schools of Nursing, supported the commissioner's views on this matter: 'The current paradigm shift in health care confirms what Aboriginal people have always believed about health and healing. For example, Primary Health Care is the World Health Organization's framework for health care in today's society ... The Principles of Primary Health Care are similar to those of the Circle of Life or the Medicine Wheel, which have served as a guide for health care for generations of some of Canada's Aboriginal People' (RCAP, 1996: 3: 220–1).

Referring to this and similar statements submitted to the Royal Commission, Warry (1998: 88), argues that 'holism' is increasingly being used by thoughtful First Nations health policy analysts to refer to a broad understanding of the socio-economic and historic determinants of health. Warry notes the commonality with social-scientific thinking reflected in such statements:

> In these quotations, 'holism' ... [is] an understanding ... that crosses artificial conceptual boundaries – social, political or economic – to encompass an explanation incorporating all these factors.
>
> Holism may be translated as an attempt to find comprehensive solutions to problems, as opposed to Band-Aid approaches that treat the symptoms of social dis-ease. The solution to alcohol abuse might (rather) be found in the provision of employment, adequate housing, or recreational opportunities, strategies that confront the root cause of people's dissatisfaction with life, rather than through the provision of alcohol counselling programs. (1989: 88–9)

Comprehensive, community-based approaches to health promotion have a number of advantages (Bracht, 1990: 21). The burden of chronic, environmentally caused diseases cuts across most sectors of community life, a fact which calls for intersectoral solutions. Most diseases result from a complex set of causal factors and, for the most part, they are rooted in socio-economic phenomena. To confront the social-environmental complexity of disease causation, community approaches are mobilized. Such an effort is designed to impact on the social milieu of individuals presenting health problems. Community-oriented approaches attempt to modify the norms, values, and policies that provide the context for and shape behavioural patterns leading to disease. Better integrated into the total community and its existing service infrastructure than individually focused approaches, community approaches shift the focus away from isolating individuals or sub-groups as the target of change and expert intervention. By contrast, community health development approaches emphasize shared, community-wide responsibility for preventing and overcoming health problems and efforts to augment the capacity of individuals to change.

Part Two

Rebuilding and Renovating Alcohol
Prevention Strategies in First Nations

12

An Effective Alcohol Abuse Service System for First Nations: Philosophical Foundations

It was argued in Part One of this book that the alcohol abuse prevention and intervention system dedicated to the First Nations people living in reserve settlements in Canada begs for fundamental change in both theory and practice. Planning for such change has long been in the works, 'on the drawing board,' so to speak, but change itself has proceeded very, very slowly. At the time of this writing it is fair to say that the disease model and a 'treatment' paradigm based on the assumption that all problem drinkers are alcoholics still predominates. Challenging this older view, I have called for a strategic, multitiered effort directed at each of the macro-, mezzo-, and micro-levels of system change. The burden of the remaining pages is to outline a specific philosophical and methodological foundation for an effective First Nations alcohol abuse prevention and intervention strategy. The analysis thus shifts from the negative to the positive, from critical deconstruction to creative reconstruction.

In my view, a fundamental commitment to a consistently applied value framework in the field of alcohol prevention and intervention is required by both the leadership and the community health workers serving First Nations. That consensual commitment must undergird policy and programming dedicated to addressing alcohol abuse specifically and addictions issues more generally. Such a value framework must also factor in not only the sensibilities of first peoples as the bearers of traditional North American cultures, but their aspirations to participate wholly and equally as bicultural citizens of Canada as well. As suggested in the final chapter of Part One, the bridge to such an integrative value framework can be found in a simultaneous reading of current public health policy literature and descriptions of the philosophical and spiritual foundations of traditional indigenous cultures in North America. The bridge is located in the term 'holistic health.'

When aboriginal health and social development workers speak of a return to tradition, they now also speak of holistic approaches to the solution of community health problems, including problem drinking and addictions. Admittedly, the term is frequently misunderstood. Often it is used simply to refer to administrative arrangements seen as the ideal alternative to the compartmentalization of programs associated with federal or provincial government funding sources. Funding programs frequently establish standardized criteria for addressing a specific social problem or health problem in isolation from various other problems endemic to the social and economic environment. It is often very difficult for communities to integrate new program interventions into existing services in a fashion that is well adapted to local realities and designed to best meet distinctive community needs. The word holistic is thus used to suggest an alternative to service segregation. Often those advocating a 'holistic' alternative are seeking global funding arrangements rather than a variety of separately earmarked program sources, and increased flexibility for local health service design and management. The implication is that if services were to be organized locally in a way that is responsive in a comprehensive or holistic way to distinctively defined local needs, then more effective and efficient local service arrangements could be organized.

Yet holistic means far more than global funding. When the word is used most thoughtfully by aboriginal leaders and community workers it denotes approaches that integrate wider socio-economic, educational, and community development initiatives, as well as direct service responses, integrated in a way that reflects a balance of spiritual, physical, mental, and emotional needs. These are the core qualities associated with the four directions of the Medicine Wheel, which was a spiritual and philosophical organizing symbol for many indigenous cultures. Thus, as the personnel involved in the Four Worlds Development project in the Lethbridge area have long emphasized, individual action, recovery, awareness, and volition are believed to derive from the balance or harmony among these spheres of the human experience (Four Worlds Development Project, 1985).

Traditional indigenous North American thinking linked history and environmental conditions to individual problems and needs. As Barbara Barnes, a spokesperson from the Akwasasne First Nation in Ontario, explains: 'Our perspective of healing is a holistic one in that it deals with the complete person as a functioning member of society and does not treat only the symptoms of the problem. In order for us to heal individuals and communities, it is vital that we pursue all possible ways in which we can bind our communities back together with a clear knowledge of who we are and where we have come from. In his way, we may be better able to chart the course of where we are going from this point onwards' (quoted in Warry 1998).

A holistic approach to health is very similar to the *social systems* approach in clinical and applied sociology and the *ecological frame of reference* in social work. It is also very similar to the most credible branches of public health and community health promotion.

Holism, from the traditional Native American cultural perspective, at least as it is being interpreted today, can best be viewed as an attempt to find comprehensive solutions to problems, as opposed to approaches that focus on attacking the most immediate 'trigger' (i.e., direct cause) of a particular symptom. Thus, fundamental solutions to alcohol abuse may be found in opening up reserve-based development to formerly excluded members and off-reserve band members; it might also involve working with urban agencies to directly address the problem of teens who have migrated from the reserve and are involved in gangs or the street sex trade. Holistic health strategies might also involve the development of band or tribal visioning sessions that focus on challenging a dependent thinking style that has the people of an entire community in its grip. It might also involve opening up opportunities for a renewed and expanded role structure established on reserves, through a more expansive and more equitable distribution of employment and voluntary, honorific roles.

Holistic health strategies might be found through a reactivation of the positive elements of a traditional kinship structure, or through the provision of adequate housing, with band members actively involved in the building process. They might also be expressed through the establishment of recreational activities centred on healthy socializing, exercise, or skill development as a positive alternative to substance abuse and addictions. In community action, a holistic perspective is best reflected in approaches that transcend specific program areas. It is possible, for instance, to speak of service coordination and case management efforts that approach individual or family issues from different vantage points, or through team approaches based in consultation, collaboration, and coordination.

Holism obviously embodies an emphasis on inclusion; it reflects the idea that all segments of the community contribute to the community's health and well-being. Young and old, strong and weak, female or male: all have an important contribution to make, and the balance of community life in its various dimensions is maintained by their collective contributions. An excellent example is found in discussion of child abuse by Native health workers. If it takes an entire village to raise a child, and since the future of a community depends upon the healthy nurture of children, abuse must be directly controlled by all members of the community. It cannot be simply turned over to a worker from a provincial department of social services or to a First Nations child and family services agency. Similarly, if someone who abuses alcohol also abuses other people, a holistic perspective would suggest that it is the responsibility of the entire community to intervene. Why? Because the health and well-being of the community is placed at risk by being thrown out of balance. The imbalance is created by the lack of contribution to the community not only from the alcohol abuser but from the people whose lives he or she has disrupted. Thus, the challenge of rebalancing the situation demands that the rights of both the victim and the victimizer be addressed. Both are an integral part of the solution.

This holistic approach has been advocated actively in recent years by First Nations family workers, social workers, and corrections workers interested in a more effective way to address violence and crime issues in First Nations, Inuit, and Métis communities. And again, compared to the mainstream, much greater emphasis has been placed on mediation than on adversarial approaches, on prevention and restitution, and on a consideration of both the offender's and the victims' rights.

The preference among aboriginal health and social development workers for holistic health strategies is also evident in their emphasis on trying to get the community leadership and membership as a whole directly involved in the resolution of interpersonal conflicts through healing circles and sentencing circles. These group formations emphasize the multipartite responsibility for addressing problems and require the attendance of victim, victimizer, Elders, and other community leaders. Admittedly, early experience with these approaches has shown that manipulative individuals at odds with the law can corrupt sentencing and dispute resolution alternatives by using them to soften the punitive consequences of their actions. However, this emphasis on community involvement, mediation, and restitution must be welcomed as a refreshing turn towards resuscitating the best of traditional thinking; in it can be seen the application of the logic of traditional aboriginal problem solving to contemporary personal and community development.

In common practice, however, the lesson has not yet been widely learned, as is witnessed by the organization of current First Nations addictions programs, beginning with NNADAP and continuing on to the 'post-transfer' environment. Unfortunately, on-reserve programs tend to work in isolation, even from other on-reserve programs, despite the considerable flexibility of available funding arrangements, especially as afforded by health service transfer agreements. It appears that the specialization and compartmentalization of programs continues, like a hangover, to dominate the thinking of those who once worked under annual contribution agreements with the federal government.

Even the treatment centres exhibit very little coordination of activities, either with each other or with on-reserve programs. As a review of treatment centres in the Saskatchewan Region in 1996–7 stated in its executive summary: 'There is no system here, if by system we mean parts of an organism that are linked together in symbiotic interplay that serves a purpose greater than each of the individual parts taken separately. The treatment programs, as well as the community referral workers, are not working as parts of a system, but rather as independent agents with no necessary connection to one another or to the region as a whole ... There is no one putting the parts of the system together so that the parts fit together ... ' (Murray, 1997: 1).

Yet the holistic view is clearly taking hold in some First Nations health areas. In northern Saskatchewan community health staff in tribal councils are clear in their belief that community health promotion activities, including those targeting addictive behaviours, are best conceived as an integral element of a broadly based 'community development' process, that dependent thinking styles must be systematically and vigorously challenged in a consistent and ongoing fashion; and that the pursuit of self-efficacy must be promoted. This perspective is also reflected in the formal strategy documents of all major health organizations serving First Nations in Saskatchewan's north. A sampling of submissions to the Royal Commission on Aboriginal Peoples would indicate that similar thinking is taking root in First Nations throughout Canada. An active consultation process is now under way nationally, spearheaded by Health Canada, but with the active participation of First Nations and Inuit health workers which is considering the integration of mental health and addictions services and the links between both to other community, tribal council, and provincial government health services. These are all hopeful signs of a shift towards a more holistic perspective.

In recent years, the thinking reflected in discussions with health care providers with a holistic health orientation is familiar territory in public health circles, epidemiology, clinical sociology, and the sociology of health. A holistic orientation is also shared by a consensus of members of the World Health Organization (WHO). In fact, *community health development*, the term with the most recent currency in WHO-promoted public health policy publications, is essentially health promotion activity designed and implemented as community development. According to recent health promotion literature, which is firmly grounded in results-oriented research, community health development is the preferred methodology of public health agencies with a mandate to work with socio-economically disadvantaged populations.

Thoughtful community health service leaders have for the past decade argued that physical health promotion is intimately tied to personal development, mental health promotion, overcoming addictive thinking and behaviour patterns, and family systems development; in turn, positive developments in these human spheres are themselves viewed as both causes and effects of effective institution development, self-government, and economic development activities and strategies.

Foundations in Values and Definitions

An effective approach to problem drinking and addictions in First Nations communities must be grounded in a solid and generally accepted base of common values, definitions, and goals. Some of these values, definitions, and goals are outlined below.

- Holistic approaches to alcohol abuse and other social and health problems require a leadership that is committed to overcoming the vestiges of colonization that function as fundamental obstacles to positive change. This includes addressing and changing the systemic inequities of on-reserve stratification, the narrow focus of resource allocation to reserve settlements, and the separation of off-reserve band members from reserve-centred band development. Ultimately, it includes the articulation and implementation of post-colonial band and tribal development policies.
- The idea that the program should be based upon a holistic perspective and holism should be concretely reflected in learning, therapy,

and program organization. Leaders and health workers should take it upon themselves to demonstrate how that perspective is consistent with traditional thinking and with the best of modern public health promotion theory – and, on that basis, to pro-actively promote the establishment of a community wide commitment to utilizing that perspective not only in the organization and delivery of addictions services, but also in personal and community development generally.

- Admittedly, the substance abuse and mental health needs of clients overlap and thus services for the two should be integrated. However, the continuation of special services for substance abuse and addictions are warranted by the distinctiveness of substance abuse problems and the far less complicated demands of training substance abuse and addictions workers in comparison with the training required to teach comprehensive mental health intervention skills.
- At all levels, from community prevention and counselling through in-patient treatment to regional and national support organizations, problem drinking and addictions programs should be built around specific, concrete risk reduction and personal abstinence or sobriety management goals – and individuals and service providers should be evaluated in terms of their measured goal achievement.
- Substance abuse programming should work from a clear and consistently accepted set of *working definitions* of *problem drinking* and *addictions* that are consistent with the evidence provided by good research.
- At the individual level, *self-efficacy* should be the organizing principle for health education and intervention programming.
- At the community level, *community empowerment* and a *health-promoting environment* should serve as goals of alcohol abuse programming.

Holistic Thinking and Programming

As indicated above, the holistic philosophy of Native American tradition should come alive in a practical way in programming, with the biological, psychological, social, and spiritual dimensions given full sway and a necessary balance accorded both prevention and intervention.

Holism at the individual level should be promoted in specific ways and can reasonably be understood in programming terms as a problem-solving and personal development program that promotes self-work and supportive counselling.

Holism, Society, and Community

At the level of *society*, as mediated and guided by representative aboriginal organizations and central and subcentral levels of Canadian government, and at the *community* level, a holistic approach should be promoted in specific ways. The dimensions of community that must be addressed in program organization and delivery are described below.

THE ECONOMIC DIMENSION
Sober and mentally healthy living, as contrasted to past substance abuse, requires not only self-efficacy but sufficient alternative rewards to make life without problem drinking or addiction worthwhile. Obviously, the key to this reward system in contemporary society is job and career opportunities. Such opportunity creation must contend with the larger economic realities of Canada and its specific regions and local areas. At present, as argued in Part One of this book, far too much emphasis in First Nations economic development is placed on the development of reserve-based economies. This emphasis originated with reserve settlement strategies and federal government policies that regard reserves as their entire jurisdiction for service provision, and the focus on reserves continues to the present. When a member of a First Nation leaves the reserve to reside outside of lands with reserve status, he or she must secure services from a provincial or territorial government. Consequently First Nations leaders have generally come to accept and work within the reserve-centred approach. But, again as argued above, most reserves simply do not have the resources to sustain the populations that reside on them, and given the distance of most from major commercial centres, they cannot be expected to serve as the foundation for a full employment policy. Economic development must therefore increasingly focus outward. Reserve residents must be encouraged to spend at least some of their working lives in off-reserve employment. Bands must shift to a reserve-centred but geographically far-flung investment strategy. It must also give emphasis to promoting school achievement, training and retraining, and getting students in to university and technical institute programming. Without a more broadly based economic development strategy, the unemployment levels of 30 to 90 per cent, which have been relatively constant before and after economic development program expenditures, will continue long into the future – and widespread unemployment is strongly correlated with a high incidence of addictions and problem drinking cases.

THE POLITICAL DIMENSION

It has been my experience that program weaknesses and doubts about the efficacy of alcohol abuse programs have made the majority of First Nations leaders sceptical of the therapeutic value of alcohol and drug abuse programs. Typically, establishing a program or getting a treatment centre on a reserve or in a tribal council area is seen as a major *coup*, justifiably considered as important from an institution-building perspective. Establishing a program is viewed as a significant part of the overall community development effort and securing a treatment program is seen as a mark of good leadership. It is also seen as a way of creating employment and, in truth, on reserves where work is scarce, even one solid job is nothing to scoff at. But beyond the point of securing the program, the principles of effective prevention and intervention are often severely compromised by their subordination to local political and social needs. The unhappy result is that, all too often, even the most minimum levels of program effectiveness go unrealized. There is a now well-established history in aboriginal alcohol abuse programming of hiring recovered alcoholics with limited education, training, or skills but who display a serious commitment to the 'recovery movement.' In the absence of any supportive evidence in the relevant research literature, conventional wisdom in the Native alcohol intervention field has held that their personal experience in overcoming alcoholism has endowed these individuals with special intuitions. One can undoubtedly gain special insights from the experience of problems, but such insights hardly form the basis of a comprehensive approach to counselling. Most First Nations leaders recognize that effective alcohol counsellors require more skills than can be gained from personal recovery and Health Canada short courses. Unfortunately, while leaders almost universally express an interest in seeing the upgrading of programs and the expertise of personnel, all too often their decisions reflect lip service rather than tangible commitment. With unacceptable frequency, alcohol abuse prevention and intervention positions are allocated to satisfy various personal familial and political ends. It is therefore important for specific accountability criteria to be built into program administration, with consideration given to:

- establishing small, elected boards with technical expertise in addictions or health promotion,
- ensuring that program outcome data is collected and summarized and reviewed openly with community 'watchdog' groups,

- conducting ongoing and summative program evaluations,
- creating a special section in annual health reports that details how all moneys are spent,
- requiring NNADAP staff to have professional qualifications or a fully referenced, demonstrated track record of effective experience in a relevant, related program area, and
- securing and maintaining accreditation for on-reserve programs.

Another political factor of particular significance to effective programming is the integrity of leadership. I have heard or examined the opinions of hundreds of First Nations health workers and individuals responding to adult health surveys with a critical view of local leaders. Consistantly, these key informants have stressed that until the leadership practises a sober and exemplary lifestyle, and adopts ethical governance practice by rather than routinely responding, primarily, to interest group pressure or personal interest, little progress will be made in lowering problem drinking rates and addictions in the First Nations population. This same body of opinion suggests that far too many chiefs, councillors, and senior committee representatives are themselves guilty of problem drinking and/or addictive behaviours, and those behaviours are widely known by their band members – and, until such leaders embrace sober lifestyles, there will not be sufficient enthusiasm in communities to seriously tackle the problem.

THE CULTURAL DIMENSION

Reserve communities and their extensions in the inner cities of Canada have frequently been described in sociological terms as 'anomic': which means that, relative to a vital, well-functioning community, there are few norms that govern social relations. While there is obviously a dense web of mutual expectations and rules that act as guides to interactions between Native people, the web is far less articulated than it should be. Social expectations are not firm, meaning that, because people have little confidence in predicting the translation of the stated intentions of others into expected outcomes, they become socially disoriented and apathetic. They have little confidence that others will do what they say they will do, whether it involves completing a task, repaying a debt, or maintaining a house at standards formally set for a reserve housing program. This shallowness of norms has much to do with the historical process of cultural disintegration that virtually every First Nation community in Canada has experienced. More immediately, it has much to do with unemployment and wel-

fare. Without the discipline of self-reliance and the pride of workman-
ship that grows out of hunting, food-gathering, craft production, or
modern, specialized employment, there is little pressure for a new and
sufficiently elaborated normative structure to emerge. Instead, the
local norms grow up around economic marginality, informality, and
economic dependency. In such an environment, individuals have little
incentive to meet an elaborate set of obligations. Yet meeting the challenges of daily obligations is a key preventive of alcohol abuse. It is
very difficult to maintain a job and consume too much alcohol every
day. At the community level, it is essential that leaders, Elders, and
health workers consciously work towards creating a politics of inclusion that involves all band members in a dense web of both obligations
and rights. Those norms are, ultimately, the basic fabric of community.

THE SOCIAL DIMENSION

In most reserve communities across Canada, outlets for social and recreational activities are few and far between. In fact, in the community
health studies conducted on reserves by this writer, the paucity of positive substitutes for recreational drinking, promiscuous sex, gambling,
and other troublesome and addictive behaviours is viewed as a primary cause of the widespread occurrence of those very problems.
Many reserves lack even organized team sports, despite the popularity
of such activities in First Nations. Very few have a varied range of social
and recreational outlets, be they commercial, public, or voluntary, that
offer activities other than team sports and bingo. There can be little in
the way of valid argument against the view that an active community
life is an effective antidote to socially destructive behaviours.

The informal social life of a community must also be a primary target of community organization aimed at reducing alcohol abuse, and
the goal of such organizing has to be to encourage group formation in
which sobriety is the status quo. When problem drinkers change the
groups to which they belong, they become, in a sense, different people.
One way for problem drinkers to overcome their drinking problem is
to modify their environments by separating themselves from those
people who encourage their drinking and establishing bonds with
those who practise sober lifestyles. Community health service programs should facilitate community change that promotes the following opportunities for problem drinkers:

• ready access to a 'sober hangout' – a location at which sober people
  spend time casually socializing on a regular basis;

- participation in a program assisting individuals with making choices about educational and career development opportunities;
- outlets and support for participating on a regular basis in recreational games, hobbies, and sporting activities;
- participation as decision makers on a volunteer board or committee that oversees some activity or services made available for the benefit of community members;
- participation in a volunteer activity that directly contributes something to the community, such as coaching, or assisting the physically or mentally challenged; and
- ongoing, problem-focused self-help groups, such as healing circles, rational recovery groups, or family therapy programs.

Holism and Strategies Focused on the Individual and Family

THE BIOLOGICAL DIMENSION: DETOXIFICATION, PROPER NUTRITION, AND EXERCISE

Effective personal development and programming that supports it requires that the physical health of the individual must be addressed. Detoxification, which can typically be handled outside of a hospital setting, is essential before serious personal transformation begins. Similarly, the issues of proper nutrition and exercise must be addressed. Appropriate diets can dampen addictions. Obesity has become a major problem with First Nations people and it is implicated in diabetes and heart disease (Thatcher, 2001). Exercise is an effective antidote to obesity, and individuals who display addictive behaviours or problem drinking patterns should be encouraged to participate actively in exercise programs. At the community level, of course, community health workers should work to ensure that appropriate counselling regarding these issues is readily available and that abundant, health-promoting exercise activities are offered. At present, such counselling and opportunities are extremely underdeveloped on most reserves.

THE PSYCHOLOGICAL DIMENSION

A person with a drinking problem has the capacity to overcome that problem through the development of rational, healthy choices, geared to the long-term acquisition of a healthy lifestyle. Destructive drinking behaviours are learned and they can be unlearned, however difficult that process may be (and it is more difficult for some than others). No one other than the affected individual can make the choices necessary for establishing a sober lifestyle. It is true that people with drinking problems often have one or a number of other problems, some rooted in the same dysfunctional thinking that encourages their addictive behaviours or the acting-out behaviour that accompanies drinking sessions. Such individuals should receive support for dealing with various emotional and cognitive problems that affect them – and counselling that is sufficiently sophisticated to detect these multiple problems and to assist the individual in tackling them should be available.

As suggested above, the key to overcoming the psychological problems that limit one's capacity to overcome a drinking problem is termed self-efficacy. The concept is of sufficient importance to the perspective advocated in this book that it is given special treatment below.

THE SOCIAL DIMENSION: FAMILY, SOCIAL ROLES, AND RELATIONSHIP BUILDING

In the great majority of cases, problem drinking is associated with specific types of social milieu. Family systems, social networks, and drinking venues are all critically implicated. It is therefore essential that individuals seeking to avoid problem drinking, as well as those charged with helping them, recognize the importance of avoiding or transforming social networks that trigger drinking as a coping mechanism. Effective self-help and therapy necessarily focuses on family systems and social networks supportive of sobriety and incorporates the learning of avoidance behaviours in relation to 'drinking crowds' and 'rough bars;' it also involves positive relationship building, effective communication skills, and problem-solving strategies. Relapse prevention efforts must also incorporate family systems, social milieu, social role, and relationship building considerations into strategies designed to assist problem drinkers whose problems have revisited them.

THE SPIRITUAL DIMENSION: MORALITY AND HOLISTIC BALANCE

In keeping with aboriginal North American tradition, a holistic approach to overcoming problems connected with problem drinking should include a spiritual dimension. In the cultures indigenous to North America, the spiritual aspect of living involved the way that people conceptualized and understood their personal relationship and the relationship of their community to different aspects of nature. It was also a basic form of causal thinking: all aspects of nature were viewed as having a spirit which had the capacity to influence outcomes. Consequently, respecting all elements of nature for their uniqueness and contribution to the environment as a whole was a practical necessity. In most North American aboriginal cultures spiritual emphasis was also placed on the balance between an individual's life and its different parts, and there was a faith in the existence of a certain order of things in the natural world that should be respected and not be disrupted. Thus, while recovery from many emotional and physical illnesses was thought to be aided by specific medicines and herbal remedies, the identification of imbalances in personal living patterns and the necessity of restoring balance was considered essential. This view is similar to the view of addictions held by many mental health workers in recent years. In what has been referred to as a 'balance of life' model, addictions such as alcohol or drug overuse or gambling are viewed as a misdirected attempt to meet a fundamental, unmet need. These unmet needs are losses on one's psycho-social development path that the individual has not been able to replace with mature, compensatory substitutes. The addict or individual with other mental health problems is seen as being 'stuck' in his or her maturation at an adolescent stage. Until balance can be restored with appropriate grief work and healthy, realistic lifestyle alternatives, the addiction continues to be troublesome; in some cases it becomes a progressively expanding preoccupation that leaves less and less time for significant others or for work, education, and family.

Spirituality has also almost universally been connected to human morality. Our sense of the spiritual provides the cognitive and emotional fuel that guides our moral behaviour. Unfortunately, this connection has all too often been lost; in fact, in recent years, it has almost been forgotten under the sway of a parade of self-help gurus, each convincing us that we must find our present faults in past injustices, and that our health, which is equated with freedom from guilt and past emotional baggage, is *not* connected with responsibility. This separation of spirituality and morality is misguided and very risky, and it tends to encourage self-care at the expense of one's obligations to one's dependents and community. Surely the meaning of life in its best sense is to be found in the connections we make to others through respect and the meeting of obligations, not in a perpetual search for remedies for self-improvement gained without due attention to the needs of those who constitute our immediate web of human intercourse.

Clearly, a moral framework that can sustain long-term abstinence or moderation management in relation to alcohol links spirituality, self-responsibility, and obligation. Responsibility to others is a cornerstone of sobriety and it must become a cornerstone of health promotion in First Nations' communities.

The Importance of Client Responsibility: A Core Issue, Both for the Problem Drinker and His/Her Helpers

As I have argued repeatedly above, the emphasis in the disease model on 'alcoholism' frames the problem as one of 'afflicted individuals' who have no control over their inappropriate use of alcohol and this conception has a dark side. While long hailed not only as a scientific advancement but as a progressive social attitude inspiring sympathy rather than scorn for the 'alcoholic,' this view attributes no blame to the problem drinker. With the assumption of blamelessness, of course, comes the attribution of powerlessness. As Marlatt and Gordon have argued:

> If alcoholics come to view their drinking as the result of a disease or phys-
> iological addiction, they are more likely to assume the passive role of vic-
> tim whenever they engage in drinking behaviour if they see it as a
> symptom of their disease ... Relapse is the turning point ... If an alcoholic
> has accepted the belief that it is impossible to control his or her drinking
> (as embodied in the AA slogan that one is always 'one drink away from a
> drunk'), then even a single slip may precipitate a total, uncontrolled
> relapse ... drinking under these circumstances is equated with the occur-
> rence of a symptom signifying the re-emergence of the disease, [and] one
> is likely to feel as powerless to control this behaviour as one would with
> any other disease symptom. (1985: 7–8)

The alarming thing about the disease model and its principal corol-
lary beliefs is that the counselling intended to provide relief and encourage recovery may actually reinforce the alcohol problem itself by contributing to the client's feelings of powerlessness. Thus the sense of limited self-control imported through such counsel can fundamentally interfere with an individual's ability to cope with difficulties or to resolve problems. For first peoples, who have been, as a group, so pro-
foundly victimized by historical circumstances, this can serve as a sort of 'double dose' of psychological paralysis.

Under the assumption that people can cope more effectively with their problems if they believe in their own potential for mastery, Stensrud and Stensrud argue convincingly that counsellors should help cli-
ents 'take personal control of their lives, accepting stress as a challenge rather than a harm-loss-threat factor, finding personal meaning within stressful situations' (1983: 216).

As noted above, the fullest formulation of the principle behind the notion of the importance of competence to personal problem solving is captured in the term 'self-efficacy' (Bandura, 1982), which is a general ability to deal with one's environment, to mobilize one's cognitive and behavioural skills, when necessary, to master even difficult situations. Self-efficacy entails the individual's belief that he or she can cope with the environment, to stand up to most challenges. A person who lacks self-efficacy tends to avoid challenges rather than facing them with optimism. The problem drinkers most likely to achieve and maintain behaviour changes are those who have a positive sense of self-efficacy: 'When coping skills are underdeveloped and poorly used because of disbelief in one's efficacy, a relapse will occur. Faultless self-control is not easy to come by for pliant activities, let alone for addictive substances. Nevertheless, those who perceive themselves to be inefficacious are more prone to attribute a slip to pervasive self-regulatory inefficacy. Further coping efforts are then abandoned, resulting in total breakdown in self control' (Bandura, 1982: 129–30).

But does the act of discarding the assumption that alcoholism is an uncontrollable disease not simply shift the blame for the problem back to the person experiencing the addiction, and thus constitute a return to the older practice of victim blaming? Such a turn of events would surely be doubly cruel for the first peoples, whose language, culture, social institutions, and economy have been overwhelmed, maimed, or destroyed by the white settler society that has enveloped them. But such a shift is not necessary. When considering where the primary responsibility for alcohol abuse should lie there are a number of options. The *moral model* holds that people are responsible for creating and solving their own problems. The *medical model* essentially holds that people are neither responsible for their problems nor for discovering the solutions to those problems. The *enlightenment model* holds that people are responsible for creating their problems, but not for solving them. Finally, the *compensatory model* holds that people are not responsible for creating their own problems, but they are responsible for solving them (Brickman et al., 1982).

While the moral model sees the individual with an alcohol abuse problem as having created the problem and thus bearing responsibility for mustering sufficient fortitude and willpower to overcome it, the medical model suggests that the drinking problem is generated by something beyond the volition of the individual, and thus the individual cannot justifiably be blamed for acquiring the problem or expected to be able to solve it alone. The enlightenment model suggests that people do bear responsibility for their past behaviours but they can be helped by surrendering personal power to a higher authority that is stronger than themselves. While it does not encourage problem drinkers to blame themselves, what the writers call the compensatory model does encourage them to take control of their problem, often with the help of a counsellor or social support network. The compensatory model tends to see individuals with alcohol problems as having acquired the problem through the learning of inappropriate coping skills, often in stressful social environments.

It is the compensatory model, stressing, as it does, self-efficacy as the key to sober living and recovery from addiction, that clearly deserves the support of addictions and problem drinking programming serving first peoples. A substance-abusing client can become the master of his or her addiction, and the potential for that mastery in turn depends upon self-perceived efficacy. Problem drinkers must seek and are encouraged to seek this sense of mastery. The Harvard social psychologist Stanton Peele, who has been among the strongest critics of the disease model, has argued that this sense of mastery may be the most critical determinant of an individual's recovery. According to Peele, 'people recover to the extent that they (1) believe an addiction is hurting them and wish to overcome it, (2) feel enough efficacy to manage their withdrawal and life without addiction, and (3) find sufficient alternative rewards to make life without the addiction worthwhile' (1985: 156).

Resilience and Self-efficacy: The Recommended, Central Principles of Assisted Skill Development to Overcome Problem Drinking

It is essential for First Nations to shift away from a disease model of alcohol abuse intervention, in which the 'client' is viewed as a permanent victim, towards a model in which the individual's inner strength is emphasized. Clients should be assisted in reorienting their thinking in accordance with the following recommendations:

• They should be encouraged to overcome a preoccupation with the past and the problems they experienced that may have led to their problem drinking.
• While learning to recognize the origins of their current problems in previous difficulties that were not of their own making, they should

not be encouraged to blame their parents or substitute caregivers for their present problems.
- They should learn to avoid 'victim thinking,' which means not being preoccupied with inaction in solving personal problems by using the excuse that they were victims.

From a positive perspective, they should:

- Identify their own strengths and learn to build on them as part of their personal development strategy.
- Consciously and methodically define an ideal lifestyle and work towards achieving it.

Clients should also be advised of the following principles of effectiveness in overcoming addictions:

1 *Self-motivation to change.* The most crucial factor in accomplishing positive change is the desire to change, or motivation, which is located inside the individual. If motivation is weak, addictive temptations remain strong and victorious.
2 *Reinforcement of the desire to change.* Those things that are most important to an individual contain the best sources of influence to support a desire to change. Resilience is connected to pleasure, aptitude, and strength. Positive motivations include the desire to treat intimates well, to do well in school or training or at work, to feel better physically, or to secure a healthy spiritual frame of mind. In attempting to reinforce a desire to change, the individual who wants to overcome alcohol abuse problems is well advised to mobilize all of these sources in a plan that will reinforce the motivation to alter addictive habits or even occasional episodes of high-risk drinking.
3 *Improving social skills.* Drinking often begins as a lubricant for dormant social skills. Once the drinking stops, the awkwardness, shyness, and loneliness return. Acquiring social skills through such exercises as role playing and participating in organized social activities in which sobriety is the rule is extremely important. Addressing the issue of social skill deficits is often the linchpin of successful attempts at sobriety.
4 *Building self-confidence through competency training.* Self-efficacy does not just fall from the sky; it is learned. Clients should therefore be

encouraged to take on specific skill-building strategies, especially in areas that are crucial to their positive, basic functioning and to the education and employment prospects that may be possible once they have overcome their problem drinking habits.

This new model of alcohol abuse intervention must be conveyed to clients, who are likely to have internalized the disease explanation. To accomplish this, the terminology of the medical model, including 'treatment' and 'pathology,' should be cleansed from common use by counsellors and group leaders and replaced with terms that emphasize learning, skill development, and personal empowerment. Clients should be given credit for success and counsellors only credit for helping them get there. Ultimately, clients should be encouraged by counsellors and psycho-educational trainers to believe that they are personally able to manage most of the situations they face. As long as goals are realistic, achievement is always within one's reach.

Measuring Progress

First Nations alcohol abuse programming has for too long escaped appropriate scrutiny regarding its progress. On-reserve and urban programs should work according to plans, with goals broken down into measurable objectives – and that applies to both prevention and intervention programming. Measurement should include population and client coverage aims, including measures of the numbers of people exposed to health promotion (group education) programs and media campaigns, and the numbers participating in constructive recreational programs and self-help groups; it should also include the numbers participating in residential programs and out-patient programs and the varying circumstances under which they have participated. In addition to program exposure goals, objectives should be set and measurements taken of the outcomes of prevention and intervention programs. While health promotion is extremely difficult to measure, except over a very long period, general trends can be calculated in the short run through local and regional data collection processes and, eventually, that data can afford long-term comparison.

It is also vital for both non-residential and residential programs to establish efficient and accurate methods of measuring the relative success of different approaches and methods with various population subgroups.

Looking Outward to the Available Research Literature

First peoples have the same right as all other cultural groups in Canada to obtain the advantages of the knowledge gained from the best research available on alcohol abuse prevention and intervention. That should mean that programs in the field serving First Nations should be expected to keep abreast of the research that is available internationally. While the adoption of methods that have proven effective elsewhere should not be blindly accepted, they must be assessed for their potential for adoption in terms of local and regional social and cultural realities

Program managers and therapists must also be accountable for exploring and implementing innovations in the field. It should not be acceptable for program directors, managers, and personnel to provide second-rate, outdated services when more effective methods are available.

The Principles of Traditional Healing Methods Should Also Be Implemented and Evaluated

While it is typically viewed as heresy to even question traditional healing methods, in recent years increasing demands have been made for public support for the payment of traditional healers. This is necessarily a thorny issue, however, given the fact that public payments are provided on the basis of fiduciary obligations, which means that providing moneys for health services is part of the federal government's role as a legal trustee of Crown responsibility to First Nations. The legitimacy of this obligation is fairly clear so long as the money is paid for services that are carefully regulated under the protection of public legislation and professional regulatory bodies. These regulatory systems are in place to ensure that demonstrably effective intervention methods are being applied and that services are provided in a way that ensures that the health and safety of the client is a primary consideration. In the absence of these conditions, both the federal government and the service providers can be held liable for any health problems that might arise as a consequence of a program, method, or procedure that is promoted as health-enhancing but actually has health-diminishing consequences.

In the past several years, I have been made aware of a number of instances of unethical and unsafe actions that have taken place in the context of the counselling relationship between traditional healers and those securing their assistance, as well as within the physical confines of the sweat lodge. I am not attempting to dissuade anyone from attempting these methods. However, traditional healing activities should be framed within some of the basic health and safety standards that health consumers have come to take for granted. First peoples need some public method for determining the legitimacy of healers and whether their advice contravenes the evidence of science and the health and safety protection that corresponds to the treatment of various illness conditions – at least before any funding is provided by a responsible government in a trusteeship role, and before any management group sanctions a traditional healing service. There is a growing recognition that some form of regulation of traditional healing is required, although the subject is a very sensitive one in First Nations communities. Public comments made by Judge Murray Sinclair of Manitoba, who is himself of aboriginal ancestry, indicated a serious concern about this issue. In the late 1990s, after becoming aware of the dubious practices of several self-described 'traditional healers,' Judge Sinclair called for the formalization of a system to regulate the administration of traditional healing and the qualifications of the healers.

Like other interventions, the outcomes of traditional healing should also eventually be measured. Culture is not a static entity; it is a society's body of knowledge utilized for survival and it is always subject to questioning and adaptation to evolving and newly emerging needs. First peoples have long demonstrated a willingness to share aspects of their own cultures with other nationality groups, and they have been consistently willing to accept many aspects of European culture, from the horse, guns, steel implements, housing styles, automobiles, half-ton trucks, motor boats and ski-doos to commercial gambling businesses. It is true that much that is 'Western' and 'modern' has fit poorly with the traditions of First Nations. Yet in many instances, the marriage of the modern with the traditional has yielded undeniable benefits – witness the glorious integration of modernist abstraction with traditional aboriginal symbolism in art. In the community health field, the conceptual work developed by the Four Worlds Development Project is another impressive example of the potential for integrating traditional and contemporary ideas. Those aspects of a culture intended directly to promote health should not be exempted from scientific scrutiny.

Definition of Addiction

While a serviceable definition of drinking behaviour risks is implicit to the continuum described above in Part One, a few other definitions should be considered.

The term *addiction* appropriately refers to behaviour associated with attraction to a variety of substances and processes; it therefore includes not only alcohol and other substance use but sex, relationships, and other leisure activities that encourage intensive habits that overwhelm one's lifestyle, such as gambling, internet surfing, and electronic games. It is important that First Nations develop a definition of addiction that serves the purpose of enhancing self-efficacy rather than further promoting a victim mentality, dependency, and a sense of powerlessness. A recommended definition of an addiction is that it is a conditioned habit that undermines an individual's health, ability to learn from experience or formal education, work performance, self-confidence, self-respect, and relationships. It is a learned psychological and social method upon which one has come to depend for coping with the stresses of life, and therefore something that is very difficult to change. An addiction may be reinforced by the distinctive activities of an individual's brain chemistry, and typically by the nature of his or her social milieu. An addiction is not literally a disease, although it *is* a bio-psycho-social disorder or, in the less clinical phrasing suggested by Stanton Peele, a 'problem of living.' As such it can conceivably be overcome through the active, self-driven processes of cognitive, social, and nutritional restructuring of one's lifestyle.

Various studies have shown that many more people give up problem drinking *on their own* than through either AA or residential treatment without taking on the stigma that they suffer from a disease (Vaillant, 1983). However, it must also be recognized that some addictions may be reinforced by neurobiological mechanisms and clients should be screened for these problems. In addition, too-frequent alcohol consumption does result in significant impairment that reduces a client's ability to cope with certain types of cognitive and visospatial learning. A clinical knowledge of the client's history and abilities to gain from therapies based in analytical reasoning is fundamental to the clinical process.

Definition of an Alcohol Dependent

An alcohol dependent is an individual who is psychologically, socially and, in varying degrees, physically addicted to the ingestion of alcoholic beverages and continues to use alcohol regularly, despite the negative consequences experienced in the spheres of personal development, interpersonal relations, financial well-being, and physical and mental health. Characteristics typically associated with alcohol dependency, or 'alcoholism,' include:

1 *Increasing tolerance*: The individual requires an increased amount of the substance to achieve intoxication.
2 *Diminished effect*: With continued use of the substance, the impairing effects on individual diminish.
3 *Withdrawal syndrome*: If the individual tries to quit, the initial abandonment of alcohol results in significant social and physical discomfort.
4 *Loss of control*: While this is highly variable, many alcohol-dependents will often drink more than s/he intended prior to or in the early stages of a drinking episode.

Definition of Problem Drinking

Drinking problems come in many varieties, originating in different sets of problems and expressed in distinctive ways. Prevention and intervention programming must be tailored to meet the needs of clients with a wide range of individual differences. The continuum provided in figure 5.1 above gives a clear idea of the many types of problem drinking that exist in the Canadian population as a whole. First peoples and the alcohol abuse programs designed for them should recognize and act upon the reality of that variation. However, it is useful to separate the alcohol-dependent individual from an individual who is simply a 'problem drinker.' Borrowing from the definition of problem drinking recommended by the widely recognized researchers, therapists, and trainers Mark R. Sobell and Linda C. Sobell, the following definition is consistent with the central demarcations of the problem drinking continuum we have described above: '... problem drinkers typically have either experienced negative consequences of their drinking or drink in ways that place them at risk of such consequences; however, they usually do not drink steadily, do not show major withdrawal symptoms when they stop drinking, and sometimes drink with control, and their lives do not revolve around drinking' (1993: 5).

The importance of making this distinction is critical, because most aboriginal people who experience difficulties with drinking are not alcoholics (or alcohol-dependents) and they correctly reject such a diagnostic label rather than simply being 'in denial.' The mischief inherent in therapists' insistence on the alcohol label is that many individuals seeking help for problem drinking behaviour are repulsed, while the treatment course of others is distorted by the inaccuracy of the assessment.

13

Structural Change: Targeting the 'Root System' of Problem Drinking on Reserves

The old adage that an ounce of prevention is worth a pound of cure surely has the same ring of truth today that it did when it was first coined. Thus factors other than direct intervention services play a far more influential role in reducing the numbers of problem drinkers in a given population. There are probably more people who experience addictions and problems associated with drinking who, on their own or with a little help from their families, employers, or friends, overcome their bad habits and modify their destructive behaviours without ever seeing a counsellor or 'treatment' professional (Vaillant, 1983). Overcoming one's own drinking troubles is a normal rather than an exceptional phenomenon. The same can be said for the most widespread substance addiction of them all: habitual cigarette smoking.

The pleasurable use of alcoholic beverages is woven into the very fabric of ordinary social life in Canadian society. Effective efforts to encourage moderate use and to discourage excess must therefore also be integral to the routines of ordinary community life: they cannot be mounted and wholly executed by professionals, paraprofessionals, and volunteers in the addictions prevention field. There are far more people who never acquire habitual drinking patterns or experience frequent, high-risk drinking episodes than there are people who do – and, obviously, *something* protects the many from the troubles experienced by the few. Further, problem drinking rates vary with relative poverty. Communities with high levels of unemployment and high social assistance rates, and which experience especially stressful events, also tend to experience high problem drinking rates.

When local populations are geographically isolated, relatively unskilled, and isolated from ready access to the primary labour markets of the mainstream economy, and when unemployment becomes intergenerational, a *malaise of motivation* tends to set in. This 'malaise' is not a disease; it is a sense of hopelessness and despair. A mindset takes root that can afflict an entire population, a mindset fixed upon a short time horizon for gratification and pain avoidance. This mindset can also become a defining element of the local, collective consciousness. In the absence of a believable set of expectations for a better future, anxieties and restlessness can be quieted and boredom challenged through mind- and behaviour-altering drugs. Creating hope through education, training, and the facilitation of economic development must therefore be viewed as the most effective addictions and problem drinking prevention strategy. Stated bluntly, in communities that are stranded outside the mainstream economy, the healthy outcomes of healing processes facilitated by professional therapists or traditional healers may have great impact in the short term, but to have a lasting effect, there must also be a reason for abstinence, such as an opportunity to support oneself and one's family through economic activity. If there is no opportunity and no real hope, relapses or a switch to substitute addictions are predictable.

When we consider which prevention programs are more effective than others, intuition would suggest that we always keep in mind the way that ordinary people routinely prevent themselves from beginning or continuing to engage in addictive and inappropriate drinking-related behaviours. The challenge appears to be to distance oneself from what we understand to be a normal range of significant risk factors, from whom we associate with to where we hang out to the relative comfort or discomfort of our moods. The most fundamental task is to identify the factors that seem to have the most influence within a family, community, or targeted group. If possible, prevention should be built around a knowledge of these risk factors; the challenge is to prevent or reduce the risk factors that correlate with unhealthy, high-risk drinking practices and to increase the prevalence or intensity of those factors that protect people against the temptations of addictions and binge-drinking episodes.

As repeatedly noted above, population health researchers have proven that, in the absence of a 'healthy' economy and the education, nutrition, and other material and social benefits that flow from it, modern, individualized health interventions can have relatively little impact on the health status of a population. A healthy economy refers not only to abundant food and relative material affluence; it also refers to development strategies guided by a keen sensitivity to market signals but checked by democratic choices framed by values of distributive justice. A healthy economy is also based on widespread, realistic access to a distribution of work roles and a balance of work benefits, rights, and obligations among groups that is accepted rather than resented. The health of populations is further influenced by the availability of recreational and life-long learning resources for all age groups.

As a population health problem, rates of alcohol abuse are indirectly affected by all of these fundamental health determinants, which can be referred to as 'structural' factors, a term used to signal the fact that they are built into the foundation of the social order itself. In addressing alcohol abuse in First Nations with preventive strategies, structural factors must be manipulated and the problem must be directly addressed through programming and educational messages. The term 'structural' is used in a sociological sense; it refers to fundamental aspects of social organization, supported by deeply rooted norms, rules, laws, and public policies which inadvertently or deliberately give rise to a socially problematic behaviour pattern.

A solution to the economic underdevelopment of First Nations is obviously beyond the scope of this book, but an outline of some approaches that might be taken in this area is warranted. The overwhelming impact of the economy on aboriginal substance abuse demands some thoughtfulness by virtually anyone who wishes to address this problem in a meaningful and strategically significant fashion. This chapter thus outlines some primary prevention strategies targeted on structural change, macro- and mezzo-level strategies that indirectly rather than directly impact on problem drinking rates in First Nations.

National Policy and the Social Problems of First Nations

While the recommendation may strike the reader as melodramatic, it is apparent to many who work in the mental health and addictions fields that First Nations people must be considered one of the uppermost priorities in a national development policy for Canada in the new millennium. The reserve system and an insensitive, racist, and underfunded assimilation policy were part of Canada's first National Policy: the policy of railroads, western agricultural development and settlement, and protective tariffs to bolster central Canadian manufacturing and finance capital. The policy accomplished the goal of setting the 'Indian problem' aside to make way for the development of a political and administrative framework to support capital accumulation for Euro-Canadian business elites. However, it failed in its pursuit of a goal that was, admittedly, considered rather minor at the time: the assimilation of Canada's indigenous peoples. Due to insufficient attention, a lack of understanding, bad choices, and underfunding, the policy resulted in several generations of social, economic, and cultural isolation of First Nations people from the larger society.

Canada's 'Indian policy' has not only failed in terms of its assimilationist intentions, it has also proven to be the antithesis of what the chiefs who signed the treaties intended. Assistance in replacing the economic culture they had once practised with the new economic culture imported by the Europeans was not forthcoming. Partially as a result of many decades of neglect by government, and partially the result of the apartheid nature of the reserve system itself, that expectation was never adequately realized. The lack of economic integration of First Nations people stands out in the history of public policy in Canada as the most substantial failure to date of the Canadian nation-building project. The endurance of the firewater complex is nourished by the segregation, isolation, and lack of economic integration that has followed from that failure – and by the antipathy towards the larger society provoked by that historic misanthropy.

It is true that the reserve system is now thoroughly entrenched and there is a plethora of legislative, administrative, and attitudinal support for the status quo. Yet, as all those who give serious thought to the nature of social problems on reserves understand, a population health and community development strategy focused primarily on social assistance, community health development, and 'growing the administrative infrastructure' on reserves must be abandoned. At some point, reserve-centred development must become a thing of the past.

As part of Canada's new national policy to guide the country's strategic development in the first quarter of the new millennium, a First Nations strategy is required that supports the revisitation of the federal government's treaty and aboriginal rights and obligations. Economic integration, combined with some form of cultural continuity, was surely the intention of the indigenous leaders who signed the original treaties. The continuous existence of the reserve system as the primary focus of First Nation development policies should be viewed as a fundamental violation of the very purpose and spirit of the treaties. If the system does not work, then it should be changed, despite its deep entrenchment.

The unavoidable conclusion is that the reserve-centred strategy and attempts to develop a parallel system of government and services to sustain reserve residents fly in the face of basic economic logic. For First Nations capital and labour to thrive, both must find a place in the larger economy, including in local, regional, provincial, national, and even international entry points, where goods and services can be exchanged at sustainable rates in the real marketplace. Most reserves have long proven that they cannot support a growing population on their land allotments. Yet reserves are the basic building blocks of the entire national policy aimed at addressing the needs of indigenous people. Those building blocks create constraints rather than opportunities for the elimination of isolation, poverty, dependency, alcohol abuse, and other social problems.

It is true that the economic elite on many reserves benefit greatly from the perpetuation of the current system. Yet for most residents, the reserve offers little hope for escape from intergenerational low income, welfare dependency, and being directly implicated in the tragic outcomes of rampant social problems. If abnormally high levels of alcohol and other substance abuse and the high rates of ill-health, violence, injuries, homicide, and suicide that so often follow it are to be eliminated, the current administrative configuration of community development, population support, and community administration must be revised and renewed. If alcohol abuse and other addictions are to decline substantially, leadership cannot continue to function in a perverse, symbiotic relationship with the fact of dependency on the part of the majority of community residents. Infrastructure expansion on reserves that cannot possibly support even a large minority of their residents cannot go on forever: neither the local, impoverished on-reserve residents nor Canadian taxpayers as a whole will allow it for more than one or two additional generations.

Instead of the status quo policy framework, treaties must be renovated to embrace realistic approaches to development. Legislation must be reframed, current programs redesigned, and financial support refocused. Much greater emphasis must be placed on the promotion of the type of development that is realistically linked to the productivity values and demand signals of the marketplace, as well as the real needs and demands of the public sector, in which aboriginal people should be playing a much more expansive role.

To ensure that the federal government is willing to undertake the policy development activity required to 'bring First Nations in' as full partners in the country's economy, First Nations leaders will have to make a number of concessions. They will have to accept and support some fundamental changes and probably the loss of at least some of their relative privileges and powers. In addition to expanding their focus of development beyond the reserve system, they will have to abandon the paradigm of parallelism. Making all development dependent upon public transfers to create parallel First Nations facilities and services in virtually every key institutional sector is not only cost-prohibitive, it might also, intentionally or otherwise, limit the access of First Nations people to the wide range of choices available to other Canadians. While the matter has its ethical complexities, parallelism often produces a 'second rate separatism' that limits opportunities for most First Nations people and, as such, represents a significant violation of their fundamental human rights and rights of Canadian citizenship.

Affirmative Business Action and Affirmative Employment Action

Although there have been many excellent examples of economic development in First Nations, overall, a candid assessment would have to describe a situation of overwhelming failure. New and drastic action is required if significant economic integration is to occur over the next several generations. Let us consider some promising new directions that might be followed.

A principal element of a renewed First Nations economic development strategy might involve what I will refer to as *affirmative business development*, by which I mean a form of affirmative action aimed at creating special business opportunities for First Nations. Much like the protective tariff against incoming manufactured goods that enabled the development of Canada as a national society, protection for aboriginal business development is essential to the integration of First Nations as economic partners.

In the policy of federal 'set asides' and direct purchases of rental space and services by INAC from First Nations organizations and people, this idea of creating affirmative business action to create First Nations employment is, in limited form, already a part of federal policy. Provincial governments have also, on occasion, bypassed the tendering process and secured the agreement of unions and their own civil servants to contract directly with First Nations to provide services. This approach needs to be enlarged in size and scope, and it must become far more innovative.

One approach that the federal government could take to promote economic development in First Nations involves the concept of 'charter companies.' Just as the Hudson Bay Company was given a special charter by the British Crown to explore, conduct business, and exercise authority in what is now Canada, so might First Nations be given charters to conduct specific businesses and public sector activities. Emphasis in such charters should be given to business that can meet one of two criteria: (1) those that can generate substantial profits for the purposes of reinvestment in aboriginal businesses, and (2) businesses and public services that are labour intensive and can employ large numbers of people. Current, extremely high rates of unemployment demand such special corporate designations, perhaps with a specific time horizon. The significant employment development that has occurred as a result of special authorities to operate casinos gives some indication of the potential that lies in this direction.

Another approach might involve the establishment of a protective tariff regime for companies providing a designated list of goods and services made available in the market through private or public First Nations businesses. Providing a share of royalties on all mineral extraction and sales to create a development fund for strategic investments in on- and off-reserve businesses also deserves further consideration. Rather than being limited to a specific time frame, such a fund could remain in place until certain measurable indicators of parity are achieved.

Finally, while aboriginal people have been a target group for federal and provincial employment equity policies, far-reaching affirmative action legislation in large companies and the public sector is also a potential source of workforce integration. To be effective, such policies require considerable workforce cooperation and, therefore, a substantial effort at diversity training and workplace hosting for nontraditional workers. To make such a policy work, the educational supply side of the equation must be given far greater emphasis. A comprehensive and innovative human resource development strategy is badly needed to realize this goal.

Promoting Distributive Justice

As argued above, it has become the primary administrative role of many if not most First Nations leaders to maintain and develop facilities, programs, and services in their home communities. Most have given but secondary attention to off-reserve economic opportunities and band members living away from the reserve. It has also been argued that on reserves where long-standing economic elites have formed, the primary function of elected leadership has often been to funnel federal funds to programs that provide basic income, shelter, and educational support to the majority of community residents who have few if any local job prospects. As Boldt writes, 'Although the rhetoric of those who promote on-reserve economic development always stresses job creation, despite the significant cumulative sums of money expended to introduce economic development on to reserves ... even where they have succeeded, with rare exceptions [they] have provided only tokenistic employment opportunities ... [The] band/tribal labour supply far exceeds the jobs created by such endeavours' (1993: 231).

Economic development efforts guided by on-reserve leadership in partnership with government funding agencies have been made over several decades. These strategies have been initiated with a mix of grant and loan support through DIAND, joint federal/provincial seed funds, and special programs like the former Native Economic Development Program (NEDP) and the current Aboriginal Business Canada (ABC). As Boldt further notes, despite years of on-reserve economic development efforts, 'the level of unemployment on most reserves (60 to 90 per cent) has remained relatively constant, even with out-migration' (1993: 231). The truth of that observation has not changed significantly since he wrote.

Not surprisingly, many reserve leaders have grown sceptical of economic development initiatives in recent years, and are increasingly aware of the considerable risks of such ventures, exposed as they are to the realities of the market place. Many if not most band councils now place their emphasis on simply managing local infrastructure and services and allocating discretionary funds for social housing, post-secondary education, and programs focused on healing from the effects of various forms of abuse and addiction.

In my opinion, few, if any, reserve leaders consciously intend to suppress opportunities for educational and employment for their band membership; in fact, the disservice in which they are implicated has little to do with their intentions. Most elected leaders of First Nations are passionately committed to improving the lot of their bands. However, over time, these leaders have become captives of the system in which they function, and that system has a very low threshold for job opportunity expansion. Local leaders have uncritically accommodated to this system, at least in part because it yields such obvious and substantial personal and family benefits and because individually they have little power to change the system.

Consciously or otherwise, by engaging in this local service and infrastructure management, band and tribal leadership function to maintain the status quo. In assuming this role, the leadership is essentially promoting social harmony within the reserve, as well as between the reserve residents and the outside world. They ensure basic income support, housing, and other services for those band members whom they regard as worthy and who want to stay on the reserve. Simultaneously, band leaders promote their own interests and the interests of their kin and, in most instances, the reserve economic elite, which tends to consist of family members and the members of politically loyal social networks. In discharging its functions, local leadership may provide some significant benefits to a minority of band members, but by doing so they inadvertently perpetuate poverty, dependency, and social problems among the majority.

It is essential that the current, primary function of reserve leadership be transformed, shifting in emphasis to the promotion of human resource and economic development for all band members and away from simply 'funnelling resources' from the federal government to various band service and infrastructure needs on reserves. Substantial improvement of the mental and social health of the peoples of the typical First Nation requires new approaches. The current focus on establishing wholly serviced and successively improving community infrastructures amid vacant economic opportunities must be redirected. The redesign of these arrangements could benefit substantially by adopting the recommendations made by the so-called Harvard Project. The project involved research into a wide variety of tribal governments to determine their comparative success in promoting economic development. The study reached the following conclusions about successful tribal governments (Cornell and Kalt, 1992):

- Tribal governments were characterized by a clearly defined and consistently maintained separation of powers, with an independent judiciary and a strong chief executive elected for longer than two years and whose policy decisions did not depend on the approval of council.
- Successful tribal administrations maintained stable norms of property rights to encourage investment.

• Elected politicians were kept away from the day-to-day involvement in business enterprises.

On Canadian reserves, long-term development goals are rarely pursued with a consistent commitment over time because they are so often derailed by the turnover of band councils every two years. The observers of social stratification systems on reserves are not blind: economic elites have been formed on most reserves. It is true that there are factions within many reserve elites and outside groups which aggressively contest band elections, and that the specific largesse of elected leadership is fickle in the short run. However, its fidelity to a small minority of the most advantaged reserve residents tends to be secure in the long term despite the temporary lapses of 'electoral wild cards.'

Elected leadership is very powerful. As we have seen, chiefs not only have local authority, they also sit on tribal council boards, regional associations, and the national First Nations organization, the Assembly of First Nations (AFN), all of which pay expenses and sizable gratuities. Band councillors tend to sit on virtually every committee in the community, including key economic development initiatives and land entitlement oversight bodies, whether or not they have any experience or knowledge of the matters to be overseen. Obviously, much could be learned from a reading of the results of the Harvard Project.

Business affairs are not the only aspect of band and tribal administration that could benefit from a separation of governance powers; the entire regime of tribal and band administration would profit from such a reorganization. I have drawn this conclusion after conducting and coordinating evaluations of the community health service systems of many First Nations and on the basis of conversations about management issues with First Nations health workers from various parts of Canada. Community services tend to suffer from micro-management and from the direct involvement of band councils as a whole or from specific councillors with key portfolios. The devolution of oversight and management control to the people who are trained and hold direct responsibility for carrying out the work of providing services is critical. As one influential management theorist has suggested, the key role of management is, ultimately, to protect an organization's core technology (James D. Thompson, 1967). In the case of social services and health services, that core technology is the workforce and its knowledge, ideas, and skills shared primarily through communications with clients. Direct involvement by band councillors results in a number of problems, as outlined below.

1 Band councillors become directly involved in the hiring of staff, regardless of their awareness of the knowledge and skill requisites of a particular occupation. This opens the door to patronage and increases the risk of poor judgment in hiring. It also makes staff feel somewhat beholden to the councillor involved in the hiring.

2 The authority of staff employed to manage is routinely undermined, as operational management decisions, sometimes very routine, are made by councils or heavily influenced by a portfolio councillor.

3 The mentoring and teaching functions of management and professional supervisors are undermined by the overall devaluation of the positions of managers and professional supervisors.

4 Sound planning in technical areas is very difficult when internal management is unclear about its authority.

5 Staff tend to bypass internal authority when senior approvals are needed, carrying out 'end runs' which further undermine not only internal authority but work team (group) solidarity within the staff. In addition, relations between staff and internal management become strained.

6 Substantial amounts of program funding are routinely siphoned off to support oversight structures which are almost entirely unnecessary. In one medium-sized First Nation for which I had been approached by Health Canada to execute a third-party management agreement, the band leadership wished to continue with management support funding for council meetings related to health, health committee meetings, a full-time position for a health portfolio councillor, a health director, and the proposed third-party management contract itself. While I declined the contract offer, my preliminary estimates indicated that the annual management support payments within a $1.25 million budget were in the range of $250,000 to $300,000 annually. That funding could have supported a full-time physician for the reserve, a superior ambulance service, or a small bus company that could facilitate the off-reserve employment of dozens of band members.

Population-Oriented Development Rather Than Reserve-Oriented Development

The sights of economic, education, and development initiatives must increasingly be refocused beyond the geographic confines of reserve boundaries. They must aim at a much more distant horizon that includes the area surrounding the reserve, the wider economic catchment area within which the reserve is situated, the region, the nation and, of course, in some instances (i.e., business development and technical education), in a globalizing economy, the world. I am *not* suggesting that reserves should be abandoned; they are and will long be seen as homelands. But the very idea of a reserve is not a traditional concept and it is counterproductive to view it as the symbolic core of First Nations development. Surely treating band membership as a whole, including those living off-reserve, as the central organizing body and ultimate focus of economic and social development strategies fits better with both good development sense and tradition.

Comprehensive Human Resource Development

As part of macro- and mezzo-level social change strategies designed to overcome the generative conditions of alcohol abuse, the problem of permanent welfare dependency must be tackled. Many community leaders argue that social assistance income is a treaty right. Various community leaders who have discussed this matter with me privately have insisted that social assistance for employable First Nations people is a justifiable 'guaranteed annual annuity income.' This income is said to be needed because of high levels of unemployment in First Nations and it is justified as an exchange for land rent. Apart from the contradiction of this viewpoint with the oft-repeated First Nation argument that mother earth's land cannot be 'owned,' the idea of permanent welfare support is problematic for several reasons.

Even the most expansive interpretation of the treaties only obliged the federal government to provide income support for the unemployable. Providing social assistance as income support for a permanently immobile labour force is simply not tenable as a permanent feature of Canadian society and it is unlikely to be legally defensible as a treaty right. Morally, it raises many doubts by yielding examples that offend basic principles of distributive justice. In effect, it divides the country into two classes of citizens and privileges. According to that division, a non-aboriginal low-income mother with limited education or job experience would be required to engage in low-wage employment while a young, able-bodied, and intellectually gifted aboriginal male would have the right to perpetual, unearned income in cash or kind to acquire food, clothing, shelter, medical care, non-insured medical benefits, and community infrastructure and services, and to accommodate special needs. Assigning a distinctive status to the members of a 'target group' may be morally and socially acceptable during a specified and conditional developmental period, but the long-term outcomes are unattractive. If the conditions of special status are not specified and widely understood, and if that special status is viewed as permanent, latent ethnic hostilities will surface. Left unattended, current divisions could well become permanently volatile social tensions that may, at any time, erupt in violent confrontations.

The idea of a guaranteed annual income has been seriously contemplated as a national policy. On compassionate grounds alone, the idea of a basic income floor not tied to the repetitive and personally degrading screening of social assistance clerks is an attractive one. However, such a program, which would necessarily be a very expensive one, could well provide fiscal support for an underclass of the permanently unemployed by reducing incentives for the migration of workers to locations where employment demand is active. Social assistance in areas of high unemployment can come to operate like a permanent guaranteed income. It has been my experience as a former social assistance worker and student of social welfare policy that, over time, eligibility determination in high unemployment areas tends to become permissive. It is my observation that a permissive approach to welfare distribution is the rule on the many reserves I have studied. On compassionate grounds and in the face of social pressure welfare officers gradually ask for little if any indication of job pursuit by their clients. Unfortunately, this humanitarian administration provides for certain income, if a paltry one, and thus acts to inhibit workforce mobility. The dark side of this permissive eligibility screening is that the poor come to rely on that unearned income. They become geographically ghettoized, dependency attitudes become mutually reinforcing, and educational and work skill competencies fade over time as the distance from their application in the workforce widens (Wilson, 1987). Stated differently, a guaranteed income or its near-equivalent in wholly permeable social assistance screening can result in a 'warehousing effect.' Abandoned to geographic regions and neighbourhoods and 'taken care of' by government programs, the poor gradually sink out of sight and, inevitably, out of mind, becoming a forgotten segment of society.

Obviously, reserves provide ready-made catchment areas for such unseemly abandonment. This effect appears to have become a permanent feature of reserve life, and for substantial numbers of those unemployed but lucky enough to have reserve housing, permanent unemployment is now a lifestyle. Concerns about divisiveness inevitably arise. The spectre of one part of the population paying for the upkeep of another on a permanent basis is troubling, and as the population of the First Nations expands and the corresponding costs of welfare reach gigantic proportions, the willingness of the Canadian taxpayer to sanction support will inevitably decline.

The most critical and fundamental problem with current arrangements remains the crippling impact of long-term dependency on the recipient population itself. Recognition of the disastrous impact of this problem by leaders of First Nations is widespread. Helen Buckley (1993) refers to a reserve community initiative described in the *Report of the Special Committee on Indian on Self-government* (1983). While the project had an educational goal, it also clearly reflected an understanding by local leaders of the negative outcomes of welfare dependency on the reserve population. Buckley's example is a northern Alberta band council which devised a plan to require social assistance recipients to work on community projects. The performance of the band's schoolchildren, as a group, was very disappointing to teachers and local leadership; linking welfare to work among the adults was intended to motivate the children by creating better parental role models. While early results seemed positive, INAC demanded that the practice stop, citing a rule that welfare eligibility under the Canada Assistance Plan cannot be thus restricted (1993: 141).

The rights of indigenous people *as* First Nations people must not be more limited than the rights of other Canadians, and this principle must be protected by the constitution. Therefore, a redesigned First Nations income support system must either be coincident with the redesign of the entire system or it should provide certain time-bound, special authorities for band councils to allow them to operate in distinctive ways, perhaps even through the rare channel of a constitutional override. The key is to break the multigenerational cycle of social assistance dependency that has come to characterize the history of recent generations of reserve families and to create employment norms that link rights to obligations, membership contributions to community vitality, social income support to the discharge of parental obligations to children. Normally, these linkages are established directly through incentives and disincentives in the market economy but when the marketplace within the community is virtually non-existent, equivalencies must be found. Regular, gainful employment will inevitably help to reduce problem drinking in First Nations. One of the greatest disincentives to drinking at night is having to get up and face work responsibilities with a hangover the next day.

Towards an Income-and-Assets-Based Policy: Re-engineering Welfare

The key to overcoming social assistance dependency may lie in a shift from an income-based public assistance system to an asset-based system, with the entire concept centred on a massive and comprehensive First Nations education and training strategy.

In the social policy literature, the asset-based concept is largely credited to the American writer, Michael Sherraden (1991), who provided some fresh and long-awaited rethinking of social assistance programming. Sherraden argues that, while easing hardship, the prevailing approach to welfare had not altered poverty levels in the United States, and that the poor had lost confidence in the value of the program. While the existing income yielding system is exclusive to low-wage labour and social assistance transfers, the modestly affluent receive substantial amounts of their wealth in the form of acquired assets bearing interest or potentially convertible to cash, and most of the wealth of the rich consists of assets. These assets are often protected by financial shelters built into tax regulations, and the shelters themselves are a form of wealth acquisition which is far less visible than social assistance. Tax sheltering has been viewed by many as an obvious form of welfare for the rich. According to Sherraden's argument, the result of this routinely different streaming of income for the rich and poor is that the poor not only do not accumulate any economic 'stakes' in society, they are also deprived of the psychological and social beliefs and expectations that could lead them away from poverty.

Sherraden argues for the addition of a new mechanism to the social assistance system. At the core of what he refers to as an 'asset-based welfare policy' is what he calls 'Individual Development Accounts' (or 'IDAs'). The IDA would provide wealth that is gradually accumulated through deposits made at different times of an individual's lifetime and is tied to some personal income sacrifice. For a social assistance client, an IDA could be used as funding to pursue further education and training or to put a down payment on a house in a location with employment potential. The account could provide the equity required to start a small business or to join with other investors in establishing a more substantial business venture, or it could be used as a retirement savings account. Sherraden argues that, unlike welfare, the accumulation of assets creates less stigma, improves self-efficacy, encourages the risk-taking required to pursue challenging educational or employment goals, and promotes political participation and influence. It can also provide assets to pass on to maturing children.

The IDA concept is not entirely new: registered retirement savings plans with deferred tax payments are rooted in the same thinking as are matching employment wage subsidies. However, the approach has never been wholly integrated into a serious, incentives-based social assistance program. Direct retirement savings plans that match a low-income depositors' contributions with government deposits are a form of IDA, and these could be provided to support the variety of personal development goals identified above. Sherraden describes the IDA as universally available to those falling below specified income levels, and entirely voluntary. In Canada, the Canada Mortgage and Housing Corporation (CMHC) has provided support through IDAs for social housing in Calgary and Winnipeg and a national demonstration project in adult education (CMHC, 2003).

Designing a specific IDA-based strategy to promote the personal development and economic empowerment for First Nations people is beyond the scope of this book. However, the concept, or at least the thinking behind it, suggests that alternative income security policies could benefit the poor of Canada generally, and First Nations in particular. Such policies could reintroduce incentives eliminated by the bankrupting in recent decades of employment markets for unskilled and semi-skilled workes. Ostensibly, an IDA approach could effectively address the problems of intergenerational welfare dependency and its attendant social problems, including addictions.

Innovative Educational Approaches

There is a consensus among students of international development that, in modernizing economies, economic values count, even if their material base supersedes their importance. The assignment of a priority to either or both formal education and employment training sensitive to market demand is strongly correlated with the achievements, material benefits, and life chances of individuals and groups alike. It must also be recognized that, in the future, most jobs and industries will demand advanced formal education and competence in specialized skills. Unfortunately, First Nations have been burdened with a contradictory orientation to formal education and training. While at least in the numbered treaty areas, the 'white man's education' was originally viewed as a prized possession and something to pursue, the overall impact of the federal assimilation policy, as expressed most succinctly through the conscious degradation of traditional aboriginal cultures in schooling, has to some extent soured the attitudes of indigenous peoples towards the educational system. The contradictory attitude towards formal education is reflected in the co-existence of high school drop-out rates and persistent demands by First Nations right across Canada for full, comprehensive elementary schooling on reserves and for unrestricted access to post-secondary education funding. Aboriginal human capital formation strategies are still in the early stages of development. Ironically, after a solid thirty years of targeted occupational training programs and two decades of reserve self-management of housing construction and physical infrastructure, building services are still typically provided by non-aboriginals from away from the reserve.

Despite the demand for entitlements to education, educational achievement remains relatively low in First Nations. In addition, the comprehensive school buildings that are being erected on reserves across Canada are, for the most part, simply delivering the mainstream curriculum. Local education has not been redesigned to adapt to the distinct nature of reserve life or to experiment with special motivation and learning strategies.

Overcoming this conflicted attitude to schooling is a requisite for improved population health, economic development, and substance abuse prevention. While adaptation of existing schooling to the cultural sensibilities of First Nations people is essential, conscious strategies to create a positive 'formal learning culture' are also neccessary. Success will depend on the support of the entire membership of a band and the blessing and active promotion by elected leaders and Elders.

To create the conditions that place most young people on the social status curve described in chapter 10, the normative gradient that routinely encourages the decline of problem drinking with age, innovative curriculum development is fundamental. Currently, the normative role modelling in the average reserve household, in which the family head is not working, does not encourage educational or employment aspirations. Drawing at least one adult member into the workforce, or into a prestigious voluntary community activity role, should be a formal, strategic local development goal – and family-based human resource development should become the strategic core of local socio-economic policy. A team approach linking community health workers, addictions workers, and school authorities with families might incorporate the following recommendations:

- Elders and family heads would be actively involved in the process, and their approval required.
- The curriculum would be adapted to establish reserve and off-

reserve school complexes as family programming and gathering centres.

- Comprehensive assessments would be made of the interests, aptitudes, background accomplishments, and strengths of all reserve residents and, if possible, all band members. Assessments would be organized through contacts with family members, and these family HRD inventories would include individual data to be utilized for the purposes of planning service, education, and business development initiatives.

- Family support strategies would be developed in partnership with families and would include both family-oriented plans and individualized plans. These would serve as the basis for work planning by all human service workers providing local services. Such strategies would emphasize problem solving, such as therapeutic alliances to address problems in dysfunctional family systems, addictions, unproductive cognitive styles, or social skill deficits; they should also facilitate positive personal development activities, such as educational support, career development support, and participation in healthy recreation and voluntary activities.

- School-to-work transition strategies are also vital. A study by William Nothdurft comparing the impressive experience in Swedish schools with the transition process typical of other OECD countries, including Germany, Britain, the United States, and France, identified Swedish success with specific factors. After completing compulsory school at age sixteen, Swedish students who do not wish to pursue university studies can opt for highly specialized training in technological, commercial, or industrial skills, or in a stream of human care skills, such as nursing or social services, courses which generally require one to three years of study. The key to improving the school-to-work transition in the Swedish experience has been the combination of school and workplace education. Termed 'cooperative education' in Canada, this approach has become a regular part of some programming for First Nations. However, it should be continued and extended.

Overcoming False Consciousness

While most of the changes recommended have primarily implicated formal structures, specifically targeting organizational and program changes, changes in the informal culture of First Nations must also be pursued. Various First Nations health workers have made a number of observations that may be especially salient:

- The principle of non-interference must be revisited to determine its positive and negative effects. Specifically, while a judgmental attitude and gossip may be inappropriate, it is surely appropriate for community members to intervene when they see an individual developing a pattern of problem drinking or drug addiction or if they witness a pattern of family violence, child abuse, or the spectre of adolescents from the band, even pre-teens, living on their own in cities, outside of parental supervision, and involved in addictions and the sex trade.
- The distorted concept of the warrior role that may give some aboriginal men a sense of personal licence to react with violence to frustrations with other people must be collectively examined and actively rejected.
- The idea that alcohol is a legitimate excuse for carelessness, irresponsible behaviour, violence, and other forms of antisocial and criminal behaviour should be collectively rejected. Addictions prevention workers and treatment centres should never be exploited as a means of softening justifiable legal or semi-legal penalties for behaviours causing significant injury to others.

14

Effective Prevention Programming Directly Targeting Alcohol Abuse

Some prevention strategies directly targeted on reducing alcohol abuse rates in an entire population or a particular subgroup are more effective than others. In addition, some approaches tend to be effective with some populations yet ineffective with others.

National policies and overall changes in the organizational and attitudinal conditions that generate alcohol abuse are preventive and might appropriately be referred to as 'first order' prevention. However, the fields of public health, social work, and community psychology inclusively define their respective mandates as falling along a continuum of responses, ranging from primary to quaternary, which are *all* framed within specific sectors of community health, such as mental health or addictions.

This chapter examines both primary and secondary prevention strategies. Focusing on the mezzo-level of social action, by their very nature, these strategies also implicate families and individuals because they are directly and deliberately linked to the micro-level of social problem intervention.

Organizational Requirements of Community Prevention Programs

Addictions and problem drinking are best addressed by the entire community. Various approaches are possible, and a community must determine its own requirements. Some guidance is available, however, and examining the wisdom and ideas of others is rarely a bad idea.

According to the Community Prevention Framework developed by a task group made up of representatives from the federal, provincial, and territorial governments in Canada, effective prevention programming needs include:

1 careful planning and coordination;
2 a strategy that reflects an interrelationship between the target
   groups and the environment (a balance of emphasis on the individual and the environment);
3 ensuring that a number of preventive options are carried out at the
   same time and/or in a planned order and time frame; and
4 ensuring that skilled workers are available to implement the intervention strategies: (see Medical Services Branch, 1991).

The Community Prevention Framework identifies the following program development elements as being consistent with good community
prevention programming:

- A formalized community policy should be developed, agreed to by
  local leadership (e.g., a band council resolution passed by chief and
  council) and arrived at through systematic needs assessment and
  community dialogue, on the role (or non-role) that various substances, like alcohol and drugs, should play in the community, and
  which emphasizes the need to address issues of abuse in various
  ways.
- A *comprehensive plan* should be prepared that identifies priorities for
  actions, interventions to be undertaken, and individuals responsible
  for them.
- An *orientation for key community leaders* that describes the plan should
  be provided and updated at least annually.
- *Staff training* in prevention and health promotion programming is
  essential.
- Preventive actions at the community level should *combine a number
  of strategies* that together will help to reduce alcohol and/or drug
  abuse in the community. These strategies should be selected from
  more than one of the following list:
     Influence – education and persuasion programs, positive peer
     pressure, role modelling, and counter advertising.
     Control – developing and enforcing by-laws, policies, and rules,
     and limiting availability, etc.
     Skills development – teaching life skills, promoting values, parent
     education programs, improvements in water and sewage, health,
     transportation, education, adequate housing, and jobs.
     Community Services – including policing, recreation, health, social
     development, and jobs.
- Prior to implementation, proposed preventive actions should be

presented for community review and for review by experts in the field.

Now let us consider an approach to identifying local assets for program development and the merits of various types of prevention programming that appear to hold out promise for First Nations.

Resiliency Assets: Inventory-Taking and Mobilization

If the shift in emphasis away from pathology towards strength and resiliency is to take place, prevention workers, as well as other key community health workers, should initiate systematic efforts to identify local assets that can in some way contribute to prevention and intervention programs. These resources include institutional assets, such as office space, instructional space, recreational facilities, sport and camping equipment, craft materials, programming and programming funds available through schools, health programs, and aboriginal library and audio-visual resource centres, as well as local libraries. Such assets also include the many non-government organizations that can be called upon to provide services, some free of charge, some for a fee. They include employee assets, in terms of their skills and, where appropriate, their current program mandates (e.g., a guidance counsellor may be able to devote more time to after-school programming or running a youth group as part of his or her mandate). An inventory of volunteer interests, skills, and experience is also an extremely useful resource.

Prevention workers might find the manuals, guides, and articles of John McKnight and the Asset-Based Community Development Institute of Illinois especially useful in examining band assets, although considerable adaptation will be required. These publications include:

- *Building Communities from the Inside Out: A Path Towards Finding and Mobilizing A Community's Assets* (1993).
- *A Guide to Capacity Inventories: Mobilizing the Community Skills of Local Residents* (1993).
- *A Guide to Evaluating Asset-Based Community Development: Lessons, Challenges and Opportunities* (1993).

Primary Health and Social Problem Prevention: Health Promotion

Health promotion is one form of primary prevention. The term refers to what would normally be viewed as preventive intervention. In the mental health and substance abuse fields, it refers more specifically to reducing the rate at which new instances of a problem arise. Ultimately, it utilizes strategies aimed at manipulating environmental conditions in an effort to eliminate or reduce the existence of circumstances that tend to generate problems.

Health promotion involves lowering the rate of new cases of mental disorder in a population over a certain period by counteracting harmful circumstances before they have had a chance to produce a pattern of irrational or counterproductive cognitive, emotional, or behavioural patterns. It does not seek to prevent a specific person from becoming troubled. Instead, it seeks to reduce the risk levels for a whole population, so that, although some may become ill, their number will be reduced. It thus contrasts with individual client or patient-oriented counselling or psychiatry, which focuses on a single person and deals with general influences only in so far as they are combined in this unique experience.

As indicated above, ultimately, the most effective health promotion strategies are largely outside the hands of mental health and substance abuse intervention workers. Such strategies include economic development, community development and education. The relationship between health status and economic well-being is well documented; ever since the Whitehall study of civil servants in England, epidemiologists have recognized that health improves as income rises in a population (Marmot, 1986). This relationship holds for specific health behaviours, including alcoholism and problem drinking. One reason for this relationship seems to be that economic well-being enhances the spread of a sense of personal control over health among the individuals comprising a population. Various social problems, including problem drinking, are mediated by feelings of dependency and powerlessness (Elias, 1996: 14; Horwitz, 2002).

What Doesn't Work

As in other areas of systematic intervention designed to change specific health behaviours, the effectiveness of health promotion varies by strategy and target population. One example of a program ineffective for individuals from both low-income and socially marginal backgrounds but effective for a mainstream, middle-class population is *information education* (Schinke, Botvine, and Orlandi, 1991). The strategy is based on the concept that once individuals are taught that there are specific, adverse consequences of alcohol and drug abuse, they will develop anti-drug attitudes and thus tend to make a conscious decision to abstain. Such an approach is typically carried out by advocacy organizations and governments, and organized as a specific campaign through the media or through speakers in institutional settings such as schools. Information programs may include fear-inducing elements and they tend graphically to show the serious consequences of alcohol and drug abuse. Most studies have suggested that such programs are ineffective with at-risk young people unless they are linked to broadly based community changes in norms reinforced by public policy, and to parent-organized campaigns.

According to Hanson (1995), the following health promotion strategies do not work in preventing alcohol abuse:

- macro-systemic policies aimed at control-of-consumption and focused on forceful and exaggerated claims and forced prohibition;
- attempts to stigmatize alcohol as inherently harmful.

Instead, Hanson argues:

- responsible drinking with the choice of abstinence should be the focus of alcohol use education;
- efforts should be made to clarify the distinctions between acceptable and unacceptable drinking;
- unacceptable drinking should be confronted with strong negative sanctions, both legally and socially;
- parents should be permitted to serve alcohol to their children in order to teach them how to enjoy it in moderation; and
- educational programming should promote responsibility and moderation in drinking, treating appropriate drinking behaviour as a sign of maturity, and thus displacing current views that drunken comportment is a virtual rite of passage through adolescence.

Effective Early Intervention Programs Targeting Alcohol Abuse

An early intervention (or 'secondary' prevention) program plan is comprised of strategies aimed at those who are just beginning to experience problems. Some programs targeted on early stages of alcohol abuse in non-aboriginal communities address the issue of drunk driving (Eliany and Rush, 1992). One such volunteer-based program that might be adapted for First Nations if there is sufficient community support is MADD ('Mothers Against Drunk Driving'), a community-based approach implemented by volunteers. The strategy should include parents, schools, and community organizations in raising awareness through gritty, often shocking presentations of outcomes, community discussions fielded by trained student spokespersons who may themselves have been victims, or impaired drivers whose behaviours have created other victims. MADD also involves training youth in the acquisition of drug- and drink-resistant skills (i.e., 'Just say No'). While this program can be effective, the bankruptcy of voluntarism now typical of First Nation communities would make it very difficult to launch on most reserves. As with many programs, the magic lies in the activation of local volunteer capacities: *if* there are volunteers and broadly based community support, programs like MADD can be very effective. An even greater probability of success can be expected from a peer-driven program of this type, such as Students Against Drunk Driving (SADD), because it is linked to the relatively structured support for students provided by schools. Student-managed programs addressing both alcohol and tobacco abuse at the Onion Lake reserve on the Alberta-Saskatchewan border near Lloydminster have been showing promise, according to conversations between this writer and band health workers.

A review of the relevant literature would indicate that the following early intervention strategies are most strongly supported by the available research and by widely recognized experts in the fields of addictions prevention, education, and mental health (see, for example Hawkins, and Cabalano Jr, Associates 1992; and Thatcher, 2001):

- Programming and activities that promote nurturing family systems, free of co-dependent relationships that reinforce rather than discourage problem drinking.
- Programs that teach early childhood development principles to young parents.
- Programs that teach assertive parenting skills. Assertive does not mean 'aggressive,' of course; it refers to childrearing that provides a secure, structured framework for the child's own learning by establishing a consistent, non-authoritarian but firm approach to discipline that emphasizes the child's participation in setting behavioural rules, fairness in mediating disputes and assessing evidence regarding rule violations, and predictable consequences for the infraction of rules.
- Programs that teach and promote childcare practices that nurture self-efficacy in children.
- Provision of high-quality group childcare and 'Head Start' programming that teaches both cognitive and social learning skills to pre-

schoolers and as a supplement to the early years of primary schooling, and which actively involves parents as learners and participants in programming.

- Pro-active, broadly based community socio-economic development. Increased levels of formal and informal education, business enterprises in the community, job opportunities and employment, and income are all direct contributing factors to reductions in substance abuse in a population.
- Promotion and enactment of behaviours associated with positive, sober role models in the community, especially among elected, professional, and informal community leadership and other people of influence.
- Establishment and enforcement of control policies that reduce accessibility and create disincentives, including increasing the minimum drinking age, product price increases, training of bar waiters and waitresses, and supervision of adolescent social events. While prohibition policies (e.g., Band Council Resolutions [BCRs] establishing 'dry reserves') have generally not proven effective and can even have the opposite effect to the one intended, limiting drinking at all social functions and providing an increased range and frequency of social outlets that do not allow drinking (or drugs) can make a difference by establishing 'legitimate competition' for events and activities involving alcohol and drug use and abuse.
- School prevention education programs, but only if they are linked to broadly based community programming that limits opportunities for abuse, provides constructive alternatives, and in other ways reinforces sober lifestyles.
- Provision of extensive recreational outlets that support healthy lifestyles for both children and adults.

Early intervention programs are intended to identify people using alcohol or other drugs who are just beginning to experience problems related to that use. They are intended to divert early-stage abusers before the problems reach a crisis or the abuse becomes habitual. Services and activities in this category usually include 'primary' programs targeted on 'at risk' young people or 'secondary prevention' programs targeted on children and youth who have already begun to experiment with alcohol, street drugs, or solvents. They also include early intervention programs for adults provided outside health care and social service settings; programs for impaired drivers; workplace programs; and detection/case-finding services.

Hawkins and colleagues (1992) suggest that early intervention programs for at-risk or already abusing children and youth can be effective in reducing substance abuse and promoting pro-social behaviour if they are designed to enhance the child's sense of *attachment* (bonding/positive relationships with others), encourage *optimism* about the future, teach *self-efficacy*, and deal with *moral issues*, stressing an understanding of right and wrong. The *major environments impacting on the child's life* should also be linked to the strategy, including the home, the school, and community. Formal leaders such as chiefs and councillors, health board members, and influential educational, cultural, and sports leaders, should believe in the program and actively express their support for it.

Early Intervention in Correctional Settings

Educational and therapeutic programs associated with correctional sentencing can be effective with social drinkers who occasionally engage in high-risk behaviours such as driving after drinking, but they have little demonstrated impact on habitual drinkers or extreme problem drinkers.

A number of valid and reliable screening instruments for the early detection of people with alcohol and drug abuse problems are of particular use in health and social service settings that involve considerable interaction with at-risk clients. The best detection tests of early-stage problem drinkers are scales based on self-administered questionnaires targeted on psycho-social facts and issues (research evidence generally supports the view that non-chemical screening tests are superior to chemical tests). Brief and easy to administer, these tests are also economical. Well-received instruments for alcohol and drug problems are discussed in the next chapter.

Parenting Education and Community School Programs

Factors that come into play throughout the human life cycle impact on the acquisition of problem drinking and addictions, beginning even prior to birth itself, and they also impact on the very physical health of the foetus and the child through the risks of foetal alcohol spectrum disorder (FASD) and inherited physical addictions. When risk-reducing and protective factors surrounding the foetus or young child are underdeveloped, children will predictably begin and continue life with such heavy social and/or physical baggage that they cannot be expected to be fully responsible contributing members of their own families and communities or society at large.

Promoting Healthy Attitudes towards Conception and Families in Youth

Youth who respect the dignity and care that should attend maternity, the needs of babies and children, and the efficiencies of an intact nuclear and extended family system are far more likely to make decisions about having babies and forming families that reduce the risks of recycling problem drinking and addictions from one generation to the next. The education of children in these matters must begin in the family, but it can be buttressed in schools through informative and engaging sex education and family life education programs. Presentations that link the traditions of the past to the realities of today and speak out against chauvinistic perspectives of sex roles and the wrong-headedness of verbal, physical, and sexual abuse are critical components of such a pedagogy (or, to be more politically correct, 'androgogy').

Reviving the Involvement of the Elders

Approaches that revive the role of Elders in the education process can be very effective, although this depends on the respect of children for the Elders. Elders consistently complain of the lack of respect and even contempt that they are accorded by their own family members and by young people in general. Prevention programs should therefore actively work to revive traditional respect for Elders. However, respect is earned, and communities must revisit traditional criteria for selecting elderly people to play the role of advisers rather than simply equating being old with wisdom: there is now and probably never was a direct correlation between the two. As any nursing home worker or family member who has taken care of an elderly person will observe, egocentric behaviour in the form of a self-centred, child-like regression may be as much or more characteristic of the aging process as thoughtfulness and insight.

Parents, Health Care Workers, and Community School Programs

The link of parents to the education of their children through active involvement as school trustees or advisory group members, in the curriculum development process, through parent discussion groups and as teacher support aides, can be a particularly effective way of communicating the needs of the foetus, infants, toddlers, and school-age children, as well as supporting active involvement in effective early childhood parenting and education strategies. The foundations of these types of programs, already in place in many forms, include:

- The team approach to prenatal and early infant care education and support provided to mothers through the community health nurse (CHN) and community health representative (CHR) on reserves and equivalent types of programs in urban centres. While careful supervision and role clarification of the CHR position is often an issue on reserves, when this program works it works very well. In fact, the on-reserve health education program may be responsible for the dramatic decline in infant mortality on reserves in the past two decades.
- Community school programs, such as those long established in the inner cities of Manitoba and Saskatchewan, that actively involve parents, often through proactive outreach work, and include free school breakfasts, lunches, and meal preparation education for parents.

Early Childhood Education

Drinking styles that are self-destructive and antisocial are correlated with hopelessness and poverty, both of which often have roots in the economic circumstances, socialization, and education that occurs in early childhood. Reducing such risk factors through economic development and family support and providing protective factors that give children safe places to bond with adults and to socialize and learn in supervised environments are critical aspects of community nurture. Early childhood education programs can be particularly effective in providing these latter protective factors.

The Head Start program, which was developed in the United States during the 'War on Poverty' years of the administration of President Lyndon Johnson in the 1960s, has been the most thoroughly evaluated program of this type, and it has proven to be an especially useful approach, when it is designed to fit the general criteria defining the conceptual model, directly involves parents as well as children, and is operated competently. As Lisbeth B. Schorr has observed, 'The basic Head Start model has proved to be sound. When three to five-year-old children are systematically helped to think, reason, and speak clearly; when they are provided hot meals, social services, health evaluations, and health care; when families become partners in their children's learning experiences, are helped toward self-sufficiency, and gain greater confidence in themselves as parents and as contributing members of the community, the results are measurable and dramatic' (1988: 192).

The evidence that Head Start participation results in risk reduction and enhanced protection against risks of addictions and problem drinking is drawn from the most fully evaluated programs. Follow-up of participants in the Perry Pre-school Project, one of the programs with detailed outcome data, found that when participating children were tracked to their twenty-first year, the rate of high school drop-outs among them was one-third less than in a control group and that children in the control group were placed in special education classes six times as often as Perry project participants. At the age of nineteen, differences in employment and education between the Perry Pre-school Project participants and a control group were especially noteworthy. Control group participants were only half as likely to be employed or attending college or further training as the nineteen-year-olds who had participated in the Perry project. Schorr (1988) and Rickel and Allen (1987) provide reader-friendly summary reviews of this and other similar research on the outcomes of early intervention and pre-school child development programs.

In recent years, the federal government has established funding for both on- and off-reserve Head Start programs and this development holds great promise. Funding has also been made available in both reserve settings (by the federal government) and off-reserve (by provincial day care programs) to support licensed day care centres operating with trained day care workers. However, it is critical that these workers be qualified to provide early childhood education, and there is evidence that, in reserve settings, far too many unqualified staff are being hired to operate both day care and Head Start programs.

Intensive, Community-Based Early Intervention Programs for Children and Adolescents

A review of the relevant literature suggests that *affective education* approaches and *alternatives* programs, both of which are targeted on children and youth, tend to have no significant impact. Affective education approaches, which are often delivered through the school system, are oriented to increasing self-esteem, responsible decision making, and interpersonal growth. They also present facts about alcohol and the effects of excessive drinking. The alternatives approach involves diverting children from alcohol and drug abuse by establishing drop-in centres and other recreational services. As the name suggests, it is primarily geared to providing positive activities as substitutes for social situations associated with alcohol and drug abuse. While these programs make good sense in theory, they not only have little impact but they may actually increase substance abuse due to the interaction of high-risk children in the group setting. The key to overcoming this problem lies in the organization, supervision, and intensity of the program.

Two types of skill training that may act as preventives of both initial substance abuse and relapse after successful therapy for adults as well as young people are *resistance skills training* and *personal and social skills training*. Both types of training are also effective for intensive in- and outpatient therapy programs.

Resistance skills training focuses on the influences that shape perceptions of normal, acceptable, and desirable behaviour. Often involving role playing and using peer leaders as facilitators, the approach gives students the tools to identify, manage, and/or avoid situations and advertising messages in which temptations to drink are strong. As well as being effective in training people to avoid alcohol and marijuana use, resistance skills training has proven effective in reducing the rate of smoking.

Personal and social skills training presents an individual with a broad range of skills for coping with life. These programs typically include general cognitive skills, problem-solving skills, self-control skills, assertiveness skills, socializing skills, and skills for resisting peer pressure or advertisements. The approach has been shown to have significant behavioural effects, especially in terms of increasing abstinence from alcohol and smoking.

These two types of training are built into the fabric of the specific program approaches described below.

Round Lake Treatment Centre: Early Intervention Pilot Project

While only one of the four First Nations communities in British Columbia participated fully in a demonstration solvent abuse prevention project initiated in 1994 by the Round Lake Treatment Centre, the project did provide significant lessons about potentially effective programming (Round Lake Treatment Centre, 1994). The community that was most actively involved closely engaged the Elders, community agencies, youth, and families in the project. The same community was also the only one to take full advantage of the resources available, and it developed a sense of ownership and commitment to the project goals.

In the three communities that were less engaged and committed the project still had some benefits, including increased local awareness of the problem and some skill development among those who participated. Further, community intervention plans were established and implementation begun. The project also referred several youth to in-patient solvent abuse treatment programs. The effectiveness of the project in one community was limited, because that community was facing an ongoing youth suicide crisis at the time. In the other two communities, the commitment of time required to reap substantial benefits from the project was not made.

A formal evaluation of the demonstration project suggested that ten primary elements may be critical to this type of program. To be successful, a program requires

1 a clear set of principles, as well as a clear plan and strategy;
2 visible commitment by chief and council through word and action;
3 a qualified full-time community liaison worker;
4 a skilled and cohesive specialist team;
5 clinical and project management support;
6 external treatment resources for solvent abusers and their families;
7 a realistic time frame;
8 proficiency by the specialist team in the aboriginal language most common to clients;
9 a holistic community-based training program (including team building) for the community intervention team, chief and council, police, medical personnel, and other health personnel; and
10 an internal and external agency coalition to collaboratively address solvent abuse and other related health problems.

Communities That Care

The Communities That Care drug risk reduction strategy was developed by a group of sociologists at Washington State University in the United States and is described in a book of the same title (Hawkins, Catalano Jr, and Associates 1992). This approach has been held up as a model for community youth intervention to prevent delinquency and drug abuse. It involves comprehensive community-wide interventions. Four community mobilization processes are used to reduce risk factors and increase factors that protect youth from the likelihood of drug abuse:

1 Recruitment and orientation of key community leaders.
2 Community advisory board formation.
3 Direct board involvement in risk and resource assessment.
4 Action planning and implementation of interventions in the family, school, and community.

The following principles form the core of the *Communities That Care* strategy (Hawkins, Catalano Jr, and Associates, 1992):

1 Interventions should be targeted on known risk and protective factors.
2 Interventions should be designed to respond to the needs of children at different levels of development.
3 Prevention of drug abuse and delinquency should start early in the lives of children, including the major components that should be delivered before drug use initiation occurs.
4 Interventions should reach people at high risk.
5 Interventions must address multiple risk factors across the several domains of individual, family, school, peer group, and community.

The Rights of Passage Experience (ROPE) Program

Another American program, developed by David Blumenkrantz in Connecticut, is the Rights of Passage Experience Program (1992), commonly referred to by its acronym, 'ROPE.' Less formal or systematically linked to risk factors than Communities that Care, the ROPE program is centred on facilitated group and camp experiences in which youth participate in games; practical, traditional skills often drawn from local cultures; traditional rites of passage, and physical and social challenges. Blumenkrantz emphasizes the importance of establishing an effective, enthusiastic core group in a community to animate the program and localize it within the sociocultural context that serves as the background for the everyday realities of participating youth. The program's author has done some work in Canada with First Nations in the Battlefords Tribal Council.

Vision Seekers

Inspired by both Communities that Care and ROPE, and originating in some preliminary work for a pilot project at Carry the Kettle (Assiniboine) First Nation in southern Saskatchewan, the Vision Seekers Program is directly targeted on twelve to fourteen-year-old First Nation adolescents at risk of alcohol and drug abuse, delinquency, and opportunity-foreclosing lifestyles. While designed for extensive local input and modification to suit local realities and cultural traditions, the program has been outlined in extensive detail in a reference text and an accompanying volume of social group work exercises keyed to its development (Thatcher, 2000a, 2000b).

The two-year Vision Seekers pro-social personal development program is organized around individual and group goal-setting and combines social learning, recreation, academic support, and community project work, as well as a summer camp experience that includes youth in camp management, traditional learning, and a vision quest experience prior to program completion. The program is grounded in available social learning research derived from applied social science and social work, as well as the author's extensive experience in working with First Nations communities. It has not, however, been systematically evaluated.

Principles to Guide the Development of Early Intervention Programs for Children and Youth: A Summary

There are some common lessons in all of these programs, each of which holds out considerable promise for the early intervention efforts of First Nation communities. It appears that early intervention programs for either at-risk or already abusing children and youth can be effective in reducing substance abuse and pro-social behaviour if they have the following characteristics:

- The program should be designed to enhance the child's sense of attachment (bonding/positive relationships with others).
- It should encourage elements that actively promote the child's belief in and commitment to an optimistic future.
- The program should teach self-efficacy, a self-confident orientation to problem-solving in all core sectors of routine living.

- The program should nurture a child's belief in what is right and wrong and encourage an orientation to positive moral behaviour and action.
- The major environments that affect the youth (school, community, and family) should collaborate in promoting the program and reinforcing the child's commitment to it.
- An effective program requires some family or extended family involvement in support of child participation.
- Programs should actively assist and, in a friendly way, encourage parents in their attempts to support the child's participation.
- Formal community leaders, such as chiefs and councillors, health board members and influential educational, cultural and sports leaders should believe in the program and actively express their support for it.
- The program is more likely to be successful if it has the support of the informal peer leadership among children and youth.
- Competent staff are mandatory.
- Staff should have the respect of children, both as leaders and as role models.

Early Intervention for Adults

The most effective and cost-effective early therapeutic intervention programs for adults are based on brief, behaviourally oriented therapies with a strong self-help component (Heather, 1995: chap.105). These approaches are often very effective, both in terms of reducing frequencies and amounts of drinking (managed drinking) and for supporting abstinence goals. Most problem drinkers who have not developed an acute dependency can benefit from a regimen of brief counselling aided by self-help. Research has been very encouraging regarding brief therapies, especially those involving what is called 'motivational assessment and training.' This type of intervention is based on the view that a sizeable proportion of individuals with alcohol problems can solve their problems by themselves if they are sufficiently motivated and are provided with some guidance and support. Heather refers to the work of Miller and Sanchez (1993) in identifying six keys to motivating clients to change through a schedule of brief therapy. The elements of the program are keyed to the acronym 'FRAMES,' which stands for Feedback, Responsibility, Advice, Menu, Empathy, and Self-Efficacy. The meaning of each term is outlined below.

1 *Feedback*: With the assistance of an intake evaluation, a respected counsellor can not only identify the severity of a problem but have a significant influence on an individual who is questioning whether or not s/he has a problem and could benefit from change. NNADAP counsellors, if trained in motivational interviewing and counselling, can certainly utilize this method.

2 *Responsibility*: The counsellor should emphasize the client's personal responsibility and freedom of choice in deciding to change and in choosing what type of change strategy s/he will choose. Research has consistently shown that treatment is more effective if the client is involved in choosing the change method. This, of course, flies in the face of the approach taken in most NNADAP treatment centres.

3 *Advice*: Clear and direct advice on the dangers of problem drinking or substance abuse can be very effective, especially if the counsellor is seen as having expert knowledge in the field.

4 *Menu*: Concrete alternatives must be understood by the counsellor and presented to the client.

5 *Empathy*: A counsellor should listen to the client and demonstrate insight and understanding in providing feedback. He or she should be sympathetic, warm, supportive, and non-judgmental.

6 *Self-efficacy*: Without some degree of optimism that change can be achieved, there is no motivation. Fear of negative consequences is not enough, and effective motivational interventions have included the message: 'You can change.' The counsellor's own optimism is important in this regard. Unfortunately, our survey work has found that NNADAP workers tend to reflect a very real pessimism about client motivation to change.

Controlled Drinking Programs

Accommodating those problem drinkers who seek to achieve the goal of moderate drinking is a worthwhile endeavour, despite the vehement arguments of the alcohol intervention counsellors who view alcohol problems as a singular, progressive syndrome that can only be arrested through total abstinence. In fact, moderation management programs have been pioneered in Canada at the Addiction Research Foundation in Ontario (now the Centre for Addiction and Mental Health).

Martha Sanchez-Craig at the (former) Addiction Research Foundation of Ontario studied moderation goals with low-dependence problem drinkers, demonstrating that such goals are preferable to abstinence

(1980). Randomly assigning problem drinkers to two similar behavioural conditions that differed mainly in terms of treatment goal – abstinence, or moderate drinking – the researchers asked clients to abstain during a period of treatment that included six individual ninety-minute sessions. When the treatment period was complete, Sanchez-Craig and colleagues found that the clients with a moderate drinking goal had drunk only one-third the amount of alcohol that the abstinent groups had imbibed; they had also drunk on significantly fewer days and less often to excess. Since that time several studies have demonstrated relative success with moderation management programs, which are sometimes called BSCT training – behavioural self-control training – and certain elements have now been identified as being effective when linked in a single curriculum or strategy. These include:

- Setting limits on the number of drinks per day, per session and on blood alcohol consumption levels.
- Self-monitoring of drinking behaviours.
- Changing the rate of drinking.
- Practising assertiveness in refusing drinks.
- Establishing self-imposed reward and punishment schedules geared to goal maintenance.
- Maintaining an active involvement with a counsellor who will monitor and provide encouragement, support, and assistance with positive interpretations of 'slips.'
- Learning which cognitive and situational factors produce high levels of immediate drinking motivation and which ones encourage moderation.
- Acquiring other personal habits and social skills to substitute for drinking.
- Learning relapse prevention skills.

Various programs in moderation management are available for First Nations people. Some of the most scientifically reputable programs are those prepared by Miller and Munoz (1976) in their manual, *How to Control Your Drinking*; Sanchez-Craig's *Drinkwise* (1995, based on a manual first published in 1974), which is available commercially and includes a comprehensive cluster of elements, including screening procedures, assessment, a BSCT training program, follow-up, and quality assurance advice; and Sobell and Sobell's *Problem Drinkers: Guided Self-Change Treatment* (1993).

Controlled drinking should be presented as a clear choice to problem drinkers by counsellors. Although it is probably the most rational choice for them, most problem drinkers will simply not accept the goal of total abstinence. But many who learn moderation come to find that the entire issue of drinking disappears. A single drink at the occasional event gradually evolves into no drinking at all with the passage of time. Some people, however, should be strongly discouraged from consideration of controlled drinking:

- clients who are severely alcohol-dependent
- clients with liver dysfunction, stomach problems, an ulcer, or any other gastrointestinal disease
- clients with any physical illness or condition that would be negatively affected by alcohol consumption
- clients diagnosed with alcohol idiosyncratic disorder intoxication
- clients who are committed to abstinence
- clients who are pregnant
- clients who have a consistent (as opposed to occasional) record of losing control of their behaviour when they drink
- clients who have been physically addicted to alcohol
- clients using any medication or drug that is dangerous when combined with alcohol
- clients who have successfully abstained from alcohol for more than six months and strongly believe that if they drink they will return to problem drinking
- individuals lacking at least one close relationship with a person who will support their moderation management efforts
- individuals who have tried a competently administered moderation-oriented treatment and failed.

Those who are more likely to succeed with controlled drinking include:

- those who assertively choose controlled drinking
- young adult drinkers without a lengthy history of alcohol problems
- those who are actively employed
- those with family members or close friends who are not co-dependent and are available to lend support
- those who have experienced relatively little physical, mental, and social harm from drinking

- those who show few signs of physical dependence.

Summary

Primary and secondary prevention programming can be highly influential in reducing problem drinking rates in First Nations' communities. The most significant interventions involve changes to the social and economic environments that nourish high rates of acute problems of living. Most of these types of changes lie outside or only partially within the mandate of alcohol intervention workers. Fortunately, a few potentially effective health promotion and early intervention programs can be utilized with reserve populations. All of them must be mounted with the support of committed leaders and administrators and by skilful and committed health workers – and all of them must be specifically adapted to the local and historical realities that define the cultural context of the community life in which they must be implemented.

15

Principles and Issues in Direct Intervention: An Overview

This chapter provides an overview of the requirements for establishing an effective system of services dedicated to directly assisting First Nations people with alcohol problems through counselling and other forms of therapeutic and educational programming.

The Issue of In-Patient versus Out-Patient Intervention

The comparative effectiveness of in-patient and outpatient programming has not been clearly demonstrated in the relevant literature. Further, to date, there has been no systematic, scientific evaluation of residential versus community-based programs serving First Nations. However, the international research literature does show that outpatient programming is generally as effective as in-patient programs, and it has the advantage of allowing for more population coverage and thus being more cost-efficient. Outpatient programming is particularly useful for problem drinkers who are not alcohol dependent. Health Canada's most recent review of best practices for substance abuse treatment and rehabilitation concludes that, 'Research continues to support the relative cost-effectiveness of treatment provided on an outpatient basis to that provided on a residential basis ...' (Health Canada, 1999: 28), while acknowledging that some people with substance abuse problems are best assisted with short- or longer-term supportive accommodation. Programs that can be delivered without the need for overnight facilities are generally far more cost-effective and flexible than residentially based programs, although for many clients on reserves, unless the program is administered locally, transportation can be a major obstacle.

Out-patient programs also have the advantage of ensuring that the client works out his or her problem in the context of that client's normal environment. The solutions can therefore be more realistic. For some clients, however, the drinking problem is so environmentally charged that relief from the home and community environment is critical, at least for an initial period. Residential programming offers more structure and human support, and both can be necessary for clients with severe dependency problems who live in family and social environments that trigger 'self-medication' as a stress relief method or which actively encourage drinking. Through the use of supervised group homes and intensive family and network support, out-patient programs can in many ways overcome these difficulties.

Whether residential or community-based venues are employed, programmers must be careful not to create negative group reinforcement for alcohol abuse, the abuse of other drugs, and for the exacerbation of other interpersonal and mental health problems of clients. Just as hospitals carry their own risks of disease transfer by concentrating the ill in close proximity to each other, alcohol abuse intervention programs can inadvertently establish new drinking networks for socially isolated and needy people.

Economic realities and the potentially larger client coverage potential of out-patient services strongly suggest that out-patient services must comprise a significantly larger share of any comprehensive alcohol, drug abuse and addictions service system if target populations are to be adequately served.

Finally, for clients on reserves with a very poor history of participation in community health programs, it is essential that psycho-educational instructors and counsellors are skilled and stimulating in order to elevate participation levels. Low participation levels for group health events are very common on reserves.

Essential Elements of an Effective Intervention Program for Alcohol Abuse

The elements of an effective alcohol abuse intervention model should fulfil the requirements of a full *continuum of care*, following a client through initial assessment, detoxification if needed, referral, treatment or psycho-educational course participation, exit planning, and aftercare and relapse prevention. A relatively exhaustive general treatment of programming standards is provided in the American substance abuse program accreditation guide edited by Elizabeth D. Brown et al. (1997); the key elements can be summarized as follows:

- Well-trained and *highly skilled human resources* should be available to manage programs and to provide intervention services. Counselling and teaching skills can be learned formally and they can be evaluated in objective terms – and training programs are available throughout the country. There is no excuse for a lack of such expertise in communities or residential therapy centres. First Nations programs in Canada are desperately in need of dramatic personnel knowledge and skills upgrading.
- An adequate *human resource development strategy* should be established to ensure that a sufficiently deep pool of First Nations people, preferably local to each community needing services, is available to draw upon to supply employees to programs.
- An adequate *volunteer network* should be developed and made available to assist with community programs. Volunteers are needed to serve as mentors to individuals with drinking problems and to assist with detoxification supervision and support. They are also needed to serve in a supportive capacity with dependants of individuals separated from them to allow participation in residential therapy.
- An *adaptable set of methods of intervention* responsive to changing needs and new findings in the relevant scientific literature is required. At present, NNADAP treatment programs tend to offer a standardized treatment curriculum, almost identical for all clients. Best practice literature calls for treatment tiering, with interventions matched to individual client needs and motivation levels and goals agreed upon by clients (Health Canada, 1999c; Miller and Hester, 1995).
- *Detoxification* services should be available. These services cannot be left entirely to the client, because such a basic commitment is fundamental to treatment success. Out-patient detoxification is most appropriate for highly committed, non-ADS clients, individuals with (willing and able) family support, and in situations where some monitoring by a human service professional is available. Significant numbers of individuals never make it into treatment because detoxification services outside of hospital settings are not available – and in-patient detoxification in hospitals is becoming increasingly difficult to access.
- *Initial problem identification is a must.* Staff and assessment procedures must be in place to accurately identify problems and solutions with

the active involvement and agreement of the client. Staff must be sufficiently knowledgeable and skilled to determine if different types of addictions are in play and if personality eccentricities and psychoses are part of the client's make-up. Lack of such knowledge can result in grossly misdirected interventions and, at times, insignificantly elevated risk levels not only for the client himself but for other clients and the staff.

- Once the type of treatment is identified, an *efficient, effective and timely referral process* should be in place.
- *Comprehensive assessment* should be undertaken as a basis for a problem-solving and healing strategy for each individual to identify the full range of problems and plan suitable responses.
- *Intervention should neither be standardized nor forced.* Self-help groups, cultural elements, residential treatment, and short-term out-patient counselling should only be used as needed and as agreed to by the client.
- *Skilled administrators* should be hired to manage the business affairs of the organization, whether full-time or part-time, depending on the size, scope, and nature of the program.
- *Health and safety standards*, as defined in the professional literature, should be in place, and appropriate health and safety codes should be followed. All too often there is far too relaxed an approach to health and safety issues in First Nations treatment centres.
- *Case management* procedures should be in place to coordinate multiple services, some of which may be provided by other social and health agencies or outside of the community.
- *Aftercare* services, including relapse prevention counselling, and 'recharge' sessions, such as short respite stays in a residential treatment centre, should be provided.
- *Adequate program documentation*, including medical screening records, background information on clients, health/problem history, the treatment plan and treatment progress is required.
- *Adequate program evaluation* methods that include data on client progress during treatment, outcome data (progress after treatment), occupancy rates, and management efficiency should be utilized.

Showing Respect for Culture

While there are various local cultural attributes to which therapists serving First Nations must be sensitive, some general 'cultural rules-of-thumb' can guide appropriate therapist/aboriginal client interactions. These include

- avoidance of good-bad judgments about First Nation cultures and lifestyles.
- exhibiting respect for the Elders
- minimizing direct eye contact
- drawing heavily upon family influence if and when possible
- avoiding stereotypes and respecting the individuality of First Nation people
- not forcing a relationship
- spending considerable time in small talk
- participating in humorous exchanges and tapping into humour to make observations and therapeutic points
- allowing leeway on punctuality and plenty of time for discussion, answers to questions, and dialogue
- allowing clients to know who you are as a person
- not engaging in excess flattery of other band members
- beginning the relationship with small, concrete services before moving on to more complex and demanding elements of intervention
- learning how to work appropriately with Elders, Medicine Persons, and Natural Helpers.

Screening, Assessment, and Intervention Planning

One especially promising assessment process and several clusters of intervention methods have received the most support in the research literature on intensive alcohol and drug abuse intervention. These should be given careful consideration in the development of First Nations programs.

Screening

The best detection tests of early-stage problem drinkers are scales based on self-administered questionnaires targeted on psycho-social facts and issues. The following instruments have proven to be highly effective with the general North American population (the third has been specifically designed to neutralize cultural influences):

- CAGE (Ewing, 1984), which is based on a scale in an information form that is brief and highly sensitive to potential problems (the name is an acronym derived from questions in the test).

- MAST (the Michigan Alcoholism Screening Test) (Selzer, 1971) and SMAST (the Short Michigan Alcoholism Screening Test) (Pokorny, Miller, and Kaplan, 1972). The latter, which is brief, economical, and well supported scientifically, is composed of seventeen yes-or-no questions chosen as the most discriminating items from the longer version of MAST.
- The Comprehensive Drinker Profile (Miller and Marlatt, 1984), which is useful for assessing motivation for treatment, as is URICA (University of Rhode Island Change Assessment), used by the 'motivation for change' theorists Prochaska and DiClemente (1986).
- ADS (The Alcohol Dependence Scale), which involves a set of twenty-five questions that can be used to determine alcohol dependence, as distinguished from problem drinking. The questions are derived from a more comprehensive inventory. It is self-administered and noted for high levels of accuracy (Skinner and Horn, 1984).
- ASI (The Alcohol Severity Index), a well-known, widely used instrument applicable for both primary alcohol and other drug areas. The ASI (McLellan et al., 1990) involves a forty-minute interview built around eight subscales measuring severity in different problem areas.
- The Diagnostic and Statistical Manual of Psychiatric Disorders (DSM-IV) criteria for determining alcohol dependency and differentiating dependency from other alcohol problems.
- ASIST (a structured addictions assessment interview for selecting treatment), an Assessment Handbook published by the Addiction Research Foundation (ARF) of Ontario, now the Centre for Addictions and Mental Health (CAMH) (1984).

As noted above, research evidence generally supports the view that non-chemical screening tests are superior to chemical tests.

ADOLESCENT SCREENING TESTS

Special instruments have been devised to screen adolescent problem drinkers. They are intended to provide early warning signs of adolescents developing problems with alcohol that warrant special attention in prevention and intervention programming. These tests include:

- The Adolescent Drinking Index (ADI) (Harell and Wirtz, 1989), a twenty-four-item screening instrument that focuses on four domains of problem drinking: loss of control, social indicators, psychological indicators, and physical indicators.

- The Problem Oriented Screening Instrument for Teenagers (POSIT), a 139-item yes-or-no questionnaire that measures functioning in ten different areas of living (Tarter, 1990).
- The Adolescent Alcohol Involvement Scale (AAIS) (Mayer and Filstead, 1979), a fourteen-item screening questionnaire.

In using these screening tests, consideration must be given to localized cultural factors.

Assessment

While 'diagnosis,' strictly speaking, is a job for professional psychologists, most intensive intervention programs can benefit from an initial diagnostic screen of clients. In particular, identifying those individuals who have no physical dependency, those who are truly alcohol or drug dependent or who have a multiple-substance dependency, and those who combine substance dependencies with severe neurosis, psychosis, or antisocial tendencies may be critical to effective treatment – not only for the individual client, but for the treatment process as a whole. The Diagnostic and Statistical Manual of Mental Disorders utilized by psychiatrists is of particular value here. The need for such screening criteria will typically be signalled by the information yielded by the assessment, especially from the checking of collateral resources and the client's own biographical statements and mental state analysis. If a client's presentation is eccentric, or the biographical material suggests significant mental health problems, a diagnosis is probably called for. Further, if a client has an antisocial or violent history, the staff should be aware of the risks posed. In some instances, declining the referral or making special security arrangements might be in order. Typically, screening criteria can be used to enable counsellors to arrive at a preliminary understanding of a disorder, especially if a professional psychologist is not involved in the program. If a preliminary diagnosis indicates complications that may be beyond the immediate capacities of the staff, a local psychiatrist should be engaged to provide treatment guidance, actual treatment or, in some cases, to hospitalize the client.

Assessment in an alcohol abuse program should focus on eight domains:

1 the individual's history and current pattern of alcohol use (frequency, levels of inebriation per episode, typical drinking situations);
2 relevant behavioural attributes, such as manipulative behaviour, trust/distrust expectations, tendency to violence, history of psychotic episodes (if any), and social sensitivities (e.g., hostility towards individuals of other cultures, people of the opposite sex, particular individuals);
3 the negative consequences of his/her use;
4 whether or not the individual is alcohol dependent;
5 the individual's family history, including the family's history of alcohol use; and
6 the individual's extra-familial social history (education, employment, friendship network(s), both current and historical);
7 negative consequences of use on personal life (and consequences for family and friends); and
8 impacts on physical health.

In addition, the individual's psychological and social motivators for drinking and *motivation for change* should be assessed through a careful interview.

Intervention Planning

The intervention (or 'treatment') plan is the foundation for effective problem solving; it gives both the counsellor and the client a structure for the individual work and their mutual engagement. The plan clarifies expectations, thus limiting misunderstandings. It also ensures the active participation of the client in determining goals and problem-solving strategies, thus facilitating the client's commitment. Without that commitment, the intervention has little value. The individual intervention plan allows counsellors to specify goals clearly and to observe and evaluate the client's success in a concrete way. Similarly, it allows the client to self-evaluate and demands that she be honest with herself and with the counsellor. In the absence of such a plan, the problem-solving process is unfocused and the counselling relationship is likely to lack clarity and to be characterized by unnecessary deception, disappointment on the part of client and counsellor, and frustration on the part of the counsellor.

Whether simple or elaborate, an intervention plan should address all

the problems connected to the substance abuse. It must, that is, be customized to the actual needs of the client. However, it is important to
articulate short-term goals for issues that can be addressed in a few
weeks, intermediate goals for problems that can be addressed in six
weeks to three months, and goals for problems that can only be
addressed over several months or years, and which are likely to require
ongoing monitoring, perhaps for the duration of the client's life.

Intervention services are currently dominated by in-patient facilities
lacking out-patient counselling linkages. Yet ultimately, the effectiveness of services to clients must determine how services are provided.
Obviously, far more weight must be given to community-based learning, counselling, and social support in the distribution of addictions
program resources. While there is no fool-proof means of determining
appropriate length, according to Miller and Mastria (1977), the length
of time to be covered by intervention and self-help goals should be
determined by a balance of the following factors:

• the seriousness and extent of the individual client's problem;
• the degree to which the client is motivated to overcome the problem;
• the setting of the plan;
• the projected time required for intervention;
• the preference of the client;
• the preference of the therapist; and
• the cooperation of significant others, such as family and friends.

The basic structure of an effective intervention plan need not be
complex, although the goals may be numerous and the means of
addressing them elaborate. A useful format is suggested in figure 15.1.

Counsellor Qualities and Skills

One of the prevailing beliefs in First Nations communities is that members who want to overcome alcohol abuse problems have clear and
overriding preferences for aboriginal counsellors. This view is also
given support in the research literature on counselling, which indicates
minority groups generally prefer to see counsellors with whom they
have easy sociocultural familiarity. Such a preference should not be
mistaken for evidence that anyone who is aboriginal can be more effective than a non-aboriginal counsellor. Community health needs assessment surveys on a significant number of First Nations reserves in

Figure 15.1 Treatment plan for an alcohol abuser

Client's name _____
Date _____
Age _____ Home Address _____

Last predominant activity (employment, schooling/education, homemaker)

Current source of income _____
Predominant source of income in past 2 years _____
Aptitudes, skills, interests (brief summary) _____
1. _____ 2. _____
3. _____ 4. _____
Date entered program _____Sex _____ Birth date _____
Significant personal contacts _____
Next of kin _____
Frequency of review _____
First week _____*Subsequent* _____
Name of Referral _____ Address _____ Phone Number _____

Presenting problems (according to client or referee)

DSM-IV Diagnosis (*if appropriate, as indicated by assessment and referral data*)
Axis I _____
Axis II _____
Axis III _____
Axis IV _____
Axis V _____

History sketch (No more than 4 paragraphs)

Brief outline of presenting problem

Short-term goals	Response	Time frame	Evaluation indicators	Goal met (yes, partially, no)

Intermediate goals	Response	Time frame	Evaluation indicator	Goal met

Long-term goals	Response	Time frame	Evaluation indicators	Goal met

General comments (dealing with motivation, prognosis [probability of success], noteworthy considerations)

Updates
Review update 1 (Date _____, ____, _____):

Review update 2 (Date _____, ____, _____):

Review update 3 (Date _____, ____, _____):

Saskatchewan suggest that, while the ethnicity of counsellors is an important consideration, other qualities are more important. Competence appears to be the primary concern; specifically, in these surveys First Nations' community residents tended to refer to empathy, warmth, and genuineness, a non-judgmental attitude, and trust in the counsellor's maintenance of confidentiality. These same traits are considered in the research literature as essential to a good counselling relationship.

Perceptions of confidentiality breaches by addictions workers have long been a major concern in reserve communities. Key informants on the reserves I have studied suggest that a fear of confidentiality breaches has tended to keep large numbers of reserve residents away from NNADAP counsellors.

When they contemplate seeking help for alcohol problems, First Nations people, like non-aboriginal peoples, want confident, insightful, knowledgeable, clearly understood, and empathetic counsellors who can be trusted and who work in settings that ensure confidentiality. Unfortunately, First Nations people all too often find the services available to them wanting in one or more of these characteristics. Substantial upgrading of personnel skills is required in the NNADAP program or a similar program directly under First Nations authority (Addictions Research Foundation, 1989; Regional Advisory Board, 1994).

Counsellors serving First Nations clients would also do well to heed the following advice before sitting down in a counselling session (Lawson, Ellis, and Waters, 1984):

- Demonstrate genuine interest in the client. Ensure the sanctity of the appointment hour; do not accept calls during counselling, and hang out a Do Not Disturb sign.
- Keep your office organized and relatively neat.
- Review the client's file before each session and not during the session itself.
- Endeavour to keep your client calm. Discuss what is happening and why it is happening. Don't force the client to continue if he or she does not want to.
- Do not be an inquisitor – 'why' questions don't work well. Be open-ended and avoid triggering the defences of the client. If he or she says no or disagrees with you, simply move on and come back to the issue later.

- Clearly specify the time limits of your sessions and don't break these limits arbitrarily.
- Do not engage in personal or sexual relationships with your clients.
- Do not act superior to your clients.
- If possible, meet each week at the same time. Explain in advance how long each counselling session will be and how many such sessions can be expected.
- Listen to the client carefully. Clients need to be respected; don't be too ready to dismiss the value of what they are saying as the product of denial or rationalization.
- Explain confidentiality, and protect the confidentiality assumed in the relationship.
- Be comfortable *not* being the expert on everything. When you don't know something, feel free to say, 'I don't know, but I'll check into it.'
- Consistently begin to end the session five minutes before its conclusion. Summarize and answer questions during this period.

In addition to the previously noted qualities of empathy, genuineness, immediacy, and warmth, respect, self-disclosure, confrontation, silence, therapy organization and movement skills, and cognitive restructuring can all contribute to counselling success (Lawson, Ellis, and Waters 1984; Small, 1983).

Communication Format: 'One-to-One' Counselling versus Group Counselling

Most communities and intervention programs should make both individual counselling and group counselling available as formats for education, information sharing, and therapeutic guidance. Individual counselling and support is vital at various stages of the intervention process, but group formats are essential and cost-effective for psychoeducational approaches and, obviously, the essence of self-help groups. The research support that distinguishes the effectiveness of individual and group therapy is not sufficiently weighed in favour of one or the other to make a confident recommendation regarding choice (see Graham et al., 1996; and Sobell et al., 1995). Groups, apart from offering a cost-effective method of providing treatment, do have the advantage of adding leverage and exploratory insights to the efforts of an individual therapist. They also provide an accepting, non-judgmental atmosphere that helps the client overcome feelings of isolation and embarrassment.

Strategies for Encouraging Compliance with Intervention Plans

Client noncompliance with alcohol abuse counselling plans is notorious, with relatively few clients continuing beyond the second counselling session. Unfortunately, dropping out of counselling because the problems have been solved independently of the counselling process explains only a small percentage of the drop-out rate. If counselling is to be effective, clients must come to the appointments and, when they come, they must be willing to follow through with the planning conducted jointly with the counsellor. The question is therefore: If clients tend to drop out of counselling inappropriately early, or fail to comply with agreements made in counselling, what can the counsellor do to encourage improvements in client compliance with both scheduling and goal-seeking?

Rooney's work (1992) on increasing engagement in counselling with involuntary clients suggests that the following advice might help counsellors assisting individuals with alcohol problems:

- Assume that clients will drop out after one or a few sessions of therapy, unless something occurs to bond them to the process.
- Provide some direct positive experiences with sobriety that are not directly linked to purposeful therapy (e.g., a night out at a movie followed by a fun social (dry) gathering).
- Have the client set specific goals to achieve, with the ultimate goal being a sober and healthy lifestyle.
- Emphasize specific rather than global changes, with more easily achievable changes at the front end of the problem-solving effort.
- Attribute the causes of behaviour to the individual's circumstances rather than the person.
- Avoid labelling.
- Emphasize the view that, ultimately, it is the client's own concrete goal-seeking behaviours that will alter his or her lifestyle. Others, including the counsellor, can help, but only the individual with the problem can ultimately solve it. And only the individual working directly on his or her own problem can ultimately take credit for its solution.
- Suggest more than one alternative as means of achieving goals.
- Don't overemphasize changes. Considerable time is often needed to effect change, and if changes are not made quickly, the client is likely to drop out in frustration.

- Identify available choices and the constraints that impose limits on them.
- Support the individual's choices.
- Emphasize the positive aspects of sobriety and assist the client in attempts to directly experience them.
- Reward efforts and progress.

Clients can be caught in an internal, approach-avoidance conflict that tends to repel them from seriously engaging in a therapeutic process. Gottman and Leiblum (1974) describe a number of possible reasons for internal conflict, including general fear of the unknown; a specific, expected loss (loss of the comforting aspects of drinking, which may provide relief from severe psycho-social pain); and loss of secondary gain or reinforcement for maladaptive behaviours (e.g., loss of normal co-dependent family behaviours that provide emotional support as well as reinforcing alcohol abuse). The same writers offer a number of specific suggestions for addressing such problems, most of which involve communication within the therapeutic relationship itself and the counsellor's need to display high levels of empathy, warmth, and genuineness (Gottman and Leiblum, 1974: chap. 10). Client-counsellor communication should emphasize an exploration of the client's perceptions and feelings about change and how these thoughts and behaviours, unless modified, become barriers to positive change. Another way of dealing with internal conflicts that serve as barriers to change is to employ *cognitive restructuring* methods to alter misperceptions or specific techniques to decrease anxiety, such as *systematic desensitization*.

Skill deficiencies can also frustrate clients and disengage them from the therapeutic process. To address this problem, counsellors and programs should have the capacity to train clients to perform tasks through such methods as role playing, modelling, and behavioural reversal. As Goldstein, Heller, and Sechrest (1966) have noted, counselling clients with skill deficiency barriers should be oriented towards accepting and utilizing the role behaviours in which those clients are already proficient. Based on an extensive review of research from social psychology, they offer several specific suggestions for dealing with communication barriers that are impeding the motivation of clients for full participation.

- Use impersonal therapies initially for clients who avoid close interpersonal relationships.

- Employ action therapies initially for non-introspective clients.
- Introduce 'deeper' explorations gradually. Barriers may be reduced as the threat of therapeutic communications declines.
- Provide strong arguments that clients can use to counter the pressure towards relapse from friends and co-dependent family members.
- Don't demand immediate compliance. Encourage clients to 'just think about the content' of a communicated message.
- Train clients to see the counsellor as a positive but discriminating reinforcer, rather than just a person who is always supportive, and possibly someone who is easy to manipulate and therefore of little real use. This encourages respect for the counsellor and the counselling process.
- Provide role modelling of sober behaviours.

Significant barriers to compliance include an unwillingness on the part of those in the client's everyday environment to support the client's intervention plan, and even active attempts to sabotage it, as well as environmental problems such as lack of time, location, or resources for implementing the plan. Special problems with 'mediators' (significant others included in the intervention plan as potentially supportive parties) may also work against compliance. Failure to take proper account of environmental factors controlling or affecting the problematic behaviour can itself act as a negative influence on compliance. Fischer (1978: 289) suggests that to enhance adherence to a treatment plan, the primary counsellor might take a two-pronged approach to the client's problems, working directly not only with the client but with significant others to enable them to support the plan. The work with significant others might require a separate, complementary plan.

Continued follow-through in the work indicated in a plan, as opposed to dropping out of treatment, is commonly viewed as an index of a client's motivation to change. According to W.R. Miller (1995: 90–5), a counsellor *can* and *should* take certain actions to motivate clients to change. They should not waste time blaming clients for lacking motivation, nor should they wait until the client has 'bottomed out' (an old AA belief). Miller suggests there are five keys to motivation for change. First, personal feedback must be provided through structured interviews at the front end of an intervention process. Second, emphasis must be placed on personal responsibility and freedom of choice in goal setting and treatment planning. Alternatives must therefore be available. Third, clear and direct advice must be given. Fourth, the counsellor must empathize with the client's situation. Being 'in recovery' will not of itself guarantee empathy. In fact, a counsellor in the early stages of recovery may have less empathy for his or her clients than someone who has not experienced problem drinking. Finally, Miller argues that an emphasis on self-efficacy is essential. Without some degree of optimism that things can change, motivation levels tend to be low. Counsellors should encourage optimism and show that change is possible if the plan is followed.

16

Effective Therapies for Problem Drinkers and Alcohol-Dependent Clients

The most promising intervention approaches for alcohol-dependent and high-risk drinkers tend to emphasize the acquisition of psychological and social skills for the dual purpose of self-analysing the causes and triggers of one's problem drinking and overcoming the problem itself by eliminating its causes and precipitants. Many effective therapies are now available, and, like the skills associated with being a good counsellor, the newer methods are quite teachable.

There is also considerable evidence to indicate that brief episodes of highly focused counselling can be of great benefit to problem drinkers. The advantages of brief therapies include the potential coverage and the relative economies that can be achieved through the delivery of such services.

The research literature and my own experience in the field suggest that aboriginal peoples would best be served by counsellors/educators who are able to transmit the skills based in *cognitive-behavioural therapy* (which is the basis of most brief therapies) and in *social problem-solving* and *social role change*. Apart from this educational function, counsellors can best play a role as family and network therapists and in providing ongoing support for the client's struggle to prevent relapse and the family's attempts to manage their affairs in a healthy, sober fashion.

Controlled Drinking versus Abstinence-Only Programs

Before proceeding with a discussion of intervention techniques, the controversial matter of setting abstinence or controlled drinking as a goal must briefly be revisited. As noted above, despite the conventional view in First Nations alcohol intervention programming, controlled drinking is a possibility for many problem drinkers. This position has long been argued by what is now a wide variety of highly respected addictions researchers. To ensure that the concept of personal choice – and therefore personal power – is understood as the ultimate driving force in a personal problem-solving strategy designed to address alcohol abuse, controlled drinking should be presented as a clear alternative for problem drinkers. Many who learn moderation come to find that problem drinking ceases to be an issue. They learn to set limits on alcohol intake and not to exceed these limits except under safe and highly controlled circumstances.

How People Change: Beyond the Jellinek Formulation

A variety of research has suggested that a problem drinker need not be treated as someone who must be motivated or that s/he must 'bottom out' before beginning a formal strategy to overcome a troublesome drinking pattern. Motivation is now understood to be the product of an interaction between the drinker and those around him or her. This is excellent news; it means that there are things the therapist can do to increase motivation for change.

A particularly helpful model for understanding the way that individuals overcome addictions is the 'stages of change' theory (first described by Prochaska and DiClemente (1983). These researchers studied how change occurs in those who have overcome an addiction outside of formal treatment relationships. They found that change of this kind is rarely a sudden event, but rather tends to occur through a sequence of stages. A person overcoming an addiction tends to move through the following stages of change:

- *Precontemplation:* At the precontemplation stage, which is the earliest stage of change, individuals are either unaware of problem behaviour or unwilling to or discouraged from changing it.
- *Contemplation:* In the contemplation stage, the person acknowledges that he or she has a problem and begins to think seriously about solving it. Contemplators struggle to understand their problem, to identify its causes, and to think about what the solutions to the problem might be. Yet contemplators are often far from making a commitment to change. This stage can last for years.
- *Preparation:* At the preparation stage, individuals with a drinking

problem are ready to change in the near future. Now ready to take action, they may have learned valuable lessons from past failures to overcome their problem.

- *Action*: At the action stage, problem drinkers overtly modify their behaviour. They pour the beer down the sink, avoid meeting with drinking friends, and get involved in a treatment program or self-help group.
- *Maintenance*: Maintenance is the final stage in the process of change. Sustaining behaviour change is not easy. Thus, at the maintenance stage, the person works to consolidate gains made during the action stage and adopts techniques to avoid relapse. Relapse is not an infrequent occurrence among problem drinkers, so a strong, active commitment to maintenance and effective relapse prevention techniques are essential to sustaining sobriety. However, a 'slip' is not treated as a full relapse but as an warning signal to get back on course.

This new perspective on how people actually overcome substance abuse problems can be especially informative for designing intervention methods to meet the distinctive needs of individual clients at different stages in the process of change.

Brief Intervention Techniques

The available research suggests that most problem drinkers can benefit from a regimen of brief counselling aided by self-help techniques, so long as they do not view themselves as having a chronic disease over which they have little or no control. This fact should be incorporated into the very essence of First Nations substance abuse intervention program designs. The majority of problem drinkers of First Nations ancestry are not alcohol dependants and, as with other problem drinking populations, they are at different stages of a potential change process. They are therefore good candidates for brief counselling.

While I was unable to find credible scientific research evaluating brief counselling programs for aboriginal clients, the general research literature has been very encouraging, especially with respect to brief therapies involving 'motivational assessment and training.' This type of intervention is based on the belief that many individuals with alcohol problems can solve their problems by themselves if they are sufficiently motivated and provided with guidance and support. Brief counselling is not likely to work for alcoholics. However, it is often all that is required for problem drinkers whose difficulties have not reached the point where they are placing their health or social or psychological security and stability at risk.

Cognitive-Behavioural Skill Development Therapies

The work of problem solving must be the central focus for the individual attempting to overcome difficulties associated with drinking alcoholic beverages. Several writers have isolated a number of general processes of problem solving (for a sampling, see Ellis et al., 1988; Beck et al., 1993). Growing primarily out of the work of rational-emotive therapy (RET), these processes include mental set; problem definition; generation of potential solutions; decision making; verification; and feedback.

The term 'mental set' refers to an individual's generalized, overall approach to problem solving; it is the instrumental cognitive framework that guides the individual in the routines of daily living. A healthy mental set encourages flexibility and an openness to a variety of solutions rather than being inhibited by prejudices, rigid 'ways' of doing things, or other self-defeating thought processes. Counterproductive mental sets create a tendency towards:

- *Overgeneralization* – in which, for example, taking one drink is seen as signifying a total loss of control. Often alcohol abusers, influenced by the disease model adopt a style of *all-or-nothing thinking*, which makes them believe that if they have a drinking problem they must be an alcoholic with a permanent disease. It might also lead them to believe that if they slip even once from an abstinence strategy they have relapsed and must undertake a therapy plan that restarts the therapeutic cycle from the very beginning.
- *Fatalism* – a belief in the inevitability of circumstances rather than a realistic understanding of how one's own beliefs, commitments, and behaviour can alter circumstances and cause change. Thus, some alcohol dependents believe that they will never overcome their addiction.
- *Catastrophization* – in which, for example, one bad event is treated as a sign that everything about the person is wrong, and nothing will ever help.
- *False positive outcome expectancies* – in which an individual tends to highlight positive memories associated with potentially destructive

behaviour, such as becoming inebriated, and to ignore negative experiences.

- *Jumping to conclusions* – in which, based on limited evidence, an individual tends to have negative expectations regarding anticipated outcomes, despite a wide variety of possible conclusions, including positive ones.

- *'Shoulds'* – Some problem drinkers organize much of their cognition around unrealistic goals and feel that they are under constant pressure to realize them. Having a specific, unrealistic view of how the world around them should work, they turn to heavy drinking as a release from their persistent, self-created pressure. Linking all of these ideas is the client's inability to detach him or herself from fixed goals or beliefs, the inability to see that, beyond these presumably fixed goals and expectations, realistic alternatives can be substituted. What the individual needs is the flexibility to perceive these alternatives and to escape such rigid thinking, which becomes a trap that only encourages escape.

A client's problem definition relates to his/her mental set, in that many people see their problems in very general terms rather than in concrete, manageable, specific ways. Only when a problem is translated into precise terms will the boundaries be made clear and solutions appear.

Once problems have been defined, the generation of potential solutions involves brainstorming to open up a range of possibilities that might not have been previously considered.

The next step is *decision making*, the selection, after brainstorming, of a small number of solutions that might be achievable, and eventually of one from that list of options that might be workable. Then comes *verification*, testing the chosen solution by talking it through with other people, imagining it, role-playing, or attempting it in real life. The final step involves *feedback*, assessing the relative effectiveness of the chosen strategy, with the help of others, and re-evaluating its usefulness in light of that assessment.

This general approach to problem solving is advocated by representatives of a school of applied psychology commonly referred to as 'cognitive-behavioural' therapy. It has also been referred to as simply 'cognitive therapy' and, in the longest standing variant of the approach, as 'rational-emotive' therapy. Given the strength of support for this type of therapy in dealing with various addictions and mental health problems, health boards wishing to institute an effective, community-based counselling program would be well-advised to draw substantially on cognitive-behavioural methods in the provision of individual counselling (Miller et al., 1995: chap. 2).

Cognitive-behavioural therapy has grown out of the joining of behaviouristic therapeutic models with the cognitive therapy of Albert Ellis (the founder of RET) and Aaron Beck. In recent years, some cognitive therapists have also embraced constructivist counselling. This latter approach assumes that our social biographies involve a 'narrative' (a subjectively interpreted memory of our personal biography) that shapes us and is, in turn, shaped by our past interactions with established social structures and their patterns of power, authority, dominance, and social differentiation. Constructivist theory assists clients in devising a new interpretation of past events and establishing a new and empowering narrative to enable future personal development and social involvement (see McNamee and Gergen, 1992 for a good introduction to constructivist counselling theory).

Early behaviourists emphasized the reinforcement of behaviours through associational learning. The behaviour of human beings, they showed, was heavily determined by the rewards and punishments that were intentionally or unintentionally associated with their actions. The early behaviourists were primarily concerned with two types of behavioural learning: classical conditioning and operant conditioning. *Classical or respondent conditioning* is a form of associational learning in which a stimulus, previously inadequate to produce a response, becomes adequate through simultaneous or nearly simultaneous association with an adequate stimulus. In this sort of training situation, the intervener looks for positive associations (rewards) to produce a pattern of desired behaviour that will persist even after the rewards (the conditional stimulus) are removed. *Operant or instrumental conditioning* differs from classical conditioning in that the organism is guided by the consequences of its acts. In classical conditioning a new stimulus is 'hooked up' to an adequate stimulus before the organism responds. By contrast, in operant or instrumental conditioning, the organism is trained by what follows from his or her actions. Behaviourists use reinforcement techniques (i.e., schedules of rewards and punishments) to reshape problem behaviours.

The Bridge to Cognitive-Behavioural Integration

Bandura (1982) went further than traditional behaviourists, arguing that environmental manipulation was not the sole determinant of behaviour; the behaviour of others also played a significant role in learning. He hypothesized that behaviour could be changed simply by observing the behaviour of others and the consequences of that behaviour. Learning theorists such as Skinner (1938) and Bandura went on to elaborate a theoretical base on which wide-ranging interventions could be devised for disorders as diverse as child behaviour problems, eating disorders, weight loss, and agoraphobia. Both Skinner and Bandura set the stage for the evolution of cognitive-behavioural models, calling for a psychological science that considered cognition itself to be behaviour. Bandura helped pave the way for cognitive-behavioural therapy with his concept of 'reciprocal determinism' in which cognition, behaviour and the environment are seen as interdependent.

While Skinner and Bandura did not deal with emotions, Aaron Beck (1976) has done much to bring once-taboo mentalistic terms and concepts like thoughts and feelings to the attention of the behaviourist therapist. As Beck puts it, 'The thesis that the special meaning of an event determines the emotional response forms the core of the cognitive model of emotions and emotional disorders. The meaning is encased in a cognition - a thought or an image' (1976: 2). His model of emotional disorders suggests that those affected characteristically misinterpret their daily experiences in self-defeating fashion. Adverse experiences are over-selected, overmagnified, and attributed to personal deficiencies in self or others that have no apparent likelihood of being overcome.

Cognitive-Behavioural Therapy Is 'Culturally Friendly' to First Peoples

Citing several writers, Heilbron and Guttman (2000) have argued forcefully that, compared to more directive approaches, cognitive-behavioural approaches are more relevant and acceptable to First Nations clients. They argue that the following 'basic premises' of cognitive-behavioural therapy are compatible with traditional First Nations values:

1 Human attitudes and behaviours are learned.
2 Emotional troubles arise out of inadequate or self-defeating mental reactions to events; these mental reactions are themselves either 'behaviours' or immediate triggers of behaviour.
3 Learning is strongly influenced by specific associational processes,

including instrumental conditioning, operant conditioning, and modelling.

4 Because behaviour and cognition are learned responses, they can be substituted through relearning.

5 Cognitive-behavioural therapy involves conscious attempts by counsellors and clients to work together to eliminate or reduce the frequency or intensity of undesired self- or other-defeating thoughts and behaviours and, consequently, to eliminate their undesired emotional consequences, and/or to learn or enhance desirable behaviours and thoughts, and hence to create positive, functional emotional responses.

Cognitive-behavioural therapists believe that verbal and nonverbal means of providing attention and recognition can be termed 'social reinforcement' (as contrasted with food or sex, which are referred to as primary reinforcers). Social reinforcement represents the most important source of motivation for human behaviour. Often significant social reinforcement, presented as care and concern for an individual who is acting in an antisocial fashion, is inadvertently communicated to the deviant individual as positive reinforcement of antisocial behaviour. The individual is sent the message: 'So long as you continue to reproduce this undesirable behaviour (symptoms), we will be interested in and concerned about you.' Receipt of such messages leads to the development and maintenance of symptomatic deviant behaviour and to deviant statuses. Individuals with a conscious awareness of these contingencies are frequently termed 'manipulative' by observant family members and mental health professionals because they are adept at generating social reinforcement for their maladaptive behaviour. But this learning can also occur without an individual's awareness or insight, in which case we view the maladaptive behaviour as being unconsciously motivated.

The three major areas of technical concern for the therapist are: (1) creating and maintaining a positive therapeutic alliance; (2) making a behavioural analysis of the problem(s); and (3) implementing the behavioural principles of reinforcement and modelling in the context of ongoing interpersonal interactions. Cognitive-behavioural therapy is recommended because the research evidence strongly supports its effectiveness in a variety of personal development areas, including attempts to overcome problematic drinking habits. Admittedly the research supports purely behaviourist therapies more strongly, but cognitive approaches are far more 'user-friendly' in most counselling situations (purely behaviourist approaches are better accommodated by training situations in highly controlled environments).

The goal of cognitive-behavioural therapy is to help the client identify, examine, test, and correct cognition and schemas at the root of current emotional, behavioural, or coping difficulties and, at times with the assistance of direct behavioural conditioning or modelling, to overcome those difficulties.

In counselling, the *behavioural change* repertoire includes systematic desensitization, extinction, positive and negative reinforcement, punishment, shaping, modelling, and time-out. It also involves the creation of 'token economies' in family settings and institutional therapeutic environments.

Cognitive approaches such as rational-emotive therapy, cognitive therapy, reality therapy, and transactional analysis (TA) have had a powerful impact on the counselling profession in North America. Rational-emotive therapy, developed by Albert Ellis in the 1950s, purports that when a highly charged emotional consequence (C) follows a significant activating event (A), A may seem to, but actually does not, cause C. Instead, emotional consequences are largely created by B, the individual's belief system. Because the undesirable emotions can be traced to irrational beliefs, these beliefs can be attacked rationally, thus eliminating the disturbed emotions (Ellis, et al., 1988).

The goal of RET is to convey unconditional acceptance of clients while trying to correct their illogical beliefs and irrational feelings. The RET counsellor adopts an authoritative stance, acts in a very directive manner, and tries to teach clients self-analysis. RET combines cognitive therapy to alter beliefs, emotive-evocative therapy to change core values, and behaviour therapy to help clients change their dysfunctional symptoms. It employs such techniques as role play, modelling, and even humour. RET is used for individual, group, marathon encounter, marriage and family, and brief therapy.

Cognitive therapy proper, developed and tested by Aaron Beck, has gained wide acceptance over the past fifteen years, especially for the treatment of phobias and depression. According to Beck, the client's problem stems from a distorted construction of reality. These distortions occur at three levels: (a) view of self, (b) view of experiences, and (c) view of the future. Beck asserts that changes in thinking produce biochemical changes in the brain, which in turn make the client feel less depressed.

Techniques of Cognitive-Behavioural Therapy

In practice, the cognitive therapist uses a variety of techniques, such as Albert Ellis's 'disputing' with the client regarding his/her irrational thoughts and/or consciously substituted 'self-talk' statements, a technique that involves supplanting negative thoughts with positive ones. It helps clients examine automatic, illogical thoughts, evaluate those thoughts, and modify the assumptions underlying them. Clients are trained to keep a daily log of their dysfunctional thoughts. This provides the problem drinker with basic cognitive skills to identify the situation, specify the emotion aroused, articulate the automatic thought, identify a rational response, and evaluate the outcome. Thus the client can identify illogical thoughts and work with the counsellor to generate alternative, more satisfying thoughts and behaviours.

In addition to self-talk and therapist thought disputes, some of the more common techniques include:

- *Tape-recorded disputing.* The client records a disputing sequence on audiotape, playing both the role of irrational self and rational self. The goal of this technique is to ensure that his or her rational self persuades the irrational self that the rational beliefs are more logical, more consistent with reality, and that they will achieve better results.
- *Rational coping self-statements.* Here the client repeatedly reminds him- or her self of his or her rational beliefs as stated in short coping self-statements. The client may be encouraged to write such statements on 5' × 3' cards which s/he can carry around and use as cue cards or reminders of the appropriate, rational messages.
- *Semantic precision.* The client is made aware of his or her constant use of self-defeating language, which reinforces self-defeating behaviour patterns, by replacing such statements as 'I can't quit drinking' with statements such as 'I haven't had a drink for three weeks.'
- *Disputing irrational beliefs.* The client asks him- or her self five questions and provides answers which are relevant to the irrational belief that he or she has targeted to challenge and change:

  1) What irrational belief do I want to dispute and surrender?
  2) Can I rationally support this belief?
  3) What evidence exists of the truth of this belief?
  4) What are the worst possible things that could actually happen to me if what I am demanding must not happen actually happens?

5) What good things could happen or could I make happen if what I am demanding must not happen actually happens?

- *Psycho-educational methods*. These involve the client reading and listening to audiotape cassettes containing cognitive-behavioural thinking messages.
- *Cognitive homework forms*. Tasks are assigned as homework to reinforce therapeutic lessons and recorded on pre-designed forms. The performance record becomes the basis for therapist and group reinforcement.
- *Creative imagery*. This technique involves structured rehearsals of deliberate visual imagery associating negatively (aversively) with substance abuse and substance abuse situations and positively with constructive alternatives.
- *Humorous exaggeration methods*. These are used to encourage the client to see the amusing aspects of his or her irrational beliefs.

Coping/Social Problem-Solving Skill Development

Within the alcohol abuse intervention literature, *Social Skills Training* has been ranked as the therapeutic approach for alcohol abusers needing more than brief intervention most fully supported by the scientific evaluation literature (see Miller et al., 1989). The methodology includes the training of alcoholics in a cluster of social problem-solving skills packaged into a specific learning curriculum. Further, there is a growing recognition that the social structure of the family and the role configurations within it are critical targets of problem identification and problem solving in alcohol abuse recovery. Not only is social skills training an essential element of alcohol abuse intervention, but the nature of social roles and the specific configuration they take in a family has become a major focus for the therapeutic exploration and problem-solving process in contemporary alcohol intervention.

Social Problem-Solving Skill Clusters

The following coping/social skills training skill clusters are common to the better alcohol abuse intervention programs organized around personal skill development:

1 setting rational and realistic goals;

2 learning communication skills, including how to give positive feed-back; how to give constructive criticism; good listening skills; conversation skills; and non-verbal communication;

3 acquiring drink refusal skills;

4 developing conflict resolution skills (with special emphasis on conflict with intimates, educators, employers);

5 positive social network building (i.e., establishing relationships with people who support one's sobriety and detaching oneself from those who encourage drinking);

6 finding positive means of expressing feelings;

7 learning to be assertive;

8 learning general refusal skills regarding unhealthy or domineering requests;

9 learning how to receive criticism;

10 cognitive-behavioural mood management training;

11 developing balanced thinking styles, which involves learning to challenge and overcome distorted, negative thinking and replacing it with positive thinking styles;

12 learning how to identify, cope with, and avoid cognitive and environmental triggers to drinking (including actual exposure to alcoholic beverages and drinking episodes).

These skills are taught through a combination of lectures, group discussions, and rehearsals that directly involve the problem drinkers participating in the program.

Social Role Change

There is growing evidence that, for individuals with acute emotional and mental health problems, including those expressed as addictive behaviours and alcohol abuse, both the source of psychological and behavioural dysfunction and the solution lie in the manner in which they engage in the social realm. Scientific examinations of non-pharmaceutical therapies for depression have strongly indicated that an emphasis on interpersonal relations is essential for effective recovery. Gerald Klerman, the most well-known psychiatrist and psychiatric theorist utilizing this approach, refers to his model as interpersonal therapy (or 'IPT'). Klerman and his colleagues (Klerman, 1992) focus on 'social and interpersonal relations' which 'involve interactions in social roles with other persons' and are based on learning originating in childhood experiences, concurrent social reinforcement, and social skill mastery issues, as well as psychological traits and skill sets that partially determine how people react socially to their learned, childhood experiences.

While partially represented in various schools of family therapy, unfortunately, the overall process of role change has not been directly formalized and applied in the alcohol intervention field. However, the field of clinical sociology has much to offer in initiating this process. The most comprehensive theoretical and practical outline of role change as a guided, therapeutic process is offered by Fein in *Role Change: A Resocialization Perspective* (1990). A brief summary of Fein's approach follows.

Fein argues that social roles are 'the preeminent human arrangement for allowing people to do things together ... [They] organize human interactions,' which is why they are essential to the achievement of human needs (1990: 5). He describes a role as a complex pattern of human behaviour constructed out of both our own motivations and plans and the responses of others. This pattern, according to Fein, is the product of ongoing negotiations and, consequently, role products have varying degrees of stability. Roles are adjustable, because they are the outcomes of negotiation. Rather than being rigidly scripted and consistently defended, roles are adjusted through a process of trial and error framed by the realistic limits of the social and material capital available to us. Thus, 'to the degree that people are frozen into patterns they find difficult to alter, they are often trapped in dysfunctional behaviours' (Fein, 1990: 5).

Challenging much of the psychotherapeutic literature that utilizes psychiatric labels, Fein argues that a static nature of mental health problems is implied by the diagnostic labels in DSM-IV. He suggests that many problems identified as psychoses actually have their origins, and therefore their solutions, in the functioning of social roles. Solutions can be achieved through resocialization, which involves a therapeutic process of shedding dysfunctional roles and constructing new, more functional roles through conceiving, planning, and renegotiation with significant others.

Frequently, individuals have developed their socializing skills and indeed their roles in conjunction with social drinking in their youth and young adult years. Without drinking, they experience great shyness or anxiety when dealing with strangers, employers, or even acquaintances whom they do not often encounter. Dysfunctional roles generated within the context of drinking episodes include the Tough Guy role, the Yappy Guy, the confident Lady's Man, or the Easy Woman. Sometimes these roles can only be activated when drinking, and when a drinking situation is not available, the individuals who adopt them feel paralysed in the company of others. In other circumstances, the roles which become associated with comfort in a bar setting are extended into other settings because alternatives have not been learned in association with sobriety.

Comprehensive Programs That Combine Effective Therapeutic Strategies

Approaches that combine knowledge acquisition, counselling, and practical social and psychological skill training, including cognitive-behavioural approaches and resocialization, have been called Broad Spectrum Skills Training (BSST) and the empirical evidence supports their use (Miller et al., 1995). One such program highly regarded in the alcohol intervention field is the Community Reinforcement Approach (CRA) (Azrin, 1976); it is a comprehensive program that enhances the coping and social skills training described above. Key enhancements beyond BSST include marital and family therapy, recreational activities, job counselling, and participation in a self-help group. Let us consider why the CRA approach is so highly regarded by intervention professionals.

The Community Reinforcement Approach (CRA)

Treatments that prepare clients to face the social and economic realities of their post-treatment environment are rare. Azrin's Community Reinforcement Approach, initially developed in a hospital setting in 1976, is exceptional in its effectiveness, according to several evaluations that have made comparisons with control groups participating in conventional treatment programs based on the Jellinek model and AA. It is also unusual in its comprehensiveness. The treatment consists of the following components:

- *Educational and job counselling*: This involves helping clients to explore and identify their aptitudes and to set goals for education/ training and/or jobs or careers. This treatment can be sustained in an out-patient and aftercare situation through the establishment of a Job Club facilitated by a NNADAP or other community worker.

- *Sobriety socialization and recreation*: This involves arranging alcohol-free social and recreational activities consciously structured to allow clients the opportunity to learn and practise social interactions and recreational pursuits that are satisfying unto themselves. Extensive practice essentially conditions the client not only to develop basic communication and leisure time skills, but to form enjoyable habits that are associated with sobriety.
- *Marital counselling*: This component involves providing counselling for married couples (and long-term partners) and arranging 'synthetic' families for unmarried alcoholics.
- *Problem prevention rehearsal*: This involves teaching clients how to handle situations that might otherwise lead to drinking.
- *Early warning system*: This involves providing a mail-in or drop-off Happiness Scale to be used daily by clients. Just as a blood glucose monitor allows for an ongoing measure of blood sugar levels in a diabetic, the Happiness Scale acts as an ongoing measure of a client's psychological well-being. If the scale scores at the lower levels, both the client and his or her primary counsellor are prompted to take steps to deal with troubling issues.
- *Disulfiram*: The program arranges for and supports clients who can benefit from Antabuse for impulse control.
- *Group counselling*: This component involves providing supportive group sessions that can develop into social or recreational groups after in-patient or intensive out-patient treatment is provided.
- *Buddy procedure*: This component involves assigning recovering peer advisers to work closely with each client. AA participants will be familiar with this component, as it is similar to the 'Sponsor' concept.
- *Contracting*: This procedure involves using written contracts to formalize agreements between counsellors and clients regarding the program's procedures and the client's responsibilities.

A multidimensional approach like CRA is built on recognition of the very real pressures faced by clients when they return to their familiar social and work environments. The CRA model has much to offer First Nations. It has been evaluated in a controlled study with alcohol-dependent and problem drinkers, and in conjunction with Antabuse medication and has been found to be extremely effective: at two years after treatment completion, 90 per cent of CRA 'grads' were still abstinent (Azrin, 1976). If adapted to the realities and needs of First Nations, CRA may prove to be an ideal-type to be used as a key reference in designing new residential and community-based therapy programs for alcohol problems.

Robert J. Meyers and Jane Ellen Smith, of the University of New Mexico, have provided the most extensive account of the CRA methodology to date (1995). In more recent work, these authors have extended the CRA method to include family training, an approach referred to as Community Reinforcement and Family Training (CRAFT).

The CRA method has been adapted at the Na'nikzhoozhi Center, Inc. (NCI) in Gallup, New Mexico, which primarily serves the Navajo (Diné). Raymond Daw and the staff at NCI have developed an intensive sixteen-day residential program for chronically alcohol-dependent Native Americans who have not responded to Minnesota-style treatment programs. Robert Meyers describes the adaptation as follows: 'Among the Diné, clan ties remain strong even when trust has been broken repeatedly. Working through the close family and community networks is thus quite culturally appropriate. The NCI program also connects or reconnects the person with Native American spirituality through the Eagle Plume Society. Traditional practices, such as the talking circle and sacred use of tobacco, are built into the process of recovery, replacing alcohol with the Diné way of 'walking in beauty.' A special compound built adjacent to the Center includes ceremonial grounds, teepees and sweat lodges' (correspondence with the author, July 2000).

According to Meyers, for many Navajo, a very long and painful road led them to NCI. Most were unemployed, traumatized, hopeless, and depressed after multiple treatment failures. At six-month follow-up in the first evaluation of the Eagle Plume Society Program, 43 per cent had continuous abstinence, while others were problem-free, despite occasional drinking (15 per cent), or much improved, despite some continuing problems (15 per cent).

The Harm Reduction Approach to Chronic Alcohol Dependency Problems

Harm reduction in the alcohol and drug abuse field is part of an international public health movement and has been advocated as part of Canada's drug strategy (Canadian Parliamentary Sub-committee on the Non-medical Use of Drugs, 2002). An extensive discussion of the subject is available in a recent reader edited by G. Alan Marlatt (1998) and, in that reader, chapter 9 (Daisy, Thomas, and Worley, 1998) is devoted specifically to aboriginal communities. Harm reduction strategies are premised on the unwelcome fact that many people with acute substance dependence who also habitually engage in high-risk behaviour are unlikely to overcome their addiction.

In the past, programs grounded in the disease model have required a strong expression of commitment by severely addicted alcoholics, and that commitment simply was not there in many cases, perhaps in the majority of cases. As street-savvy intervention workers and long-time reserve addictions workers will often wearily admit, some people are unlikely to achieve sobriety for many years and many will never overcome their alcohol dependency. For too long it has been presumed that these people must fit the mould of a willing, recovering alcoholic or wait until they are sober and ready for help. But this insistence on a 'do it our way or take the highway' approach means that severely addicted alcoholics often do severe harm to themselves. Under the prevailing treatment principle, service providers have essentially abandoned these most unhealthy, vulnerable people to their toxic habits and extremely high-risk lifestyles.

Increasingly, service providers are deciding that it is only humane to reach out to alcoholics with little if any motivation for change. The approach taken with such people focuses on reducing the risks they face and the risks they pose for others and for society as a whole.

Agreement on what constitutes a 'harm reduction' approach in the substance abuse field has not been reached among researchers and addictions professionals. However, all seem to concur that substance abuse is highly predictable in some communities and neighbourhoods and that, with some groups and individuals, policies and programs are better directed to efforts to increase the health and safety of addicts than on those intended solely to eliminate the dependency. The argument is not that the goal of ultimately becoming drug free should be entirely abandoned. However, in some cases we simply do not have programs or counselling methods that are sufficiently effective with unmotivated individuals with intense chemical dependencies to clinically support permanent sobriety as a probable outcome of intervention. Rather than abandoning those who suffer, goals must be revised to place a priority on increasing the health and safety of the addicts and of those with whom they associate.

Harm reduction in the alcohol abuse field has been heavily influenced by the stages-of-change theory which, in recent years, has been accepted by most reputable intervention professionals. Evidence of the employment of this strategy in other areas is found in seat-belt promotion campaigns and legislation, condom hand-outs at health clinics, vaccination programs, and health screening fairs. Safety equipment worn in the workplace and in sport are likewise examples of harm reduction approaches.

In the substance abuse field, examples can be found in attempts to come up with a more humane and safe alternative to a police 'drunk tank,' and in clean needle exchanges intended to reduce the lethal risks of injection drug use, especially the transmission of HIV/AIDS or the hepatitis C virus. Yet another example is provided by methadone maintenance treatment for heroin addicts. While this approach is controversial because it involves substituting one drug for another, there are strong reasons for supporting the intervention. Methadone has advantages in that it can be taken by mouth, has a slow onset of action, does not result in continuing tolerance, does not cause euphoric or sedating effects, permits a relatively constant dose over time, is long acting, and it blocks the euphoric effects (high) of heroin. Methadone is also medically safe when appropriately prescribed and dispensed, even when used on a long-term basis. Research indicates that criminal activities related to heroin use result in social costs that tend to be at least four times higher than the cost of intervening in the lives of injection opiate users through methadone maintenance treatment (Health Canada, 2002).

In alcohol abuse intervention, harm reduction can include outreach 'protection patrols' that remove severely intoxicated individuals to protective shelters or detoxification centres, the use of Antabuse to support detoxification, special courts to deal with repeat offenders who commit petty crimes, and drop-in day centres or evening shelters with hot lunch programs and counseling and client advocates on hand.

The following basic principles for implementing harm reduction strategies have consistently been identified:

1 The philosophical basis of intervention shifts from moral judgment to compassionate and pragmatic approaches to reducing the consequences of harmful behaviour.
2 Alternatives to abstinence, such as needle exchanges and Antabuse (disulfiram), are deemed acceptable if wisely and competently managed and appropriately introduced to host communities.

3 Rather than being based on top-down decisions, harm reduction requires client input into treatment goal setting and activity planning.
4 Harm reduction emphasizes easy access to treatment as well as welcoming staff and user-friendly approaches in order to reduce barriers to treatment.

Crisis Intervention in Extreme Risk Adolescent Group Substance Abuse Situations

First Nations and Inuit communities have experienced several crises in which apparently unsupervised children and youth have turned, as a group, to extremely high-risk solvent abuse and alcohol and drug abuse practices. These tragic situations, in which local leaders and parents are either unable or unwilling to take control, have received national media attention on several occasions. Unfortunately, the response has largely been to 'ship' the children and youth out of the community to receive intensive residential treatment.

The National Youth Solvent Abuse Program, which the operators refer to as the YSACs (the Youth Solvent Abuse Centres), the National Native Addictions Partnership Foundation (NNAPF Inc.), and the First Nations and Inuit Health Branch (FNIHB) of Health Canada are currently attempting to tackle this issue. Informed by the experience of the Round Lake outreach program and the growing experience gained by the YSAC network's outreach work, an attempt is now being made to develop a national, regional, and community-based crisis intervention capacity operated by First Nations people.

With NNAPF Inc. assuming the lead and undertaking to work with the YSACs, a new program will develop involving a national team of intervention specialists who will also play a significant role in training teams in each FNIHB health region to provide intervention and local crisis intervention training.

Primary Source of Methodological Underpinnings

While the capacity-building aspect of the First Nations youth crisis intervention approach of NNAPF is original, the specific intervention approach is largely an adaptation of multisystemic therapy (MST), which originated in South Carolina under the authorship of Scott Henggeler and his colleagues (1998). The leading advocate and practitioner of MST in Canada is Alan Leschide of the University of Waterloo in London, Ontario.

MST was developed by the Family Services Research Centre at the Medical University of South Carolina. The approach involves a social-ecological strategy premised upon the fact that antisocial behaviour is multicausal and, therefore, effective interventions should address its multiple sources. These sources are found not only in a young person's values, attitudes, social skills, or biology, but in that person's social ecology: his or her family, school, peer group, and neighbourhood.

It is also a premise of MST that community-based intervention is both more cost-effective than residential therapy and more effective in the long term. Why? Research has shown that when programs attempt to modify antisocial behaviour in isolation from the family, the peer group, and the school and neighbourhood social systems, gains made during therapy quickly erode upon the child's return to the community. Custodial care has the added disadvantage of congregating troubled children in a way that ferments an antisocial culture.

MST is based on a family preservation approach in which social workers work intensively with a child or youth and his or her family in setting and achieving goals in all the ecological spheres that contribute to the deviant behaviour pattern. It is home-based, family- and community-centred, and time-limited. MST is essentially a dynamic form of family therapy, with social workers or trained family support workers helping the child and his or her family identify and extinguish undesirable behaviours that are a problem not only for those who have identified the youth as needing help, but also for the family and the child him- or herself. MST works with the family as a whole and in collaboration with local health, social service, law enforcement, and education personnel.

While the initial involvement of MST therapists is intensive, the ultimate goal is to empower the parents and the youth to be their own problem solvers. On the evidence of systematic evaluation studies, the NNAPF Inc. approach appears to be very promising. The approach also meets the urgent need for building response capacities within communities.

Continuing Care and Support: Avoiding the 'Revolving Door'

Returning to problem drinking behaviour is obviously one of the greatest problems facing both the individuals afflicted with such troubles and the counsellors employed to serve them. Continuing care is therefore an important aspect of an intervention program that claims to provide a full continuum of care. Continuing care, or 'aftercare,' as it is sometimes called, may involve many elements, but the most significant types of continued support and intervention include the following:

1 *Follow-up calls or visits.* Clients who have completed an intensive therapy program for alcohol abuse often experience feelings of abandonment when the program ends. Telephone or in-person visits can be critical to continuation of sobriety management practices. If the individual does not have a phone or, as is most often the case, the treatment program was residential and located at a great distance from the client's home, a 'proxy' visit by a community counsellor (i.e., typically funded by NNADAP) can fully serve the purpose. The community worker should liaise with the treatment program counsellor in the home community who worked directly with the client to develop an aftercare plan.

2 *Community worker participation in final days of residential program.* To prepare a plan for out-patient self-management and support, it is advisable that a substance abuse counsellor visit the residential centre and work with the client and staff to develop the plan.

3 *Regular refresher sessions.* In community-based day and evening programs, integrate follow-up participation into the personal development plan within a reasonable schedule of 'fading' interviews (e.g., after one month from completion, then after two months, then every six months for two years, then once a year to Year five, and finally, once every two years). For in-patient clients, participation with on-reserve or area counsellors should be encouraged, with 'booster' sessions held at least once a year initially and less frequently beyond that period. Choices in these matters are all subject to practical considerations, including the client's success with abstinence or controlled drinking.

4 *Continuation of marital and/or family therapy.* If marital/family therapy has been a part of a community-based, intensive counselling program, serious consideration should be given to its continuation. Even casual meetings on a monthly basis can be of considerable value. If the substance abuse therapy has been provided on a residential basis and marital and family therapy has not, the inclusion of this type of intervention can be most useful as an element of aftercare.

5 *Educational and career counselling.* To sustain sober living, an individual needs to look forward to a future that is better than one involving the pleasure, escape, and medication against loneliness and psychological pain for which alcohol consumption can be used.

Building a future through furthering education, securing employment, and establishing a career can be vital to maintaining a sober lifestyle, because it provides that hope. Participation in educational counselling sessions and seriously seeking out employment are important elements of self-managed aftercare, and they can also be built into a community-based program.

6 *Sober social clubs.* One of the core elements of the widely praised Community Reinforcement Approach to alcohol problems is that of a job/recreation club. These clubs can provide a regular buddy group that can function as a self-help group, as well as an outlet for socializing. Many facilitators of CRA programs establish the clubs and invite graduands of in-patient and community programs to participate. These clubs often hold sober social events, like dances or other outings, much like AA does.

7 *Relapse prevention skill development.* The most noteworthy element of aftercare supported by the research literature is referred to as *relapse prevention.* The approach is of such major significance that the balance of this chapter shall be devoted to describing its rationale and methodology.

Relapse Prevention

In the alcohol abuse intervention field, a 'relapse' is essentially an uncontrolled return to problem drinking after a successful sobriety management course has been followed by the individual, or after a competent intervention program has been completed and a period of sober living has occurred. Indeed, American researchers have provided evidence that 90 per cent of clients treated for substance abuse in professional settings relapse within one year of their discharge from the program. While that figure is obviously daunting, it did not until recently inspire programs to focus extensively on challenging the relapse process itself. It is clear that if the revolving door pattern of treatment is to be prevented, programming must give far greater emphasis to the relapse experience and how it can be resisted. Unfortunately, the AA approach and the disease model have presented far too dramatic a conception of what relapse means, and far too narrow and intimidating a view of what is really required to overcome the temptations to relapse. Fortunately, more recent approaches provide individuals with a set of concrete skills that can be reinforced by counsellors – and they do *not* require the reworking of all the twelve steps of AA!

Redefining Relapse: From Total Failure to a 'Slip'

A relapse could be a major binge or a minor event, such as a slip in which drinking has recurred once for someone with a total abstinence goal, or a problem drinker who has had a drunken episode. In the conventional view, any slip, no matter how small, is of enormous significance, because it is thought that the drink or episode inevitably fully reactivates the dormant 'disease process' and that the individual must therefore start again at the 'beginning' of recovery. The prospect of having to start the twelve-step or similar program all over again is very foreboding and may tend to discourage people from working on the relapse until they have developed a far more intense program. As one aboriginal veteran of in-patient treatment programs who became very critical of their fundamental approach said to me, 'It can sort of keep you drinking when you know you've got to go through all that pain and rigamarole again just 'cause you've taken a few drinks. Like, you're thinking, why start all that again until you've bottomed out?' Might as well enjoy the ride down.'

The notion that for many people 'the ride down' is more tempting than a return to an intensive, lengthy recovery process is the most compelling indicator that an alternative approach to relapse prevention should be adopted. More recent thinking suggests that the very belief may encourage a serious pattern of full-scale relapse. For problem drinkers who will not – and most often *should* not – accept the label 'alcoholic' as a self-descriptor, the 'return to the beginning' strategy offers virtually nothing. Even for the more chronically dependent alcohol abuser, who can be expected to have frequent slips before achieving abstinence, the idea of repeated, full-scale, intensive treatment that goes over the same issues must act as a repellant rather than a magnet to therapy. For these reasons, and on the basis of the research and conceptual work of Marlatt and Gordon (1985), various writers (Lewis et al., 1988: 194) have argued that a true relapse should be differentiated from a slip.

A true relapse is a re-established, serious pattern of drinking that occurs following a slip, when that slip has not been effectively managed psychologically or behaviourally. According to Marlatt, when an individual is influenced by conventional alcoholism therapy, a slip will trigger what is called the *abstinence violation effect* (AVE), which involves a frequently overwhelming experience of conflict, guilt and acute anxiety, decreased self-esteem, and a pervasive sense of shame –

in short, a depressive, self-defeating effect that encourages intensive relapse. A slip can therefore be redefined as a 'learning experience' rather than a clear sign of failure.

In the view of cognitive-behavioural relapse prevention theorists, a slip is a sign of a need for more focused work on abstinence or sobriety management, but it can be embraced by and included as a part of treatment, rather than seen as a mark of disease reactivation. If a client relapses for two or three weeks after a hundred days of sobriety, he or she simply learns to compare the quantitative difference between, say twenty-one days, and a hundred days, rather than feeling guilty. That client is then psychologically free to get on with the serious task of learning skills that can prevent slips and relapses.

Determinants of Relapse

The good news contained in this more recent approach to relapse prevention is that by identifying determinants of relapse one can also identify their opposites and teach problem drinkers and alcoholics the skills required to avoid overwhelming temptations to drink or to reestablish a lifestyle that encourages drinking.

Marlatt and Gordon (1985) have identified what they refer to as 'lifestyle imbalances' which occur when an individual's balance between external demands (his or her 'shoulds') and pleasure and self-fulfilment ('wants') is weighted to the side of the shoulds. When this happens clients begin to feel imposed upon and deprived, and they are likely to begin to believe that they deserve indulgence and gratification. People who feel 'put upon' may well believe that they deserve to fully indulge themselves at night by getting intoxicated. According to the Marlatt and Gordon model, these people would, following their desire for indulgence and gratification, begin to have increasingly strong urges and cravings for their preferred substance. As cravings and urges increase, the client will begin to think positively about the immediate effects of the substance (making self-talk statements such as: 'I'll feel so relaxed; it'll taste so good'). As the urges and cravings continue to grow and the desire for indulgence increases, clients will begin to rationalize ('I owe myself ...') and to deny any possible negative outcomes that could be associated with initiation of substance use.

As their thinking processes change clients move ever closer to the high-risk situation, and as this movement occurs, they begin to make what Marlatt calls 'Apparently Irrelevant Decisions' (AIDS). These AIDS are thought to be a product of rationalization ('What I'm doing is okay'), certain choices that lead inevitably to a relapse. In this respect, AIDS are best conceptualized as 'mini-decisions' that are made over time. Examples of AIDS include the refusal by a recovering alcohol user to clear her house of liquor on the basis of the excuse that her problem should not incovenience other people. An analogous example might be the smoker who refuses to tell his office mate that he has quit smoking because, 'It's nobody's business but my own.' This person may neglect advertising his resolution so that he can more easily approach a co-worker for a cigarette ('Oh crumb, I've run out'). As AIDS are developed, the substance abuser moves closer and closer to a possible high-risk situation. This situation, if not averted by a coping response, can, and quite often does, lead to a slip (i.e., what Marlatt and colleagues call an 'Abstinence Violation Effect' [AVE]), and then to a full-blown relapse. How can it be prevented? Marlatt and Gordon (1985) have provided specific intervention techniques to be used after a client is exposed to a high-risk situation following a period of initially successful treatment, as well as what they call 'global intervention strategies.'

Specific Intervention Strategies

Skill acquisition strategies are intended, as a treatment goal, to become a part of the routine repertoire of clients. They include:

- *Self-monitoring,* which involves training clients how to recognize high-risk situations by looking back and forth to consider tempting situations and the feelings associated with those situations.
- *Direct observation,* another set of techniques that help identify high-risk situations. Clients are presented with a comprehensive list of situations and asked to rate them for the degree of temptation they present and the level of confidence they think they would have in avoiding relapse in each specific situation.
- *Coping skills,* considered by Marlatt and Gordon and other researchers to be the single most important set of skills in the relapse prevention repertoire. Rather than a strategy based on willpower, these emphasize the client's preparedness for avoiding high-risk situations. Relaxation training, assertiveness, stress management, and proper communication are coping skills. Stress management

involves (1) learning to take one thing at a time, (2) working tension off physically, (3) learning not to be a perfectionist, (4) seeking outside help when needed, (5) humour, (6) spending some time alone, (7) developing hobbies and other activities not involving substance use, (8) moderation rather than rigidity in thinking patterns, (9) sleeping and eating in healthy ways, and (10) balancing the costs and benefits of different aspects of life and life itself. Another strategy is *efficacy-enhancing imagery,* by which clients are asked to fully relax, presented by their counsellor with images of possible relapse situations, and asked to practise imagining themselves controlling their behaviour in the high-risk situation.

- *A decision matrix.* This method teaches clients how to use a pencil and paper technique for identifying the pros and cons of relapse. When one or a few relapse incidents have occurred, before continuing, clients are trained to write down the pros and cons of drinking or, in other words, the positive and negative consequences of drinking.
- *Behavioural contracting.* This technique involves a simple, straightforward behavioural contract focused on setting some basic limits on the client's participation in high-risk situations and drinking itself. It is particularly useful for the client who is in the process of relapsing and having difficulty with long-term goals.
- *Reminder cards.* This method involves giving all clients reminder cards that can fit into a wallet. The cards have tips and suggestions on what to do should a slip occur. They outline coping skills and positive thoughts, and contain supportive telephone numbers to call.
- *Programmed relapse.* This technique involves a client taking that first drink after treatment, followed by abstinence under the supervision of a counsellor and, in so doing, learning to control his/her behaviour (i.e., taking additional drinks, etc.).
- *Cognitive restructuring.* If clients are advancing through the relapse process and experiencing the guilt and other feelings and self-defeating thoughts that comprise the abstinence violation effect, one more powerful technique is available to them: positive mental attitude training, or cognitive restructuring. A slip is not defined as a profound mark of weakness but as a mistake that can be learned from. Rational, objective thinking processes are taught, so that irrational, overwhelming thoughts can be systematically substituted for with positive thinking and attitudes.

Global Intervention Strategies

Global self-control strategies are intended to increase a client's overall capacity to deal with stress and to cope with high-risk situations with an increased sense of self-efficacy. Individuals are trained to identify situational and internal (psychological) early warning signals and to utilize self-control strategies to reduce the risk level of any situation that might trigger a slip.

The initial goal of treatment with global intervention strategies is to resist the onset of an imbalanced lifestyle. Clients are taught to effectively balance their 'shoulds' and 'wants' in such basic areas as work and recreation, good times and bad, happiness and sadness, pain and pleasure. Such a balance can best be effected by showing clients that, while they may feel overwhelmed by the details of everyday life, which can create enormous frustration and a sense of inability to accomplish all that is expected of them, by carefully managing those details, and by ensuring that there are plenty of 'good things' to balance the bad, the need for an escape into alcohol can be avoided.

The next step in the relapse process is to find alternative indulgences to excessive drinking, meaning things or activities that truly give pleasure. Global intervention strategies also involve techniques for dealing with cravings and denial in the face of relapse and careless exposure to high-risk cues.

Marlatt and Gordon's work is well-supported in the research literature, and relapse prevention should become a standard part of post-intervention support. It is the therapist's responsibility to educate clients about relapse and to provide them with wide-ranging treatment focused on relapse prevention.

Terrence Gorski, who established the CENAPS Corporation in large part to promote relapse prevention, has also written extensively on 'signs' of impending relapse and on practical techniques for preventing it (see, for example, Gorski and Miller, 1986). While many of Gorski's individual strategies may be effective, the overall approach has not been independently evaluated with a strong scientific methodology.

17

Conclusion

In this book I have attempted to describe and explain the emergence of a pervasive, enduring, and destructive presence in the reserve communities of the First Nations of Canada. I have referred to this phenomenon as the 'firewater complex,' a cultural construct, which, I believe, has become integral to the social reality of reserve life. As I have perceived its behavioural base and ideological superstructure, the firewater complex provides and tacitly encourages lay excuses and even professional justification for destructive drinking norms in First Nations.

Beverage alcohol consumption norms have long posed significant physical, psychological, spiritual, and social health risks in reserve communities. Those norms include binge drinking in a social context and an accompanying drunken comportment – a norm that is often explained away or excused in terms of a distinctive, aboriginal sensitivity to beverage alcohol.

I have argued that the firewater complex grows out of policy and programming designed singularly to address alcohol abuse but, by extension, its coverage has been generalized, replicated in form and spirit, if not in letter, to guide organized efforts to explain and address all manner of social problems and public health concerns. It has been argued that the essence of the firewater complex has been widely adopted by First Nations leaders, addictions workers, and social and health service personnel to explain and remedially intervene in virtually any social problem plaguing reserve communities.

One element of the firewater complex that has been generalized well beyond concerns about alcohol problems is the assumption that First Nations are incapable of healthy adaptation to the products of contemporary leisure-time culture they are exposed to, whether alcohol or other drugs, commercial sex, gambling, juvenile subculture formations, or high-sugar or fatty foods. Other key elements of the firewater complex include the belief that addressing maladaptation to these products is dependent upon new public programming and specialized, external expertise rather than the choices, motivations, ideas, commitment, and work of reserve residents themselves. In my view, this entire way of thinking is dangerously flawed. The pessimism it reflects regarding the potential of First Nations to solve their own problems is self-defeating. It disguises a fundamental paternalism towards First Nations and implicit in such thinking is an assumption that they are and might always be dependent populations rather than independent or interdependent and equal cultural, social, economic, and political partners within Canadian society. The approach also flies in the face of what sound psychology, social psychology, military leaders, and coaches of athletic teams all tell us: negative expectations doom a group or population to failure.

The firewater complex originated in the speculations of early European explorers, military personnel, and settlers about aboriginal drinking comportment. Later referred to by anthropologists as the 'firewater theory,' this more formal idea purported that a racial trait best explained the emotionally charged, careless, aggressive, and often violent behaviour witnessed among members of indigenous North American tribes during drinking episodes. That same belief was apparently adopted by indigenous people themselves. Yet even the historical record shows that the earliest reception to, and behaviour associated with, alcohol use by indigenous peoples in North America varied widely. Attraction to alcohol was not universal among indigenous peoples, and violent behaviour was not a uniform reaction upon their first exposure to European beverage alcohol. In the more southern climes of America, where beverage alcohol was used in pre-Columbian times, social controls had been in place, including prohibition. However, at least in the area that is now Canada, either immediately or gradually, an attraction to beverage alcohol was acquired and careless and explosive drinking episodes did become a normative drinking style in the communities of First Nations.

Shortly after the middle of the twentieth century, the firewater theory became a scientific hypothesis, ostensibly linking aboriginal genetics to cravings for and hyper-reactivity to beverage alcohol. However, by the 1970s, science had separated fact from fiction, and the firewater theory was found wanting. In scientific discourse, the firewater theory became the 'firewater myth.'

Having discarded the firewater theory as a serious explanation of drinking problems in First Nations, I reviewed the spectrum of macro-, mezzo-, and micro-sociological data and ideas for alternatives. My gathering of various interrelated propositions about the creation and maintenance of problem drinking norms linked alcohol use and abuse to the political economy of Canada's nation building and 'Indian affairs' policies. It was argued that the most outstanding failure of Canadian nation building was the alienation of First Nations men from traditional economic roles and the substitution of welfare for work on isolated reserve settlements with no significant opportunities for real economic growth. This lack of opportunity and the multigenerational unemployment, poverty, despair, and lack of social attachment it engenders are the social-structural factors that breed problem drinking and its associated social problems.

I have argued that, within limits, experimenting with drunkenness is a normative aspect of social life for adolescents and young adults; it is a sort of 'rite of passage' experience that tends to decline with time, without any assistance from 'treatment professionals.' Irresponsible and destructive drinking behaviour is normally left behind with the growth of the enhanced obligations and significant rewards that mark the gradients of a typical male and, increasingly female adult role trajectory in Canadian society. However, for the majority of First Nations residents on reserves, that career trajectory is non-existent. As a result, reserve members do not acquire the stakes in sobriety that deter them from such behaviour. Those who do acquire such stakes through reserve employment tend to leave their problem drinking behaviour behind.

I have also argued that current support policies for First Nations defy development logic, continuing, as they do, to centre on reserves. Despite considerable evidence that off-reserve movement correlates with significant improvement in educational achievement and employment opportunities for band members, federal policy makers and First Nations leaders insist on this catastrophic status quo. The only reasonable explanation for this stubborn refusal of the federal government to redirect policy is that, in the short term, it is easier and less expensive to put off the inevitable reckoning with the overwhelming challenges that must someday be confronted to establish a new national aboriginal development policy. I have also been forced by the evidence to conclude that the cooperation of First Nations leadership with the prevailing federal strategy can only be explained by the substantial social and material benefits that flow to reserve elites and incumbent leadership as a result of current arrangements.

My review also found that shortly after its debunking by science, the firewater theory was, unfortunately, given new life in First Nations through the influence of the disease model of treatment. This occurred inadvertently, through the process of recruiting unqualified indigenous prevention and treatment personnel who were, typically, recovered alcoholics, to work in federally funded community programs and a network of in-patient centres that now stretches across Canada. Indoctrinated in the disease concept of treatment, typically through their own personal experience of 'recovery,' most First Nations addictions workers were and are passionately committed to the disease model and the treatment approaches informed by that model. Despite the literature on evidence-informed, alternative 'best practices' of prevention and intervention, the personnel and programs directly serving reserve members were and continue to be locked into the DCT. With virtually all clients referred for 'treatment' being defined as alcoholics, the notion that First Nations people have a special, genetic vulnerability to alcohol re-emerged without any conscious intent.

The firewater complex has largely grown out of paternalistic, federal responses to social problems in First Nations. This paternalism has been specifically reflected in protectionist social control policies aimed at alcohol abuse. Targeted prohibition laws that suspended the citizenship rights of First Nations people to use alcohol were in place until the early 1960s. That prohibition was followed by a decade and a half of inaction. Then, in the late 1970s, alcohol abuse prevention programs were funded on reserves. These programs were aimed at convincing residents to abstain completely from drinking. Further, the network of in-patient treatment centres established across the country has almost exclusively offered abstinence-oriented programming based on the disease concept of treatment, and the centres have typically been linked to or supported by local chapters of Alcoholics Anonymous. While some minor elements of aboriginal tradition and ceremony were integrated into alcohol abuse programming offered to First Nations, the approach was essentially adopted, almost wholesale, from the mainstream addictions treatment program models prevalent in the 1970s and early 1980s.

Growing out of and elaborating upon the DCT, an all-embracing 'recovery movement' has emerged in First Nations that has demonstrated enormous potential for addressing psychological malaise. However, it has also set in motion a misguided, perpetual search for therapeutic solutions, offered by either psychologists or traditional healers, to virtually any personal problem originating in difficult social relationships. Fundamental to all preferred solutions are those which, like the DCT, awkwardly combine pseudo-science and spirituality. Typically, these approaches fail to give any serious thought to the relative effectiveness of interventions or to the strategic, cost-efficiency of funding allocation.

Guided by the assumption that First Nations will suffer for years to come from the legacy of past victimization, the problem-solving approach that has evolved has been founded on an assumption of dependence. Thus permanent social assistance support has been substituted for serious, market-oriented economic development, and individualized therapy and spiritual healing for alternative, more demanding psycho-educational programming. Yet with increasing repetition, the evidence suggests that what is needed is the facilitation of cognitive and social coping skills that promote self-efficacy, resiliency, and personal empowerment. These are the factors that a growing body of psychological and sociological literature indicates can break the cycle of poverty, dependency, and addictive lifestyles characteristic of economically marginalized and geographically isolated populations.

I have also argued that, for alcohol abuse and other related social problems to be successfully overcome in First Nations, fundamental social reorganization must take place. The reserve-centred development policy framework is destined for failure as a result of insufficient economic potential on most reserves, and it must be redirected to embrace direct linkages to the wider economy and society. Biculturalism and robust and pro-active economic integration through partnerships and investments in enterprises in the surrounding areas, regions, and national and global marketplace are needed, as well as far more coordinated working partnerships with other levels of government. Isolation, segregation, and dependency cause rather than prevent the health risks of acute and widespread alcohol abuse and related social problems.

The persistence of the firewater complex is largely a by-product of Canada's failure to integrate First Nations people into the economic system that displaced their traditional modes of production and distribution. Continued, primary emphasis on the reserve system as the target of socio-economic development and community health promotion virtually ensures majority unemployment and multigenerational welfare dependency. Most reserves have an insufficient economic base to sustain more than a small fraction of their current membership – and while reserve populations continue to grow slowly, increasing numbers of First Nations people, recognizing the opportunity vacuum on the reserve, sensibly migrate to the cities for education, job opportunities, and, in some instances, access to housing. Yet with a logic that defies reason, the bulk of federal developmental assistance to First Nations remains focused on reserves. At the same time, the size of the off-reserve First Nations population has long outgrown its reserve counterpart.

The lack of hope for a better future on reserves nurtures a variety of social problems, including alcohol abuse and other addictions. The primary, generative conditions for problem drinking are found in long-term, multigenerational unemployment, not in an 'Indian alcohol gene.' Most First Nations drinkers are not alcoholics (or, better stated 'alcohol dependants'); their problem drinking behaviours are learned and socially reinforced reactions to a social environment characterized by acute community and personal powerlessness. Yet misinformation about First Nations drinking patterns has served to ensure that the majority of First Nations people who abuse alcohol but are not alcohol dependent have no appropriate services at their disposal. The misinformed and misguided beliefs of First Nations addictions workers have contributed in a substantial way to sustaining the firewater complex beyond its deserved termination.

In the preceding pages I have argued that the type of prevention education and institutional, in-patient treatment now available may often be appropriate for intervening in acute alcohol dependency (although, in such cases, treatment tailored to individual needs rather than boilerplate, Minnesota-model treatment is required). This assertion must be qualified, in that a much more varied service profile is also needed by alcoholics in treatment: some require longer care than is now provided and some can only benefit from harm reduction approaches that offer them a degree of safety if and until their motivation for change increases. For the great majority of problem drinkers who are not alcohol dependent, however, the DCT is counterproductive. It mistakenly explains their destructive behaviours as permanent addictions, which allows them to avoid confronting their real problems. Further, the DCT does not help them explore how their moral and rational choices, and their social bonds, are the keys to healthy living and sobriety. The DCT also relieves policy makers and community leaders of responsibility for seriously addressing the political and economic realities underlying the segregation and unemployment that have nourished alcohol abuse in reserve communities.

By 'pathologizing' alcohol abuse and other social problems, the fundamental organizational change needed can be ignored. By transforming problem drinking in First Nations into a problem that demands an individualized service response, the burden of solution is shifted to therapeutic personnel, and away from government and community leaders who have the capacity to undertake fundamental changes in development policy. By relying so heavily on the counsel of experts or self-help groups, the alcohol-abusing client is also relieved of responsibility for personal change and a sober lifestyle.

Rejecting the present therapeutic orientation, I have proposed fundamental social reorganization and greater emphasis on personal empowerment through cognitive and social coping skills development, and advocated a holistic development approach keyed to the spirit rather than the letter of traditional community health promotion. Such an approach is in keeping with the conclusions of the well-received Royal Commission on Aboriginal Peoples.

Despite the daunting nature of the challenge, transformation of the structural conditions that give rise to alcohol abuse and addictions in reserve communities is essential. The current, reserve- centred developmental focus must be abandoned. Real development potential is situated in partnerships with, and far more active linkages to, the wider market place and public sector – and democratic reason and demographic realities demand that such a development orientation must be inclusive of both on- and off-reserve band members. However, it is also acknowledged that to achieve such organizational change, in many, perhaps most, reserve communities, local concentrations of power must be redistributed. In sociological terms, existing stratification functions to maintain the advantages of an administrative and, in many instances, deeply entrenched, economic elite. Unfortunately, the benefits accruing to that elite are acquired at the expense of an economically and socially stranded population resident on the reserves or, increasingly, in low-income neighbourhoods of inner cities. Ultimately, local leadership has been assigned to administer services and filter financial support to members of communities that have virtually no room for substantial growth; they are functioning in the capacity of gatekeepers and maintenance managers in the country's most unconscionable instance of 'warehousing' the poor.

Solutions wholly dedicated to the prevention of, and intervention into, alcohol abuse in First Nations have also been advocated. While current arrangements are primarily organized around the DCT, an effort has been made to identify more effective and cost-efficient strategies. Selection was guided by an attempt to promote methods that are both socially and culturally appropriate and evidence-based. A shift is encouraged that moves beyond an almost exclusive emphasis on short-term, four-six-week in-patient treatment in centres located outside the client's community towards an emphasis on employment development, community-based prevention programs, out-patient counselling, and psycho-educational programs. Social learning strategies with cognitive and social coping skills are also advocated. Such an approach emphasizes personal and community strengths rather than assuming weakness and promoting dependency on experts and the victimization of 'clients.' Despite the benign surface of these latter concepts, in their ubiquitous application to troubled First Nations people, taken together they constitute a neo-colonial vocabulary of response to social problems. The newly acceptable vocabulary in lay and professional discourse regarding alcohol prevention and intervention should reject words like disease, illness, pathology, dependence, and damage and replace them with social re-organization, resiliency promotion, self-efficacy development, personal empowerment, and responsibility. These words would better constitute the terminology of a post-colonial psychology and political economy for First Nations.

The approaches recommended throughout this book are not the product of the author's fancy, nor did they originate in a vacuum. The strategies espoused have been gleaned from a wide body of applied social theory and from the professional addictions and substance abuse literature on best practices. They were also heavily influenced by the passionate, caring, and intellectually keen First Nations alcohol abuse prevention and intervention service personnel I have encountered in the field. Ultimately, the ideas advanced in Part Two are a synthesis of the ideas of others.

Summary of Key Arguments

1 Alcohol abuse patterns in First Nations are primarily learned; they do not originate in a distinctive, race-based genetic profile.
2 The destructive, drunken comportment that accompanies conventional social binge drinking in First Nations was originally learned from and has been reinforced by interactions with Europeans and non-aboriginal Canadians. It has also been reproduced through social learning within reserve communities and sustained by illogi-

cal development policies. Those policies primarily bolster residential settlement on reserve lands which are, for the most part, bereft of any significant opportunities for attaining levels of economic growth that could support even a small percentage of the membership in current populations.

3 The disease model of alcoholism has been discredited by scientific inquiry and replaced by the bio-psycho-social model that assumes there are many causal paths leading to alcohol problems. It also assumes there is a continuum of alcohol-related problems ranging from occasional bouts of excess drinking causing minor problems to addiction and acute, life-threatening health problems.

4 Contradicting the Jellinek concept of predictable and inevitable stages of problem intensification, the available research evidence indicates that alcohol problems may evolve through various shifts of intensification and diminution, and that they can remain stable in a specific pattern.

5 Heavy drinking does not necessarily cause either the normal drinker or the alcoholic to 'go out of control,' nor does it cause the violence and antisocial behaviour that is so often identified in statistical studies as being coupled with it, whether in the non-aboriginal population or among First Nations people. The relationship appears to be spurious; it is mediated by other variables, such as the reasoning and attitudes of the individuals going into a drinking situation, the expectations of drinking partners, and the reputation of the drinking venue. Thus, being drunk is a poor excuse for careless driving, beating or killing another human being, or neglecting one's children.

6 Problem drinking in First Nations remains a significant social health problem. Current services do not begin to address the needs of the majority of problem drinkers on reserves, who are not alcohol dependent. The service delivery system is underdeveloped on the prevention side and it is primarily centred on assisting the alcohol dependent who has exhibited a pattern of legal, relational, or health crises associated with drinking habits. It ignores most binge and other high-risk drinkers. Further, the delivery system has responded in a far too narrow way to existing needs. For example, it has not addressed the special needs of youth, women with violent partners, criminal offenders, drinkers with dual disorders, dual drug users, and foetal alcohol spectrum disorder (FASD) survivors. It has failed to adequately develop a harm reduction strategy for chronic alcoholics, and it has not considered the special issues of the homeless or

skid-row, chronic alcoholics. All of these needs should be addressed in the renewal of programming and the training of personnel who provide services.

7 It is useful to conceive of high problem drinking rates in First Nations as being defined by a cultural complex that unites actual behavioural norms with explanations that serve as a popular excuse for (and therefore reinforce) drunken behaviour and also informs public interventions. Beginning with the firewater theory and probably reinforced by fears associated with smallpox and tuberculosis epidemics, there is a popular impression both within and without First Nations that indigenous Canadians have a special and permanent vulnerability to both diseases and commercial recreation originating in European and modern North American culture. In keeping with these assumptions, protectionist policies, once imposed in the form of prohibition and, more recently, in the form of therapeutic intervention, have been implemented by the federal government. The paternalism at the core of those policies has not only come to define public responses to alcohol abuse, it also frames social problem-solving strategies in reserve communities generally.

8 To overcome alcohol abuse and related social problems in reserve communities the firewater complex must be challenged, through social reorganization and a renovated alcohol abuse strategy. Social reorganization must be centred on education and training, and on practical, population-based economic development rather than reserve-centred development. A renewed alcohol prevention and intervention strategy must be based on an approach to personal change in keeping with traditional First Nations health promotion philosophies. Alcohol abuse reduction strategies should emphasize individual, family, and community resilience and strength rather than damage and disease. They should also foster school-based and informal youth and adult training in cognitive, social, and practical education and skill development, rather then promoting alcohol avoidance as a permanent strategy.

References

AADAC (Alberta Alcohol and Drug Abuse Commission: An Agency of the Government of Alberta), Inhalant Abuse Northern Field Services. n.d. *Adolescent Inhalant Abuse.*

Adams, Ian, Peter Cameron, Brian Hill, and William C. Penz. 1970. *The Real Poverty Report.* Edmonton: Hurtig.

Addiction Research Foundation (ARF). 1984. *A Structured Addictions Assessment Interview for Selecting Treatment.* Toronto: ARF.

– 1987. *Drugs and Drug Abuse: A Reference Text.* 2nd ed. Toronto: ARF.

– 1989. *Final Report of the Evaluation of Selected NNADAP Projects.* Ottawa: Medical Services Branch, Health and Welfare Canada.

Alcohol Concern. 1989. *Volunteer Alcohol Counsellors: The Minimum Standards.* London: Alcohol Concern.

Alden, L.E. 1978. Evaluation of a Preventive Self-Management Programme for Problem Drinkers. *Canadian Journal of Behavioural Science* 10:258–63.

Alibrandi, L.A. 1978. The Folk Psychotherapy of Alcoholics Anonymous. In *Practical Approaches to Alcoholism Psychotherapy,* ed. S. Zimberg, J. Wallace, and S. Blume, 163–80. New York: Plenum Press.

American Psychiatric Association (APA). 1994. *Diagnostic and Statistical Manual of Mental Disorders.* 4th ed. Washington, DC: APA.

Anderssen, Erin. 1998a. Fearing Big Costs, Ottawa Stalls Native Land Promise. *Globe and Mail,* 16 Nov.

– 1998b. How the Sawridge Millions Tore Apart a Native Community. *Globe and Mail,* 16 Nov.

Annis, H.M. 1979. The Detoxification Alternative to the Handling of Public Inebriates. *Journal of Studies on Alcohol* 30:196–210.

– 1986a. 'Is Inpatient Rehabilitation of the Alcoholics Cost Effective? Con Position. *Advances in Alcohol and Substance Abuse* 5:175–80.

– 1986b. A Relapse Prevention Model for Treatment of Alcoholics. In *Treating Addiction Behaviours*, ed. W.R. Miller and N. Feather, 407–33. New York: Plenum Press.

Annis, H.M., and C.S. Davis. 1988. Self-Efficacy and the Prevention of Alcoholic Relapse: Initial Findings from a Treatment Trial. In *Addiction Disorders: Psychological Research on Assessment and Treatment*, ed. T.B. Baker and D. Cannon, 88–182. New York: Pergamon Press.

– 1989a. *Handbook of Alcoholism Treatment Approaches*, 170–82. New York: Pergamon Press.

– 1989b. Relapse Prevention. In *Handbook of Alcoholism Treatment Approaches*, ed. R.K. Hester and W.R. Miller, 170–82. New York: Pergamon Press.

– 1989c. Relapse Prevention Training: A Cognitive-Behavioural Approach Based on Self-Efficacy Theory. *Journal of Chemical Dependency Treatment* 2 (2): 81–103.

Armor, D.S., J.M. Polich, and H.B. Stambul. 1978. *Alcoholism and Treatment*. New York: Wiley.

Austin, Gregory A. 1988. Substance Abuse Among Minority Youth: Native Americans. *Prevention Research Update* 2 (Winter).

Azrin, N.H. 1976. Improvements in the Community Reinforcement Approach to Alcoholism. *Behaviour Research and Therapy* 14:339–48.

Azrin, N.H., W. Sisson, R. Meyers, and M. Godley. 1982. Alcoholism Treatment by Disalfiram and Community Reinforcement Therapy. *Journal of Behaviour Therapy and Experimental Psychiatry* 13:105–12.

Bandura, A. 1982. Self-Efficacy Mechanism in Human Agency. *American Psychologist* 37:122–47.

Banton, Michael. 1987. *Racial Theories*. London: CUP.

Barnett, M.L. 1955. Alcoholism in the Cantonese of New York City: An Anthropological Study. In *Etiology of Chronic Alcoholism*, ed. O. Diethelm, 179–227. Springfield, IL: Charles C. Thomas.

Battlefords Indian Health Centre, Inc. 1984. *Alcohol and Drug Abuse In-patient Treatment Centre Study*. 18 Jan.

Battlefords Tribal Council Indian Health Services, Inc. (BTCIHS) 1993. *Adult-Band Member Health Survey. Battlefords Tribal Council Bands: Original Survey Data.*

Beauvais, Fred, and Steve LaBoueff. 1985. Drug and Alcohol Abuse Intervention in American Indian Communities. *International Journal of the Addictions* 20 (1): 139–71.

Beavis, Mary Ann, Nancy Klos, Tom Carter, and Christian Douchant. 1997. *Literature Review: Aboriginal People and Homelessness*. Prepared for Canada Mortgage and Housing Corporation (CMHC). Winnipeg: Institute of Urban Studies.

Beck, Aaron T. 1976. *Cognitive Therapy and the Emotional Disorders.* New York: Meridian.

Beck, Aaron T., Fred D. Wright, Cory F. Newman, and Bruce S. Liese. 1993. *Cognitive Therapy of Substance Abuse.* New York and London: Guilford Press.

Beckham, E.E., and W.R. Leber, eds. 1985. *Handbook of Depression: Treatment Assessment and Research.* Homewood, IL: Dorsey Press.

Begleiter, Henri, and Bernice Porjesz. 1988. Potential Biological Markers in Individuals at High Risk for Developing Alcoholism. *Alcoholism: Clinical and Experimental Research* 12 (4): 488–93.

Berg, B.J., and W.R. Dubin. 1990. Economic Grand Rounds: Why 28 Days? An Alternative Approach to Alcoholism Treatment. *Hospital and Community Psychiatry* 41:1175–8.

Berger, Peter L., and Thomas Luckmann. 1967. *The Social Construction of Reality: A Treatise in the Sociology of Knowledge.* Garden City, NY: Anchor Books, Doubleday and Company.

Blake, B.G. 1967. Follow-Up of Alcoholics Treated by Behaviour Therapy. *Behaviour Research and Therapy* 5:89–94.

Blaszczynski, A., N. McConaghy, and A. Frankova. 1991. A Comparison of Relapsed and Non-Relapsed Abstinent Pathological Gamblers Following Behavioural Treatment. *British Journal of Addiction* 86:1485–9.

Blum, K. 1984. *Handbook of Abusable Drugs.* New York: Gardner Press.

Blum, Kenneth, and Helga Topel. 1986. Opioid Peptides and Alcoholism: Genetic Deficiency and Chemical Management. *Functional Neurology* 1:71–83.

Blume, S.B. 1986. Alcoholism Rehabilitation: Getting Involved – A Memoir of the 60s. In *Alcohol Intervention: Historical and Sociocultural Approaches,* ed. D.L. Strug, S. Priyadarsini, and M.M. Hyman, 75–80. New York: Haworth Press.

Blumenkrantz, David G. 1992. *Fulfilling the Promise of Children's Services: Why Primary Prevention Efforts Fail and How They Can Succeed: The Rite of Passage Model.* San Francisco: Jossey-Bass Publishers.

Boldt, Menno. 1993. *Surviving as Indians: The Challenge of Self-Government.* Toronto: University of Toronto Press.

Borg, Stefan, et al. 1983. Clinical Conditions and Concentrations of MOPEG in Cerebrospinal Fluid and Urine of Alcoholic Patients with Withdrawal. *Science* 213:1135–7.

Bowden, K.M., et al. 1958. A Survey of Blood Alcohol Testing in Victoria (1951–56). *Medical Journal of Australia* 2:13–15.

Bracht, Neil, ed. 1990. *Health Promotion at the Community Level.* Newbury Park, CA: Sage Publications.

Bracht, Neil, and Lee Kingsbury. 1990. Community Organization Principles in

Health Promotion: A Five Stage Model. In *Health Promotion at the Community Level*, ed. Neil Bracht, 66–88. Newbury Park, CA: Sage Publications.

Bradshaw, John. 1988. *Bradshaw on the Family: A Revolutionary Way of Self-Discovery*. Dearfield Beach, FL: Health Communication, Inc.

Brandsma, J.M., M.C. Maultsby, and R. Welsh. 1980. *The Outpatient Treatment of Alcoholism: A Review and Comparative Study*. Baltimore, MD: University Park Press.

Bremner, Robert. 1965. 'Shifting Attitudes.' In *Social Welfare Institutions: A Sociological Reader*, ed. Mayer Zald, 23–37. New York: Wiley.

Brennan, John G. 1990. Redefining Alcoholism. *Addiction and Recovery* (June): 26–9.

Brickman, P., V.C. Rabinowitz, J. Karuza Jr, D. Coates, E. Cohn, and L. Kidder. 1982. Models of Helping and Coping. *American Psychologist* 37:368–84.

Brill, L. 1981. *The Clinical Treatment of Substance Abusers*. New York: Free Press.

Brody, Hugh. 1977. Alcohol, Change and the Industrial Frontier. *Inuit Studies*, 1 (2): 31–47.

Brodsky, Archie. 1995. Extract from a workshop presentation and adapted on the basis of a personal communication from with the author.

Bronfenbrenner, Urie. 1997. Reply to John McKnight's 'A 21st Century Map for Health Communities and Families.' *Families and Society: The Journal of Contemporary Human Services*. 78 (2) (March/April): 124.

Brook, R.C., and P.C. Whitehead. 1980. *Drug-Free Therapeutic Community*. New York: Human Services Press.

Brower, K.J., F.C. Blow, J.P. Young, and E.M. Hill. 1991. Symptoms and Correlates of Anabolic-Androgenic Steroid Dependence. *British Journal of Addiction* 86:759–68.

Brown, C., and J. Thompson. 1990. *An Evaluation of the Lander Model for Addictions Treatment*. Edmonton: Alberta Alcohol and Drug Abuse Commission.

Brown, Elizabeth D., Timothy J. O'Farrell, Stephen A. Maisto, Karen Boies-Hickman, and Richard Suchinsky, eds. 1997. *Substance Abuse Program Accreditation Guide*. Thousand Oaks, CA, London, and New Delhi: Sage Publications.

Brown, S.A. 1990. Adolescent Alcohol Expectancies and Risk for Alcohol Abuse. *Addiction and Recovery* 10 (5/6): 16–19.

Brown, S.A., V.A. Creamer, and B.A. Stetson. 1987. Adolescent Alcohol Expectancies in Relation to Personal and Parental Drinking Patterns. *Journal of Abnormal Psychology* 96:117–21.

Brown, S.A., M.S. Goldman, A. Inn, and L.R. Anderson. 1980. Expectations of Reinforcement from Alcohol: Their Domain and Relation to Drinking Patterns. *Journal of Consulting and Clinical Psychology* 48:419–26.

Brown, S.J. 1990. Adolescent Alcohol Expectancies and Risk for Alcohol Abuse. *Addiction and Recovery* 10 (5/6): 16–19.

Bruhn, John G., and Howard M. Rebach. 1996. *Clinical Sociology: An Agenda for Action*. New York and London: Plenum Press.

Buckley, Helen. 1993. *From Wooden Ploughs to Welfare: Why Indian Policy Failed in the Prairie Provinces*. Montreal and Kingston: McGill-Queen's University Press.

Cahalan, D. 1970. *Problem Drinkers: A National Survey*. San Francisco: Jossey-Bass.

– 1987. Studying Drinking Problems Rather than Alcoholism. In *Recent Developments in Alcoholism*, ed. M. Galanter, 363–72. New York: Plenum Press.

Cahalan, D., and Robin Room. 1974. *Problem Drinking among American Men*. New Brunswick, NJ: Rutgers Center of Alcohol Studies.

Canada, 1971. *Poverty in Canada: Report of the Special Senate Committee Report on Poverty*. Ottawa: Queen's Printer.

Canada Mortgage and Housing Corporation. 2003. Homesave: Building Investments in Housing Assets. *Research Highlights*. Socio-economic Series. April, Issue 03-001.

Canadian Parliamentary Sub-Committee on the Non-Medical Use of Drugs. 2002. *Policy for the New Millennium: Working Together to Define Canada's Drug Strategy*. Ottawa: Minister of Public Works and Government Services Canada.

Canter, Lee (with Marlene Canter). 1974. *Assertive Discipline for Parents*. New York: Harper and Row.

Carpenter, E.S. 1959. Alcohol in the Iroquois Dream Quest. *American Journal of Psychiatry* 116:148–51.

– 1970. *Problem Drinkers: A National Survey*. San Francisco: Jossey-Bass Publishers.

Carr-Saunders, A.M., and P.A. Wilson. 1933. *The Professions*. Oxford: Clarendon Press.

Carter, Sarah. 1990. *Lost Harvests: Prairie Indian Reserve Farmers and Government Policy*. Montreal and Kingston: McGill-Queen's University Press.

Chan, Arthur K. 1986. Racial Differences in Alcohol Sensitivity. *Alcohol and Alcoholism* 21 (1): 93–104.

Chandler, Michael J. 2001. The Time of Our Lives: Self-Continuity in Native and Non-Native Youth. In *Advances in Child Development and Behavior*, ed. H.W. Reese, 175–221. New York: Academic Press.

Chaney, E.F., M.R. O'Leary, and G.A. Marlatt 1978. Skill Training with Alcoholics. *Journal of Consulting and Chemical Psychology* 46:1092–1104.

Charness, M.E., R.P. Simon, and D.A. Greenberg. 1989. Ethanol and the Nervous System. *New England Journal of Medicine* 321 (7): 442–54.

Cheney, Peter. 1998. The Money Pit: An Indian Band's Story. *Globe and Mail*, 24 Oct.

Chiauzzi, E. 1990. Breaking the Patterns that Lead to Relapse. *Psychology Today* 23 (12): 18–19.

Chrisjohn, Roland D., and Sherri Young. 1994. *The Circle Game: Shadows and Substance in the Indian Residential School Experience in Canada*. Ottawa: Report of the Royal Commission on Aboriginal People.

Cleveland, F.P. 1955. Problems in Homicide Investigation IV: The Relationship of Alcohol to Suicide. *Cincinnati Journal of Medicine* 36:28–30.

Cloninger, Robert C. 1983. Genetic and Environmental Factors in the Development of Alcoholism. *Journal of Psychiatric Treatment and Evaluation* 5:487–96.

Cloninger, C.R., M. Bohman, and S. Sigvardsson. 1981. Inheritance of Alcohol Abuse: Cross-Fostering Analysis of Adopted Men. *Archives of General Psychiatry* 38:861–8.

Cloninger, Robert C., Soren Sigvardsson, and Michael Bohman. 1988. Childhood Personality Predicts Alcohol Abuse in Young Adults. *Alcoholism: Clinical and Experimental Research* 5 (4): 494–505.

Coggins, Kip. 1990. *Alternative Pathways to Healing: The Recovery Medicine Wheel*. Deerfield Beach, FL: Health Communications, Inc.

Cohen, M., I. Liebson, L. Faillace, and R. Allen. 1971. 'Alcoholism, Controlled Drinking and Incentives for Abstinence. *Psychological Reports* 28:575–80.

Cook, C., and C.H. Cook. 1988. The Minnesota Model in the Management of Drug and Alcohol Dependence: Miracle, Method or Myth, Part II: Evidence and Conclusions. *British Journal of Addiction* 83:735–48.

Cornell, Stephen, and Joseph P. Kalt, eds. 1992. *What Can Tribes Do? Strategies and Institutions in American Indian Economic Development*. Los Angeles: American Indian Studies Center.

Coser, Lewis. 1956. *The Functions of Social Conflict*. New York: Free Press.

Critchlow, B. 1986. The Powers of John Barleycorn: Beliefs About the Effects of Alcohol on Social Behaviour. *American Psychologist* 41:751–64.

Cummings, C., J.R. Gordon, and G.A. Marlatt. 1980. Relapse: Prevention and Prediction. In *The Addictive Behaviors*, ed. W.R. Miller, 291–321. New York: Pergamon Press.

Cutler, R., and N. Morrison. 1971. *Sudden Death: A Study of Characteristics of Victims and Events Leading to Sudden Death in British Columbia with Primary Emphasis on Apparent Alcohol Involvement and Indian Sudden Death*. Vancouver: Alcohol Foundation of British Columbia.

Cutler, R., and T. Storm. 1973. *Drinking Practices in Three British Columbian Cities*. Vol. 1. *General Population Survey*. Vancouver: Alcoholism Foundation of British Columbia.

Dailey, R.C. 1968. The Role of Alcohol Among North American Indian Tribes as Reported in the Jesuit Relations. *Anthropologica* 10:45–57.

Daisy, Fransing, Lisa R. Thomas, and Charlene Worley. 1998. Alcohol Use and Harm Reduction with the Native Community. In *Harm Reduction: Pragmatic Strategies for Managing High-Risk Behaviors*, ed. G. Alan Marlatt, 327–50. New York and London: Guilford Press.

Davies, D.L. 1962. Normal Drinking in Recovered Alcoholics. *Quarterly Journal of Studies on Alcohol* 23:94–104.

Davis, Arthur K. 1971. Canadian Society and History as Hinterland vs. Metropolis. In *Canadian Society: Pluralism, Change and Conflict*, ed. Richard J. Ossenberg, 6–32. Scarborough, ON: Prentice-Hall.

DenHartog, G. 1982. *A Decade of Detox: Development of Non-Hospital Approaches to Alcohol Detoxification – A Review of the Literature*. Substance Abuse. Monograph Series. Jefferson City, MO: Division of Alcohol and Drug Abuse.

Denning, Patt. 2000. *Practicing Harm Reduction Psychotherapy: An Alternative Approach to Addictions*. New York and London: Guilford Press.

DIAND – Department of Indian Affairs and Northern Development. 1980. *Indian Conditions: A Survey*. Ottawa: Department of Indian Affairs and Northern Development.

Dineen, Tana. 1996. *Manufacturing Victims: What the Psychology Industry Is Doing to People*. Westmount, QC: Robert Davies Publishing.

Ditman, K.S., G.G. Crawford, E.W. Forgy, H. Maskowitz, and C. MacAndrew. 1967. A Controlled Experiment on the Use of Court Probation for Drunk Arrests. *American Journal of Psychiatry* 124:160–3.

Dorpat, T.L. 1985. *Denial and Defense in the Therapeutic Situation*. New York: Jason Aronson.

Doweiko, Harold F. 1993. *Concepts of Chemical Dependency*, 2nd ed. Pacific Grove, CA: Brooks/Cole Publications.

Drake, R.E., and G.E. Vaillant. 1985. A Validity Study of Axis II of DSM III. *American Journal of Psychiatry* 142 (5): 553–8.

Dreikurs, Rudolf, Shirley Gould and Raymond J. Corsini. 1974. *Family Council*. Chicago: Contemporary Books.

Driver, Harold. 1969. *Indians of North America*. 2nd ed. Chicago: University of Chicago Press.

Dryden, Windy. 1989. *Rational-Emotive Counselling in Action*. London: Sage Publications.

Dubourg, G.O. 1969. Aftercare for Alcoholics: A Follow-Up Study. *British Journal of Addiction* 64:155–63.

Dulfano, Celia. 1992. *Families, Alcoholism and Recovery*. New York: Jossey-Bass.

Dunning, R.W. 1964. Some Problems of Reserve Indian Communities: A Case Study. *Anthropologica* 4:3–38.

Duran, Eduardo, and Bonnie Duran. 1995. *Native American Postcolonial Psychology*. Albany: State University of New York Press.

Eastman, M. 1915. *Church and State in Early Canada*. Edinburgh: University of Edinburgh Press.

Edwards, G., J. Orford, S. Egert, S. Guthrie, A. Hawker, C. Hensman, M. Mitcheson, E. Oppenheimer, and C. Taylor. 1977. A Controlled Trial of 'Treatment' and 'Advice.' *Journal of Studies on Alcohol* 38:1004–31.

Eliany, Marc, ed. 1989. *Licit and Illicit Drugs in Canada*. Ottawa: Health and Welfare Canada (Cat. No. 39-159/1989E).

Eliany, Marc, and Brian Rush. 1992. *How Effective Are Alcohol and Other Drug Prevention and Treatment Programs? A Review of Evaluation Studies: A Canada's Drugs Strategy Baseline Report*. A Technical Report Prepared for the Health Promotion Studies Unit, Health Promotion Directorate, Health Services and Promotion Branch. Ottawa: Health and Welfare Canada.

Eliany, Marc, Scott Wortley, and Ed Adlaf. 1992. *Alcohol and Other Drugs Use by Indian Youth*. A National Alcohol and Other Drugs Survey (1989) Report. Prepared for the Health Promotion Studies Directorate, Health Services and Promotion Branch. Ottawa: Health and Welfare Canada.

Elias, Peter Douglas. 1996. Worklessness and Social Pathologies in Aboriginal Communities. *Human Organization* 55 (1): 13–24.

Ellis, A., J.F. McInerney, R. DiGiuseppe, and R.J. Yeager. 1988. *Rational-Emotive Therapy with Alcoholics and Substance Abusers*. New York: Pergamon.

Ellis, Albert, and W. Dryden. 1987. *Practice of Rational-Emotive Therapy*. New York: Springer.

Employment and Immigration Canada. 1993. *Labour Market Review: Fourth Quarter Report, January to March, 1993*. North Battleford, SK: Canada Employment Centre (CEC).

Escalona, S.K. 1982. Babies at Double Hazard: Early Development of Infants at Biologic and Social Risk. *Pediatrics* 70 (5) (November): 670–6.

Etzioni, Amitai. 1969. *The Semi-Professions and their Organization: Teachers, Nurses and Social Workers*. New York: Free Press.

Evans, Robert G., Morris L. Barer, and Theodore Marmer, eds. 1994. *Why Are Some People Healthy and Others Not?* New York: Aldine De Gruyter.

Ewing, J. 1984. Detecting Alcoholism: The CAGE Questionnaire. *Journal of the American Medical Association* 252:1905–7.

Federation of Saskatchewan Indians (FSI). 1985. *Alcohol and Drug Abuse among Treaty Indians in Saskatchewan*. Prepared for the FSI Health and Social Development Commission by WMC Research Associates, Saskatoon.

Fein, Melvin L. 1990. *Role Change: A Resocialization Perspective*. Westport, CT, and London: Praeger.

Feldman, O.L. et al. 1975. Outpatient Alcohol Detoxification: Initial Findings on 564 Patients. *American Journal of Psychiatry* 132:407–12.

Fenna, D., L. Mix, O. Schaeffer, and J.A.L. Gilbert. 1971. Ethanol Metabolism in Various Racial Groups. *Canadian Medical Association Journal* 105:472–5.

Ferguson, Jack. 1971. Eskimos in a Satellite Society. In *Minority Canadians: (Volume 1), Native Peoples*, ed. J.L. Elliott, 15–28. Scarborough, ON: Prentice Hall.

Ferrence, R.G. 1984. Prevention of Alcohol Problems in Women. In *Alcohol Problems in Women*, ed. S. Wilsnack and L. Beckman, 413–42. New York: Guilford Press.

Fiddler, S. 1985. *Suicides, Violent and Accidental Deaths among Treaty Indians in Saskatchewan: Analysis and Recommendations for Change*. Regina: Federation of Saskatchewan Indian Nations.

Fingarette, Herbert. 1988a. Alcoholism: The Mythical Disease. *Utne Reader* 30:64–9.

– 1988b. *Heavy Drinking: The Myth of Alcoholism as a Disease*. Berkeley: University of California Press.

First Nations and Inuit Regional Health Survey National Steering Committee. 1999. *First Nations and Inuit Regional Health Survey: National Report*. Ottawa: Health Canada.

Fischer, Joel. 1978. *Effective Casework Practice: An Eclectic Approach*. New York: McGraw-Hill.

Fisher, A.D. 1987. Alcoholism and Race: The Misapplication of Both Concepts to North American Indians. *Canadian Review of Sociology and Anthropology* 24 (1): 81–98.

Fisher, R.S. 1951. Symposium on the Compulsory Use of Chemical Tests for Alcohol Intoxication. *Maryland Medical Journal* 3:291–2.

Flach, Frederich. 1988. *Resilience: Discovering a New Strength at Times of Stress*. New York: Fawcett Columbine.

Flavin, Daniel K., and Robert M. Morse. 1990. What Is Alcoholism? Current Definitions and Diagnostic Criteria and Their Implications for Treatment. *Alcohol Health and Research World* 15 (4): 267–9.

Flores, John Philip. 1985–6. Alcoholism Treatment and the Relationship of Native American Cultural Values to Recovery. *International Journal of the Addictions* 20 (11 & 12): 1707–26.

Foucault, Michel. 1975. *The Archaeology of Knowledge*. London: Tavistock.

Four Worlds Development Project. 1983. *The Sacred Tree: Teacher's Guide*. Lethbridge, AB: Faculty of Education, University of Lethbridge.

- 1985. *Overview*. Lethbridge, AB: Faculty of Education, University of Lethbridge.

Frederickson, P.A., J.W. Richardson, M.S. Esther, and S. Lin. 1990. Sleep Disorders in Psychiatric Practice. *Mayo Clinic Procedures* 65:861–8.

Freedberg, E.J., and W.E. Johnson. 1978. *The Effects of Assertion Training ... and The Effects of Relaxation Training ... (both) ... Within the Context of a Multi-Model Alcoholism Treatment Program for Employed Alcoholics*. Substudies No. 796 & 988. Toronto: Addiction Research Foundation.

Freeman, Edith M., ed. 1993. *Substance Abuse Treatment: A Family Systems Perspective*. Newbury Park, CA: Sage Publications.

Freidson, Eliot. 1970. *Profession of Medicine*. New York: Dodd and Mead.

Frideres, James S. 1993. *Native Peoples in Canada: Contemporary Conflicts*. Scarborough, ON: Prentice-Hall.

Gabrielli, W. et al. 1982. Electroencephelograms in Children of Alcoholic Fathers. *Psychophysiology* 19:402–7.

Galanter, Marc. 1993. *Network Therapy for Alcohol and Drug Abuse*. Expanded ed. New York and London: Guilford Press.

- 1989. *Cults: Faith, Healing and Coercion*. New York: Oxford University Press.

Garcia-Andrade, Consuelo, Tamara L. Wall, and Cindy L. Ehlers. 1997. The Firewater Myth and Response to Alcohol in Mission Indians. *American Journal of Psychiatry* 154 (July): 7.

Genazzani, A.R. et al. 1983. Central Deficiency of B-endorphin in Alcohol Addicts. *Journal of Clinical Endocrinology and Metabolism* 55:583–6.

Gfellner, B.M., and J.D. Hundleby. 1995. Patterns of Drug Use among Native and White Adolescents: 1990–93. *Canadian Journal of Public Health* 86:95–7.

Glaser, P.D., and A.C. Ogborne. 1982. Does A.A. Really Work? *British Journal of Addictions* 77:88–92.

Goffman, Erving. 1961. *Asylums: Essays on the Social Situation of Mental Patient and Other Inmates*. Garden City, NY: Anchor Books.

Goldstein, A., K. Heller, and L. Sechrest. 1966. *Psychotherapy and the Psychology of Behavior Change*. New York: Wiley.

Goldstein, Avram. 2001. *Addiction: From Biology to Drug Policy*. 2nd ed. Oxford and London: Oxford University Press.

Goldstein, Dora. 1983. *Pharmacology of Alcohol*. New York: Oxford University Press.

Goldstein, P. 1990. Drugs and Violence. Paper presented at the 1990 meeting of the American Psychological Association. Cited in Doweiko (1993).

Goodwin, D.W., F. Schulsinger, and L. Hermansen. 1973. Alcohol Problems in Adoptees Raised Apart from Alcoholic Biological Parents. *Archives of General Psychiatry* 28:283–43.

Gorski, Terence T., and Merlene Miller. 1982. *Counselling for Relapse Prevention.* Independence, MO: Herald House, Independence Press.

– 1986. *Staying Sober: A Guide for Relapse Prevention.* Independence, MO: Herald House, Independence Press.

Gottheil, E., A. Alterman, T.E. Skoloda, and B.F. Murphy. 1973. Alcoholics' Patterns of Controlled Drinking. *American Journal of Psychiatry* 130:418–22.

Gottheil, E., L.O. Corbett, J.C. Grassburger, and F.S. Cornelison. 1972. Fixed Interval Drinking Decisions, I.: A Research and Treatment Model. *Quarterly Journal of Studies on Alcohol* 33:311–24.

Gottlieb, A.M., J.D. Killen, G.A. Marlatt, and C.B. Taylor. 1987. Psychological and Pharmacological Influences in Cigarette Smoking Withdrawal: Effects of Nicotine Gum and Expectancy on Smoking Withdrawal Symptoms and Relapse. *Journal of Clinical and Consulting Psychology* 55:606–8.

Gottlieb, Benjamin H., ed. 1988. *Marshaling Social Support: Format, Processes and Effects.* Newbury Park, CA.: Sage Publications.

Gottman, J.M., and S. Leiblum. 1974. *How to Do Psychotherapy and How to Evaluate It.* New York: Holt.

Graham, K., H. Annis, P. Brett, and P. Venesoen. 1966. Women Aged 65 and Over: Alcohol and Drug Use. In *Women's Use of Alcohol, Tobacco and Other Drugs in Canada*, ed. N. Adrian, C. Lundy, and E. Eliany, 82–103. Toronto: Addiction Research Foundation.

Gray, James H. 1982. *Baccanalia Revisited: Western Canada's Boozy Skid to Social Disaster.* Saskatoon: Modern Press.

Green, Lawrence W., and John Raeburn. 1990. Contemporary Developments in Health Promotion: Definitions and Challenges. In *Health Promotion at the Community Level*, ed. Neil Bracht, 29–44. Thousand Oaks, CA: Sage Publications.

Grotberg, Edith Henderson. 1999. *Tapping Your Inner Strength: How to Find the Resilience to Deal with Anything.* Oakland: New Harbinger Publications, Inc.

Groves, Mark. 1990. The Nature of Inhalant-Solvent Abuse and American Indian Youth: Implications for Intervention and Treatment. Unpublished paper, Eden Youth Inhalant Abuse Training and Information Project, Minneapolis.

Guillory, B.M., E. Willie, and E.F. Duran. 1988. 'Analysis of a Community Organizing Case Study: Alkali Lake. *Journal of Rural Community Psychology* 9 (1): 27–36.

Hagan, John. 1977. *The Disreputable Pleasures.* Toronto: McGraw-Hill Ryerson.

Hallowell, A.J. 1955. *Culture and Experience.* Philadelphia: University of Pennsylvania Press.

Hanson, David J. 1995. *Preventing Alcohol Abuse: Alcohol, Culture and Control.* Westport, CT: Praeger.

Harrell, A.V., and P.W. Wirtz. 1989. *Adolescent Drinking Index Test and Manual.* Odessa, FL: Psychological Assessment Resources.

Hawkins, J. David, Richard Catalano, Jr; and Associates. 1992. *Communities That Care: Action for Drug Abuse Prevention.* San Francisco: Jossey-Bass Publishers.

Hawthorn, H.B., ed. 1966. *A Surrey of the Contemporary Indians in Canada.* 2 vols. Ottawa: Queen's Printer.

Hayshida, M. et al. 1989. Comparative Effectiveness and Costs of Inpatient and Outpatient Detoxification of Patients with Mild-to-Moderate Alcohol Withdrawal Syndrome. *New England Journal of Medicine* 320 (6): 358–65.

Heath, Dwight B. 1964. Prohibition and Post-Repeal Drinking Patterns Among the Navejo. *Quarterly Journal of Studies on Alcohol* 25 (1): 119–35.

Health Canada. 1993. *Prevention Framework for First Nations Communities.* Prepared by the Prevention Task Group. Ottawa: Addictions and Community Funded Programs, Medical Services Branch.

– 1999a. *Ten Years of Health Transfer: First Nation and Inuit Control: April 1989 to March 1999.* Ottawa: Minister of Public Works and Government Services.

– 1999b. *Profile: Treatment and Rehabilitation in Canada.* Prepared by Gary Roberts and Alan Ogborne. Ottawa: Minister of Public Works and Government Services.

– 1999c. *Best Practices: Substance Abuse Treatment and Rehabilitation.* Prepared by Gary Roberts and Alan Ogborne. Ottawa: Minister of Public Works and Government Services.

– 2002. *Literature Review: Methadone Maintenance Treatment.* Prepared by Bruna Brands, David Marsh, Liz Hart, and Wanda Jamieson of Jamieson, Beals, Lalonde & Associates, Inc. Ottawa: Minister of Public Works and Government Services.

Health and Welfare Canada. 1991. *Health Status of Canadian Indians and Inuit: 1990.* Ottawa: Mental Health Division, Health Programs Service Branch, Health Canada.

Heath, D.W. 1975. *A Critical Review of Ethnographic Studies of Alcohol Use.* New York: John Wiley & Sons.

– 1982. Alcohol and Drug Use among North American Indians: A Cross-Cultural Survey of Patterns and Problems. In *Research Advances in Alcohol and Drug Problems,* ed. R.G. Smart, F. Glaser, V. Israel, R.E. Popham, and W. Schmidt, vol. 7. New York: Plenum Press.

Heather, N., and J. Tebbutt, eds. 1989. *The Effectiveness of Treatment for Drug and Alcohol Problems: An Overview.* Monograph Series No. 11. Canberra: Australian Government Publishing Service.

Heather, Nick. 1995. Brief Intervention Strategies. In *Handbook of Alcoholism*

Treatment Approaches, 2nd ed., ed. Reid K. Hester and William R. Miller, chap. 6, 105–22. Boston: Allyn and Bacon.

Heather, Nick, and Ian Robertson. 1981. *Controlled Drinking*. New York: Methuen.

– 1997. *Problem Drinking*. 2nd ed. Oxford and New York: Oxford University Press.

Heilbron, Carrie L., and Mary Alice Julius Guttman. 2000. Traditional Healing Methods with First Nations Women in Group Counselling. *Canadian Journal of Counselling* 34 (1) (January): 3–13.

Henggeler, Scott, Sonja K. Schoenwald, Charles M. Borduin, Melisa D. Rowland, and Phillippe B. Cunningham. 1998. *Multisystemic Treatment of Antisocial Behaviour in Children and Adolescents*. New York and London: Guilford Press.

Henshel, Richard L. 1976. *Reacting to Social Problems*. Don Mills, ON: Longman Canada, Ltd.

Herman, S., and Noam Chomsky. 2002. *Manufacturing Consent: The Political Economy of the Mass Media*. New York: Pantheon Books.

Hester, R.K. 1995. Behavioural Self-Control Training. In *Handbook of Alcoholism Treatment Approaches: Effective Alternatives*, 2nd ed., ed. R.K. Hester and W.R. Miller, 148–9. Needham Heights, MA: Allyn and Bacon.

Hester, R.K., and W.R. Miller. 1989. Self-Control Training. In *Handbook of Alcoholism Treatment Approaches*, ed. R.K. Hester, and W.R. Miller, 141–9. New York: Pergamon Press.

Hilton, M.E. 1987. Drinking Patterns and Drinking Problems in 1984: Results from a General Population Survey. *Alcoholism: Clinical and Experimental Research* 11:167–75.

– 1991. A Note on Measuring Drinking Problems in the 1984 National Alcohol Survey. In *Alcohol in America: Drinking Practices and Problems*, ed. W.B. Clark and M.E. Hilton, 51–70. Albany: State University of New York Press.

Hislop, Gregory T., William J. Threllfall, Richard P. Gallagher, and Pierre R. Band. 1987. Accidental and Intentional Violent Death Among British Columbia Native Indians. *Canadian Journal of Public Health* 78:271–4.

Holman, Adele. 1983. *Family Assessment*. Sage Service Guides (33). Newbury Park, CA: Sage Publications.

Horton, John. 1966. Order and Conflict Theories of Social Problems as Competing Ideologies. *American Journal of Sociology* 71 (May): 701–13.

Horwitz, Allan V. 2002. *Creating a Mental Illness*. Chicago: University of Chicago Press.

Howay, F.W. 1942. The Introduction of Intoxicating Liquor to the Indians of the Northwest Coast. *B.C. Historical Quarterly* 4 (3): 157–69.

Hull, Jeremy. 2001. *Aboriginal People and Social Classes in Manitoba*. Ottawa: Canadian Centre for Policy Alternatives.

Illich, Ivan. 1971. *Deschooling Society*. New York: Harper and Row.

– 1976. *Medical Nemesis: The Expropriation of Health*. New York: Pantheon Books.

Institute of Medicine. 1990. *Broadening the Base of Treatment for Alcohol Problems*. Washington, DC: National Academy Press.

Irwin, Eugene. 1987. Recent Research in Animal Behavioral Genetics. Paper presented at the National Alcoholism Research Conference, May, 1987, Chapel Hill, North Carolina.

Irvin, M., M. Schuckit, and T.L. Smith. 1990. Clinical Importance of Age of Onset in Type 1 and 2 Primary Alcoholics. *Archives of General Psychiatry* 47:320–4.

Jarvis, Gordon K., and Menno Boldt. 1982. Death Styles among Canada's Indians. *Social Science and Medicine* 16:1345–52.

Jellinek, E.M. 1960. *The Disease Concept of Alcoholism*. New Brunswick, NJ: Millhouse Press.

Jenike, M.A. 1989. Drug Abuse. In *Scientific American Medicine*, vol. 13, ed. E. Rubinstein and P.D. Federman, 1–8. New York: Scientific American.

Jessor, R., and S.L. Jessor. 1977. *Problem Behavior and Psychosocial Development: A Longitudinal Study of Youth*. New York: Academic Press.

Jilekaal, L. 1974. Psychosocial Aspects of Drinking among Coast Salish Indians. *Canadian Pychiatric Association Journal* 19 (4): 357–61.

Johansson, S.R. 1982. The Demographic History of the Native Peoples of North America: A Selective Bibliography. *Yearbook of Physical Anthropology* 24:133–52.

Jock, Richard. 1998. *Final Report. General Review: Nationqal Native Alcohol and Drug Abuse Program*. Ottawa: Health Canada.

Johnson, Terence J. 1972. *Professions and Power*. London: Macmillan.

Johnson, Vernon E. 1986. *Intervention: How to Help Someone Who Doesn't Want Help*. Minneapolis, MN: Johnson Institute Books.

Johnston, Patrick. 1983. *Native Children and the Child Welfare System*. Ottawa: Canadian Council on Social Development.

Josephson, E., et al. 1972. Adolescent Marijuana Use: Report on a National Survey. In *Proceedings of the International Conference on Student Drug Surveys*, ed. S. Einstein and S. Allen, 1–8. Farmingdale, NY: Baywood.

Julien, R.M. 1988. *A Primer of Drug Addiction*. 5th ed. New York: W.H. Freeman and Co.

Kalant, Harold. 1996. Intoxicated Automatism: Legal Concent vs. Scientific Evidence. *Contemporary Drug Problems* 23 (Winter): 631–47.

Kaminer, Wendy. 1993. *I'm Dysfunctional, You're Dysfunctional*. New York: Vintage Books.

Kandel, D.B. 1978. *Longitudinal Research on Drug Use: Empirical Findings and Methodological Issues*. New York: Hemisphere-Wiley.

Kaplan, Harold I., and Benjamin J. Sadock. 1991. *Synopsis of Psychiatry: Behavioral Sciences and Clinical Psychiatry*. Baltimore, MD: Williams & Williams.

Kassinove, Howard, ed. 1995. *Anger Disorders: Definition, Diagnosis and Treatment*. Washington, DC: Taylor and Francis.

Katz, Stan J., and A.E. Liu. 1991. *The Codependency Conspiracy: How to Break the Recovery Habit and Take Charge of Your Life*. New York: Warner Books, Inc.

Kazemipur, A., and S.S. Halli. 2000. *The New Poverty in Canada: Ethnic Groups and Ghetto Neighbourhoods*. Toronto: Thompson Educational Publishing Inc.

Kendell, R.E. 1965. Normal Drinking by Former Alcohol Addicts. *Quarterly Journal of Studies on Alcohol* 26:247–57.

Keso, L., and M. Salaspuro. 1990. Inpatient Treatment of Employed Alcoholics: A Randomized Clinical Trial on Hazelden-type and Traditional Treatment, *Alcoholism: Clinical and Experimental Research* 14:584–9.

Kissin, Benjamin, and Meredith Hanson. n.d. The Bio-Psycho-Social Perspective in Alcoholism. From SADAC Files; book source unknown (probably late 1980s).

Klerman, G.L. 1992. Interpersonal Psychotherapy: Efficacy and Adaptatins. In *Handbook of Affective Disorders*, 2nd ed., ed. E.S. Paykel, 5501–10. New York: Guilford Press.

Kobasa, S.C. 1979. Stressful Life Events, Personality and Health: An Inquiry into Hardiness. *Journal of Personality and Social Psychology* 37:1–11.

Koenigsberg, H.W., R.D. Kaplan, M.M. Kaplan, and A.M. Cooper. 1985. The Relationship between Syndrome and Personality Disorder in DSM-III: Experience with 2,462 Patients. *American Journal of Psychiatry* 142 (2): 207–12.

Kretzman, John P., and John L. McKnight. 1993a. *Building Communities from the Inside Out: A Path Towards Finding and Mobilizing a Community's Assets*. Evanston, IL: Asset-based Community Development Program.

– 1993b. *A Guide to Capacity Inventories: Mobilizing the Community Skills of Local Residents*. Evanston, IL: Asset-based Community Development Program.

– 1993c. *A Guide to Evaluating Asset-Based Community Development: Lessons, Challanges and Opportunities*. Evanston, IL: Asset-based Community Development Program.

Krystal, H., and R. Moore. 1963. Who Is Qualified to Treat the Alcoholic? *Quarterly Journal in the Study of Alcoholism* 27:705–19.

Kunitiz, Stephen J., and Jerrold E. Levy. 1987. A Suicide Prevention Program for Hopi Youth. *Social Science and Medicine* 25:931–40.

– 1994. *Drinking Careers: A Twenty-five Year Study of Three Navajo Reservations*. New Haven, CT, and London: Yale University Press.

– 2000. *Drinking Conduct Disorder and Social Change: Navajo Experiences*. New York: Oxford University Press.

Lane, Phil, Jr. 1986. Interview reported in *The Ronan Pioneer*. Alcoholism an Obstacle to Growth. 30 Apr.

Lawson, G.W., D.C. Ellis, and P.C. Rivers. 1984. *Essentials of Chemical Dependency Counselling*. Rockville, MD: Aspen Systems Corp.

Lazarus, A.A. 1980. The Stress and Coping Paradigm. In *Competence and Coping in Adulthood*, ed. L.A. Bond and J.C. Rosen, 28–74. Hanover, NH: University Press of New England.

Leavitt, F. 1982. *Drugs and Behavior*. 2nd ed. New York: Wiley.

Le Dain, Gerard. 1973. The Treatment of Alcoholism. In *Alcohol and Other Drugs: Perspectives on Use, Abuse, Treatment and Prevention*, ed. Paul C. Whitehead et al., 74–88. Toronto: Holt, Rinehart and Winston. Repr. from *Treatment*, a segment of the Report of the Royal Commission of Inquiry into the Non-Medical Use of Drugs, 1972. Ottawa: Queen's Printer.

Leland, Joy. 1976. *Firewater Myths*. Monograph 11. New Brunswick, NJ: Rutgers Center of Alcohol Studies.

Lester, David. 1998. Genetic Theory: An Assessment of the Heritability of Alcoholism. In *Theories on Alcoholism*, ed. C.D. Chaudron and D.A. Wilkinson, 17. Toronto: Addiction Research Foundation.

Levine, H.G. 1978. The Discovery of Addiction: Changing Conceptions of Habitual Drunkenness in America. *Journal of Studies on Alcohol* 39:143–74.

Levy, J.E., and S.J. Kunitz. 1971. Indian Reservations, Anomie and Social Pathologies. *Southwestern Journal of Anthropology* 27:97–128.

– 1974. *Indian Drinking: Navajo Practices and Anglo-American Theories*. New York: John Wiley and Sons.

Lewis, Judith A., Robert Q. Dana, and Gregory A. Blevins. 1988. *Substance Abuse Counselling: An Individualized Approach*. Belmont, CA: Brooks/Cole Publishing Co.

Lewontin, R.C. 1972. The Apportionment of Human Diversity. *Evolutionary Biology* 6:381–96.

Lightfoot, L., et al. 1982. *Final Report of the Kingston Developmental Research Project*. Submitted to Health Promotion Directorate, Health and Welfare Canada. Toronto: Addiction Research Foundation.

Lin, T., and D.T. Lin. 1982. Alcoholism among the Chinese: Further Observations of a Low-Risk Population. *Culture, Medicine and Psychiatry* 6 (2): 109–16.

Lingeman, R.R. 1974. *Drugs from A to Z: A Dictionary*. New York: McGraw-Hill.

Loughran, N. 1990. Economy, Social Structure and Development among the Cree and Ojibwa of Northern Manitoba. Unpublished paper.

Luborsky, L., A.T. McLellan, G.E. Woody, C.P. O'Brien, and A. Auerbach. 1985. Therapist Success and Its Determinants. *Archives of General Psychiatry* 42:602–11.

Lux, Maureen K. 2001. *Medicine That Walks: Disease, Medicine, and Canadian Plains Native People, 1880–1940*. Toronto: University of Toronto Press.

MacAndrew, C., and R. Edgerton. 1969. *Drunken Comportment: A Social Explanation*. Chicago: Aldine Publishing.

MacLeod, William Christie. 1928. *The American Indian Frontier*, ed. C.K. Ogden. London: Kegan Paul, Trench, Trubner & Co.

Mann, Karl, Derik Hermann, and Andreas Heinz. 2000. One Hundred Years of Alcoholism: The Twentieth Century. *Alcohol and Alcoholism* 35 (1): 10–15.

Mao, Y., B.W. Moloughney, and R.M. Semenciw. 1992. Indian Reserve and Registered Indian Mortality in Canada. *Canadian Journal of Public Health* 83 (5): 350–3.

Marlatt, G.A. 1985. *Relapse Prevention*. New York: Guilford Press.

– 1988. Matching Clients to Treatment: Treatment Models and Stages of Change. In *Assessment of Addictive Behaviours*, ed. D.M. Dopnauer and G.A. Marlatt, 474–83. New York: Guilford Press.

Marlatt, G. Alan, ed. 1998. *Harm Reduction: Pragmatic Strategies for Managing High-Risk Behaviours*. New York and London: Guilford Press.

Marlatt, G.A., and W.H. George. 1984. Relapse Prevention: Introduction and Overview of the Model. *British Journal of Addiction* 79:261–74.

Marlatt, G.A., and J.R. Gordon, eds. 1985. *Relapse Prevention*. New York: Guilford Press.

Marmot, M.G. 1986. Social Inequalities in Mortality: The Social Environment. In *Class and Health: Research and Longitudinal Data*, ed. R.C Wilkinson, 21–3. London: Tavistock.

Matuschka, P. 1985. The Pharmacology of Addiction. In *Alcoholism and Substance Abuse: Strategies for Clinical Intervention*, ed. J.E. Bratter and G.G. Forest, 49–73. New York: Free Press.

May, P. 1982. Substance Abuse and Native Americans: Prevalence and Susceptibility. *International Journal of the Addictions* 17 (7): 1185–1209.

Mayer, J., and W.J. Filstead. 1979. The Adolescent Alcohol Involvement Scale: An Instrument for Measuring Adolescents' Use and Misuse of Alcohol. *Journal of Studies on Alcohol* 40:291–300.

McConnell, H. 1981. A Tale of Two Cities. *The Journal*. Toronto: Addiction Research Foundation. 1 Aug.

McCormick, Rod M. 2000. Aboriginal Traditions in the Treatment of Substance Abuse. *Canadian Journal of Counselling* 34 (1) (January): 25–32.

McEvoy, J.P. 1982. The Chronic Neuropsychiatric Disorders Associated with

Alcoholism. In *Encyclopedic Handbook of Alcoholism*, ed. E.M. Pattison and E. Kaufman, 169–79. New York: Gardner Press.

McGuire, L. 1990. The Power of Non-Narcotic Pain Relievers. *RN* 53 (4): 28–35.

McHugh, M.J. 1987. The Abuse of Volatile Substances. *Pediatric Clinics of North America* 34 (April): 333–40.

McKim, W.A. 1986. *Drugs and Behavior: An Introduction to Behavioral Pharmacology*. Englewood Cliffs, NJ: Prentice-Hall.

McKnight, J., and J. Kretzman. 1993. *Building Communities from the Inside Out*. Chicago: ACTA Publications.

McKnight, John L. 1994. *Community and Its Counterfeits*. An Idea Series Broadcast. Toronto: Canadian Broadcasting Corporation.

– 1997. A 21st Century Map for Health Communities and Families. *Families and Society: The Journal of Contemporary Human Services* 78 (2) (March/April): 117–27.

McLellan, A.T., G. Parikh, A. Bragg, J. Cacciola, B. Fureman, and R. Incmikofki. 1990. *Addiction Severity Index Administration Manual*. 5th ed. Philadelphia: Penn-VA Center for Studies in Addiction.

McNamee, Sheila, and Kenneth J. Gergen, eds. 1992. *Therapy as Social Construction*. London: Sage Publications.

Medical Services Branch. 1991. *Community Prevention Framework*. Ottawa: Health Canada.

Medicine, Institute of. 1990. *Broadening the Base of Treatment for Alcohol Problems*. Washington, DC: National Academy Press.

Mello, N.K., and J.H. Mendelson. 1972. Drinking Patterns during Work-Contingent and Noncontingent Alcohol Acquisition. *Psychosomatic Medicine* 34:139–64.

Mendelson, J.H., and N.K. Mello. 1985. *Alcohol Use and Abuse in America*. New York: Little Brown.

Merton, Robert K. 1957. *Social Theory and Social Structure*. Glencoe, IL: Free Press.

Meyers, Robert. 1985. Multiple Metabolite Theory, Alcohol Drinking and the Alcogene. In *Aldehyde Addicts in Alcoholism*, ed. Michael Collins, 201–20. New York: Allen R. Lis, Inc.

Meyers, Robert J., and Jane Ellen Smith. 1995. *Clinical Guide to Alcohol Treatment: The Community Reinforcement Approach*. New York: Guilford Press.

Milam, James R., and Katherine Ketcham. 1983. *Under the Influence*. New York: Bantam.

Milardo, Robert M., ed. 1988. *Families and Social Networks*. Newbury Park, CA: and Sage Publications.

Miles, Robert. 1982. *Racism and Migrant Labour*. London: Routledge and Kegan Paul.

Milke, Mark (and staff of the Canadian Taxpayers Federation). 2002. *Tax Me, I'm Canadian: Your Money and How Politicians Spend It*. Calgary: Thomas & Black Publishers.

Miller, J.R. 1997. *Shingwauk's Vision: A History of Native Residential Schools*. Toronto: University of Toronto Press.

Miller, Norman S. 1998. The Alcohol and Multiple-Drug Dependent. In *Clinical Textbook of Addictive Disorders*, 2nd ed., ed. Richard J. Frances and Sheldon I. Miller, chap. 11, 262–88. New York and London: Guilford Press, 1998.

Miller, P.M., and M.A. Mastria. 1977. *Alternatives to Alcohol Abuse: A Social Learning Model*. Champaign, IL: Research Press.

Miller, W.R. 1995. Increasing Motivation for Change. In *Handbook of Alcoholism Treatment Approaches: Effective Alternatives*, 2nd ed., ed. Reid K. Hester and William R. Miller, 89–104. Boston: Allyn and Bacon.

– 1995. Treatment for Alcohol Problems: Toward an Informed Eclecticism. In *Handbook of Alcoholism Treatment Approaches: Effective Alternatives*, 2nd ed., ed. Reid K. Hester and William R. Miller, 1–12. Boston: Allyn and Bacon.

Miller, William R., Janice M. Brown, Tracy L. Simpson, Nancy S. Handmaker, Thomas H. Bien, Lorenzo F. Luckie, Henry A. Montgomery, Reid K. Hester, and J. Scott Tonigan. 1995. What Works? A Methodological Analysis of the Alcohol Treatment Outcome Literature. In *Handbook of Alcoholism Treatment Approaches: Effective Alternatives*, 2nd ed., ed. Reid K. Hester and William R. Miller, 12–44.

Miller, W.R., C.A. Taylor, and J.C. West. 1980. Focused versus Broad-Spectrum Behavior Therapy for Problem Drinkers. *Journal of Consulting and Clinical Psychology* 4 (8): 590–601.

Miller, W.R., and R.K. Hester. 1980. Treating the Problem Drinker: Modern Approaches. In *The Addictive Behaviours: Treatment of Alcoholism, Drug Abuse, Smoking and Obesity*, ed. W.R. Miller, 11–141. Oxford: Pergamon Press.

– 1986. The Effectiveness of Alcoholism Treatment: What Research Reveals. In *Treating Addictive Behaviors: Processes of Change*, ed. W.R. Miller and N. Heather, 175–203. New York: Plenum Press.

Miller, W.R., and G.A. Marlatt. 1984. *Manual for the Comprehensive Drinker Profile*. Odessa, FL: Psychological Assessment Resources.

Miller, W.R., and R.F. Munoz. 1976. *How to Control Your Drinking*. Rev. ed. Englewood Cliffs, NJ: Prentice-Hall.

Miller, W.R., and V.C. Sanchez. 1993. Motivating Young Adults for Treatment and Lifestyle Change. In *Issues in Alcohol Misuse by Young Adults*, ed. G. Howard, 555–82. Notre Dame, IN: University of Notre Dame Press.

Milloy, John S. 1999. *A National Crime: The Canadian Government and the Residential School System, 1879 to 1986*. Winnipeg: University of Manitoba Press.

Monti, Peter M., David B. Abrams, Ronald M. Kadden, and Ned L. Cooney.
   1989. *Treating Alcohol Dependence: A Coping Skills Training Guide*. New York:
   Guilford Press.
Mosher, V., J. Davis, D. Mulligan, and F.L. Iber. 1975. Comparison of Outcome
   in a 9-Day and 30-Day Alcoholism Treatment Program. *Journal of Studies on
   Alcohol* 36:1277–81.
Moskowitz, J.M. 1989. The Primary Prevention of Alcohol Programs: A Critical
   Review of the Research Literature. *Journal of Studies on Alcohol* 50:54–8.
Murray, Glen. 1997. *The Status of NNADAP Treatment Programs in the
   Saskatchewan Region*. Prepared for the Regional Advisory Board (RAB) to
   NNADAP in Saskatchewan.
Myers, Robert D. 1985. Multiple Metabolic Theory, Alcohol Drinking and
   the Alcogene. In *Aldehyde Adducts in Alcoholism*, ed. Michael Collins, 201–
   20.
Nace, E.P. 1987. *The Treatment of Alcoholism*. New York: Brunnel/Mazel.
Nace, E.P., C.W Davis, and J.D. Gaspari. 1991. Axis II Comorbidity in the Sub-
   stance Abuse Sample. *American Journal of Psychiatry* 18 (1): 118–20.
Nace, E.P., and P.G. Isbell. 1991. Alcohol. In *Clinical Textbook of Addictive Disor-
   ders*, ed. R.J. Frances and S.I. Miller, 43–68. New York: Guilford Press.
Najavits, L.M., and R.D. Weiss. 1994. Variations in Therapist Effectiveness in
   the Treatment of Patients with Substance Use Disorders: An Empirical
   Review. *Addiction* 89:679–88.
Naranjo, C.A., E.M. Sellers, K. Chater, P. Iversen, C. Roach, and K. Sykova.
   1983. Non-pharmacologic Intervention in Acute Alcohol Withdrawal. *Clini-
   cal Pharmacological Therapy* 34 (2): 214–19.
Naranjo, Claudia A. et al. 1984. Zimelidine-Induced Variations in Alcohol
   Intake by Nondepressed Heavy Drinkers. *Clinical Pharmacological Therapy*
   35:374–81.
Nathan, P.E. 1988. The Addictive Personality in the Behavior of the Addict.
   Journal of Consulting and Clinical Psychology 56:183–8.
National Association of Friendship Centres (NAFC). 1985. *Urban Research
   Project. Phase I and II, Alcohol, Drugs and Solvent Abuse*. Ottawa: NAFC.
Nelsen, Jane, Riki Intner, and Lynn Lotti. 1992. *Clean and Sober Parenting: A
   Guide to Help Recovering Parents*. Rocklin, CA: Prime Publishing.
Nettler, Gwyn. 1976. *Social Concerns*. New York: McGraw-Hill.
NNADAP, Saskatchewan Region. 1989. Challenges for the 90s: The NNADAP
   Program in Saskatchewan – A Discussion Paper. March.
North Battleford. 1993. *Community Profile*. North Battleford, SIC: City of North
   Battleford Administration.
Northwest Territories Bureau of Statistics. 1996. *1996 NWT Alcohol and Drug*

Survey: Rates of Use for Alcohol, Other Drugs and Tobacco. Yellowknife: Government of the Northwest Territories.

Oei, T., and P. Jackson. 1980. Long-Term Effects of Group and Individual Social Skills Training with Alcoholics. *Addictive Behaviours* 5:129–36.

Ogborne, Alan C., and F.B. Glaser. 1985. Evaluating Alcoholics Anonymous. In *Alcoholism and Substance Abuse: Strategies for Clinical Intervention,* ed. T.E. Bratter and G.G. Forrest, 43–68. New York: Free Press.

Ogilvie, Heather. 2001. *Alternatives to Abstinence: A New Look at Alcoholism and the Choices in Treatment.* New York: Hatherleigh Press.

Ohlms, David. 1990. The Disease of Alcoholism. *Alcoholism: Clinical and Experimental Research.* New York: Grune and Sutton.

Ordorica, Patricia I., and Edgar P. Nace. 1998. Alcohol. In *Clinical Textbook of Addictive Disorders,* 2nd ed., ed. Richard J. Frances and Sheldon I. Miller, 91–119. New York and London: Guilford Press.

Ortner, Catherine N.M., Tara K. MacDonald, and Mary C. Olmstead. 2003. Alcohol Intoxication Reduces Impulsivity in the Delay-Discounting Paradigm. *Alcohol and Alcoholism* 38 (2): 151–6.

Parkman, F. 1885. *The Jesuits in North America in the Seventeenth Century.* Boston: Little, Brown & Co.

– 1901. *The Old Regime in Canada.* 2 vols. Boston: Little, Brown & Co.

Parsons, Talcott. 1951. *The Social System.* Glencoe, IL: Free Press.

Pattison, E.M. 1966. A Critique of Alcoholism Treatment Concepts with Special Reference to Abstinence. *Quarterly Journal of Studies in Alcohol* 27:49–71.

Pearlman, S. 1984a. Early Experiences with Primary Care. In *A System of Health Care Delivery, Vol. II. Primary Care Assessment,* ed. F. Glaser, et al., 35–48. Toronto: Addiction Research Foundation.

– 1984b. Primary Care on Weekends. In *A System of Health Care Delivery,* vol. 2. *Primary Care Assessment,* ed. F. Glaser et al., 67–9. Toronto: Addiction Research Foundation.

Pearson, Richard E. 1990. *Counselling and Social Support: Perspectives and Practice.* Newbury Park, CA: Sage Publications.

Pedigo, Jill. 1983. Finding the 'Meaning' of Native American Substance Abuse: Implications for Community Prevention. *Personnel and Guidance Journal* 83 (January): 273–7.

Peele, Stanton. 1985. *The Meaning of Addiction: An Unconventional View.* San Francisco: Jossey-Bass Publishers.

– 1995. *Diseasing of America: How We Allowed Recovery Zealots and the Treatment Industry to Convince Us We Are Out of Control.* 2nd ed. San Francisco: Jossey-Bass.

– 1990. Research Issues in Assessing Addiction Treatment Efficacy: How Cost

Effective Are Alcoholics Anonymous and Private Treatment Centres? *Drugs and Alcohol Dependence* 25:179–82.

– 1989. *Diseasing of America*. Lexington, MA: D.C. Heath.

Peele, S., Archie Brodsky, and M. Arnold. 1991. *The Truth about Addiction and Recovery: The Life Process Program from Outgrowing Destructive Habits*. New York: Simon and Schuster.

Perlman, Art. 1990. *Rational-Emotive Therapy: Understanding Your Personal Power to Change – Thoughts, Feelings, Actions*. Center City, MN: Hazelden Educational Materials.

Philips, Paul C. 1961. *The Fur Trade*. 2 vols. Norman, OK: University of Oklahoma Press.

Pickens, R.W., et al. 1991. Heterogeneity in the Inheritance of Alcoholism: A Study of Male and Female Twins. *Archives of General Psychiatry* 48:19–28.

Pittman, D.J., and R.L. Tate. 1969. A Comparison of Two Treatment Programs for Alcoholics. *Quarterly Journal of Studies on Alcohol* 30:889–99.

Pokorny, M.D., B.A. Miller, and H.D. Kaplan. 1972. The Brief MAST (or SMAST): A Shortened Version of the Michigan Alcoholism Screening Test. *American Journal of Psychiatry* 129 (3): 342–5.

Polsky, Andrew. 1993. *The Rise of the Therapeutic State*. Princeton: Princeton University Press.

Porter, John. 1965. *The Vertical Mosaic: An Analysis of Social Class and Power in Canada*. Toronto: University of Toronto Press.

Potter-Efron, R.T. 1989. Differential Diagnosis of Psychological, Psychiatric and Sociocultural Conditions Associated with Aggression and Substance Abuse. *Journal of Chemical Dependency Treatment* 3:37–59.

Powell, B.J., et al. 1985. Comparison of Three Outpatient Treatment Interventions: A 12-Month Follow-Up of Men Alcoholics. *Journal of Studies on Alcohol* 46 (4): 309–12.

Price, John A. 1978. *Native Studies: American and Canadian Indians*. Toronto: McGraw-Hill Ryerson.

Prochaska, J.O., and C.C. DiClemente. 1983. Stages and Processes of Self Change of Smoking: Toward an Integrative Model of Change. *Journal of Consulting and Clinical Psychology* 51:390–5.

– 1986. Toward a Comprehensive Model of Change. In *Treating Addictive Behaviors and Processes of Change*, ed. W.R. Miller and N. Heather, 3–27. New York: Plenum.

Ray, A.J. 1974. *Indians in the Fur Trade: Their Role as Trappers, Hunters and Middlmen in the Lands Southwest of Hudson's Bay, 1660–1870*. Toronto: University of Toronto Press.

Ray, O.S., and C. Cassiere, 1987. *Drugs, Society and Human Behavior*. 4th ed. St Louis: C.V. Mosby.

Reed, T. Edward, Harold Kalant, Robert J. Gibbins, Bushon M. Kapur, and James E. Rankin. 1976. Alcohol and Acctalerhyde Metabolism in Caucasions, Chinese and Americans. *Canadian Medical Association Journal* 115:851–5.

Regional Advisory Board to NNADAP (Saskatchewan). 1994. *Addictions Intervention Needs of First Nations: 1994 and Beyond*. Regina: Regional Advisory Board to NNADAP, Saskatchewan Region.

– 2000. *Moving to First Nations Control: Literature Review*. April. Regina: First Nations and Inuit Health Branch, Health Canada, Saskatchewan Region.

Regional Advisory Board, Strategic Planning Group. 1993. *Regional Strategic Plan for the Provision of Alcohol and Substance Abuse Programming for First Nations in Saskatchewan*. Saskatchewan: NNADAP.

– 2000. *Moving to First Nations Control: Addiction Intervention Needs in 2000 and Beyond*. Saskatchewan: NNADAP.

Reid, John G., with Audrey Dewit and Rae Matonovich. 1980. *Public Drunkenness in Regina: A Search for Determinants and Solutions – Final Report*. Regina: Alcoholism Commission of Saskatchewan.

Reuler, J.B., D.E. Girard, and T.G. Cooney. 1985. Wernicke's Encephalopathy. *New England Journal of Medicine* 316:1035–9.

Rich, E.E. 1967. *The Fur Trade and the North-West to 1857*. Toronto: McClelland and Stewart.

Rickel, Annette U., and Allen LaRue. 1987. Preventing Maladjustment from Infancy through Adolescence. *Developmental Clinical Psychology and Psychiatry*, No. 11 in Monogram Series. Newbury Park, CA: Sage Publications.

Robson, R.A., I. Paulus, and G.G. Clarke. 1965. An Evaluation of the Effects of a Clinic Treatment Program on the Rehabilitation of Chronic Alcoholic Patients. *Quarterly Journal of Studies on Alcohol* 26:264–78.

Rogers, Carl. 1965. *Client Centered Therapy*. London: Constable.

– 1969. *Freedom to Learn*. Columbus, OH: Merrill.

Rogers, D.D., and N. Abas. 1988. A Survey of Native Mental Health Needs in Manitoba, *Arctic Medical Research* 47 (supp. 1): 576–80.

Room, Robin. 1983. Sociological Aspects of the Disease Concept of Alcoholism. In *Research Advances in Alcohol and Drug Problems*, ed. R.G. Smart, F.B. Glaser, Y. Israel, H. Kalant, R.E. Popham, and W. Schmidt, 7. New York: Plenum.

Rooney, Ronald H. 1992. *Strategies for Work with Involuntary Clients*. New York: Columbia University Press.

Rose, K.J. 1988. *The Body in Time*. New York: J. Wiley.

Rosenthal, R., and L. Jacobson. 1968. *Pygmalion in the Classroom*. New York: Holt, Rinehart and Winston.

Ross, David, Katherine Scott, and Mark Kelly. 1996. *Child Poverty: What Are the Consequences?* Ottawa: Canadian Council on Social Development, Centre for International Statistics.

Round Lake Treatment Centre. 1992. *Research on Native Adolescents and Substance Abuse*. Armstrons, Next Generation Native Adolescent Substance Abuse Project.

– 1994. *A Demonstration Program to Test a Community Based Solvent Abuse Intervention Model*. Armstrons, Next Generation Solvent Abuse Project.

– 1996. *Client Outcome Study: Final Report*. Armstrons, Next Generation Solvent Abuse Project.

Royal Commission on Aboriginal Peoples, Report of. 1996. *Gathering Strength*. vol. 3, Ottawa: Minister of Supply and Services. Canada Communication Group Publishing.

Russell, Mary Nomme. 1990. *Clinical Social Work: Research and Practice*. London: Sage Publications.

Rutledge, Don, with Rita Robinson. 1992. *Center of the World: Native American Spirituality*. North Hollywood, CA: Newcastle Publishing.

Ryan, William. 1971. *Blaming the Victim*. New York: Pantheon Books.

SADAC (Saskatchewan Alcohol and Drug Abuse Commission).

– 1993. *Focus Sheet: SADAC Client Profile 1991/92: Aboriginal People in Treatment*. April. Regina: Government of Saskatchewan.

– 1989. *Public Drunkenness in Regina*. Regina: Government of Saskatchewan.

Sadler, P.O. 1977. The 'Crisis Cult' as a Voluntary Association: An Interactional Approach to Alcoholics Anonymous. *Human Organization* 36:207–10.

Saggers, Sherry, and Dennis Gray. 1998. *Dealing with Alcohol: Indigenous Usage in Australia, New Zealand and Canada*. Cambridge: Cambridge University Press.

Sanchez-Craig, M. 1975. A Self-Control Strategy for Drinking Tendencies. *Ontario Psychologist* 7:25–9.

– 1976. Cognitive and Behavioural Coping Strategies in the Reappraisal of Stressful Social Situations. *Journal of Counselling Psychology* 23:7–12.

– 1980. Random Assignment to Abstinence or Controlled Drinking in a Cognitive-Behavioural Program: Short-Term Effects on Drinking Behaviour. *Addictive Behaviours* 5:35–9.

– 1995. *Drinkwise: How to Quit Drinking or Cut Down*. Toronto: Centre for Addictions and Mental Health.

Sanchez-Craig, M., K. Spivak, and R. Davila. 1991. Superior Outcome of Females over Males after Brief Treatment for the Reduction of Heavy Drinking: Replication and Report of Therapist Effects. *British Journal of Addiction* 86 (7 July): 867–76.

Sanchez-Craig, M., and K. Walker. 1974. Teaching Alcoholics How to Think Defensively: A Cognitive Approach for the Treatment of Alcohol Abuse.

Paper presented to the North American Congress on Alcohol and Drug Problems, San Francisco.

Santé Quebéc. 1994. A Health Profile of the Cree. In Carole Daveluy, et al., *Report of the Santé Quebéc Survey of the James Bay Cree*. Montreal: Santé Quebéc.

Saskatchewan Alcoholism Commission. n.d. *Fast Facts I: A Summary of Answers to Frequently Asked Questions*.

Sask-Trends Monitor. 1992. 9 (3) (March): 5.

Satzewich, Vic, and Terry Wotherspoon. 1993. *First Nations: Race, Class and Gender Relations*. Scarborough, ON: Nelson Canada.

Scarpetti, Frank R., and Margaret L. Andersen. 1989. *Social Problems*. New York: Harper and Row.

Schaefer, J.M. 1981. Firewater Myths Revisited: Review of Findings and Some New Directions. *Journal of Studies on Alcohol* 9:99–115.

Schaler, Jeffrey A. 1989. *Social Problems*. New York: Harper and Row.

– 1995. Cult-Busting. *The Interpsych Newsletter* (5) (June): 1–11.

– 2000. *Addiction Is a Choice*. Chicago and LaSalle: Open Court.

Schinke, S., G. Botvine, and M. Orlandi. 1991. *Substance Abuse in Children and Adolescents*. London and Newbury Park, CA: Sage Publications.

Schinke, Steven Paul, et al. 1985. Preventing Substance Abuse with American Indian Youth. *Social Casework: The Journal of Contemporary Social Work* (April).

Schorr, Lisbeth B. 1988. *Within Our Reach: Breaking the Cycle of Disadvantage*. New York: Doubleday.

Schuckit, M.A. 1987. Studies of Population at High Risk for the Future Development of Alcoholism. *Progress in Clinical and Biological Research* 241:83–6.

Schur, Edwin M. 1979. *Interpreting Deviance: A Sociological Introduction*. New York: Harper and Row.

– 1971. *Labeling Deviant Behavior: Its Sociological Implications*. New York: Harper and Row.

Schwartz, R.H. 1987. Marijuana: An Overview. *Pediatric Clinics of North America* 34:305–17.

Science Digest. 1989. Nightcap Dangers. 2 (5): 90.

Scott, Kim. 1994. Substance Use among Indigenous Canadians. In *Aboriginal Substance Use: Research Issues*, 9–41. Ottawa: Canadian Centre on Substance Abuse.

– 1997. Indigenous Canadians. In *Canadian Profile: Alcohol, Tobacco and Other Drugs*, ed. D. McKenzie, R. Williams, and E. Single, 133–64. Toronto: Centre for Addiction and Mental Health.

– n.d. *Indigenous Canadians: Substance Abuse Profile*. Prepared for Kisht Ana-quot Health Research and Program Development and the National Native Alcoholism and Drug Abuse Program.

Segal, R., and B.V. Sisson. 1985. Medical Complications Associated with Alcohol Use and the Assessment of Risk of Physical Damage. In *Alcoholism and Substance Abuse: Strategies for Clinical Intervention*, ed. T.E. Bratter and G.G. Fared, 137–75. New York: Free Press.

Selzer, M.L. 1971. The Michigan Alcoholism Screening Test: The Quest for a Diagnostic Instrument. *American Journal of Psychiatry* 127:1653–8.

Services, Legislative, Saskatchewan Justice. 1993. *Social Implications of Gaming: A Literature Survey*. Regina: Department of Justice, Province of Saskatchewan.

Shaffir, William B., Robert A. Stebbins, and Allan Turowetz. 1980. *Fieldwork Experience: Qualitative Approaches to Social Research*. New York: St Martin's Press.

Sherman, Howard J., and James L. Wood. 1979. *Sociology: Traditional and Radical Perspectives*. New York: Harper and Row.

Sherraden, Michael. 1991. *Assets and the Poor: A New American Welfare Policy*. Armonk, NY, and London: M.E. Sharpe.

Shkilnyk, Anastasia M. 1985. *A Poison Stronger Than Love: The Destruction of an Ojibwa Community*. New Haven, CT: Yale University Press.

Single, Eric, Linda Robson, Xiaodi Xie, and Jürgen Rehm. 1996. *The Costs of Substance Abuse in Canada: A Cost Estimation Study*. Ottawa: Canadian Centre on Substance Abuse.

Single, E., L. Robson, and K. Scott. 1996. *Morbidity and Mortality Related to Alcohol, Tobacco and Illicit Drug Use among Indigenous People in Canada*. Ottawa: Canadian Centre on Substance Abuse (CCSA) for NNADAP.

Single, E.W., and D. McKenzie. 1997. *Canadian Profile: Alcohol, Tobacco and Other Drugs*. Ottawa: Canadian Centre on Substance Abuse.

Skinner, B.F. 1938. *The Behavior of Organisms*. New York: Appleton.

Skinner, H.A., and J.L. Horn. 1984. *Alcohol Dependence Scale (ADS) User's Guide*. Toronto: Addiction Research Foundation.

Small, J. 1983. *Becoming Naturally Therapeutic*. Austin, TX: Eupsychian Press.

Smart, R.G. 1996. *Northern Spirits: A Social History of Alcohol in Canada*. Toronto: Addiction Research Foundation.

Smart, R.G., and Alan C. Ogborne. 1977. Changes in Alcoholic Beverage Sales after Reductions in the Legal Drinking Age. *American Journal of Drug and Alcohol Abuse* 4:101–8.

– 1986a. Cocaine Use and Problems in North America. *Canadian Journal of Criminology* 28:109–28.

– 1986b. Solvent Use in North America: Aspects of Epidemiology, Prevention and Treatment. *Journal of Psychoactive Drugs* 18 (2) (April – June): 87–96.

Smart, R.G., and G. Gray. 1978. Minimal, Moderate and Long-Term Treatment for Alcoholism. *British Journal of Addiction* 73:35–8.

Smith, James W. 1982. 'Treatment of Alcoholism in Aversion Conditioning Hospitals.' In *Encyclopedic Handbook of Alcoholism*, ed. E.M. Pattison and E. Kaufman, 874–84. New York: Gardner Press.

Sobell, L.C., M.B. Sobell, J.Brown, and P.A. Cleland. 1995. A Randomized Trial Comparing Group versus Individual Guided Self-Change Treatment for Alcohol and Drug Abusers. Paper presented at the 29th annual convention of the Association for the Advancement of Behaviour Therapy, Washington, DC.

Sobell, L.C., M.B. Sobell, and W.C. Christelman. 1972. The Myth of 'One Drink.' *Behavioural Research and Therapy* 10:119–23.

Sobell, Linda C., J.A. Cunningham, and Mark B. Sobell. 1996. Recovery from Alcohol Problems with and without Treatment: Prevalence in Two Population Surveys. *American Journal of Public Health* 86 (7): 966–72.

Sobell, Mark B., and Linda C. Sobell. 1993. *Problem Drinkers: Guided Self-Change Treatment*. New York: Guilford Press.

Spitzer, Steven. 1975. Toward a Marxian Theory of Deviance. *Social Problems* 22:638–51.

Spoonley, Paul, David Pearson, and Cluny McPherson, eds. 1966. *Nga Patai: Racism and Ethnic Relations in Aotearoa/New Zealand*. Palmerston North: Dunmore.

Spotts, J.V., and F.C. Shontz. 1982. Ego Development, Dragon Fights, and Chronic Drug Abusers. *International Journal of the Addictions* 18:633–80.

Stanton, M.D., and T.C. Todd. 1982. The Therapy Model. In *The Family Therapy of Drug Abuse and Addiction*, 109–53. New York and London: Guildford Press.

Statistics Canada. 1985. *Health and Social Support, 1985*. General Social Survey Analysis Series. Catalogue 11-612E, No. 1. Ottawa: Statistics Canada.

– 1993. *1991 Aboriginal Peoples Survey: Language, Tradition, Health, Lifestyle and Social Issues*. Catalogue Number: 89-533. Ottawa: Ministry of Industry, Science and Technology.

Stensrud, R., and K. Stensrud. 1983. Coping Skills Training: A Systematic Approach to Stress Management Counselling. *Personnel and Guidance Journal* 62:214–18.

Stinnett, J.L. 1982. Outpatient Detoxification of the Alcoholic. *International Journal of the Addictions* 17 (6): 1031–46.

Stocking Jr, George. 1968. *Race, Culture and Evolution: Essays in the History of Anthropology*. London: Collier-Macmillan.

Stone, J. 1991. Light Elements. *Discover* 12 (1): 12–16.

Sumner, Maggie, and Howard Parker. 1995. *Low in Alcohol: A Review of International Research into Alcohol's Role in Crime Causation*. Manchester: University of Manchester Press.

Supernault, Esther. 1995. *A Warrior's Heart*. Edmonton: Native Counselling Services.

Szabo, E.L. 1990. *A Study of Mortality Related to Alcohol Use among the Status Indian Population of Saskatchewan*. Paper presented at the 8th International Congress on Circumpolar Health, Whitehorse, Yukon, 20–5 May.

Szasz, Thomas. 1961. *The Myth of Mental Illness*. New York: Hoeber-Harper.

– 1985. *Ceremonial Chemistry: The Ritual Persecution of Drugs, Addicts, and Pushers*, rev. ed. Holmes Beach, CA: Learning Publications.

– 1987. *Insanity: The Idea and Its Consequences*. New York: Wiley.

– 1991. Diagnoses Are Not Diseases. *Lancet* 338:1574–6.

Sztromka, Piotr. 1993. *The Sociology of Social Change*. Oxford: Blackwell Publishers.

Tabakoff, B., P.L. Hoffman, J.M. Lee, T. Saio, B. Willard, and R. DeLeon-Jones. 1988. Differences in Platelet Enzyme Activity. *New England Journal of Medicine* 313:134–9.

Tafrate, Raymond Chip. 1995. Evaluation of Treatment Strategies for Adult Anger Disorders. In *Anger Disorders: Definition, Diagnosis and Treatment*, ed. Howard Kassinove. Washington, DC: Taylor and Francis.

Taiaiake, Alfred. 1999. *Peace, Power, Righteousness: An Indigenous Manifesto*. Don Mills, ON: Oxford University Press.

Tarter, R.E. 1988. Are there Inherited Behaviour Traits That Predispose to Substance Abuse? *Journal of Consultation and Clinical Psychology* 56:189–97.

– 1990. Evaluation and Treatment of Adolescent Substance Abuse: A Decision Tree Method. *American Journal of Drug and Alcohol Abuse* 16:1–46.

Tarter, R.E., P.J. Ott, and A.C. Mezzich. 1991. Psychometric Assessment. In *Clinical Textbook of Addictive Disorders*, ed. R.J. Frances, 189. New York: Guilford Press.

Tarter, R.E., and D.U. Schneider. 1976. Models and Theories of Alcoholism. In *Alcoholism: Interdisciplinary Approaches to an Enduring Problem*, ed. R.E. Tarter and A.A. Sugraman, 75–106. Reading, MA: Addison Wesley.

Taylor, William B. 1979. *Drinking, Homicide, and Rebellion in Colonial Mexican Villages*. Stanford, CA: Stanford University Press.

Tewari, S., and V.G. Carson. 1982. Biochemistry of Alcohol and Alcohol Metabolism. In *Encyclopedic Handbook of Alcoholism*, ed. E.M. Pattison and E. Kaufman, 83–104. New York: Gardner Press.

Thatcher, Richard. 1986. The Functions of Minority Group Disrepute: The Case of Native Peoples in Canada. In *The Political Economy of Crime: Readings for a Critical Criminology*, ed. Brian D. MacLean, 272–88. Scarborough, ON: Prentice-Hall.

– 1993. *Needs Assessment and NNADAP Out-Patient and Prevention Program Plan (New Path)*. North Battleford, SIC: Battlefords Tribal Council Indian Health Services (BTCIHS).

– 2000a. *Vision Seekers: Part I of a Structured Personal & Social Development Program Targeted on First Nations' Youth at High Social Risk*. Ottawa: Health Canada.

– 2000b. *Vision Seekers: Social Group Work Exercises: Part II of a Structured Personal & Social Development Program Targeted on First Nations' Youth at High Social Risk*. Ottawa: Health Canada.

– 2000c. *Moving to First Nations Control: Literature Review*. April. Regina: (Saskatchewan) Regional Advisory to NNADAP.

– 2001. *Deadly Duo: Tobacco and Convenience Foods, the Other Substance Abuse Epidemics Afflicting the First Nations and Inuit of Canada*. Muskoday First Nation Reserve: National Native Addictions Partnership Foundation.

Theodorson, George A, and Achilles G. Theodorson. 1969. *A Modern Dictionary of Sociology*. New York: Thomas Y. Crowell.

Thompson, D. 1990. A Losing Battle with AIDS. *Time* 136 (1): 42–3.

Thompson, James D. 1967. *Organizations in Action*. New York: McGraw-Hill Book Co.

Timasheff, Nicholas. 1967. *Sociological Theory: Its Nature and Growth*. New York: Random House.

Timpson, J.B., S. McKay, S. Kakegamic, D. Roundhead, C. Cohen, and G. Matewapit. 1988. Depression in a Native Canadian Community in Northwestern Ontario: Sadness, Grief or Spiritual Illness. *Canada's Mental Health* (June): 5–8.

Toby, Jackson. 1957. Social Disorganization and Stakes in Conformity: Complementary Factors in Predatory Behavior of Young Hoodlums. *Journal of Criminal Law, Criminology and Police Science* 48 (May-June): 12–17.

Torens, Nina. 1972. *Social Work: The Case of a Semi-Profession*. Beverly Hills and London: Sage.

Townson, Monica. 1999. *Health and Wealth: How Social and Economic Factors Affect Our Well-Being*. Ottawa: Canadian Centre for Policy Alternatives.

Trimpey, Jack. 1996. *Rational Recovery: The New Cure for Substance Addiction*. New York: Pocket Books.

Truax, C., and R. Carkhuff. 1967. *Toward Effective Counselling and Psychotherapy: Training and Practice*. Chicago: Aldine-Atherton.

Truscott, Richard. 1999. Native Bands: Where Has All the Money Gone? *Taxpayer* (April): 37.

Turbo, R. 1989. Drying Out Is Just a Start: Alcoholism. *Medical World News* 30 (3): 56–63.

Vaillant, G.E. 1983. *The Natural History of Alcoholism: Causes, Patterns, and Paths to Recovery.* Cambridge: Harvard University Press.

Valle, S.K. 1981. Interpersonal Functioning of Alcoholism Counsellors and Treatment Outcome. *Journal of Studies on Alcohol* 42:783–90.

Vanicelli, M. 1978. Impact of Aftercare in the Treatment of Alcoholics: A Cross-Lagged Panel Analysis. *Journal of Studies on Alcohol* 39 (11): 1875–86.

Velleman, Richard. 1992. *Counselling for Alcohol Problems.* London: Sage Publications.

Volberg, Rachel. 1992. *Gambling Involvement and Problem Gambling in Montana.* Prepared for the Montana Department of Corrections and Human Services. Minot, ND: State Government of North Dakota.

Waldram, James B., D. Ann Herring, and T. Kue Young. 1995. *Aboriginal Health in Canada: Historical, Cultural and Epidemiological Perspectives.* Toronto: University of Toronto Press.

Walker, K., M. Sanchez-Craig, and K. MacDonald. 1974. Teaching Coping Strategies for Inter-Personal Problems. Paper presented at the North American Congress on Alcohol and Drug Problems, San Francisco.

Wallace, John. 1985. Working with the Preferred Defense Structure of the Recovering Alcoholic. In *Practical Approaches to Alcoholism Psychotherapy*, 2nd ed., ed. Sheldon Zimberg, John Wallace, and Sheila B. Blume, 23–36. New York: Plenum Press.

– 1988. The Relevance to Clinical Care of Recent Research in Neurobiology. *Journal of Substance Abuse Treatment* 5:207–17.

– 1989. A Biopsychosocial Model of Alcoholism. *Social Casework: The Journal of Contemporary Social Work* 70 (6) (June): 325–32.

Warry, Wayne. 1998. *Unfinished Dreams: Community Healing and the Reality of Aboriginal Self-Government.* Toronto: University of Toronto Press.

Wax, Murray, L. 1971. *Indian Americans.* Englewood Cliffs, NJ: Prentice-Hall.

Webb, M., and A. Unwin. 1988. The Outcome of Outpatient Withdrawal from Alcohol. *British Journal of Addiction* 83:929–34.

Weisner, Thomas S., Joan Crofut Weibel-Orlando, and John Long. 1984. 'Serious Drinking', 'White Man's Drinking' and 'Teetotaling': Drinking Levels and Styles in an Urban American Indian Population. *Journal of Studies on Alcohol* 45 (3): 237–50.

Werner, E.E., and R.S. Smith. 1982. *A Longitudinal Study of Resilient Children and Youth.* New York: McGraw-Hill.

White, William. 1998. *Slaying the Dragon: The History of Addiction Treatment and Recovery in America.* Bloomington, IL: Chestnut Health Systems.

Whitehead, Paul C., and Michael J. Hayes. 1998. *The Insanity of Alcohol: Social*

Problems in Canadian First Nations Communities. Toronto: Canadian Scholars' Press.

Whiteside, Don. 1973. *Historical Development of Aboriginal Political Associations in Canada*. Ottawa: National Indian Brotherhood.

Wilensky, Harold, and Charles N. Lebeaux. 1965. *Industrial Society and Social Welfare*. New York: Free Press.

Wilkins, Richard G. 1996. *Unhealthy Societies: The Afflictions of Inequality*. New York: Routledge.

Wilkinson, Richard G. 1996. *Unhealthy Societies: The Afflictions of Inequality*. London: Routledge.

Willoughby, A. 1979. *The Alcohol-Troubled Person: Known and Unknown*. Chicago: Nelson-Hall.

Wilson, William Julius. 1987. *The Truly Disadvantaged*. Chicago: University of Chicago Press.

Wolf, S., and J.G. Bruhn. 1992. *The Power of the Clan: The Influence of Human Relationships on Heart Disease*. New Brunswick, NJ: Transaction.

Wolff, P.H. 1973. Vasomotor Sensitivity to Alcohol in Diverse Mongoloid Populations. *American Journal of Human Genetics* 25:193–9.

Wolfgang, M.E. 1958. *Patterns in Criminal Homicide*. Philadelphia: University of Pennsylvania Press.

Wolin, Steven J., and Sybil Wolin. 1993. *The Resilient Self: How Survivors of Troubled Families Rise above Adversity*. New York: Villard Books.

Working Group on Native Mental Health. 1989. *Final Report*. Ottawa: Medical Services Branch, Indian and Northern Health Services.

Wynne, L.C., R.L. Cromwell, and S. Matthysse. 1978. *The Nature of Schizoprenia: New Approaches to Research and Treatment*. New York: John Wiley & Sons.

Wyrostok, Nina C., and Barbara L. Paulson. 2000. Traditional Healing Practices among First Nations Students. *Canadian Journal of Counselling* 34 (1) (January): 14–24.

Yalisove, Daniel. 1997. The Origins and Evolution of the Disease Concept of Treatment. *Journal of Studies on Alcohol* (July): 469–76.

Young, T. Kue. 1994. *The Health of Native Americans: Toward a Biocultural Epidemiology*. New York and Oxford: Oxford University Press.

Young, T. Kue, Linda Bruce, John Elias, John D. O'Neil, and Annalee Yassie. 1991. *The Health Effects of Housing and Community Infrastructure on Canadian Indian Reserves*. Prepared for Finance and Professional Services, Indian and Northern Affairs, Canada. August. Winnipeg: Northern Health Research Unit, Department of Community Health Sciences, University of Manitoba.

Youngstrom, N. 1990. Debate Rages On: In- or Outpatient? *APA Monitor* 21 (10): 19.

Yukon, Government of. 1991. *Yukon Alcohol and Drug Survey*. Vol. 1. *Technical Report*. Whitehorse: Yukon Government Executive Council Office, Bureau of Statistics.

Zweben, A., S. Pearlmen, and S. Li. 1988. A Comparison of Brief Advice and Conjoint Therapy in the Treatment of Alcohol Abuse: The Results of the Marital Systems Study. *British Journal of Addictions* 83 (8): 899–916.

Index